BREAKTHROUGH 2.0

Singaporeans Push for
Parliamentary Democracy

BREAKTHROUGH 2.0

Singaporeans Push for
Parliamentary Democracy

Derek da Cunha

World Scientific

NEW JERSEY · LONDON · SINGAPORE · BEIJING · SHANGHAI · HONG KONG · TAIPEI · CHENNAI · TOKYO

Published by

World Scientific Publishing Co. Pte. Ltd.

5 Toh Tuck Link, Singapore 596224

USA office: 27 Warren Street, Suite 401-402, Hackensack, NJ 07601

UK office: 57 Shelton Street, Covent Garden, London WC2H 9HE

National Library Board, Singapore Cataloguing in Publication Data
Name(s): Da Cunha, Derek.
Title: Breakthrough 2.0 : Singaporeans push for parliamentary democracy / Derek da Cunha.
Other Title(s): Singaporeans push for parliamentary democracy.
Description: Singapore : World Scientific Publishing Co. Pte. Ltd, [2022].
Identifier(s): ISBN 978-981-12-2727-1 (hardcover) | 978-981-12-2931-2 (paperback) |
      978-981-12-2728-8 (ebook for institutions) | 978-981-12-2729-5 (ebook for individuals)
Subject(s): LCSH: Elections--Singapore. | Political parties--Singapore. |
      Opposition (Political science)-- Singapore. | Singapore--Politics and government--1990–
Classification: DDC 324.95957--dc23

British Library Cataloguing-in-Publication Data
A catalogue record for this book is available from the British Library.

For any available supplementary material, please visit
https://www.worldscientific.com/worldscibooks/10.1142/12018#t=suppl

Desk Editor: Jiang Yulin

Typeset by Stallion Press
Email: enquiries@stallionpress.com

ABOUT THE AUTHOR

erek da Cunha, a Singapore national, is an independent scholar. He is the author of *Breakthrough: Roadmap for Singapore's Political Future* (2012); *Singapore Places its Bets: Casinos, Foreign Talent and Remaking a City-state* (2010); and, *The Price of Victory: The 1997 Singapore General Election and Beyond* (1997). He is also the editor of *Debating Singapore: Reflective Essays* (1994, reprinted 1996); and, *Singapore in the New Millennium: Challenges Facing the City-State* (2002).

Between February 1990 and March 2006 he was on the full-time research staff of the Institute of Southeast Asian Studies, in Singapore. He left ISEAS with the rank of Senior Fellow. At ISEAS he held multiple responsibilities simultaneously. He was editor, between June 1992 and December 2003, of the journal *Contemporary Southeast Asia*; editor, between March 1990 and September 1997, of the four-page monthly pullout, *Trends*, published variously in *The Sunday Times* (Singapore), *The Straits Times*, and *The Business Times*. And, between August 1991 and February 2005, he was Coordinator of ISEAS' Regional Strategic and Political Studies Programme.

He has M.Phil. and PhD degrees in the field of International Relations from Cambridge University, and the Australian National University respectively. He was awarded an ISEAS PhD scholarship in 1986.

CONTENTS

ABBREVIATIONS

4G	fourth-generation leaders
AHTC	Aljunied-Hougang Town Council
AJCC	Aljunied Constituency Committee
ASPD	Anti-Social Personality Disorders
AWARE	Association of Women for Action and Research
BFA	barrier-free-access
BJP	Bharatiya Janata Party
BTO	Build-to-Order
CDC	Community Development Council
CEC	Central Executive Committee
CECA	Comprehensive Economic Cooperation Agreement
CEO	Chief Executive Officer
CPA	Council of Presidential Advisers
CPC	Criminal Procedure Code
CPF	Central Provident Fund
CVR	compulsory voting rules

DP	Dependant's Pass
DPM	deputy prime minister
EBRC	Electoral Boundaries Review Committee
EIP	Ethnic Integration Policy
ELD	Elections Department Singapore
ESM	emeritus senior minister
EU	European Union
FB	Facebook
FPTP	first-past-the-post
FTA	free trade agreement
GCE	General Certification of Examination
GLC	government-linked corporation
GOTV	Get-Out-the-Vote
GRC	group representation constituency
HDB	Housing and Development Board
HGCC	Hougang Constituency Committee
HR	Hugo Restall
IPS	Institute of Policy Studies
ISA	Internal Security Act

JBJ	Joshua Benjamin Jeyaretnam
KV	Karisma Vaswani
LGBT	Lesbian, Gay, Bisexual and Transgender
LHL	Lee Hsien Loong
LHY	Lee Hsien Yang
LKY	Lee Kuan Yew
LO	Leader of the Opposition
MCST	Management Corporation Strata Title
MM	Minister Mentor
MNC	multinational corporation
MOM	Ministry of Manpower
MP	Member of Parliament
MPS	meet-the-people session
MVT	Median Voter Theorem
NCMP	Non-constituency Member of Parliament
NIC	New Industrialising Country
NMP	Nominated Member of Parliament
NS	National Service
NSP	National Solidarity Party

OFW   Overseas Filipino Workers

PA   People's Association

PAP   People's Action Party

PAP IB   People's Action Party Internet Brigade

PEA   Parliamentary Elections Act

PKR   Parti Keadilan Rakyat

PM   Prime Minister

PMET   professionals, managers, executives and technicians

POFMA   Protection from Online Falsehoods and Manipulation Act

PPP   People's Power Party

PQ   Parliamentary Question

PR   proportional representation

PRs   Permanent Residents

PRPTC   Pasir Ris-Punggol Town Council

PSP   Progress Singapore Party

PV   Peoples Voice

RDU   Red Dot United

RP   Reform Party

SAF   Singapore Armed Forces

SAP   Special Assistance Plan

SDA   Singapore Democratic Alliance

SDB   social desirability bias

SDP   Singapore Democratic Party

SERS   Selective En bloc Redevelopment Scheme

SingFirst   Singaporeans First

SJW   social justice warrior

SMC   single-member constituency

SpAd   special adviser

SPP   Singapore People's Party

STI   Straits Times Index

TC   Town Council

TCB   Tan Cheng Bock

TCS   Television Corporation of Singapore

TJS   Tan Jee Say

TOC   *The Online Citizen*

TWC2   Transient Workers Count Too

WP   Workers' Party

WPCF   Workers' Party Community Fund

INTRODUCTION

his is my third book on general elections in Singapore. It follows on from my examination of the 1997 and 2011 elections, *The Price of Victory* and *Breakthrough*, respectively.[1] On the latter, i.e., GE2011, I had analysed the breakthrough by the Workers' Party (WP) in winning Aljunied Group Representation Constituency (GRC), a multi-member constituency, which the WP won through defeating two Cabinet ministers. In the general election of July 2020 (GE2020), the WP surprised again with a further breakthrough. Consequently, the WP is the central focus in *Breakthrough 2.0*. This book is not a blow-by-blow, descriptive, account of GE2020, which the reader will find in the works of other authors. Many issues which have interested other authors have been of less interest to me. I will elaborate why later.

All issues raised will thematically revolve around the WP. After all, the second opposition election breakthrough in Singapore was manifested in the WP taking another GRC in GE2020. Even the ruling People's Action Party (PAP), the party of natural government, will feature mostly in a supporting role in the narrative. Therefore, this represents an unconventional treatment of issues arising out of GE2020.

How the WP planned and executed on the campaign for GE2020 will be subjected to detailed examination. Included in these pages are accounts of how the WP navigated through a maze of pressures, not only from the PAP, but from other alternative parties and, not least, civil society activists. The WP was assailed robustly and repeatedly by the political left. The challenges facing the WP, and the prospects for

---

1 *The Price of Victory: The 1997 Singapore General Election and Beyond*, (Singapore: Institute of Southeast Asian Studies, 1997); and, *Breakthrough: Roadmap for Singapore's Political Future*, (Singapore: Institute of Policy Studies and Straits Times Press, 2012).

the party post-GE2020 are also set out in some detail. A number of key issues — including the purpose and efficacy of social media in broad political terms and, specifically, electorally; the human trait of instinctively lionising political personalities; and, the level, nature and quality of other alternative parties' interactions with the WP — will be demystified. *Breakthrough 2.0* attempts an honest appraisal of events. I take my mission as spelt out concisely by the academics Matthew Flinders and Alexandra Kelso: "[s]cholars have a public duty to correct rather than propagate the myths that surround their chosen subject matter."[2] Singapore electoral politics is my chosen subject.

At GE2011, the taking of a GRC from the PAP by the opposition was a landmark and unprecedented event in Singapore's political history. A considerable segment of Singaporeans, mostly ardent opponents of the PAP, were thus convinced that the WP's breakthrough in GE2011 marked a sea-change in Singapore's evolving parliamentary democracy. They felt that there was no going back to the hard-line paternalistic policies of founding prime minister Lee Kuan Yew, and that opposing voices to the PAP which, at a national level, range from anywhere between 25% and 40% of adult citizens, would eventually be represented proportionately in the Singapore Parliament. Much stock was, therefore, placed on the subsequent election, held in 2015, to confirm the apparent trend in Singapore politics. However, at GE2015, there was no enhancement of the WP's breakthrough. In fact, the opposite was the case. In a surprise, there was a broad national swing towards the PAP of almost 10% of the popular vote, with the ruling party re-capturing a single-member constituency — Punggol East — which it had lost to the WP in a by-election in January 2013. The WP's breakthrough at GE2011 thus took a sudden, almost screeching, pause in GE2015.

---

2 Matthew Flinders and Alexandra Kelso, "Mind the Gap: Political Analysis, Public Expectations and the Parliamentary Decline Thesis", *British Journal of Politics and International Relations*, Vol. 13, No. 2, 2011, p. 265.

But if politics is unpredictable, then it showed that side again when, in the general election in July 2020, the WP took a second GRC, Sengkang, from the PAP, surprising even some of those within the WP itself.[3] The WP's breakthrough had, therefore, resumed. This book is, in consequence, titled *Breakthrough 2.0*, to analyse GE2020 and to provide observations of the likely trajectory Singapore politics will take over the near-to-medium term. Subsequent to the publication of the original *Breakthrough*, I had posted online my analysis of political issues, which gave me a small following in cyberspace. Those analytical pieces were useful in distilling some key issues I felt were germane but often ignored in public discourse on electoral politics in Singapore. In *Breakthrough 2.0* I will elaborate in detail, and with supporting empirical evidence some of the issues I had made brief references online since 2011. This book is also cast widely to include events since the original *Breakthrough* was published back in January 2012, and also other issues that impact on electoral politics. In fact, to fully understand political developments in the Singapore of today, you need to understand certain developments from the early 1990s onwards. There is an obvious continuum and, more significantly, as will be demonstrated in this book, things tend to come in cycles, i.e., a lot of the same issues which dominated the politics of the 1990s are still apparent today, even if they have taken on different manifestations. To that extent, there is significance in a phrase commonly invoked in British parliamentary politics: "The opposition occupies the benches in front of you, but the enemy sits behind you."[4] Here, "opposition" is not taken in the literal

---

3 The WP chair, Sylvia Lim, in an interview with Bloomberg TV on 12 July 2020, i.e., just two days after the general election, conceded that when the party began its election campaign it did not expect to win Sengkang GRC. See, "Singapore's Opposition Party Pleased with Vote of Confidence", *Bloomberg*, 12 July 2020, https://www.bloomberg.com/news/videos/2020-07-13/singapore-s-opposition-party-pleased-with-vote-of-confidence-video. Accessed on 11 December 2020.

4 It is a phrase often attributed to Winston Churchill, but it is unclear whether he actually ever uttered it.

sense as the parliamentary opposition to the ruling party. Instead, "opposition" is employed generically to indicate one's political opponent. In the way this phrase is utilised in this book, the PAP represents the opposition to the WP, but the WP's real enemy actually lies elsewhere. To be clear and upfront, what is being alluded to is the chasm between moderate opposition politics and that of radicalised elements who are against both the PAP government and those in moderate opposition to that government. Consequently, as will be repeated throughout the book, the PAP versus non-PAP binary choice, as tended to be employed by lay persons and even other analysts, is both simplistic and false.

This chasm within the broad and unwieldy movement of non-PAP forces was apparent during the 1990s. And, the contention that will be made in this book is that this chasm could likely re-emerge following GE2020 if the WP and those who support the party are not fully alive to this possibility. Before delving into substantive issues, it is worthwhile expending a few words on GE2015 — the election that did not pan-out to the predictions of most politically-engaged Singaporeans.

The results of GE2015 were completely unexpected to many. The mood of dejection, if not shell-shock, across a wide swathe of opposition supporters, was palpable. Shortly after GE2015, I was invited to participate in a forum organised by the civil society organisation, Maruah, where I was part of a panel of six speakers. Given the significance of what transpired during the Maruah forum, I will make reference to parts of it throughout the book. It was a packed-out forum, as the audience wanted to know why the results turned out so unexpectedly, and what would be the political prognosis for Singapore. I, and fellow panellists, were posed multiple searching questions as to whether it was all over for the political opposition to the PAP. Unlike most of the participants, I was still upbeat about the WP's prospects. The following is one of the points I made in answer to a question:[5]

I have already stated this shortly after the election results that the political parties in Singapore — and I hate to use the term opposition parties, because we also now must move in terms of what is the general practice in other jurisdictions. And, in other jurisdictions… in the UK, it is called Labour Party and Conservative. We must call it now in Singapore, PAP and WP. Sorry about the other parties; I've been that way all the time with the rest. And I have been proven to be absolutely correct. I was the one who said just before the 2011 general election, that the party — the opposition party — that gets the most parliamentary seats, whether it is fully elected MPs or NCMPs should never ever sit down with those other, what I call, minor parties, okay. … [T]he term "arrogance" has been raised, the arrogance derives from the minor parties thinking that they are on the same level as the WP. That is exactly the case.

Placing the WP front and centre is not hindsight analysis on my part. I have argued this point for at least a decade prior to GE2020. This is why this book will heavily focus on the WP, and not on issues or entities which I consider to be relatively inconsequential or a non-story.

But I have also got things wrong as well. At the Maruah forum, one member of the audience, a lady who described herself as a "social entrepreneur", suggested that "short of a black swan event", it would be very difficult for the opposition to chip away at the PAP and recover from the loss ground suffered in GE2015. I responded to her: "The lady just now mentioned about a black swan event. You know, I'm very

---

5   The remarks are found at the 1:14:33 to 1:15:52 mark of the following clip: "MARUAH #GE2015 Post-Elections forum — Q & A", 23 September 2016, *YouTube*, https://www.youtube.com/watch?v=Q2ngpQdwlUI&t=3257s. Accessed on 3 February 2021.

pedantic as a scholar: the fact of the matter is that by its very nature a black swan event cannot be predicted. We do not know what it is. So, I can't even answer that question." I was partly right: by its strict definition a black swan event cannot be predicted. But I was wrong in not giving the question more serious consideration which, now looking back, was so brilliantly raised by that audience member. I would say that on the point she made her political instincts were far better than mine.

The COVID-19 pandemic was the black swan event that overshadowed the July 2020 general election. The PAP saw its national vote share erode and, as mentioned, it lost another GRC to the WP. I reference this incident not merely because of the significance of the point that was raised, but also to be upfront with readers that in *Breakthrough 2.0* I will be admitting to some errors of analysis I had made previously. No one can get everything right in the highly niche and dynamic field of electoral politics. And, it is important to be upfront if one had previously committed any errors of analysis. In fact, the one lesson which should be taken from both GE2015 and GE2020 is the fluid nature of electoral politics. More specifically, the Singapore electorate is now prone to a volatility in mood swings and preferences that was simply not apparent before 2011.

The writing of the manuscript for this book and its publication was deliberately not rushed in order to include some developments that occurred subsequent to the general election, and the performance of new members in the 14th Singapore Parliament. More significantly, important statistical data was to emerge during 2021 that proved central in supporting a number of inferences that have been drawn. Bringing this book out a year after GE2020 also provided sufficient time to test the proposition as to whether Singapore's political culture was changing as a consequence of that election. That change had been mooted by some observers almost immediately following

GE2020.[6] I was sceptical about such utterances not least because they were light on details and evidence. Very simply, they were mostly bare assertions, but they were expected to be accepted because they were the popular assertions of the moment. This has contributed to post-truth politics, as is becoming a commonplace phenomenon in the 21st century.[7] No proper analyst can draw reliable inferences immediately from a single, major event, when all the variables that led up to that event had yet to be subjected to close scrutiny and the early ramifications of that event had not even panned out.

Controversy over holding an election during a pandemic

If COVID-19 was the black swan event, the ruling PAP appeared to magnify it by holding a general election right in the midst of the pandemic when the pandemic had not fully subsided. Unlike many other jurisdictions around the world which postponed elections related to political office due to COVID-19, Singapore, under the PAP, insisted on holding a mid-2020 election in spite of the fact that the parliamentary term still had some six months to run its course (after which, within a three-month period, an election must be held). As a derivative of the Westminster model of parliamentary elections, the exact timing of a Singapore general election is entirely in the gift of the prime minister of the day. As early as March 2020, as COVID-19 was making itself felt in Singapore, the widespread feeling among the politically-engaged was that Prime Minister Lee Hsien Loong would issue a writ for a general

---

6 See, for example, "GE2020 shows a new political culture of a 'kinder and gentler politics' is emerging, says Chan Heng Chee", *The Straits Times*, 15 July 2020, https://www.straitstimes.com/politics/ge2020-shows-a-new-political-culture-of-a-kinder-and-gentler-politics-is-emerging-says-chan. Accessed on 16 August 2020.

7 Peter Horton and Garrett W. Brown, "Integrating Evidence, Politics and Society: A Methodology for the Science-Policy Interface", *Humanities and Social Sciences Communications*, 17 April 2018, https://www.nature.com/articles/s41599-018-0099-3.pdf. Accessed on 10 April 2021.

election for the following month. That did not happen. Singapore's initial success in stabilising and getting control of the COVID-19 situation in February and March 2020, faltered as the virus began spreading widely through the dormitories of the huge population of lowly paid migrant workers, who toiled mostly in the construction sector, shipyards, cleaning, and other related low-skilled jobs. Thousands of these workers were infected, albeit mostly mildly, by the virus even as the death rate in Singapore due to COVID-19 remained relatively low as compared to many other jurisdictions. A general election, therefore, could not take place until the pandemic stabilised once more.

Another controversial aspect of GE2020 was that, due to the pandemic, the authorities, in the form of the Elections Department, which is part of the Prime Minister's Office, imposed significant restrictions on aspects of physical election campaigning. On the face of it, this was a major disadvantage to the parties in opposition to the PAP. The alternative parties — as they have been increasingly referred to since 2015 — had in previous elections relied heavily on physical election rallies to get their message across to voters. This book will seek to answer the question: to what extent did a mostly virtual election campaign mean that social media ultimately played a part in the election results? *Breakthrough* had shown that it was not possible for Singapore to have an internet election that could determine its outcome because of one key fact — Singapore has compulsory voting, and it is in a minority of countries that makes it compulsory for citizens to vote in legislative elections. Consequently, social media determining election outcomes become quite implausible. Chapter 3 of *Breakthrough 2.0* goes into some detail in examining the efficacy of social media at GE2020.

Theoretical framework

The chapters in this book are organised thematically. Even though my work on electoral politics has been grounded in empiricism, and I continue in that same tradition in this volume, I have also employed a theoretical framework, in order for the narrative to be more readily understood. The theoretical framework has two components. One component conceptualises the Singapore political landscape into a theoretical model, which I refer to as "authoritarian-centrism". This will be set out and analysed in detail in Chapter 1. The second component of the theoretical framework revolves around what I call the four Ps (4Ps) — Policies, Personalities, Process, and Party branding. Each of these four variables is not of equal weightage. The 4Ps operate mostly asymmetrically between the PAP, as the ruling party, on the one hand, and the alternative parties, on the other. Chapters 2 and 3 will be devoted to analysing the 4Ps.

The subsequent chapters can then be understood by the theoretical framework established in the earlier chapters. It is hoped that this theoretical framework, through which parliamentary elections in Singapore should be viewed, will contribute to knowledge on electoral politics. Just to be clear, a theoretical framework cannot constitute the truth but, if tested rigorously against the empirical evidence, it can guide one towards the truth.

The Singapore electoral system, derived from Westminster's first-past-the-post, cannot be viewed or analysed in isolation. To do so would lead to flawed inferences, because the reader would wonder why certain election phenomena occur, or tend to work, elsewhere, but not so in Singapore. Or, worse still, the reader will insist because certain things work elsewhere then they must necessarily also work in Singapore. This misreading is mostly a consequence of a cursory understanding of electoral systems in general, or of people taking snap-shots of election results elsewhere and contending that there could well be parallels with the situation in Singapore. Thus, a further tool employed is brief comparative analysis of electoral systems in a number of jurisdictions, most notably the United Kingdom. More specifically, parallels — however inexact — are drawn between the WP and the UK's Labour Party where, the contention is made, that an understanding of how the latter has evolved in philosophy and ideology has surprising similarities with how the WP has developed in its political positioning since 2001.

Outlier elections

One of the hazards of employing a theoretical framework in analysing electoral politics in Singapore is that the island-republic has had three parliamentary general elections — in 2011, 2015 and 2020 — that can be considered political outliers. As demonstrated in *Breakthrough*, GE2011 was an anomaly, not because the WP was able to achieve victory in a five-member GRC against the PAP behemoth but because the entire Singapore mainstream media coverage of GE2011 was highly unusual in nature. The print media, whether in English, Chinese, Malay or the Tamil vernacular, ran stories in the weeks leading up to that election which were more balanced in content and analysis. This was unlike previous elections where the mainstream media had been heavily skewed in its political and election coverage in favour of the PAP. In fact, in the run-up to GE2011, some local media were even running stories critical of the PAP or some of its candidates while, conversely, stories were run lauding some opposition personalities, such as Low Thia Khiang, Chen Show Mao and Nicole Seah. At the time, the conventional wisdom, especially among some younger Singaporeans, was that the sudden change in political tone of the local media was due to the influence of the millennial generation. In online socio-political blogs and forums, Singaporean millennials were openly asserting that, because they were of the internet generation, their importance to the future of the country was obvious and that the Establishment, including the mainstream media, had to be responsive to the aspirations of a generation that ostensibly gave greater weight to non-material concerns, such as personal rights, civil liberties, environmental issues, and so on. In fact, journalists from the English and Chinese media were to tell me that the entire machinery of government was changing, becoming more emollient, because it had to pander to the younger generation. At the time, I attempted to dispel such notions, saying that if there was a change adopted by the Establishment, it was a change in style, not substance.

Overlapping and self-reinforcing variables that underpin analysis of Singapore politics

When I'm invited to discuss Singapore politics with visiting academics and officials, I immediately mention to them that the starting point for any discussion lies in a number of variables that overlap and reinforce each other. One of these variables is understanding the nature of the electorate. For the most part, when it comes to socio-cultural matters and politics, the electorate is mostly conservative and risk-averse in nature. Adherence to a particular religious belief is not the only determinant that informs that outlook. Other factors appear to be at work. One of these relates to the extent to which many Singaporeans who grew up over part or all of the period from 1960 to 2010 have viewed Singapore's first prime minister, Lee Kuan Yew — specifically, his over-bearing, paternalistic style — as something which they could or should emulate? Even if they did not deliberately go out to emulate the attitude and behaviour of Lee, did his force of personality, so dominant in a city-state over half-a-century, implicitly bleed into the personalities of those who experienced his ubiquitous presence? That issue cannot be overlooked nor can its significance be underestimated. The contention here is that the durability of the ruling PAP government, with its evident soft authoritarianism, has simply been enabled by a large swathe of the population displaying similar authoritarian leanings. Further, as I argued in *Breakthrough*, Singaporeans' immigrant roots, largely of recent provenance, is a lodestar that guides much of Singaporeans' behaviour and instincts. In most things, economic motivation is the raison d'être of the vast bulk of Singaporeans, and this drives an almost accepted mercenary culture. That said, altruism is also apparent in Singapore. But in order to exist meaningfully in one of the most expensive countries in the world, the unrelenting and almost single-minded pursuit of money and wealth has been a practical necessity for most Singaporeans.

Therefore, a second variable, but one which is really a sub-set of the first is that economic motivation remains the primary driving force for a large majority of Singaporeans. To put it directly, individual mercenary instincts, in terms of what one can benefit from a particular act or situation, is preeminent and always quite apparent.

A third variable that is meshed with the first two is the reality that Singapore has been governed by one political party, the PAP, for some six decades. The PAP was a creature of Lee. He was synonymous with the party. It has taken some five years after his death for the initial signs of a waning of the high degree of respect and deference that was accorded to Lee. Irrespective of that, the fact of the matter is that, politically, his PAP is still very much in the driving seat. And, some six decades of the PAP's socialisation of Singapore's economy, politics, and society, remains a reality. PAP socialisation is manifested in the pervasiveness of the party throughout the island; in the phenomenon of state capitalism (through government-linked corporations); in tough laws and punishments handed down by the courts for breaches of law and order; and, in the general acceptance of the PAP narrative that has become a national narrative, that certain aspects of an austere, paternalistic form of governance, not found elsewhere, are necessary for Singapore because the country exists in a tough neighbourhood. It is unclear whether Singaporeans would be prepared to move away meaningfully from this existential reality, let alone whether the process of PAP socialisation can be so easily halted and reversed. Nonetheless, political opponents to the ruling party can still make inroads against the PAP, as the WP has demonstrated, if they navigate through this labyrinth and, just like a proponent of the martial art of *jiu-jitsu*, deploys the PAP's strengths against itself.

Given the fact that the book is arranged thematically, each of the 10 chapters stands on its own in examining with some degree of granularity the key issues that inform Singapore politics. Consequently, a Conclusion has been eschewed, as it would unlikely do justice to the analysis in each of the chapters. Instead, as a useful reference to all the concepts that were analysed, a Summary providing a check-list of each of the concepts and other issues of material significance, is provided at the end of the book.

A researcher investigates truth, not surface impressions. It takes the metaphorical digging of a mine-shaft to get to the truth which is buried at a significant depth. Nor does a researcher take the easy way out by retailing and embroidering a storyline spun by others simply because that is the expedient and popular narrative which they wish to claim is the answer or the truth. If researchers did so, then they would have failed in their duty to seek out, and uphold, the truth. In this book, loose ends, related to personalities whose statements and behaviour going back a number of years had significant political ramifications but who have attempted to evade accountability, will be tied up, even as other writers have either been impervious to or have found these matters far too delicate for them to address.

Acknowledgements

Even though I am an independent scholar, I do not work independently. To that extent, I owe debts of gratitude to many people, whether scholars or otherwise, who have informed my understanding of electoral politics over many years. The subject is highly specialised and constantly evolving that, in spite of having researched it for more than three decades, I still consider myself but a mere student of politics. The reference sources in each chapter provide attribution to ideas that have originated from others. Even casual remarks of intellectual significance uttered in seminars or published in social media, I have given attribution to their provenance. Let me start right now by crediting Titus Chng, a young Singaporean, for inspiring the title of this volume. Back in May 2020 I had suggested to my publisher the working title *Singapore's Pandemic*

Election. This was accepted. However, in the early hours of 11 July 2020, after the results of GE2020 were known, Titus left a comment to one of my Facebook posts. He asked whether I would be writing a new book, "Breakthrough II perhaps?" My publisher spotted the comment, immediately realised that my earlier work had been remembered and, in a nod to the terminological preference of millennials and Generation Z, suggested we go with *Breakthrough 2.0.*

As my research and writing progressed and I was in need of certain scholarly works which were not immediately accessible to me, I reached out to a number of academics for assistance. Professor Charles Pattie of the University of Sheffield, who has written extensively on political canvassing at the local level, responded immediately and generously to my request for several of his works. Equally, Professor Shane P. Singh of the University of Georgia, who is an expert on the concept of compulsory voting, came through following a similar request. The same for Associate Professor Karel Kouba at the University of Hradec, Králové, Czech Republic, and Assistant Professor Patrick Cunha Silva of the University of Washington in St. Louis, Missouri, whose separate research efforts on invalid voting substantially enriched my understanding of that phenomenon. A number of senior academics and administrators at the University of Oxford also responded promptly to my email enquiries for clarification on several matters.

The officers at the Elections Department Singapore were unfailing in their courtesy towards me and, without exception, provided me fully with data and answers to all the clarifications I had sought. Out of an abundance of caution, and to avoid inadvertently transgressing any boundaries, I have only used a small portion of that information.

Considerable thanks go to WP parliamentarians, cadres, and volunteers, who provided me with insights on a number of matters which were to disprove popular (i.e., *optimistic*) accounts of events that circulated in the mainstream and alternative media. Again, I have only used a small portion of the information that was furnished to me and, where it was appropriate, have been careful not to reveal the identities of some sources.

Members of the PAP and former Nominated MPs, also provided me with little-known observations that formed the basis of one of the sub-themes in Chapter 7. A member of the Progress Singapore Party, who had been heavily involved in the party's election efforts, brought to my attention an interesting bit of information which had escaped my attention but was highly useful to my analysis. Jose Raymond, who had been a member of the Singapore People's Party, was one of my main sources of information for what was happening across the alternative parties outside the WP. Both of us had kept in regular contact since mid-2018.

To ensure accuracy, I have attempted to independently verify the accounts of the political practitioners whose information appears in this book. Statements of material significance that were of such variance to other sources and, therefore, did not seem reliable, were discounted and not used. Like the piecing together of a jigsaw puzzle, if pieces did not fit, I did not force them into the body of the text just to formulate a particular narrative.

Whilst writing the manuscript for this book I had met up individually with half-a-dozen of my friends and acquaintances, who are not just politically-engaged, but who have stood for election to Parliament. Over meals we discussed various issues I had examined in the manuscript. I sought sounding boards to challenge some of the evidence I had unearthed and the inferences drawn.

Finally, I must acknowledge World Scientific for the opportunity to publish this book on GE2020, which also enabled me to expand my thoughts on broader political and social issues that predated that election by up to three decades. This allowed me to provide a different perspective to conventional wisdom. In particular, I wish to thank my editor, Jiang Yulin who, right from the start, encouraged me to put together this volume, and who worked closely and patiently with me to see the manuscript to its conclusion. The responsibility for errors of fact that might have crept into the text in spite of the best efforts, remains solely with me.

CHAPTER 1

An Authoritarian-Centrist Polarity Reflects Singapore's Political Landscape as Evidenced in GE2020

A major thesis of this book is that Singaporeans are, for the most part, socially and politically conservative. Consequently, the main form of electoral change which can occur in the country in the foreseeable future is through a political party that practises a moderate form of politics. Here, "moderate" is defined as something that is relative to the accepted nature of the People's Action Party (PAP) and its six decades of largely paternalistic rule over Singapore. The contention of this chapter, and this book, is that the Workers' Party's (WP) political positioning close to the centre-ground was what gained it initial support at the general election in 2011. That support was to be reinforced nine years later. The result of the general election of 2020 (GE2020) confirmed what was apparent for some time, but had yet to be captured in actual polling numbers, i.e., in its governance and socio-political leanings, Singapore is an authoritarian-centrist polity. The deep political polarisation across demographics that is found in many other countries is less apparent in Singapore.

At GE2020, the WP secured 10 out of 93 parliamentary seats, the highest number for any alternative party in decades. The WP's average percentage of the valid vote cast across the six electoral divisions — four group representation constituencies (GRCs) and two single-member constituencies (SMCs) — it contested was 50.4%. That is to say, the WP took just slightly more than half the popular vote in an aggregate of six straight fights against the PAP. Why and how the WP did so are some of the questions answered in this book. The short answer is that the WP's relatively good performance was due to its deliberate positioning in the political spectrum. The WP projected itself as a moderate alternative to the PAP. If the PAP is defined as having authoritarian leanings; and, the WP is defined as a politically moderate party, then, in theoretical terms, what best describes Singapore politically is the concept of an authoritarian-centrist polarity. But it is not a model that is immutable. New trends and data emerging in a fast-changing world could prompt the need for a new model in the foreseeable future.

Before proceeding, some definitional clarity is required. In the scholarly literature, a number of writers have tended to refer to "authoritarian populism", or employ "populism" (i.e., right-wing populism) and authoritarianism interchangeably.[1] In the political context of countries, such as Brazil, India and the Philippines, the interchangeable use of the terms is not inapt. In the case of Singapore, however, it would not be accurate to suggest that populism has been used as a political strategy, at least not as a winning strategy in parliamentary elections. Neither the PAP nor the WP can be said to be populist parties.[2]

Authoritarian-centrism: Where a moderate party is the real challenger to the incumbent

The conceptualised authoritarian-centrist theoretical model differs from the model conceived by constitutional law expert and Harvard professor, Mark Tushnet. Here, it should be stated that the theoretical construct framed in this chapter views Singapore largely through a political lens, whereas Tushnet does so largely through the lens of constitutional law. In his study published in 2015, Tushnet described Singapore as an

---

1 See, Kanishka Jayasuriya, "The Rise of the Right: Populism and Authoritarianism in Southeast Asian Politics", *Southeast Asian Affairs 2020*; and, Lars Rensmann, "The Persistence of the Authoritarian Appeal: On Critical Theory as a Framework for Studying Populist Actors in European Democracies", in J. Morelock (ed.), *Critical Theory and Authoritarian Populism*, (London: University of Westminster Press, 2018).

2 It would be calamitous if they were, as Singapore is, in its demographics, multiracial, with three-quarters of its population being ethnic Chinese, and the island-republic is geographically situated in the Malay world of maritime Southeast Asia.

"authoritarian constitutionalism".[3] He described three forms of constitutionalism other than liberal constitutionalism:[4]

> *In absolutist constitutionalism, a single decisionmaker motivated by an interest in the nation's well-being consults widely and protects civil liberties generally, but in the end, decides on a course of action in the decisionmaker's sole discretion, unchecked by any other institutions. In mere rule-of-law constitutionalism, the decisionmaker conforms to some general procedural requirements and implements decisions through, among other things, independent courts, but the decisionmaker is not constrained by any substantive rules regarding, for example, civil liberties. Finally, in authoritarian constitutionalism liberal freedoms are protected at an intermediate level, and elections are reasonably free and fair.*

That was an exercise in contrast to highlight what authoritarian constitutionalism is not so that it can be understood normatively. In a fairly indirect way, what Tushnet says in his work is that the government in Singapore is duly elected by the people; that the government enacts laws, places them on the statute book and governs on the basis of an accepted and written constitution after being duly voted in through a parliamentary general election. But, then, that government displays aspects of authoritarian behaviour, where Tushnet provides examples over many years. Much of what Tushnet describes cannot be disputed. His study is both useful and well-considered. But it is worth building on his work by providing a model that would *not* have been apparent back in 2015 but seemed to have been confirmed by the outcome of GE2020.

It is not uncommon for many researchers to place the entire onus on the PAP government to explain the political landscape in Singapore

---

3 Mark Tushnet, "Authoritarian Constitutionalism", *Cornell Law Review*, Vol. 100, No. 2, January 2015.

4 Ibid. p. 396.

and the way society is ordered. Not much attempt has been made to determine whether there is any possibility that a sizeable segment of Singaporeans might actually be predisposed to illiberal and authoritarian tendencies.[5] If not being illiberal or authoritarian, could it be said that many Singaporeans are at the very least socially and politically risk-averse, preferring to stick to the familiar which is a relic of a bygone era?[6] Some scholars are either impervious to this possibility, or find it uncomfortable to countenance. On that latter, a number of non-Singaporean scholars are unable to understand why in spite of glowing socioeconomic metrics,[7] Singapore had not joined the ranks of liberal democracies many years ago.[8] The one should follow the other, so the axiom goes.[9] That Singapore has not done so is due to an authoritarian government preventing progression towards liberal democracy, as sometimes argued by the critics. The truth is

5 For instance, one scholar has written, in relation to Singapore, "about a mutually reinforcing set of institutions subordinated to ruling party interests". Garry Rodan, *Transparency and Authoritarian Rule in Southeast Asia: Singapore and Malaysia*, (London: Routledge, 2004), p. 180.

6 The following observation was made of the Singapore middle class in 1998: "[it is] founded on political indifference mixed with high anxiety. Its most significant manifestation is the local practice of *kiasuism*. *Kiasu* behaviour is premised on the belief that 'if you are not one up you are one down' and condones otherwise antisocial activity provided the progenitor succeeds in achieving collectively desired but scarce social goods while maintaining conformist anonymity." (Since 1998, this behaviour has not changed much, if at all.) David Martin Jones, "Democratization, Civil Society, and Illiberal Middle Class Structure in Pacific Asia", *Comparative Politics*, Vol. 30, No. 2, January 1998, p. 153.

7 See, for instance, Michael D. Barr and Zlatko Skrbis, *Constructing Singapore: Elitism, Ethnicity and the Nation-Building Project*, (Copenhagen: NIAS Press, 2008); and, Garry Rodan, *The Political Economy of Singapore's Industrialisation: National State and International Capital*, (Basingstoke: Macmillan, 1989).

8 Fareed Zakaria, *The Future of Freedom: Illiberal Democracy at Home and Abroad*, (New York: W.W. Norton, 2003), p. 86. See, also, Uk Heo and Alexander C. Tan, "Democracy and Economic Growth: A Causal Analysis", *Comparative Politics*, Vol. 33, No. 4, July 2001.

9 Jeffrey A. Winters, "Wealth Defense and the Complicity of Liberal Democracy", *Nomos*, Vol. 58, 2017, p. 159.

usually never as straightforward as that. One American observer had said:[10]

> *The People's Action Party, the party of Lee [Kuan Yew], Goh [Keng Swee], and [S.] Rajaratnam, never faced any serious electoral adversary, no doubt in part because Lee and his colleagues ruthlessly crushed any potential challenger while they were still ducklings. But, in part, the citizens of Singapore were more than supportive of their government and of the PAP, which regularly won landslide majorities…*

In other polities, regime repression would often tend to elicit a strong pushback from the people. In Singapore, however, the ruling PAP's multi-track approach to fighting general elections — as sketched out in Chapter 10 — has, on-balance, given it the desired results at the polls. But, at GE2011 and GE2020, there was a measure of pushback from voters in key constituency-level contests. That said, the unmistakable fact is that there is still a majority of Singaporeans who are attracted to a type of governance in Singapore that can be described as paternalistic and authoritarian. That does not make Singapore unique in the global political landscape.

India has, since 2014, been governed by the Bharatiya Janata Party (BJP) under Narendra Modi. The BJP is a Hindu-nationalist party and an authoritarian movement.[11] In the Philippines, the populist authoritarian Rodrigo Duterte was elected as president in 2016.[12]

---

10 Gerald Hyman, "Lee Kuan Yew's Enigma: Authoritarian, Yet a Kind of Democrat", Center for Strategic & International Studies, 30 March 2015, https://www.csis.org/analysis/lee-kuan-yew%E2%80%99s-enigma-authoritarian-yet-kind-democrat. Accessed on 10 January 2021.

11 The dimensions of the BJP's authoritarianism are set out in Audrey Truschke, "Hindutva's Dangerous Rewriting of History", *South Asia Multidisciplinary Academic Journal*, 24/25, 2020; and, Lucie Calleja, "The Rise of Populism: The Threat to Civil Society?" *E-International Relations*, 9 February 2020, https://www.e-ir.info/pdf/81470. Accessed on 11 January 2021.

12 Anna Romina Guevarra and Maya Arcilla, "The Source of Actual Terror: The Philippine Macho-Fascist Duterte", *Feminist Studies*, Vol. 46, No. 2, 2020.

Duterte was helped into power by the Philippine middle-class who was said to have wallowed in "authoritarian nostalgia".[13] Significantly, around 72.4% of Overseas Filipino Workers (OFW) also voted for Duterte at Philippine diplomatic missions worldwide.[14] In the wake of Duterte's election, some Singaporean civil society activists who had, for many years, been assisting OFWs regarding employment issues were said to have been crestfallen that many did not share their own liberal values. In Brazil, a retired military officer, Jair Bolsonaro, running on a right-wing platform, was elected as president in 2018, and was to govern with a relish for authoritarianism.[15] In Europe, Hungary's Viktor Orban has led a resurgence in the popularity of far-right political parties across the continent since 2010. In 2015, Poland joined Hungary on an "illiberal development path".[16] Some might argue that the examples just cited were aberrations. But, in truth, it is difficult to dismiss the reality that impulses towards authoritarianism are alive in electorates across a diverse range of countries. For Singapore, however, European, American and Australian scholars tend to hold it to a far higher standard because the country is mostly English-speaking, has a highly-educated population and, on a per capita basis, has probably sent more of its citizens to Oxford and Cambridge and the Ivy League schools combined than any other country. Yet, in its political development, the island-republic does not appear enlightened. Instead, it leans towards authoritarianism.

13 Adele Webb, "Why are the Middle-Class Misbehaving? Exploring Democratic Ambivalence and Authoritarian Nostalgia", *Sociological Review*, Vol. 65, 2017.

14 "Duterte Victory Boosts by OFW Power", *OFW Pinoy Star Magazine*, http://www.ofwpinoystar.com/ofw-power-boosts-duterte-victory/. Accessed on 11 January 2021.

15 Ericson Crivelli, "The Rise of Right-Wing Populism in Brazil", *International Union Rights*, Vol. 26, No. 3, 2019.

16 Andras Bozoki and Daniel Hemedus, "An Externally Constrained Hybrid Regime: Hungary in the European Union", *Democratization*, Vol. 25, No. 7, April 2018, p. 1176.

To many non-Singaporean scholars this existential reality must purely be the making of the PAP government.

To give some texture to the issue, it might be useful to inject an anecdote of some relevance. In a discussion in September 2019 on Singapore politics with three journalists from *The Straits Times*, I had said words to the effect, that hardball election tactics by the PAP might sometimes be counter-productive when applied broadly as the voters were sensitive to differences across the parties, and some voters could be fair in their judgment.[17] To which, one journalist, a millennial, seemed genuinely surprised and immediately asked whether voters were interested in "fairness"? I thought that was very telling. I responded that, yes, I could see some voters being fair. Yet, the journalist's remark might in fact be reflective of a mindset pervasive amongst many Singaporeans — even across the younger generation — whereby they think mostly in terms of what they can get out of a situation, and not in terms of the general good or what might be fair and just.

The authoritarian personality is pervasive in the electorate

The distinction between a regime that displays authoritarian traits, on the one hand, and a large swathe of a population which displays outward authoritarian personality traits or simply called the "authoritarian personality",[18] on the other, needs to be made clear. The two should not be conflated. On the authoritarian personality, researchers have check-listed a number of traits.[19] These include: deference, if not subservience,

---

17 Discussion with journalists from *The Straits Times*, 5 September 2019.

18 John Levi Martin, "The Authoritarian Personality, 50 Years Later: What Lessons are There for Political Psychology", *Political Psychology*, Vol. 22, No. 1, 2001.

19 Stanley Feldman and Karen Stenner, "Perceived Threat and Authoritarianism", *Political Psychology*, Vol. 18, No. 4, December 1997, pp. 749–750; John Duckitt,

to established authority and an acceptance of hierarchy;[20] an attachment to dominant groups in society and a rejection of outgroups;[21] placing a high value on order in society but not on individual freedom;[22] demonstrating patriotism and an inclination towards social conformity;[23] and, a stress on discipline and willingness to use extreme measures on those who violate laws.[24] To this list one could add self-centredness, an obvious mercenary instinct and, most importantly, opportunism.

Taking each of the foregoing traits in turn, it is accepted that Singapore is a class-conscious society, where citizens are expected to know their place in the established hierarchy. The ingroup versus outgroup juxtaposition is a consequence of the multiracial character of the country; racial consciousness has come in cycles and has been on an up cycle since social media use became pervasive in Singapore and was further accentuated during the COVID-19 pandemic. In many jurisdictions, the impact of race is personalised in terms of lived experience, but is generally informed at three levels — the cultural, the institutional, and the individual.[25] Equally, the

---

"Authoritarianism and Group Identification: A New View of an Old Construct", *Political Psychology*, Vol. 10, No. 1, March 1989, p. 70; and, Marlies Glasius, "What Authoritarianism is… and is not: A Practice Perspective", *International Affairs*, Vol. 94, No. 3, 2018, pp. 516–517.

20 Stefano Passini, "Different Ways of Being Authoritarian: The Distinct Effects of Authoritarian Dimensions on Values and Prejudice", *Political Psychology*, Vol. 38, No. 1, February 2017, p. 73.

21 Feldman and Stenner, op. cit., p. 749.

22 Ibid.

23 Ibid., p. 750.

24 Ibid.

25 Benjamin B. Bowser, "Racism: Origin and Theory", *Journal of Black Studies*, Vol. 48, No. 6, September 2017, pp. 579–581.

significance given to race as a challenge also depends on the particular person who might raise it as an issue. To that extent, focusing on the institutional level, Chinese-Singaporean writer Zhuo Tee set out in some detail how one of the planks of a structure has systematically benefited ethnic Chinese-Singaporeans, who make up around three-quarters of the country's demographic.[26] A few other planks of race-based institutional structures,[27] have prompted some to suggest the existence of the concept of "Chinese privilege".[28] For a number of reasons, including the fact that it is employed as a derivative of the concept of "white privilege", there has been marked resistance in

---

26 In a concluding observation to his article on Special Assistance Plan (SAP) schools, Zhuo Tee says:

Of course, to ascribe all the tensions between multiracialism and meritocracy to SAP schools would be fallacious. Other systemic and cultural issues have made our society less fair, equal, and democratic. But effectively providing affirmative action for an already privileged racial majority, and guaranteeing the ascension of members of that majority to power, definitely doesn't help. Removing these vestiges that make a mockery of our democracy will allow us to truly build a multicultural society, based on justice and equality.

Zhuo Tee, "The Special Assistance Plan: Singapore's Own Bumiputera Policy", *Equality & Democracy: Singapore Political Theory in Action*, 7 December 2017, https://equalitydemocracy.commons.yale-nus.edu.sg/2017/12/07/the-special-assistance-plan-singapores-own-bumiputera-policy/. Accessed on 19 January 2021.

27 These include self-help groups, and the Ethnic Integration Programme which imposes ethnic quotas in blocks of Housing and Development Board (HDB) flats.

28 The actual provenance of the term "Chinese privilege" is uncertain. However, some have credited the Singaporean anti-racism activist, Sangeetha Thanapal, for having coined it.

accepting the phenomenon of Chinese privilege.[29] It is a highly contested concept.[30]

---

29 There was a strong pushback by panellists at a webinar organised by the Institute of Policy Studies (IPS) in January 2021, that the concept of "Chinese privilege" exists in Singapore. One panellist, sociologist Daniel Goh, said that because Chinese privilege is derived from the American concept of white privilege, "It cannot be something that is just simply equivalent to white privilege, because America had a very different history with regard to racial relations..." (Quoted in "IPS conference: racial, social identities will continue to pose a challenge, say observers", *The Straits Times*, 14 January 2021, https://www.straitstimes.com/singapore/politics/ips-conference-racial-social-identities-will-continue-to-pose-a-challenge. Accessed on 19 January 2021.) Intellectually, some people will find difficulty grappling with Goh's view. Numerous theories and concepts of sociology derive from the West, based on centuries of Western civilisation and lived experience. To what extent sociologists have claimed that those theories and concepts have entirely no applicability to non-Western societies, is not entirely clear. But what is clear is that the same set of empirical circumstances need not exist in exact form for a theory or concept to be considered valid in broad terms. What is required in proving the validity or otherwise of a theory or concept is to test it through the marshalling of empirical evidence that supports its basis balanced against countervailing evidence that refutes it. Both sets of evidence have to be adduced fully. To be disinclined to accept the concept of "Chinese privilege" simply because it derives from America's "white privilege" and, instead, to prefer some other phrase or term to describe the situation in Singapore would tend, in the view of some ethnic minorities, to water down the degree of the problem. Quite a number of ethnic minorities will maintain that the problem is real and not confected. They will also say that because the deck is so heavily stacked against them in multiple dimensions and has continued to evolve that way over several decades, they have to keep mum and accept the state narrative which has argued directly the reverse. Equally, in private discussion, a number of Singaporean ethnic minorities have said that they have to be 200% better than any ethnic Chinese to be able to achieve just 50% as much, or similar formulations. I had gathered all these views in face-to-face conservations with ethnic minority Singaporeans over a number of years.

30 Many Chinese Singaporeans, if asked about their privilege relative to ethnic minorities, are likely to respond similarly as white Americans have done when the latter were asked about the same issue. As one study observed:

... when white American individuals were exposed to evidence of white privilege, they reported greater levels of personal hardship. This suggests that privileged individuals may respond to evidence of their group privilege by emphasising personal hardship in order to mitigate the extent to which they feel undeserving of that privilege, or to distance themselves from that elevated status on an individual level.

As to the emphasis on social order over individual freedom, this tendency was mostly government-led during the 1990s and had largely been bought into by most Singaporeans.[31] Citizens' sense of patriotism is indicated by how easily Singaporeans' have internalised the need for National Service — i.e., a conscripted armed force — in defence of the country. On harsh punishments for aberrant behaviour, the population's general support for corporal and capital punishment are noteworthy. Finally, as to mercenary instincts, the degree to which money has tended to buy loyalty and has created an all-too-obvious culture of sycophancy in the island-republic, is also noteworthy.

Divining what has contributed to the authoritarian personality traits of many Singaporeans will be open to contention. Based on studies elsewhere around the world, scholars have posited that the authoritarian personality could be caused by innate and genetic factors, or is possibly "the product of social learning".[32] One scholar has also noted that as "economic inequality increases, people are more and more trained by the market to expect command and obedience".[33] All these factors are interesting but might not fully explain the strong strand of authoritarianism that runs through Singapore's population. The wellspring of authoritarian leanings amongst Singaporeans could really be said to be the result of social and cultural conservatism. It has been analysed in some detail by Joseph B. Tamney in *The Struggle Over Singapore's Soul: Western Modernization and Asian Culture*.[34] Though published in 1996, that

---

Alexandra Murdoch and Kareena McAloney-Kocaman, "Exposure to Evidence of White Privilege and Perceptions of Hardships Among White UK Residents", *Race and Social Problems*, 11, 2019, p. 206.

31 See Chua Beng Huat, *Communitarian Democracy in Singapore*, (London: Routledge, 1997).

32 Frederick Solt, "The Social Origins of Authoritarianism", *Political Research Quarterly*, Vol. 65, No. 4, December 2012, pp. 703–704. See, also, Stanley Feldman, "Enforcing Social Conformity: A Theory of Authoritarianism", *Political Psychology*, Vol. 24, No. 1, 2003.

33 Solt ibid., p. 704.

34 Joseph B. Tamney, *The Struggle Over Singapore's Soul: Western Modernization and Asian Culture*, (Berlin: Walter de Gruyter, 1996).

work still retains validity a quarter-of-a-century later. The social and cultural conservatism of many Singaporeans partly derives from the civilisational aspects of the country's "Chineseness".[35] Another aspect pointing to the conservative character of the country is the fact that a vast proportion of Singaporeans are relatively traditional in their value system, being adherents of one of the major religions.[36] Singapore's population census — an exercise conducted every 10 years — noted in its 2020 survey that 80% of Singaporeans and Permanent Residents (PRs) aged 15 and above had a religious affiliation.[37] However, the mainstream media, perhaps not seeing that as newsworthy, preferred to focus on the fact that the number professing no religion rose by three percentage points to 20% from 17% a decade earlier.[38] Commenting on this aspect of the census, two observers were to note that: "… the continued significance of religion should not be understated. Despite

---

35 The general concept of "Chineseness", the sources that inform it, and its ramifications, especially in relation to other ethnicities, was highlighted by one scholar in 1994, who had noted that "the systematic investigation of racism and discriminatory exclusions" in a number of East Asian countries, including Singapore, had "become a matter of great urgency". Frank Dikötter, "Racial Identities in China: Context and Meaning", *The China Quarterly*, No. 138, June 1994, p. 412.

36 That religious belief underpins conservative attitudes is replete in the body of research. In an article published as long ago as 1913, one scholar stated that, "All experience proves that conservatism is an immense power in human nature, and in religion probably more than in any sphere of human life." The writer went on to say that, "The power of conservatism affects doctrine, ethics, ceremonial and liturgical forms, and polity in unequal degrees, although it affects them all very greatly." E. Albert Cook, "Conservatism in Religion", *The Harvard Theological Review*, Vol. 6, No. 2, April 1913, p. 185.

37 Due to the fact that Permanent Residents (PRs) make up a materially large proportion of the Singapore resident population, they tend to be included in surveys. This is at a variance from other countries where PR numbers are not significant enough to warrant such inclusion.

38 "More S'poreans have no religious affiliation: Population census", *The Straits Times*, 16 June 2021, https://www.straitstimes.com/singapore/more-sporeans-have-no-religious-affiliation-population-census. Accessed on 16 June 2021; and, "20% of Singapore residents have no religion, an increase from the last population census", *CNA*, 16 June 2021, https://www.channelnewsasia.com/news/singapore/census-2020-more-residents-no-religion-15023964. Accessed on 16 June 2021.

the decline in overall proportions of adherents, faith will continue to retain its relevance and play a sizeable role in shaping [Singapore] society."[39] To put things in some context, for advanced countries such as the United Kingdom, Germany, Australia, and the United States, the proportion of the population reporting as having no religion was 52.8% (in 2017), 37% (2017), 30% (2016), and 26% (2019) respectively.[40]

The think tank, the Institute of Policy Studies (IPS), has regularly taken the pulse of the Singapore body politic, including on issues of morality and religiosity. Though its surveys have shown movement towards acceptance of more liberal attitudes, the bulk of the population is still conservatively anchored. This was affirmed in a 2019 IPS study based on a survey of attitudes related to *Religion, Morality and Conservatism in Singapore*.[41] (The sample size of the survey was 4,015, comprising Singaporeans and PRs, and was fairly representative of its ethnic and religious diversity.[42]) Though the study confirmed that Singapore remained a relatively conservative society when it came to social mores, there was significant movement towards more liberal

---

39 Mathew Matthews and Melvin Tay, "Fading faith? Fathoming the future of Singapore's religious landscape", *The Straits Times*, 22 June 2021.

40 Elizabeth Clery, John Curtice and Roger Harding (eds.), *British Social Attitudes 34*, (London: NatCen Social Research 2017), p. 197, https://www.bsa.natcen.ac.uk/media/39196/bsa34_full-report_fin.pdf. Accessed on 16 June 2021; "What Germany Believes", 7 September 2017, https://www.deutschland.de/en/topic/life/religious-faith-in-germany%3Amany-germans-are-leaving-the-church. Accessed on 16 June 2021; Australian Bureau of Statistics, "2016 Census: Religion", https://www.abs.gov.au/AUSSTATS/abs@.nsf/mediareleasesbyReleaseDate/7E65A144540551D7CA258148000E2B85. Accessed on 16 June 2021; and, Pew Research Center, "In US Decline of Christianity Continues at Rapid Pace", 17 October 2019, https://www.pewforum.org/2019/10/17/in-u-s-decline-of-christianity-continues-at-rapid-pace/. Accessed on 16 June 2021.

41 Mathew Matthews, Leonard Lim and Shantini Selvarajan, *Religion, Morality and Conservatism in Singapore*, May 2019, IPS Working Papers No. 34, p. 23, https://lkyspp.nus.edu.sg/docs/default-source/ips/ips-working-paper-34---religion-morality-and-conservatism-in-singapore.pdf. Accessed on 20 January 2021.

42 Ibid. p. 7.

attitudes from a similar survey conducted in 2013.[43] But those who take the view that there is an inexorable progression towards liberalism on socio-cultural issues could well be ignoring countervailing factors and, consequently, there might not be a linear progression. The main countervailing factor is the large number of newly arrived immigrants to Singapore who take up permanent residency and who might later then become naturalised citizens. According to government figures released in January 2020, between 15,000 and 25,000 new citizenships are granted annually.[44] Previous research into, and analysis of, naturalised Singaporeans, have indicated that many were predisposed towards being conservative in their social attitudes and were sympathetic to the government of the day — i.e., the PAP.[45] In fact, one reason which prompted quite a number of them to become Singapore citizens was the attraction to the socially conservative basis of the country, with its stress on discipline and a no-nonsense attitude towards law and order. The country's demographic profile which, to some extent, they could identify with, was also another reason. Many of the new waves of immigrants to Singapore from the turn of the millennium were also — like many born and bred Singaporeans before the millennial generation — enamoured of Singapore's founding prime minister, Lee Kuan Yew.

It could be said that substantial numbers of Singaporeans have had a symbiotic relationship with the PAP. And, in their traits, many have role-modelled themselves after Lee, whose influence over Singaporeans for over half-a-century was pervasive and omnipresent. This

---

43 Ibid. p. 23.

44 "Are Singaporeans Renouncing Their Citizenship and Rapidly Being Replaced?" 19 January 2020, https://www.gov.sg/article/are-singaporeans-renouncing-their-citizenship-and-rapidly-being-replaced#:~:text=Between%2015%2C000%20and%2025%2C000%20new,Asian%20Countries%20such%20as%20Malaysia. Accessed on 15 January 2021.

45 Derek da Cunha, *Breakthrough: Roadmap for Singapore's Political Future*, (Singapore: Institute of Policy Studies and Straits Times Press, 2012), p. 253.

role-modelling effect that Lee had across a significant swathe of Singaporeans, is an under-rated and under-studied phenomenon. Yet, it might be a better frame to understand Singapore society. To that extent, could such a dominant personality overseeing the evolution of a small country over a protracted period, have had any other effect? The outcome of GE2015, where the PAP secured 69.9% of the popular vote (a surge from 60.14% at GE2011), and which followed just months after Lee's death was attributed to an "LKY effect" — a sympathy vote for the PAP in gratitude to Lee and his contributions to Singapore.[46] Viewed through another lens, that election was deemed by some observers as a vote for authoritarianism.[47] Lee was effectively synonymous with independent Singapore. He was at once charismatic and authoritarian, successfully melding the two into a "heroic leadership" that steered the country through his sheer force of personality.[48] Singaporeans who were enamoured of Lee would say that they viewed his charisma — manifested in diligence, vision, intellectual brilliance and oratory — as an example to them. Few would ever admit that they might have sub-consciously been emulating — and still emulate — someone who was authoritarian

---

46 "PAP won GE2015 before campaign began: Polling firm Blackbox Research", *The Straits Times*, 5 February 2016, https://www.straitstimes.com/politics/pap-won-ge2015-before-campaign-began-polling-firm-blackbox-research. Accessed on 19 February 2021.

47 See "Singapore's Stubborn Authoritarianism", *Harvard Political Review*, 29 September 2015, https://harvardpolitics.com/singapores-stubborn-authoritarianism/. Accessed on 19 February 2021; and, Lily Rahim, "Fear, smear and the paradox of authoritarian politics in Singapore", *The Conversation*, 28 September 2021, https://theconversation.com/fear-smear-and-the-paradox-of-authoritarian-politics-in-singapore-47763. Accessed on 19 February 2021.

48 One scholar has noted that charisma is based on the aura of the exceptional or exemplary quality of a leader, and that leadership is attributed to the inner life of the leader, a personal vision, an imagination and fantasies, where self-confidence and theatricality are employed to impress and persuade followers. (To that extent, it is noteworthy that short video clips that show Lee Kuan Yew confidently delivering bombastic, assertive speeches and without a script, gesticulating authoritatively and holding his audience in thrall, are replete online and have been repeatedly re-posted on various websites after his death.) Tuomo Antero Takala, "Charismatic Leadership and Power", *Problems and Perspectives in Management*, August 2004, p. 50.

by nature. It could be said that Lee's greatest legacy was to leave behind for many Singaporeans — those who, by GE2020, were 40 years old or above — a particular attitude of mind that was anything other than liberal or progressive.[49]

So, though Tushnet's theoretical model of authoritarian constitutionalism has considerable merit, and was a fairly accurate portrayal at the time it was espoused, what is postulated here is that following GE2020 Singapore can, in political terms, more accurately be described as an authoritarian-centrist polity, where the forces of conservatism/authoritarianism are in contention with the forces of moderation/centrism. The analysis that follows attempts to explain in more granular terms why this theoretical model has intellectual utility.

The left-right polarity does not apply to Singapore even as it explains other polities

It has been acknowledged in the growing body of research that, as a semantical concept, the left-right polarity remains relevant in describing the political preferences of voters in many countries.[50] The work of two scholars, writing in 2018, reinforced that view: "Previous findings have shown that left and right political ideologies can serve as vessels through which inclinations, values, and preferences of individuals are organized

---

49 Around 70% of Singaporean voters were aged 40 years old or above at GE2020.

50 See, for instance, H.F. Bienfait and W. E. A. van Beek, "Right and Left as Political Categories: An Exercise in 'Not-so-Primitive' Classification", *Anthropos*, Vol. 96, No. 1, 2001; and, Andre Freire and Kats Kivitstik, "Mapping and Explaining the Use of the Left-Right Divide", *Brazilian Political Science Review*, December 2013. It has also been observed: "While still typically invoked for analytical purposes rather than as a distinctive object of study, Left and Right have been given detailed consideration in several works of the last two decades. Almost all contributions have felt it necessary to discuss, though they have often disputed, the possibility that these categories are on the wane." Jonathan White, "Left and Right as Political Resources", *Journal of Political Ideologies*, Vol. 16, No. 2, 2011, p. 123.

and find expression in individuals' political action."[51] And, another scholar has pointed out that, in Western Europe, social, value-based, and partisan components continue to structure a left-right schema.[52] In extrapolating these variables to four polities in East Asia, the following findings were arrived at: "value-based factors exert most influence on left-right orientations in Japan and Korea, partisan factors in Taiwan, and that neither play a significant role in the Philippines."[53] But it has also been noted by others that the rise of identity politics and populism might actually be eclipsing the traditional left-right cleavage as a key descriptive concept to explain political divides.[54] Putting that last point aside, the fact remains that the left-right divide is still regularly employed by academics to conceptualise the broad political landscape. But what is relevant for our purposes is that, though the left-right divide exists in other countries, it does not exist in Singapore. This is a strawman argument, some might contend. On the contrary, since GE2020, there have been attempts by liberals and left-leaning elements on social media and the blogosphere to either reframe the WP's gains at that election as some sort of liberal/progressive reaction to PAP authoritarian rule; or, if not that, then an attempt to push the WP to stand with those who consider themselves as having suffered repression by the Establishment.[55]

---

51 Gian Vittorio Caprara and Michele Vecchione, "On the Left and Right Ideological Divide: Historical Accounts and Contemporary Perspectives", *Advances in Political Psychology*, Vol. 39, Suppl. 1, 2018, p. 51.

52 Willy Jou, "The Heuristic Value of the Left-Right Schema in East Asia", *International Political Science Review*, Vol. 31, No. 3, 2010, p. 387.

53 Ibid.

54 Abdul Noury and Gerard Roland, "Identity Politics and Populism in Europe", *Annual Review of Political Science*, Vol. 23, 2020, p. 422.

55 Two examples can be cited. One related to remarks online decrying why the WP did "not contribute even one cent" to the fund-raising efforts of Leong Sze Hian, a member of the Peoples Voice party, who had been sued by Prime Minister Lee Hsien Loong for defamation and had to pay damages. Another example can be found in "Non-profit arts group asks whether LO Pritam Singh will raise PJ Thum issue in Parliament", *The Independent SG*, 25 September 2020, https://theindependent.sg/non-profit-arts-group-asks-whether-lo-pritam-singh-will-raise-pj-thum-issue-in-parliament/. Accessed on 8 May 2021.

The left-right polarity had existed in Singapore in the late 1950s/ early 1960s, but ended with the left, as represented by the Barisan Socialis, losing out to the right, as represented by the PAP, in the battle for the spoils of a post-colonial Singapore. Remnants of the political left continued to be vanquished in the 1970s, exemplified in the crackdown on university students attempting to represent workers' interests.[56] From the 1980s onwards, Singapore was in a phase of political transition. At the 1991 general election, the Singapore Democratic Party (SDP), led by the moderate Chiam See Tong, secured three seats, the largest number for an opposition party in three decades. Those gains were mostly lost at the subsequent election — GE1997 — when the SDP was led into that election by the more combative Chee Soon Juan. It is worth reprising what was written in the book *The Price of Victory*, on GE1997:[57]

Another point to raise is that which was first broached by academic Walter Woon on the Nomination Day special on TCS [Television Corporation of Singapore]. He said that, because in his view, Opposition MP Mr Chiam See Tong had moved a bit too close to the PAP he would lose votes and that it would be interesting to see the level of spoilt votes in Potong Pasir to bear out his contention: in other words, the voters of that constituency would rather spoil their ballot or return a blank ballot than cast it for one, of what they perceive to be, two similar candidates. Since that election, other people, like journalist Cherian George; Simon Tay and Zulkifli Baharuddin of the non-partisan discussion group The Roundtable; and academics Hussin Mutalib and Chua Beng Huat, have also made the similar point. They seem to say that what they want in an Oppositionist is someone who is confrontational in his approach or who is able to provide a markedly

---

56 Kevin Hewison and Garry Rodan, "The Decline of the Left in Southeast Asia", *The Socialist Register*, Vol. 30, 1994, p. 250.

57 Derek da Cunha, *The Price of Victory: The 1997 Singapore General Election and Beyond*, (Singapore: Institute of Southeast Asian Studies, 1997), p. 58.

distinct identity from that of the PAP. I would suggest that this is a flawed observation.

One could argue just the reverse, the more moderate the Oppositionist and the greater the similarity to the PAP the greater likelihood of being elected. The view is based not merely on the experience of 2 January 1997, but also on that of the previous general election, of 31 August 1991, more than five years earlier. In the previous election, the SDP secured 3 seats and came very close to securing another 2, not because it was perceived as a confrontational party. On the contrary, it did relatively well in 1991 because it was viewed by many people as being very similar to the PAP. People who now say otherwise — who say what is needed in an Opposition politician is a confrontational style — are mistaken and perhaps have short memories.

The centrality of this point cannot be over-stated. Equally, that a clutch of Singaporean intellectuals publicly took its obverse side, is telling. The observations of 1997 have stood the test of time. In fact, there has been a clear political continuum since the early 1990s to three decades thence. How GE2020 was conducted and its ultimate outcome bear out the essential validity of *The Price of Victory*. Similarly, if memories of the politically-engaged were short just before and after GE1997, they have become even shorter in the two decades that have elapsed, given the effects of the Digital Age.

In an increasingly complex world, the polarisation of left and right might not quite accurately capture the varied nature of the electorate.[58] This was observed in an article in the January-March 2021 issue of *The Political Quarterly*. It provided an analysis of the report *Britain's Choice: Common Ground and Division in 2020s Britain*. Instead of left

---

58 Paula Surridge, "Britain's Choice: Polarisation or Cohesion", *The Political Quarterly*, Vol. 92, No. 1, January–March 2021, https://onlinelibrary.wiley.com/doi/epdf/10.1111/1467-923X.12943. Accessed on 10 May 2021.

and right, it was suggested that core beliefs, values and identities could be more instrumental to political choices.[59] It noted:[60]

> *Neither the 'old' politics of left and right, nor the 'new' politics of open and closed (liberal and authoritarian or nationalist and cosmopolitan) fully explain political preferences. Instead, the distinct combinations of these core beliefs give rise to distinctive groups within the electorate that do not easily match onto existing party structures. This reinforces the utility of the approach used in this report, which defines segments of the electorate rather than positioning along two (or more) value dimensions and seeking to choose the most important of them.*

These observations are also germane to Singapore, where a more nuanced mapping of the electorate tends to point to the variables of core beliefs, values and identities. They also partly explain why the WP attained disproportionate support at GE2020 while the other alternative parties lagged behind. In short, it is a tendency on the part of voters to gravitate towards the centre or the median. Yet, there are some who still think in terms of a simplistic pro-PAP and anti-PAP binary and, for them, the anti-PAP component must necessarily be synonymous with the political left. They are unable to grasp the point that the aggregate of protest votes against the PAP does not translate into seats in Parliament for an alternative party. For an alternative to win against the PAP, that party needs the combination of votes cast positively for it (i.e., pro-party votes) plus protest votes against the ruling party. (See Chapter 3.) Thus, one can identify a significant segment of pro-WP voters, i.e., a pro-party phenomenon, that is not as apparent — or at least to the same extent — in the other alternatives to the PAP.

---

59 Ibid.

60 Ibid.

The beliefs of ardent WP supporters

The lack of a left-right political divide does not suggest that a partisan component is absent in an identifiable pro-WP segment within the electorate.[61] In fact, such a partisan component exists to the extent that if, hypothetically, the WP was not the alternative to the PAP in the constituencies of Aljunied GRC, Hougang SMC and Sengkang GRC, it is doubtful that any alternative party could win in those same constituencies. In other words, much of the WP's pro-party vote will *not* be transferred to another opposition party. In ongoing research conducted since just before GE2011, I have concluded that the ardent WP supporter is typically passionate about the party. That supporter sees in the WP qualities which s/he can identify and associate with. These include the old school virtues of humility, hard work, friendship, and creating a sense of community. Political provocation and confrontation do not sit well with those supporters. In totality, all this can be referred to as a belief system,[62] which waxes and wanes with prevailing norms.[63]

To that extent, within the WP strongholds of Aljunied GRC and Hougang SMC, ardent WP supporters would not generally describe themselves in ideological terms, as attested by on-ground data collection over the decade 2010–2020.[64] But, if pressed, they would say that, on

---

61 My analysis differs somewhat from what is found in the scholarly literature. That is to say, the literature appears to suggest that a partisan component is mostly a product of a left-right political divide. See, for example, Oddbjorn Knutsen, "The Partisan and the Value-based Component of Left-Right Self-Placement: A Comparative Study", *International Political Science Review*, Vol. 18, No. 2, April 1997, p. 195.

62 Delia Baldassarri and Amir Goldberg, "Neither Ideologues nor Agnostics: Alternative Voters' Belief Systems in an Age of Partisan Politics", *American Journal of Sociology*, Vol. 120, No. 1, July 2014, p. 47.

63 Here, I draw on the work of Giovanni Sartori, "Politics, Ideology, and Belief Systems", *American Political Science Association*, Vol. 63, No. 2, June 1969, p. 401.

64 This observation was gathered in discussions with identified WP supporters on three occasions, i.e., just before GE2011, GE2015 and GE2020.

the one hand, in social terms they are generally conservative and, on the other, in economic terms, they are socialist. Simplified further, many WP supporters are adherents of one of the main organised religions; they believe in law and order and that tough penalties ought to be meted out on those who break the country's laws; and, most have little time for culture wars. (See Chapter 8.) But where many of the supporters are progressive socially it is in the area of race relations; they see the struggles of many working families as an issue that cuts across ethnic lines. That could not be otherwise for a party that, in 2018, chose a Sikh as its leader. The WP's cadres, members and ardent supporters have at first-hand witnessed the work of their leader, Pritam Singh, in cultivating the ground within the Eunos division of Aljunied GRC and how residents there had been positive in their interactions with him.

By natural instinct, Singh is a person who does not go out of his way to be politically hostile but, instead, often strives to make allies. Since becoming leader of the WP, he has been pivotal in the party's efforts to knit together a coalition of voters across most demographics. That attempt, at reaching out, has at times incurred the wrath of those in implacable opposition to the PAP who feel that the WP should merely make allies exclusively with anti-PAP elements.

Photo-ops are an example where this is sometimes played out. When Singh agrees to have a picture taken with someone from another alternative party and this picture is subsequently published, it is read deeply by anti-PAP elements as somehow amounting to the seeds of an anti-PAP pact being planted, and elation ensues. On the other hand, when Singh has a picture taken with a PAP personality, he will be roundly attacked by anti-PAP elements for somehow enabling the PAP. Thus, a simple act of courtesy is re-constructed by others into an event of considerable political significance.

On the economic side of the ledger, many ardent WP supporters subscribe to nationalisation of key public services which they believe ought to be run on merely a cost-recovery basis. They believe in redistribution (with far heavier taxes levied on higher income earners). They desire greater government subsidies to cover the bulk of healthcare costs. Significantly, some younger supporters are also less enamoured of the idea of property ownership and, if given a choice, say they prefer to live in a rental Housing and Development Board (HDB) flat; they want the HDB to dramatically expand the number of such flats, and to rent them out at nominal rates.

If one could draw a parallel with the United Kingdom, it would not be totally inaccurate to say that the ardent WP supporters of Aljunied GRC and Hougang SMC are in political outlook not dissimilar to the traditional supporters of the Labour Party in its deindustrialised heartlands of the Midlands, Yorkshire and North England versus the mostly young left-wing intellectuals of the inner cities, the latter handily referred to as the "metropolitan liberal elite".[65] Where the new WP support base of Sengkang GRC falls in terms of what informs its support for the WP is not entirely clear even one year after GE2020. But the WP leadership might well decide to be cautious in not falling into the same predicament of pursuing fashionable trends that, ultimately, enfeebled the Labour Party after 2010. The issue confronting Labour — as it could the WP — was best summed up by a Labour Member of Parliament (MP), Khalid Mahmood, who wrote an opinion-piece for the think tank Policy Exchange shortly after the Labour Party suffered a catastrophic by-election loss on 6 May 2021 in Hartlepool, a one-time safe and traditional Labour heartland seat. Mahmood reflected:[66]

---

65 "How Labour failed to connect with the British working class", *The Conversation*, 16 December 2019, https://theconversation.com/how-labour-failed-to-connect-with-the-british-working-class-128082. Accessed on 11 January 2021; Rushanara Ali, "Can Labour reach beyond the metropolitan elite?" *Fabian Society*, 25 January 2017, https://fabians.org.uk/can-labour-reach-beyond-the-metropolitan-elite/. Accessed on 11 January 2021; and, "The metropolitan elite: Britain's new pariah class", *The Guardian*, 20 May 2015, https://www.theguardian.com/politics/2015/may/20/metropolitan-elite-britains-new-pariah-class. Accessed on 11 January 2021.

66 Khalid Mahmood, "Hartlepool is a Wake-Up Call for my Party", *Policy Exchange*, 7 May 2021, https://policyexchange.org.uk/hartlepool-is-a-wake-up-call-for-my-party/. Accessed on 12 May 2021.

> *[I]n the past decade, Labour has lost touch with ordinary British people. A London-based bourgeoisie, with the support of brigades of woke social media warriors, has effectively captured the party. They mean well, of course, but their politics — obsessed with identity, division and even tech utopianism — have more in common with those of Californian high society than the kind of people who voted in Hartlepool yesterday. The loudest voices in the Labour movement over the past year in particular have focused more on pulling down Churchill's statue than they have on helping people pull themselves up in the world. No wonder it is doing better among rich urban liberals and young university graduates than it is amongst the most important part of its traditional electoral coalition, the working-class.*

These observations cut to the heart of the issues that have plagued the UK Labour Party, and it is not the only party in opposition to a conservatively-ingrained status quo that faces such a challenge.[67] As already noted, shortly after GE2020, signs emerged of some anti-PAP elements attempting to hijack the WP's moderate agenda.

The main voting blocs in the Singapore electorate: Refined from three to four

Much of what finds in the scholarly literature on electoral politics, voting behaviour, and the determinants of voting outcomes, relates to voter turnout. That is to say, what decides the level of voter turnout. And, in many jurisdictions, politicians during election campaigns will normally make the standard remark, which goes something like this: "The outcome of this election will be determined on the basis of turnout."

---

67 Chapter 7 draws further parallels, however indirect and inexact, between the Labour Party and the WP.

What is meant by that is that the actual level of voting by the *identified supporters* of the candidate and his/her party will decide the election. Thus, much of the scholarly literature on psephology revolves around the dynamics of GOTV — Get-Out-the-Vote.[68]

The relative effectiveness of GOTV campaigns has an inherent volatility in predicting election outcomes in many jurisdictions where rates of voter turnout can range anywhere from the mid-50% to the mid-80%.[69] Singapore, on the other hand, has an election system based on compulsory voting, where any Singaporean, not disqualified by law, and at least 21 years of age as of the cut-off date for the Registers of Electors, can — and must — vote in parliamentary or presidential elections. The actual turnout rates in Singapore general elections have tended to hover around 94% of registered voters. At GE2020, the turnout rate was 95.81%.[70]

In *Breakthrough*, three main voting blocs in Singapore pre-GE2011 were identified from polling data derived from previous elections. Those blocs are represented in Table 1.1.

---

68 A good example of this is found in Kevin Arceneaux and David W. Nickerson, "Who is Mobilized to Vote? A Re-Analysis of 11 Field Experiments", *American Journal of Political Science,* Vol. 53, No. 1, January 2009. Another example is the study by Ryan D. Enos, Anthony Fowler and Lynn Vavreck, "Increasing Inequality: The Effect of GOTV Mobilization on the Composition of the Electorate", *The Journal of Politics*, Vol. 76, No. 1, January 2014.

69 The average global voter turnout was 66% of registered voters during the period 2011–2015. This figure is sourced from Abdurashid Solijonov, *Voter Turnout Trends Around the World,* (Stockholm: International Institute for Democracy and Electoral Assistance, 2016), p. 24.

70 The figure does not include rejected ballots. Elections Department Singapore, "Press Release: Total Votes Cast at Singapore General Election 2020", 15 July 2020, https://www.eld.gov.sg/press/2020/Press_Release_on_Total_Votes_Cast_at_Singapore_General_Election_2020.pdf. Accessed on 20 January 2021.

Table 1.1
Singapore main voting blocs, 2011

Bedrock of PAP voters (the "true believers")	40%
Wavering middle ground voters	35%
Irreducible core of anti-PAP voters	25%

SOURCE: Derek da Cunha, Breakthrough: Roadmap for Singapore's Political Future, (Singapore: Institute of Policy Studies and Straits Times Press, 2012), p. 36.

Since the publication of that book, the emergence of new data and further research into the subject have made modification of the voting blocs necessary. It ought to be stressed that in interpreting data, one should err on the side of caution. To that extent, inferences have been drawn not from a single set of data but from a combination of three datasets.

The first dataset of significance are the results of the August 2011 presidential election (PE2011), which provided a fairly accurate reflection of voting segments in Singapore because three of the four candidates contesting that election had, either implicitly or otherwise, positioned themselves as, variously, Establishment favourite (Tony Tan), moderate alternative (Tan Cheng Bock), and the candidate furthest from the status quo (Tan Jee Say).[71] The presidential election results were to break as 35.2%, 34.85%, and 25.04% of the valid votes cast respectively. One has to remember the context of these results: they occurred just less than three months after GE2011 and the WP's taking of Aljunied GRC from the PAP. Heavily anti-PAP elements were intoxicated by the GE2011 feat and were convinced that momentum was on their side. Consequently, they instinctively flocked to the candidate furthest from the status, Tan

---

71 The fourth candidate, Tan Kin Lian, did not, or failed to, define himself politically in voters' minds. He tended to be defined largely by the fact that, previously, he had been Chief Executive Officer of the insurer, NTUC Income, and his strength was in dispensing financial advice, a not insignificant attribute but, in voters' minds, coming out so quickly after the highly-charged atmosphere of GE2011, was not relevant politically, and so his candidacy was largely ignored.

Jee Say, in the hope of landing a further major blow on the Establishment. Tan Jee Say was overwhelmingly favoured on social media. But all that did was to rally around him the irreducible core of anti-PAP voters and not much more, while Tony Tan and Tan Cheng Bock split between them the rest of the voter segments.

The contention here is that PE2011 was the best and most accurate polling survey of voters' political preferences in Singapore in a long while because ample choice was provided to the electorate and three candidates were perceived to have conveniently positioned themselves along three points across the political spectrum. The numbers of voters in implacable opposition to the PAP had also finally revealed themselves. That 25% figure was what I had actually put forward as being the irreducible core of anti-PAP voters at a public seminar at the Singapore Management University on 19 April 2011 just weeks before GE2011. More significantly, the results of PE2011 indicated that the alignment of political forces in Singapore is mostly between conservative and moderate-leaning voters. The alignment is not between moderates and heavily anti-PAP voters.

The other election data that emerged to prompt a re-evaluation of the voting blocs was the result in Aljunied GRC at GE2020. Due to the fact that it is a five-member GRC with 150,303 voters on the electoral register,[72] the sample size in Aljunied can be considered large enough to draw a reasonable inference, which would not have been possible in the case of a smaller-sized constituency. The total number of ballots cast — including overseas and rejected ballots — was 143,145, making for a turnout rate of 95.24%.

A third set of election data takes into consideration wider constituency-level results at GE2020.[73] Those other constituency-level

---

72 *White Paper on The Report of The Electoral Boundaries Review Committee*, 13 March 2020, https://www.eld.gov.sg/pdf/White_Paper_on_the_Report_of_the_Electoral_Boundaries_Review_Committee_2020.pdf. Accessed on 8 April 2021.

73 The PAP's popular vote at GE2020, calculated on valid votes cast, was 61.23%.

Table 1.2
Singapore main voting blocs, 2020

A.	Bedrock of PAP voters (the "true believers")	35%
B.	Moderate PAP voters	15%
C.	Wavering middle ground voters	25%
D.	Irreducible core of anti-PAP voters	25%

SOURCE: Derek da Cunha.

results are significant in a number of ways, not least in providing for a contrast to the fortunes of other alternative parties relative to the WP. Appendix 1 provides a breakdown of the results of GE2020 on the basis of *valid* votes cast.

Taking the three datasets together, and extrapolating from them, the voting blocs within the Singapore electorate are reformulated, and expanded — or refined — from three to four. This is shown in Table 1.2.

It is worth pointing out that three constituency-level results at GE2020 tend to confirm that one of the main voting blocs, D, the "Irreducible core of anti-PAP voters", not only retains its fundamental characteristic but also, in terms of proportion — 25% — has remained remarkably steady over the span of a decade. The opposition contesting in Jurong GRC, Mountbatten SMC and Radin Mas SMC garnered 24.88%, 25.50% and 25.09% of *total* votes cast respectively,[74] indicating that 25%, with a variance of plus or minus 0.5%, is the floor level for anti-PAP votes nationally. In absolute numbers, 25% of the turnout at GE2020 is represented in 635,090 voters, and this conveys more starkly the magnitude of the irreducible core of anti-PAP voters. Still, given

---

74 See Appendix 3 for a full breakdown of total votes cast. Total votes cast, which include rejected votes, is a more precise measurement of support levels, instead of the usual "valid votes cast". Chapter 3 will provide an argument as to why this is the case.

the fact that the percentage has remained stable for the period of a decade, this would not be a concern to the PAP. If the proportion had grown, even marginally, say, by 3% to 28%, then that would be another matter. It could be argued that such growing implacable opposition would call into question the PAP's narrative of the party as a national movement.

Three variables, which can be considered as scaffolding that helped to construct Table 1.2, provides a relatively high degree of accuracy to the percentages presented in the table. The first variable relates to Singapore's system of compulsory voting: this automatically generates not only a predictable voter turnout rate of over 90% at elections, but that turnout rate also skews the vote towards certain directions. The second variable relates to the fact that the PAP government under Lee Kuan Yew had fairly early on decided that — with minor exceptions — each constituency would, in its demographic composition, of ethnicity and class structure, represent a microcosm of Singapore. (No opposition party could thus carve out wins by relying on ethnic or social class enclaves.) GRCs were subsequently to become a key element incorporating just the right demographic balance, each being fairly representative of the nation at large. The third variable is the election system of first-past-the-post (FPTP) where, to win, a candidate/party must garner a plurality of votes, resulting in a high bar being set for any challenger to the incumbent. As scaffolding, the three variables constitute the inferential framework that allows for the construction of Table 1.2. Identifying voting blocs to any degree of precision in other jurisdictions that practise aspects of democratic politics, becomes less apparent because of the absence of this inferential framework.

What the four voting blocs in Table 1.2 indicate is that in straight fights between the PAP and a second or third tier alternative, the PAP would secure the entirety of A plus most of B and a sizeable portion of C. However, in Aljunied GRC at GE2020, the WP — the only first tier opposition party widely perceived as moderate in its leanings — garnered the entirety of D, virtually all of C, and the largest chunk of

B, to give it 59.95% of the valid votes cast. The most significant bloc here is B — identified as "moderate PAP voters". It seems that this voting bloc was always part of the electorate but, in research prior to 2011, had not been assigned a discrete identity.

Of the four main voting blocs, those within C — wavering middle ground voters — can be considered relatively diverse. And, in point of fact, that bloc of voters can be disaggregated further into separate layers, of 2%–3% each. As one moves up the layers, the voters become increasingly sensitive to differences across the parties that are in opposition to the PAP.

The proximity model of voting

Due to what is known as the proximity model of election voting, those who populate main voting blocs B and C are presented in a party, the WP, which is in proximity to their views, offering a moderate alternative to the authoritarian-leaning PAP. To view it in the obverse: the model explains why low evaluations are given by voters to candidates and parties deemed too far from "voters' ideal points".[75] Or, as framed by two scholars: "For the proximity model, a voter compares a party's position on policy issues to the voter's own ideal point. The voter most prefers a party that is closest to the ideal point."[76] The WP of Low Thia Khiang and Pritam Singh had deliberately positioned the party in such a way that allowed it to benefit from a strategy of "vote-maximising" under the proximity model.[77] Consequently, sizeable numbers of those in main

---

75 Dean Lacy and Philip Paolino, "Testing Proximity versus Directional Voting Using Experiments", *Electoral Studies*, Vol. 29, No. 3, September 2010, p. 470.

76 Sundai Cho and James W. Endersby, "Issues, the Spatial Theory of Voting, and British General Elections: A Comparison of Proximity and Directional Models", *Public Choice*, Vol. 114, No. 3/4, March 2003, p. 279.

77 The "vote-maximising" strategy under proximity theory is explained by Laron K. Williams, "It's All Relative: Spatial Positioning of Parties and Ideological Shifts", p. 2, http://web.missouri.edu/~williamslaro/It's%20All%20Relative.pdf. Accessed on 8 April 2021.

voting bloc C and, in the case of Aljunied GRC, main voting bloc B, had been comfortable in opting for the WP.

It is the contention here that the utility of the proximity model, on the one hand, and the formulation of the main voting blocs in Table 1.2 (especially in reference to B and C), on the other, are self-reinforcing. But being in proximity to the dominant party is, in and of itself, insufficient to result in voters migrating from main voting bloc B to the WP. The proximity model must co-exist with a *conversion strategy*. The details of that strategy are set out in Chapter 3.

Any stark alternative to the PAP is not an option for many Singaporean voters. That reality is accentuated by Singapore's Westminster-style first-past-the-post election system. Adapted from what is referred to as the British Political Tradition, that system has involved a limited "liberal conception of representation and a conservative notion of responsibility",[78] translating into an emphasis on "limited democracy and, strong, centralized executive power".[79] But a stark alternative to the PAP could arise in a system of proportional representation (PR), where the threshold for election to the legislature is set so low that voters are incentivised to vote for radical alternatives because there would be a strong possibility that such alternatives can gain entry to Parliament.[80] For all the benefits of proportional representation touted by its supporters, such an election system tends to spawn cleavages along ethnic, religious and other lines. In a PR voting system, the PAP's popular vote of 61.23% at GE2020 would have translated into roughly between 55 and 60 parliamentary seats, and not the 83 seats the PAP secured at GE2020 under FPTP.

---

78 David Marsh, David Richards and Martin Smith, "Unequal Plurality: Towards an Asymmetric Power Model of British Politics", *Government and Opposition*, Vol. 38, No. 3, Summer 2003, p. 311.

79 Ibid. pp. 312–313.

80 Orit Kedar, "When Moderate Voters Prefer Extreme Parties: Policy Balancing in Parliamentary Elections", *The American Policy Science Review*, Vol. 99, No. 2, May 2005, p. 187.

For purposes of intellectual clarity, readers might be curious as to who makes up the two voting blocs which are at polar opposites — A and D. The initial point to make is that Singapore's online world of political opinion tends to be disproportionately populated by those from A and D. The make-up of A is easier to identify. It constitutes large numbers of Singaporeans who have benefited in a material and meaningful way from PAP governance, and they credit their socioeconomic situation mostly to the PAP government.

As to D, the irreducible core of anti-PAP voters, that bloc can be sub-divided into two sub-blocs:

- those who are rabidly opposed to the PAP due to their own circumstances and, in their view, unedifying experiences they have had with the state;
- and, those opposed to the PAP on progressive ideological grounds.

That first sub-bloc does not necessarily include people who are liberal/progressive by inclination. In fact, many of them appear to project nativist impulses, where they believe that well-paying jobs (in the PMET tier) should go to born and bred Singaporeans. Those who make up that sub-bloc are similar to the kinds of people who leave comments to threads and articles in a number of online portals (including *SG Talk*[81]).

---

81 *SG Talk* has had different incarnations. The forum with the extension sgtalk.org, had been one of the most popular among Singapore netizens, having been established in 2013 as the successor to the *CNA Market Talk* forum. Consequently, it carried over a large number of existing registered users. Because the forum had no moderation, it resulted in a free-for-all, with the ugliest side of human nature coming to the surface. But, at around 11am on 8 July 2021, the forum was shut down. Most members of the public would have been unaware that a police report had been filed a week earlier, on 1 July 2021, complaining about a forum thread strewn with racially incendiary remarks. The thread, which was started on 28 June 2021 and clocked 85 postings and more than 2,000 views, was deleted on the afternoon of 1 July. The contents of that thread were, arguably, the most egregious to be published on *SG Talk* (illustrating a mounting problem) and triggered the report to the police. The *SG Talk* administrator had put up a pinned post (a sticky) on 5 July 2021 with the following heading: "Pls read the forum rules. Do not slander

The second sub-bloc of the irreducible core of anti-PAP voters is quantifiably smaller and is made up of a number of liberals/progressives, civil society activists, a few prominent members of the arts community and personalities from the blogosphere.[82]

It should be obvious that the two sub-blocs are, in point of fact, at ideological logger-heads. And, this is why certain alternative parties would appeal to one sub-bloc but not the other. From this, it should also be obvious that there is a wide variation across non-PAP voters on fundamental issues. Both sub-blocs in D have unity of purpose only by being in implacable opposition to the PAP. And, as inherent in those who are rabid or ideological, they view the world mostly in Manichean terms.[83]

Yet, at GE2015, where the results were mostly the consequence of a pronounced "LKY effect", in no less than four large-sized constituencies — Ang Mo Kio GRC, Jurong GRC, Tanjong Pagar GRC, and West Coast GRC — the PAP succeeded in piercing through the bloc of irreducible core of anti-PAP voters. The irreducible core was thus, surprisingly, reduced. See Table 1.3.

---

or post racist remarks". Three days later, the forum was shut down. At its peak, the forum was bringing in vast amounts of advertising revenue for its owner. Shortly after its closure, attempts were made to replace the forum with similar ones. Eventually, the closest replacement was established on 12 July 2021 with a different extension — sgtalk.net. Many forummers from the original *SG Talk* decamped to its replacement.

82 See Chapter 5.

83 The contention has been made that "... Manichean narrative structures better comport with how some people process political information and because they provide compelling explanations for otherwise confusing or ambiguous events." Further, "... the proclivity to make casual attributions of salient phenomena to unseen forces and an attraction to Manichean political narratives — will explain why many otherwise ordinary people may embrace conspiracy theories." J. Eric Oliver and Thomas J. Wood, "Conspiracy Theories and the Paranoid Style(s) of Mass Opinion ", *American Journal of Political Science*, Vol. 58, No. 4, October 2014, p. 954.

Table 1.3
GE2015: Constituencies where the PAP cut into the irreducible core of the anti-PAP vote

Ang Mo Kio GRC	78.64% (PAP)	21.35% (Reform Party)
Jurong GRC	79.29% (PAP)	20.71% (SingFirst)
Tanjong Pagar GRC	77.71% (PAP)	22.29% (SingFirst)
West Coast GRC	78.57% (PAP)	21.43% (Reform Party)

SOURCE: *Elections Department Singapore, 2015 Parliamentary General Election Results,* *https://www.eld.gov.sg/elections_past_parliamentary2015.html.*

These results from GE2015 should be acknowledged, not ignored. Relatively small entities, represented in the Reform Party and (the now dissolved) Singaporeans First (SingFirst) Party, should ordinarily still have garnered a full one-quarter of the valid votes cast. But that did not happen. Part of the reason for the dismal results of SingFirst was that it was a new party with no branding whatsoever. As to the Reform Party, its low polled vote appears to have been related to two of its prominent members, supporting the teenager, Amos Yee who, shortly after Lee Kuan Yew's death, launched into an expletive-laden rant in an online video directed at Lee and Christianity. The "Amos Yee episode", as it became known, was politically significant. In order not to over-extend the narrative in this chapter, that episode is analysed separately in Appendix 2.

If the foregoing is accepted as reflecting reality, it should thus be clear from Table 1.2 that the elementary political arithmetic for any party intending to be a credible alternative to the PAP is that, in order to prevail, it needs to attract to its side meaningful numbers of moderate PAP voters. It simply cannot rely on the combination of D and C to make it across the finish line in the FPTP election system.

The four main voting blocs in Table 1.2 can be viewed in another way: from the baseline of D an alternative party must move upwards, slicing through layers of increasingly conservative-inclined voters in order to get a plurality of votes. After a certain threshold is reached, with each additional percentage point, the resistance against the challenger expands markedly. In *Breakthrough*, this was described as analogous to how earthquakes are measured on the Richter scale, where a constantly expanding magnitude is required to move the scale even slightly higher.[84]

At GE2020, in Aljunied GRC, the WP succeeded in inducing to its side almost two-thirds of B — moderate PAP voters. Here, two contentions are made. First, that, in the context of compulsory voting, in elections prior to GE2020, many moderate PAP voters viewed the PAP as simply their default choice. But at GE2020 the WP changed that dynamic: the PAP as the default choice for moderate PAP voters in Aljunied GRC was far less obvious. The second contention is that moderate PAP voters constitute the main voting bloc that is left for the WP to mine if it is to enhance its parliamentary numbers in any meaningful way. Thus, the path to victory for the WP is through B. For avoidance of doubt — if one takes the figures as formulated in Table 1.2 as valid — then the bloc of moderate PAP voters would be up for the WP's taking *if* the party plays its cards right. What it achieved in Aljunied GRC, by inducing two out of three moderate PAP voters onto its side, the WP can scale-up in a limited way.

The WP's poisoned chalice: The small but vocal base of liberal ideologues

On election-night GE2020, when it became clear that the WP was doing relatively well and that it had secured a second GRC, Sengkang, Prime Minister Lee Hsien Loong telephoned WP leader Pritam Singh to offer his congratulations and said that the latter would now be officially recognised and designated Leader of the Opposition (LO), with the government providing some resources to accompany the new

---

84 da Cunha, *Breakthrough*, op. cit., p. 226.

post. That call spawned elation by WP supporters and a general feeling across the political divide in Singapore that the prime minister had demonstrated magnanimity. However, in the days that followed, there were remarks posted online to the effect that Singh should reject the prime minister's offer because if he did not do so he would be "selling out" the opposition. In short, the message from some online was that the "opposition should not be bought". One commenter, a staunch supporter of the SDP's Chee, even likened the prime minister's gesture as a "Greek bearing gifts", and urged Singh to reject the offer. Some of the people making these remarks were of the same mind as those who had for years smeared the WP as "PAP-lite". It is the mistaken belief of many that this derisive term had originated from the PAP or elements associated with it. (Chapter 6 goes into the origins of this term in order to set the record straight on this matter.) Those who had come up with this term are individuals who make up the irreducible core of anti-PAP voters — i.e., being either rabidly opposed to the PAP due to their own circumstances, or opposed to the PAP on mostly ideological grounds.

If, hypothetically, at GE2020 the Progress Singapore Party (PSP) had won 10 seats and the WP was reduced to two Non-constituency MP seats, the PSP's Tan Cheng Bock would have been similarly offered the LO post and no opposition element — least of all, the most hardcore — would have even raised the slightest query or doubt about the gesture. In fact, the reaction would have been quite the reverse. Many had in the months leading up to GE2020 stridently asserted online that the PSP was the "sunrise" party and the WP the "sunset". That characterisation is placed on the record here so that it is never forgotten.

For the WP, in its relationship to some other alternative parties, the old British parliamentary cliché applies, "The opposition occupies the benches in front of you but the enemy sits behind you." This point will be elaborated at length in Chapter 8.

Jamus Lim's compassion compels a netizen to invoke the "long arc of truth"

Thus far, the analysis has attempted to dispel the notion that "the opposition" is monolithic. A dissection of main voting bloc D in Table 1.2 makes clear how illusory is the concept of "the opposition". Yet, there are those whose views are so at variance from the mainstream but who will continue to make the claim that they either represent "the opposition" in its entirety or they represent that part of the popular vote the PAP failed to secure in a general election.[85] They don't represent the 38.77% of the electorate who did not vote for the PAP at GE2020. Perhaps they represent around the irreducible core of 25% of anti-PAP voters, possibly even less. Consequently, it bears repeating, that it amounts to a false narrative for anyone to talk in terms of a PAP versus non-PAP binary choice.

In early February 2021, a spotlight was thrown on whether ideological values not represented in the PAP can somehow be represented by the WP. This arose when Jamus Lim, a star candidate for

---

85 In a Facebook post published on 1 August 2017, poet and playwright Alfian Sa'at, who has a Facebook following of close to 30,000 (the figure as of June 2021), seemed to make such a claim. He advocated for funding from the National Arts Council for artists whose views do not align with those of the state. Among other things, he said:

> *Do we think it is fair to discriminate against those whose political views do not meet state approval? There is at least 30% of the population that [sic] did not vote for the PAP in the last election. How do you ensure that their needs are met, assuming that a government has the responsibility to serve all citizens, and not only those who voted them in?*

Alfian Sa'at is a person of prodigious artistic output. But some of his views on socio-political issues are significantly at variance from the mainstream of the opposition movement — i.e., the WP — that it would be surprising if all those who cast votes against the PAP said they could identify with him or that he could represent their views through his artistic expression. Consequently, he might like to make the case for state funding of artists — of whatever persuasion — on grounds which are more intellectually sustainable and convincing.

the WP at GE2020, filed a written parliamentary question (PQ) for answer by the Minister for Home Affairs at the session on 2 February 2021. This was about the possible expansion of the Yellow Ribbon Project to allow ex-offenders of non-violent crimes to have their criminal history expunged so that they might improve their employment prospects.[86] In his official reply, K. Shanmugam noted that non-violent crimes could include "sexual grooming, outrage of modesty, criminal breach of trust, and theft in dwelling", and said that Lim's suggestion could "mean that ex-offenders could be employed in roles such as pre-school teachers or security officers, without their employers being aware of their history.[87] In an online clarification on 5 February 2021, Lim, who is known for his compassion and good intentions, acknowledged that there may need to be certain exceptions where ex-offenders of violent crimes could not be employed in particular jobs. He also said that his PQ was inspired by his "experience with some residents trying to obtain security jobs (such as being a guard at a condo or shopping mall), but who were ruled out due to a glue-sniffing or petty theft offence, perpetrated in their youth." Further, he maintained that his "one sentence question" was intended "to open up a conversation about crime and rehabilitation". Two days later (7 February 2021), Shanmugam provided a robust response. Among other things he said:[88]

The MP now seems to realise that there are difficulties with his suggestion.

Having realised that, he now says that he raised the issue in order to "open up a conversation on crime and rehabilitation". He adds that there is a

---

86 Parliament of Singapore, "Written Answers to Questions: Expanding Coverage of Yellow Ribbon Project to Include Ex-offenders of Non-violent Crimes", *Singapore Parliamentary Debates (Hansard)*, 2 February 2021, https://sprs.parl.gov.sg/search/fullreport?sittingdate=02-02-2021. Accessed on 21 April 2021.

87 Ibid.

88 K Shanmugam SC, Facebook, 7 February 2021, https://www.facebook.com/k.shanmugam.page/posts/3781393388573830. Accessed on 21 April 2021.

risk in allowing offenders to take jobs which pose a risk to society, and that there is also a risk that labelling may affect reintegration.

I am puzzled. "Open up a conversation on crime and rehabilitation"?

I am tempted to ask: Is the MP aware that we have been having that conversation for decades? He can look up the Parliamentary records. It's not a new topic, suddenly to be discovered. And our laws, policies have been heavily influenced by our approach to crime and rehabilitation, for more than 20 years.

During this period, there have been several discussions in Singapore, leading to legislation focusing on rehabilitation.

He went on to say:[89]

What we need are sensible, real world, practical suggestions, or incisive ideas, which will make a contribution to the ongoing conversations on these issues. We welcome such ideas, suggestions. For example, on the restrictions on jobs that ex-offenders may be employed in, there is a framework, which has been adapted over the years. If the MP believes that ex-offenders (be they child molesters or have convictions for housebreaking and so on, as long as it is non violent), should be allowed (for example) to be security officers in condominiums, (without their conviction record being available to employers), he can make that suggestion. And perhaps suggest some condominiums where the approach can be tested out.

This response was to lead to a flood of criticism of Lim online, mostly from members of the PAP Internet Brigade (IB). But it also generated a strong defence of Lim by his own followers. The IB's criticism turned on what they said was Lim's failure to properly research the topic before

89 Ibid.

filing his PQ, his subsequent "backtracking", and his apparent imperviousness to the general sentiment of Singaporeans regarding those who have committed criminal offences, even non-violent offences. In keeping with the authoritarian culture ingrained in many Singaporeans, it is a well-known fact that little sympathy is shown towards those who break the law. Even netizens not usually supportive of the PAP came out to say that Lim's PQ was perhaps ill-judged. One netizen, Dexter Aw, left a comment on a Facebook thread to a *Mothership SG* story on the controversy, saying:

I am not a PAP supporter but if WP keeps asking questions like this, the PAP IB hounds are going to have a field day tearing them apart.

We are in the midst of a pandemic. WP and the opposition was [sic] voted in to ask the key questions that matter: CECA,[90] jobs, healthcare related issues etc, not pander to the left wing libtards or liberal SJW.

There will be a time for these questions (and if they make sense or not), but not now. Bigger issues are at hand that need to be resolved.

On my Facebook page, on 7 February 2021, I posted a screenshot of Aw's remarks together with my own observations which were in general agreement with what he said. This spawned a minor, but useful, debate with a number of Facebook users. In particular, two commenters, Leslie Chan and Tan Jin Meng, made a number of noteworthy interventions which raised the level of debate on social media. Chan's points are worth focusing on. He had said that if Lim played it too safe then what would be his "selling point", as he would be "behaving like the rest of muted" PAP MPs. He went on to contend that, "if we believe in the long arc of truth, we should have faith that we should say the right things despite being attacked mercilessly in the short term".

---

90 CECA is the acronym for Comprehensive Economic Cooperation Agreement and, in this context, it refers to the one signed between India and Singapore.

Before dealing with Chan's more substantive point, about the "long arc of truth", it should be said that there has been a consistent tendency by some netizens stridently opposed to the PAP to dismiss WP MPs as little more than PAP clones if those MPs are not as strident in either pushing a progressive agenda or in not bringing up historical issues in Parliament related to the PAP's more than half-a-century of governance that some contend have been punctuated with abuses of power. In fact, shortly after the WP's first breakthrough at GE2011 it was not uncommon to see the following phrase online, "Then we vote for them for wat?" It ought to be asked, who is the "we" here?

What of Chan's remark that Lim's "selling point" was in advocating for such issues as ex-offenders' employability? At no stage prior to GE2020 did Lim give any indication that he was interested in a certain type of advocacy that would appeal to progressives. Lim and his WP Sengkang GRC team-mates were voted in on the basis of other reasons, as set out in Chapter 3. And, Lim's own identified strength prior to GE2020 was as an economist in academia. But, conveniently, some netizens have come up with ex-post facto justifications for what the WP and Lim are, so that it is in-line with their own understanding of "opposition".

More substantively, Chan had invoked "the long arc of truth". This was probably a paraphrase of Martin Luther King Jr.'s, dictum that, "The arc of the moral universe is long, but it bends toward justice." Here, as with Dr King, Voltaire was just as compelling when he said, "The perfect is the enemy of the good." What this means in the particular context being considered, is that those who push to achieve an ideal state become a stumbling block for the many more who would be satisfied with a less ideal, but more achievable, state. Cast differently, this can be formulated as the politics of addition versus the politics of subtraction.

A cogent example of how the striving for the perfect became the enemy of the good, was what happened at the 27 August 2011 presidential election (PE2011). As already noted, Tan Jee Say (TJS) was the candidate who positioned himself furthest from the status quo. Of all four presidential election candidates, TJS had also drawn the greatest amount of support online. Netizens gravitated to him in droves only because they were euphoric following the WP winning Aljunied GRC several months earlier at GE2011. TJS was their perfect choice. And, many netizens believed they had power — online power — to decide the outcome of PE2011 and, through electing TJS, they would metaphorically land a blow on the Establishment. I took a different view. I felt that Tan Cheng Bock (TCB) would have the greatest chance of defeating the Establishment favourite, Tony Tan, because TCB was then widely perceived as the moderate alternative and would draw support from the more numerous moderates. In that election, TCB was the good choice. Additionally, being a student of election process, it dawned on me only at the polling station that TCB had a real chance of winning when I opened my folded ballot paper and saw the ballot order placement — TCB was at the top of the ballot, and Tony Tan placed third. The names were arranged alphabetically. Known as the "ballot order-effect", two researchers have concluded that, "The impact of ballot order on the outcome of elections is not only statistically significant, but also economically and politically significant."[91] From a review of the corpus of literature on ballot order-effect, I estimate that, in the context of Singapore's compulsory voting system, TCB might have benefited anywhere from 0.5% to 2% in having his name placed at the top of the ballot paper at PE2011.[92] That he still failed to convert

---

91 Marc Meredith and Yuval Salant, *Causes and Consequences of Ballot Order-Effects*, Stanford Institute for Economic and Policy Research Discussion Paper No. 03–29, February 2007, p. 24, https://siepr.stanford.edu/sites/default/files/publications/06-29_0.pdf. Accessed on 22 April 2021.

92 See, for instance, Amy King and Andrew Leigh, "Are Ballot Order Effects Heterogeneous", *Social Science Quarterly*, Vol. 90, No. 1, March 2009; Jonathan GS Koppell and Jennifer A. Steen, "The Effects of Ballot Position on Election Outcomes", *The Journal of Politics*, Vol. 66, No. 1, February 2004; and, Barry C. Edwards, "Alphabetically Ordered Ballots and the Composition of American Legislatures", *State Politics and Policy Quarterly*, Vol. 15, No. 2, June 2015.

a favourable ballot-order placement to a win, should have really ended the matter there. But, apparently, not for him.

Returning to the main point, all that the flood of online support did for TJS was to ensure the election of Tony Tan. The lesson here is indeed, "The perfect is the enemy of the good." But to what extent has that lesson been learnt is less clear. Given the tendency to shortness of memory in the Digital Age, one does not tend to be optimistic.

This chapter has argued that to attain the politics of addition for itself, the WP must push an agenda which the broad electorate can support at this particular juncture in Singapore's political evolution. This does not mean that "the long arc of truth" should not be pursued. Instead, what it means is that, as an objective, it might just take slightly longer to get to. Ultimately, the pace towards the pursuit of that objective will be a matter for a younger generation of Singaporeans and whether they choose to break decisively from the philosophical legacy left behind by Lee Kuan Yew. For now, the WP's adherence to a Voltairian approach to its politics might be the best way forward to entrench and grow a two-party parliamentary democracy in Singapore.

CHAPTER 2
Analysing GE2020 Through the Lens of Policies, Personalities and Party Brand

his is one of two chapters focused on an analysis of the results of GE2020. It does so through the lens of the 4Ps — Policies, Personalities, Party brand and Process. The most significant P — Process — is analysed separately in Chapter 3, which explains in detail the Workers' Party's (WP's) election strategy going into GE2020. The 4Ps, as a conceptual framework, is a useful way to understand electoral politics in Singapore.

The chapter will first look at how hastiness in providing analysis of election results can lead to incorrect conclusions. It will then sketch-in the backdrop to GE2020. Next, it will flag the issues — under Policies — which were germane to the outcome of the vote. This will be followed by reference to a number of other issues which were not germane but, as will be argued, were actually strawmen broached by other observers. In examining Party brand, the "rebranding", which emerged from GE2020 as explaining the unexpectedly better performance of two Singapore Democratic Party (SDP) candidates, will be analysed. Party brand juxtaposed against Personalities will form the basis for an analysis of the results obtained by the Progress Singapore Party (PSP). The arguments for and against other political parties — the minor players — continuing to contest elections will then be set out towards the end of the chapter.

Hasty analysis leads to a dash over the cliff

Let me start with how I made a classic error in a Facebook post on 6 November 2020, where I provided some early "analysis" of the US presidential election of that year. I trot out this example to underscore the point that early "analysis" is really not proper nor serious analysis but simply a reaction. Let me quote one paragraph of that post:

> *Biden wins the presidency partly (I said "partly") due to a change in voting process: many more states allowed for mail-in (or postal) ballots, or allowed for such ballots to be made more easily available, due to the COVID-19 pandemic. Mail-in ballots have not been the norm in US elections. Republicans have in fact for decades engaged in voter suppression. Restricting the franchise has traditionally helped Republicans.*

The second portion of that paragraph was accurate, but the first was not. I was not the only person who suggested that mail-in ballots were instrumental in Joe Biden's win over Donald Trump. The early analysis by several US commentators was along similar lines, although some were even more dogmatic. Once the empirical evidence emerged, it was to support a more accurate, and completely different, assessment of the effect of mail-in ballots. To that extent, a working paper published by scholars from Stanford University in March 2021 was noteworthy:[1]

> *A conventional wisdom about vote-by-mail in the 2020 election has already congealed and is setting the terms of this debate. [...]*
>
> *Using nationwide data, we have shown that states that implemented absentee voting for the 2020 election saw no obvious, dramatic increases in turnout relative to states that did not. Indeed, turnout was up across the board in 2020, and increased markedly in states that offered no absentee voting at all.*

---

1 Jesse Yoder, Cassandra-Handan Nader, Andrew Myers, Tobias Nowacki, Daniel M. Thompson, Jennifer A. Wu, Chenoa Yorgason and Andrew B. Hall, *How Did Absentee Voting Affect the US 2020 Election?* Stanford Institute for Economic Policy Research, Working Paper No. 21–011, March 2021, p. 27.

These conclusions are also in-line with those of another scholar who noted that: "… increased absentee voting did not favor Joe Biden's candidacy. After controlling for 2016 Democratic vote margin, the prevalence of absentee voting in a state had no effect at all on 2020 Democratic vote margin."[2]

All these observations provide a salutary lesson as to why it is not a good idea to be hasty in arriving at conclusions on matters of considerable importance, that could then settle into an inaccurate or false narrative difficult to subsequently correct. Even with a tendency towards cautiousness, I made the same error.

Background to GE2020

From as early as the first quarter of 2019, there was a general feeling across Singapore's opposition parties that the election to come would be as challenging as GE2015. After the PSP was established, the view was that it would be the only party to watch because its chief, Tan Cheng Bock (TCB), had some national prominence. Much online chatter placed great store on the personality of TCB. But those hopes were to be dashed. On the other hand, the general sentiment from online chatter was that the WP was on its way out. This was because the party was deemed to be hobbled due to the significant litigation it was embroiled in over governance issues related to the Aljunied-Hougang Town Council (AHTC).

The alternative parties had not put together any electoral pact in spite of some efforts in that direction. Thus, other than the WP and PSP, the other opposition parties were of the view that they would not stand a chance to win any seat in the election. This was a view that had

---

2 Alan I. Abramowitz, "Assessing the Impact of Absentee Voting on Turnout and Democratic Vote Margin in 2020", 25 February 2021, https://centerforpolitics.org/crystalball/articles/assessing-the-impact-of-absentee-voting-on-turnout-and-democratic-vote-margin-in-2020/. Accessed on 30 April 2021.

been articulated to me by a few opposition members but, obviously, such defeatist sentiment would never be made public by them. The view that was in the ascendant in the non-WP camp for almost 18 months prior to GE2020 was that due to the WP's legal woes the party would implode at the election. In consequence, the calculations that some in the other opposition parties were making were that a few Non-constituency Member of Parliament (NCMP) seats would be up for their taking. This, therefore, partly explained why the SDP decided to let its party chief, Chee Soon Juan, and its party chairman, Paul Tambyah, contest in single-member constituencies (SMCs), Bukit Batok and Bukit Panjang respectively. This was intended to optimise their chances for an NCMP seat. And, this was a departure from GE2015 when both SDP personalities stood together in the four-member Holland-Bukit Timah group representation constituency (GRC). The Singapore People's Party's (SPP) Jose Raymond, whom I was in close contact with, had also let on that if he could not win Potong Pasir SMC outright, he was hopeful that, with the amount of effort he put into the constituency a full two years prior to the election that he could at least snag one of the NCMP seats. Similar calculations were being made elsewhere across the alternative parties. And, all those calculations turned on a possible WP implosion. This was the unsaid but evocative expectation. Not only did that expectation fail to materialise but the WP surprised by outperforming the competition at GE2020.

Policies — Economic rationality, and the WP's awareness of the broad electorate

Great store has tended to be placed by other commentators on Policies and Personalities in parliamentary elections. Not much analysis has been undertaken on matters of Party brand and Process which, the contention here, are even more deterministic of outcomes in the context of Singapore's particular parliamentary election system — the Westminster-adapted first-past-the-post (FPTP).

Within the ambit of Policies, voters around the world tend to emphasise personal economic interest.[3] Consequently, economic motivation cannot be overstated in terms of voters' priorities.[4] This is even more so in Singapore where, as was seen in the previous chapter, Singapore society is largely ingrained with a mercenary culture. To that extent, in the lead up to GE2020 many Singaporeans were hit economically because of the COVID-19 pandemic. Though the government's multiple budgets — amounting to almost $100 billion — brought relief to some, many others were aware that that relief would be temporary, that they would lose their jobs or be forced into less stable employment, including the gig economy, where income could fluctuate markedly from week-to-week. The pandemic, however, merely accentuated a long-term trend of simmering resentment by Singaporeans, especially those in their 40s and 50s, about increasing job insecurity and/or reduced income. As they saw it, the nub of the problem was the government's relatively liberal immigration policy which opened the doors to a large number of foreign nationals who displaced Singaporeans from their jobs. (See Chapter 10.) Singapore's liberal immigration policy was therefore linked to economic rationality as a key driver of how quite a number of voters cast their votes at GE2020.

What appeared to have dismayed many Singaporeans was that the government's initial success in getting control of COVID-19 in February and March 2020 gave way to a spread of the virus through

---

3 This has become even more so with the rise of what is called "economic nationalism" as a countervailing force to globalisation. A particularly useful analysis of economic nationalism and the rise of populist parties in Europe can be found in Italo Colantone and Piero Stanig, "The Surge of Economic Nationalism in Western Europe", *Journal of Economic Perspectives*, Vol. 33, No. 4, Fall 2019.

4 Economic interests tend to be paramount not only as a factor in elections but, as scholars have also pointed out, such interests have in fact shaped the nature of electoral systems. See, for instance, Thomas R. Cusack, Torben Iversen and David Sockice, "Economic Interests and the Origins of Electoral Systems", *The American Political Science Review*, Vol. 101, No. 3, August 2007.

dormitories housing many thousands of migrant workers.[5] The general public perception was that the government was distracted by some praise it had received internationally for its initial infection-control efforts. The government lapped up all the praise, and added to it with its own self-congratulation. Almost a decade earlier, in January 2011, I had publicly spoken at a conference about "a self-congratulatory attitude that's very pervasive" in Singapore.[6] My remarks were reported in a story in *Today* with the headline, "S'pore, a global city, yes. But how about humility?"[7] The contention here is that Singapore witnessed some of the worst consequences of the pervasive self-congratulatory behaviour during the COVID-19 pandemic. To add to the public perception of a government that fumbled because it was distracted with congratulating itself, was a view that it wanted to push ahead with a general election almost in the eye of the pandemic, when there was still ample time remaining to the parliamentary term. The public perception of a government wanting to exploit a health crisis for political purposes did not have a good look.

Some observers had suggested that there would be a similar situation as the September 11, 2001 (9/11) terrorist attacks on the United States, which resulted in the People's Action Party (PAP) government calling for an early election as a consequence of that attack and, thus, benefiting from it. I was less enamoured of that view. In public remarks posted on

---

5 "Singapore was a Shining Star in COVID-19 Control — Until it Wasn't", *NPR*, 3 May 2020, https://www.npr.org/sections/goatsandsoda/2020/05/03/849135036/singapore-was-a-shining-star-in-covid-control-until-it-wasnt. Accessed on 30 April 2021.

6 Years later I was to discover that the Singaporean scholar, Kenneth Paul Tan, had actually made a similar observation, but three years earlier. In consequence, he ought to be given credit. His reference to "self-congratulatory public gestures" can be found in Kenneth Paul Tan, "Meritocracy and Elitism in a Global City: Ideological Shifts in Singapore", *International Political Science Review*, Vol. 29, No. 1, 2008, p. 10.

7 "S'pore a global city, yes. But how about humility?' *Today*, 18 January 2011.

my Facebook page on Nomination Day on 30 June 2020, I said the following:

A number of people have argued that due to the pandemic, there will be a flight to safety by voters, i.e., towards the PAP. They draw a parallel with 9/11 and the calling of a general election not long thereafter, on 3 Nov 2001. I'm not sure whether many voters will view it the same way. International terrorism on a spectacular scale, as exemplified by 9/11, emerged suddenly and, justifiably, frightened most people. On the other hand, COVID-19 has now been around for some months and, as Hong Kong and Taiwan, have demonstrated, it is not beyond the wit of governments to get a handle of the pandemic. (I don't use New Zealand as an example as it is geographically remote and, thus, is able to seal its borders better.)

There was no flight to safety. In fact, some voters decided to punish the PAP for what they perceived as, being crass in wanting to exploit a health crisis for partisan purposes. In the ultimate analysis, that, together with the economic fallout of the pandemic, which adversely impacted livelihoods, took its toll on the PAP vote. In short, it could justifiably be said that if the "LKY effect" inflated the PAP vote at GE2015, then the "pandemic election effect" deflated it.

Another point to be made about Policies is in relation to the WP. Other than the PAP, the WP is the only party that has for a long time been conscious that any policy it comes up with has to be placed within the context of Singapore being a relatively conservative society. The other context the WP is fully conscious of is that elections in Singapore occur under conditions of compulsory voting, where the demographic profile of the turned-out electorate is, consequently, diverse. In that connection, as one scholar specialising on the efficaciousness of parties' campaigning within compulsory voting has observed: "[T]he wider array of voters should increase for parties the utility of broad, catchall policy programs. At the same time, it should decrease the utility of subgroup-targeted appeals."[8] Those observations explain the WP's political positioning towards the centre-ground, which facilitates proximity voting (as examined in Chapter 1). And, the observations also underpin why the WP has knitted together a *coalition of voters* as its election strategy. Contrary to the opinions of some in the blogosphere,[9] no base election — i.e., an election where a party successfully engages in subgroup-targeted appeals — can ever occur in Singapore because it is directly at odds with the logic underlying compulsory voting, where "catchall policy programmes" have to be pursued. The WP's 39-page manifesto, *Make Your Vote Count*, published for GE2020, was the most detailed manifesto put out by all the parties and, yet, to most voters, much of what it advocated would not have been considered objectionable.

The only other point regarding Policies concerns the decay of leases of Housing and Development Board (HDB) flats. It was an issue which had an adverse impact on the PAP's vote. This issue emerged as an existential political problem for the PAP because the then Minister for National Development, Lawrence Wong, had on 24 March 2017 put out a fairly blunt statement that when the leases on the flats expired the flats would revert to the HDB. In short, going into GE2020, Wong had inadvertently weaponised the issue of HDB lease decay against his own party.

Personalities

Jamus Lim. If one were to believe the comments uttered by many on election-night GE2020, one would be forgiven for thinking that the

---

8 Shane P. Singh, "Compulsory Voting and Parties' Vote-Seeking Strategies", *American Journal of Political Science*, Vol. 63, No. 1, January 2019, p. 39.

9 Here, I refer to left-leaning bloggers, including one who lauds a "clear water strategy" for those in opposition to the PAP. These bloggers have decried the WP for not being ideologically distant from the PAP and, as such, had hoped the WP would lose its entire parliamentary presence. Of course, they would have been displeased by the results of GE2020.

WP's Jamus Lim, an economics-trained academic, had single-handedly set alight the election campaign. To be certain, Lim was essential to the WP in winning Sengkang GRC. But as a factor, Lim could not operate independently. He operated as part of a confluence of factors that came together to deliver victory to the WP in Sengkang GRC. (This is analysed in Chapter 3.)

It should be said that in the Westminster system of first-past-the-post elections, personalities tend to take second place to party brand. The system has been designed that way, and is intended to have that effect. Rarely can a personality on her/his own, as a challenger, prevail against a strong party brand.[10] That is the underlying premise of the Westminster model, where voters effectively choose parties, not personalities. This, as a reality, tends to be accentuated in Singapore where there are also multi-seat constituencies — GRCs.

Lee Hsien Yang. The falling out between Prime Minister Lee Hsien Loong and his two siblings was potentially also an election issue. That falling out began publicly in 2017 and evolved into increasingly bitter acrimony right into GE2020. For some three years, Singaporeans were wondering whether the prime minister's brother, Lee Hsien Yang (LHY),

---

10 In the UK, there have been a few notable exceptions, one being the maverick politician, George Galloway. He has had a high public profile, and he has also been shrewd in understanding the election process, where in first-past-the-post, a winner needs merely to attain a plurality, not a majority, of votes to be declared winner. Also, at the 1997 UK general election, the former BBC journalist, Martin Bell, ran as an independent and defeated a sitting Conservative Member of Parliament (MP). Bell used his high profile as a well-recognised face on the BBC to challenge and defeat an unpopular MP, for the constituency of Tatton, who had been under a cloud for having asked parliamentary questions in exchange for cash. Given Bell's high profile, and also running on an anti-corruption platform, the Labour Party and the Liberal Democrats stood down their candidates in Tatton at the 1997 election in order not to split the anti-Conservative vote, thereby giving Bell a free run for the seat, and resulting in him winning by an enormous margin. In the UK electoral set-up of 650 SMCs, Galloway, Bell and a few others, have merely been the exceptions proving the essential validity of the generalisation — that party brand tends to heavily trump personality in FPTP.

would run as an election candidate on an anti-PAP ticket. Ultimately, LHY did not run for election but he became a member of the PSP and campaigned for it on the ground. From the way he was greeted by residents everywhere he visited it was clear that LHY had electoral stardust. His popularity was, therefore, obvious. LHY reflected the Lee family brand, and would have been the only personality of equal standing to a Party brand. To that extent, it is the contention here that only LHY running alongside TCB on the same PSP GRC ticket would have ensured a PSP victory in a GRC. The 1.68% which the PSP team fell short in West Coast GRC would have easily been made up for if LHY had stood on the PSP ticket there. The final point that remains to be made about LHY's involvement in GE2020, is that he was the only person who seemed to have campaigned on his father's legacy, on behalf of the PSP. Even the PAP did not go there in its campaigning.

Lim Tean. That one can viably run on one's personality in the Westminster parliamentary election system is a common misconception and was apparent in how some personalities from the alternative parties conducted themselves at GE2020. A high-profile example was Lim Tean, the head of Peoples Voice (PV). Lim stood as part of a four-member PV team for Jalan Besar GRC. However, an on-ground survey of the election efforts in that GRC on Cooling-off Day, 9 July 2020, revealed that there was a disproportionate number of large posters just showing Lim's image and seemingly far fewer posters of the four-man PV GRC team. Also, PAP posters were pervasive throughout the constituency, whereas one had to strain to spot their opponent's. Many voters in Jalan Besar GRC would have been either confused or unimpressed. One voter in the constituency indicated to me that he was not sure who the opposition was. He then asked, "The Workers' Party is not here, right?"

Lim had also placed inordinate emphasis on social media as an electioneering tool, and he had been doing that for a few years leading up to GE2020. He put out many video clips where he gave short, crisp speeches. These clips were uploaded onto Facebook and YouTube, among other portals. Undoubtedly, Lim, a lawyer by training, is a speaker who has presence. He can speak seemingly off-the-cuff without faltering, and his speeches are both sharp and eloquent. But what was the impact?

The software company, Meltwater Media Intelligence, conducted a survey of Facebook interactions during the campaign period, 30 June to 10 July 2020. This was reported in *The Straits Times* on 15 July 2021. The findings indicated that PV (effectively Lim) chalked up 125,687 interactions.[11] This was the third highest number of party interactions after the WP and the PAP, and ahead of the SDP. Just to provide further context, the 125,687 interactions were larger than the total voter turnout of 101,840 at Jalan Besar GRC at GE2020. Yet, the PV's team in that GRC garnered just 34,261 votes or 34.64% of the valid votes cast. The incidence of rejected votes in Jalan Besar GRC was at a relatively high 2.9%. The disconnect between cyberspace and the offline world is subjected to further analysis in Chapter 3.

A year after GE2020, Lim continued to post avidly on Facebook, with each of his postings regularly eliciting between 2,000 and 3,000 positive reactions. These positive reactions can balloon to 5,000 or even more and, still, it would not be surprising if Lim failed to get elected the next time round. (This assumes that he stands for re-election.) Should that come to pass, his ardent supporters will likely opine that those who gave him online support ultimately did not then vote for him. This misunderstands the issue. At GE2020, those who expressed online support for Lim *did* vote for him, but they were overwhelmingly drawn from the irreducible core of anti-PAP voters (main voting bloc D, Table 1.2, Chapter 1), and a smattering of those from the wavering middle-ground. Thus, social media mostly captures existing online support. It is a channel to allow interactions with the converted.

---

11 "By the numbers: Facebook interactions", *The Straits Times*, 15 July 2020.

A politician who has great oratory will gather the converted together in an online portal. To that extent, journalist Chong Zi Liang described Lim in relation to GE2020, as "this election season's chief provocateur".[12] Beyond speaking to the converted, Lim and his party have had no conversion strategy — a concept also examined in Chapter 3 — which is required for elections under the conditions of compulsory voting.

Strawmen issues

I do not ascribe the vote swing against the PAP to a supposed "desire for greater diversity" in Parliament as suggested by both the PAP and other observers. As a concept, the "desire for greater diversity" is too ambiguous for practical-minded Singaporeans. But it seems to have been *publicly* touted by the PAP as a reason why its vote share suffered an erosion at GE2020. That, however, simply constitutes a PAP talking point intended to distract attention from the more compelling matter that pummelled the party — increasing job insecurity by Singaporeans who had experienced displacement from stable employment due to structural changes to the economy and the influx of foreign nationals. In short, a not inconsiderable segment of voters at GE2020 were voting against what they felt were failed PAP policies. That is a reality that is less ambiguous.

The government placing on the statute book the Protection from Online Falsehoods and Manipulation Act (POFMA) was another strawman issue touted by some as having an adverse impact on the PAP's vote at GE2020. POFMA was passed into law in May 2019 after extensive debate in a special parliamentary select committee, of which the hearings were conducted a year earlier, throughout the month of

---

12 Chong Zi Liang, "Is WP's Raeesah Khan the most disliked politician on social media in Singapore?" *Art Science Millennial*, 22 July 2020, https://artsciencemillennial. substack.com/p/is-wps-raeesah-khan-the-most-disliked?fbclid=IwAR2fubHyzDbJ wb0czqYwZQ9MNiPIDJSpik5BIz34zU5XYCZrO4n9kFy_5PU. Accessed on 20 March 2021.

March 2018. POFMA is Singapore's anti-fake news law, which critics claim is a partisan device to ensure that the state's narrative is supreme. They allege that it has the effect of constraining independent journalism and forcing netizens to self-censor online. However, there is no evidence that POFMA on its own had converted some previous PAP voters to vote against the party. Those who were already stridently anti-PAP in outlook merely jumped on the passing into law of POFMA to express further outrage at the PAP. Their magnified anger — whether real or confected — at the government does not give them extra votes.

From strawmen issues and personalities, we now move on to a focus on a more substantive matter. This relates to the SDP.

SDP's "rebranding"

The SDP's Chee and Tambyah were two of the surprises to emerge from GE2020. Although both failed to get elected, they chalked up votes of significance, confounding many observers. Chee took 45.2% of the valid votes cast in Bukit Batok SMC, while Tambyah garnered 46.27% in Bukit Panjang SMC. This was a strong showing by both candidates. Previously, the party failed to breach the 40% level. The ceiling of 40%, which had held back the SDP in every constituency it contested between GE1997 and GE2015 (inclusive),[13] was breached effortlessly by the party's Secretary-General and its Chairman at GE2020. Given its significance, it deserves granular analysis.

One myth, among several, that GE2020 spawned was the suggestion made by some observers that there was a "rebranding" of the SDP. Here, if "rebranding" is taken to mean the figurative slapping on of a coat of paint to make something look fresh and new, even if in substance it is neither, then the term has some basis to it in relation to the SDP. But if "rebranding" is meant to convey the impression that the SDP had

13 This should also include the Bukit Batok by-election of May 2016.

re-positioned itself politically to move closer to the centre-ground of Singapore politics, then the empirical evidence does not support that proposition. Yet, the talk both online and offline touted an SDP "rebranding" as key to an unexpectedly strong showing by Chee and Tambyah.

For the SDP, there was merely "an evolution of image management".[14] The contention here is that the SDP has remained substantively the same even if some gained the impression of a significant change in its nature. Before getting into the evidence, this is the main point: the SDP gave an appearance of moderation in the lead up to Polling Day. And, this would affirm the analysis in the previous chapter, that the political polarity in Singapore is between the authoritarian-leaning PAP, on the one hand, and the organised opposition that is in the moderate centre-ground, on the other. Anything that looks vaguely ideologically liberal would be spurned by the voters.

The public perception of a newly minted moderate persona appears to be in juxtaposition with belligerence just beneath the surface of SDP members. The last instance where such belligerence surfaced prior to GE2020 was the expression of contempt for the Singapore judiciary by one of Chee's key lieutenants, John Tan. This was to lead to Tan's prosecution. The matter arose out of a Facebook comment Tan left to a post in April 2018 agreeing with the original poster that the Singapore courts were not as independent as Malaysia's on cases with political implications. A year later, in April 2019, a ruling was handed down on this case. Tan was fined $5,000 for contempt of court.[15] This was his

---

14 Alex Marland and Tom Flanagan, "Brand New Party: Political Branding and the Conservative Party of Canada", *Canadian Journal of Political Science*, Vol. 46, No. 4, December 2013, p. 952.

15 "Jolovan Wham, SDP's John Tan fined $5,000 for contempt of court", *CNA*, 29 April 2019, https://www.channelnewsasia.com/news/singapore/jolovan-wham-sdp-john-tan-fined-contempt-of-court-11487364. Accessed on 10 April 2021.

second conviction for the same offence. His earlier conviction was in 2008, where he received 15 days' imprisonment.[16]

Tan's $5,000 fine meant that he would be disqualified from standing as an election candidate for a period of five years as stipulated under the Singapore Constitution. This is a measure intended to filter out unsuitable candidates. (The threshold for disqualification is a minimum fine of $2,000 for a criminal offence.) Due to this provision, Tan sought a declaration by the Singapore High Court that "contempt by scandalising the judiciary" was a quasi-criminal offence and not an "offence" that would result in his disqualification as an election candidate. In November 2019, the High Court rejected the application saying, "Based on the text of the provision and the context in which it is found in the Constitution, the interpretation to be given to the term 'offence' in Art 45(1)(e) extends to cover quasi-criminal offences such as criminal contempt."[17] Tan appealed, and the matter went to adjudication by a five-judge Court of Appeal. In March 2020, the judges rejected the appeal. The Court of Appeal did not agree with Tan's preference of wanting to serve jail time instead of paying the $5,000 fine, in order to avoid disqualification as an election candidate.[18] The judges in effect said that an accused person could not choose a sentence based on that person's political considerations. Other than drawing a line under the matter, this judgment, handed down in March 2020, was just four months before GE2020. Yet, the suggestion was floated

---

16 "Singaporeans jailed for kangaroo T-shirts in courts", *Reuters*, 27 November 2008, https://www.reuters.com/article/oukoe-uk-singapore-kangaroo-idUKTRE4AQ1 V920081127. Accessed on 10 April 2021.

17 "SDP's John Tan not eligible to run in general election after contempt of court conviction: High Court", *The Straits Times*, 6 November 2019, https://www. straitstimes.com/politics/high-court-sdps-john-tan-conviction-for-contempt-disqualifies-him-from-ge. Accessed on 10 April 2021.

18 "Apex court dismisses appeals by SDP's John Tan, activist for scandalising the judiciary", *Today*, 16 March 2020, https://www.todayonline.com/singapore/apex-court-dismisses-appeals-sdps-john-tan-activist-scandalising-judiciary. Accessed on 10 April 2020.

online following the election of a "rebranding" of the SDP. It has since gained traction even though there is little evidence to support it.

Chee's negatives are "priced-in" by the voters, thus he surprises on the upside

One way of viewing why Chee exceeded expectations at GE2020 might be to look at his situation in the same way that investors tend to value companies listed on the stock market. Companies which report results showing further losses, instead of having their stock prices pummelled in reaction, actually experience price rallies. This is because investors had already priced-in negatives, and tend to look forwards, not backwards. Over several decades Chee had accumulated plenty of negatives. His proxies and ardent supporters have been adamant that he had been the victim of bad press as he valiantly opposed the PAP. It wouldn't be constructive to go through all the various things Chee had said and done which had put off many Singaporeans. However, it will be sufficient to mention just two. Chee had travelled abroad to speak at conferences and seminars, where he used the various platforms to launch attacks on the government. Yes, the PAP is not Singapore, but Singapore politicians travelling abroad to criticise their compatriots is, tactically, not considered a good idea. Many Singaporeans feel that such political exchanges should take place domestically. Second, under Chee, the SDP had engaged in a decade-long campaign of civil disobedience that seemed to have ended, or been suspended, sometime in 2009. Going into GE2020, these aspects of historical baggage did not appear to weigh Chee down.

Significantly, at GE2020 there was a noticeable change in Chee's demeanour. Politics is about optics. The unsmiling, scowling Chee, whom most Singaporeans were accustomed to seeing since the early 1990s, was less apparent. Chee's appearance at the nationally televised election debate on 1 July 2020, where he crossed swords with Minister

Vivian Balakrishnan, made him look reasonable. Ironically, it was Balakrishnan who came across as heavy-handed in terms of tone and even body language. This was apparent when Chee said the government was "toying with the idea" of having Singapore's population grow to 10 million.[19] Balakrishnan refuted the claim, calling it a "falsehood". Chee was not hurt by that live broadcast. His historical negatives had already been priced-in by the voters, and they must have been surprised that he had appeared relatively reasonable during the debate. Voters also gave him credit for raising the issue of population growth, thus compelling the government to make a public denial. At GE2020, Chee's public persona seemed at variance from just a few years earlier.

In that connection, at a rally for the Bukit Batok by-election of May 2016, of which he was a candidate, Chee gave one of his trademark emotionally-charged speeches. Video footage of a part of that speech, which the party felt was valuable politically — or personally — was uploaded online. In that segment, Chee referenced his situation:

The taunts, the insults, the punishment, the attacks, have been unrelenting. But I do not bow to those who mock me, nor will I bend to those who attack me. I will not kneel before them because one cannot stand up for one's principles, for one's beliefs, for one's people, on bended knees. As long and as hard as the struggle has been, I walk with my head held high. I can do this because it doesn't matter who the PAP says I am. What matters is what God knows who I am, my wife and my children know who I am and, most important, I know who I am.

---

19 "Singapore GE2020: Vivian Balakrishnan refutes Chee Soon Juan on SDP's 10m population claim", *The Straits Times*, 2 July 2020, https://www.straitstimes.com/politics/vivian-refutes-chee-on-sdps-10m-population-claim. Accessed on 20 January 2021.

This might have come across as somewhat Churchillian — "We shall never surrender!". But where Churchill was rallying a nation, Chee's remarks come across as a "Look at poor me!" introspective. It would be significant if at GE2020 Chee had actually moved on from all that.

The SDP under Chee has positioned itself to the left of the WP. Chee has spoken at length about why democracy and democratic values are essential. That said, there is a general convention in politics globally: someone who leads a political party into an election but fails to win any seats would do the honourable thing — resign on principle. In other words, they would fall on their sword to take responsibility for failure. (In many countries, the leader of a political party would resign if s/he failed to meet the party's basic electoral expectations, even if the party retained many parliamentary seats.[20]) This is an established practice for political parties whose claim to legitimacy is being democratic, in both letter and spirit. And, a leader of such a party would resign even though s/he would be able to demonstrate that s/he has overwhelming, if not unanimous, support within the party to stay on as leader.

The SDP emerged out of GE1991 with three seats, then in May 1993 Chee assumed its helm and took the party into GE1997, leaving it with no parliamentary representation. Chee did not resign. Instead, he led the SDP into five subsequent general elections — 2001, 2006, 2011, 2015 and 2020 — and the party continued to draw a blank. It seems that the selectorate of carefully chosen cadres in the SDP is

---

20 British political personalities, such as David Cameron and Alex Salmond, resigned as Conservative Party and Scottish National Party leader respectively when they failed to win referenda outcomes they had campaigned for. In the case of Cameron, he failed to win the 2016 UK-wide referendum to remain in the European Union. As for Salmond, he resigned when he failed to win the 2014 Scottish independence referendum. Upholding the democratic ideal and a strong sense of personal honour required both leaders to resign.

preferred over the will of the more numerous constituency-based electorate. As the scholar J. Patrick Dobel has written: "Resigning has a profound role in the moral ecology of the self."[21] This is because:[22]

The willingness to resign buttresses the moral and psychological core of integrity and responsibility. If persons become so wedded to office that they will not resign under any circumstances, they risk violating their integrity, the norms of office, and effectiveness.

On a related note, a key aspect of the democratic tradition is that those who adhere strictly to it would embrace an obvious time-limitation on the office they hold, whether it be a political office, such as party Secretary-General, or the office of head of government, i.e., prime minister or president. As two scholars have observed: "In principle, democratic time rules concern terms of action as well as terms of office. The latter delineate the temporal boundaries of public office."[23] As I write this, Chee has been Secretary-General of the SDP for an unbroken 28 years and counting. Anywhere else, where politicians' claim to legitimacy as adherents of democracy is measured by their acceptance of limits on their length in office, this would be considered beyond parody. But in Singapore, it is hyper-normalised.

At the next general election, assuming two things, that Chee is still leading the SDP and that he is allowed to participate in a televised

---

21 J. Patrick Dobel, "The Ethics of Resigning", *Journal of Policy Analysis and Management*, Vol. 18, No. 2, Spring 1999, p. 246.

22 Ibid. p. 248.

23 Andreas Schedler and Javier Santiso, "Democracy and Time: An Invitation", *International Political Science Review*, Vol. 19, No. 1, January 1998, p. 8.

debate during the campaign, the PAP representative at the debate should ask him or the SDP representative a few things:

- Does the SDP regret its previous campaign of civil disobedience (which it quietly abandoned — or put on hold — in 2009) and, if it does, will it now apologise for it?
- If any SDP candidates are elected to Parliament, will they raise the issue of ex-Internal Security Act detainees (a number of whom have been members of the party) and, if so, do they intend to press the government for "restorative justice" for the former detainees?
- Does the SDP still support the repeal of S377a of the penal code, that criminalises sex between men and, if it does, what further would the party like to see in terms of Lesbian, Gay, Bisexual and Transgender (LGBT) rights?
- Back in 2015, SDP chair, Paul Tambyah, was prominent in pushing back against the state's prosecution of the teenager Amos Yee for wounding religious feelings. (See Appendix 2.) Does the party regret or support Tambyah's intervention in that episode?
- Does the SDP accept that the Singapore judiciary is independent and impartial, or does it still support the stand taken by some party members who have tended to argue the reverse?

All these questions do not have anything to do with the centrality of economic motivation that heavily determines the voting choices of Singaporeans, that was argued at the front of this chapter. Instead, all the questions revolve around issues of civil liberties and human rights. Consequently, Chee or his party's representative giving unambiguous answers to the above questions would provide a clear indication of the extent of the SDP "rebranding", as claimed by some.

It should be noted that, as the SDP stepped up election preparations, its Chairman, Tambyah, in a speech to party members on 1 November 2019, proclaimed: "The task is tremendous. We've got the mass media, we've got apathy, we've got all the goodies that they're giving out... So, it's really, really hard. But that is something the SDP has never shied away from doing." Those remarks should be juxtaposed against an "Ask Me Anything" session Tambyah and his party colleague, Alfred Tan, conducted over the span of six hours on Reddit on 25 June 2020. As was reported in *Today*, "For its stance on LGBT and whether Section 377a — the law that criminalises sex between men — should be repealed, the SDP members did not answer any of them."[24]

We now continue the discussion of Party brand, focusing on the PSP. The PSP's failure to get fully elected MPs was due to a lack of branding.

Party brand: PSP was tripped up by a poorly designed logo

After its establishment in early 2019, the PSP was quick to forge ahead and steadily built up its membership base. It was also quick in getting a party logo. Perhaps it was too quick because no real thought appears to have gone into the logo which, effectively, represents the single most important element in party branding at the most rudimentary level. The lack of clear and simple messaging through a party logo that voters could identify with was a major pitfall for the PSP when it unveiled its logo on 11 April 2019.[25] In its report on the PSP logo, *The Straits Times* noted the following in terms of what I had said:

Political observer Derek da Cunha said a party logo is an exercise in branding. "It should be easily identifiable by the voters, easily distinguishable from the plethora of other party logos, and aspirational, if possible. As such, a party logo should speak for itself, and should not require any explanation."

---

24 See "Reddit users ask SDP members about election campaign proposals, stance on migrant labour, LGBT issues", *Today*, 26 June 2020, https://www.todayonline.com/singapore/reddit-users-ask-sdp-members-about-election-campaign-proposals-stance-on-migrant-labour-lgbt-issues. Accessed on 6 January 2021.

25 "Progress Singapore Party unveils party symbol", *The Straits Times*, 12 April 2019.

Without being explicit and obvious about it, I was critical of the PSP logo. That logo was a palm tree, with the trunk taking the form of a human body, with five fronds. In skeletal form, the logo was not dissimilar to a palm tree with nine fronds which was employed by TCB as his symbol for his presidential election bid in 2011 (PE2011). This apparent conflation of TCB the personality with PSP the party was obvious to me even as it was not obvious to many people. The latter simply do not see any problem there. But it is a major problem. What the PSP logo was conveying was not immediately apparent to the eye. The party said that each of the five fronds of the palm tree symbolised "democracy, equality, justice, peace and progress". And, according to TCB, "They also represent our multi-racial and inclusive society consisting of the four racial groups and new citizens."[26] This was a lengthy and convoluted explanation for what should have been clear and concise messaging which any skilled branding specialist could have worked out for the PSP. As is said in politics, *if you have to explain, then you have lost.*

In a walkabout in West Coast GRC two days after GE2020, TCB conceded that the party's logo had proved a problem with voters. He said: "[O]ur symbol is so new to many people. They always remember the lightning, they don't remember so much our palm."[27] A poorly designed party logo likely cost the PSP victory in West Coast GRC: a segment of politically apathetic voters compelled to turn out to vote because voting is compulsory, simply did not know what that logo was about. The PSP's logo derived from TCB's PE2011 logo, was perhaps why he had suggested that voters did not "remember so much our palm".

---

26 Quoted in ibid.

27 Quoted in "Singapore GE2020: Progress Singapore Party will continue serving residents, to decide on NCMP seats on Monday, says Tan Cheng Bock", *The Straits Times*, 12 July 2020, https://www.straitstimes.com/politics/ge-2020-progress-singapore-party-will-continue-serving-residents-to-decide-on-ncmp-seats-on. Accessed on 8 February 2021.

Do minor alternative parties play any useful role?

In the pecking order of alternative parties, the WP stands by itself as the only first tier party. As for the PSP and the SDP, they have carved out a niche for themselves amongst a segment of non-PAP voters. The other alternatives — such as the National Solidarity Party (NSP), Reform Party (RP), PV, People's Power Party (PPP), Red Dot United (RDU), and Singapore Democratic Alliance (SDA) — constitute relatively minor players in the political landscape. Yet, since these minor parties contested GE2020, they were given some significance by a number of online portals. Consequently, the question arises, do these parties play any useful role?

Before answering that question, it should be noted that there were attempts by the minor parties, together with the PSP and the SDP to put together some sort of anti-PAP pact with the WP being at its heart. However, the WP was uninterested in any association with the other parties. And, when that became clear, the PSP also decided to go its own way.

Despite the fact that the WP has not had very pleasant experience with some personalities from the other alternatives, online commentary had suggested that the WP should simply forgive and forget. It argued that the WP should be the adult in the room, rise above it all, and place national interests before narrow party interests. Deconstructing these observations, it should first be noted that, in politics, any statement or action a politician has made would remain as part of that politician's record. Politicians have to run on their record; they cannot quietly run away from their record; and, if people publicly recall parts of their record going back decades, they cannot dismiss that as a smear or an attempt at character assassination. That is one of the accepted conventions in politics. As for the point about placing national interests over that of party interests, some might say that this was simply an attempt at emotional or political blackmail of the WP.

A case can be made out that, by maintaining its distinctive identity and not muddying that identity through any association with other alternative parties, the WP is in fact putting national interest front and centre as it ensures the party's electability is maintained at the highest possible level. National interests are actually far better served if minor parties, such as the NSP, PV, PPP, RDU, RP, and SDA, dissolve, as there is little purpose for minor parties in a small country. Even the SPP has now been consigned to the fringes after Jose Raymond's otherwise valiant effort fizzled out in Potong Pasir SMC at GE2020 and his subsequent departure from the party. The continued existence of all these minor parties actually only serves one purpose — legitimising PAP rule, where the PAP can point the international community to parliamentary elections in Singapore which are *freely* contested by all and sundry.

This contention would be rebutted by the minor parties. In fact, those parties would not even accept the characterisation of being "minor", even though they have fallen well short of gaining entry into Parliament. Privately, they would concede that they are not electable, but they would still insist that they play a useful role in giving the electorate a choice through not allowing for walkovers by the PAP. If they let constituencies go uncontested, they would say that they would be disenfranchising segments of voters. Even if they fail to win any parliamentary seats, their contention might be that by contesting a general election they assist in depressing the PAP's popular vote, thereby bringing to the fore exactly the proportion of Singaporeans in opposition to the ruling party. In other words, what is publicly visible and statistically accounted for in a fully contested general election cannot be ignored by the PAP. To that extent, in the past, the PAP has tended to claim that its legitimacy to govern with the kind of paternalism not often seen in most democracies is based on the overwhelming popular support it has enjoyed in parliamentary elections.[28]

---

28 That was the general spiel often trotted out by Lee Kuan Yew in parrying away unfriendly questions from Western journalists enquiring about his authoritarian rule.

Intellectually, the minor parties do have a point. But there also exists a problem with this point: the very nature of being minor parties means that these parties and their candidates cannot garner a significant percentage of votes that would make an impression on the PAP. And, in a first-past-the-post election system, national percentages count for far less than actual parliamentary seats gained. For instance, none of the UK's main political parties has ever won more than 50% of the popular vote nationally since WWII.[29] Yet, both the Conservative Party and Labour Party have won thumping parliamentary majorities on the basis of minority popular votes. For instance, in a House of Commons of 650 Members of Parliament (MPs), the Conservatives secured 397 seats on a popular vote of 42.4% at the 1983 general election; and, Labour secured 418 seats on a popular vote of 43.2% at the 1997 general election.[30] Banner newspaper headlines on each occasion were to characterise these as "landslide" election wins for the Conservatives and Labour respectively.[31]

Of course, drawing on the UK as an example might not be completely apt for Singapore because the WP does not contest nationally. However, there is a Catch-22 here: some segment of voters in Singapore believe in the notion of a "freak election" result, whereby the PAP would be displaced as the government because those voters cannot discern between minor parties, on the one hand, and an electable alternative to

---

29 It should be noted that a reason which partly explains this is that Northern Ireland is viewed in the Westminster parliamentary calculus as a contest for local power by mostly sectarian parties, reflecting the Catholic (Irish nationalist/republican) and Protestant (British unionist/loyalist) divide there. Consequently, the Labour Party and Liberal Democrats do not contest in Northern Ireland, and the Conservative Party has only done so sporadically, polling poorly.

30 Lukas Audickas, Richard Cracknell, and Philip Loft, *UK Election Statistics: 1918–2019: A Century of Elections*, House of Commons Library, Briefing Paper CBP7529, 27 February 2020, p. 12.

31 "Thatcher wins by landslide", *The Washington Post*, 10 June 1983, https://www.washingtonpost.com/archive/politics/1983/06/10/thatcher-wins-by-landslide/045486d7-d3be-4d59-a0f9-c8117b69ce29/. Accessed on 17 February 2021; and, "After the landslide", *The Economist*, 3 May 1997.

the PAP, i.e., the WP, on the other. All they see is *opposition* contesting across the parliamentary seats. This segment of voters is a direct manifestation of elections in Singapore being compulsory whereby those who are *not* engaged politically are compelled to turn out to vote. Consequently, it is not clear-cut that a fully contested general election, with minor parties in straight fights with the PAP, will make such a material difference politically. It is noteworthy that at both GE2011 and GE2020, where the PAP was on the defensive, its popular vote still held above 60% of valid votes cast. As I had stated in *Breakthrough*, for the PAP, that figure was both statistically and psychologically important.[32] But now a new reality emerges: the importance of that figure begins to wane when the PAP has demonstrated that it can hold the line at that percentage even when it loses more seats. The ruling party's priority, therefore, is to stem a further loss of seats. And, the contention here is that the popular vote, therefore, assumes mostly symbolic significance, and not the importance once ascribed to it.

All things considered, the only effect the minor parties appear to have is threefold:

- through inadvertence they legitimise the PAP's governance;
- they make the WP look good, with voters being provided a sharper contrast between what is an electorally viable party, on the one hand, and others which are not, on the other;
- and, they provide content for otherwise information-starved media outlets, whether mainstream or alternative.

Even a party, the SPP, which, prior to GE2020, was not considered to be in the same league as the other parties referenced above, has now become insignificant for failing to make a mark for itself at that election. We complete this chapter with a brief look at the efforts of its main candidate.

---

32 da Cunha, *Breakthrough*, op. cit., p. 36.

SPP Jose Raymond's experience: A valiant effort, but an unviable brand

Since 2017, Jose Raymond had been engaging in political work for the SPP, focused on Potong Pasir SMC. This was a constituency which had been held by Chiam See Tong for some 27 years, between 1984 and 2011, first under the SDP, and later the SPP, banner. Chiam's wife, Lina, then contested the seat at GE2011 and was returned as a Non-constituency MP (NCMP). I met Raymond on 26 June 2018 to discuss his political work and strategy for potentially standing as a candidate at Potong Pasir SMC. We went through several possible scenarios. I told him candidly that, even assuming that Potong Pasir was retained as an SMC he would face an uphill battle to win the seat as the SPP lacked branding. Its party logo was not distinctive. The logo did not stand out from the mass of other logos across the minor parties, such as the NSP, SDA and RP. I said to him that if he was really interested in politics as a non-PAP candidate, the only party that mattered was the WP. He responded that the main reason why he was engaged in political work with the SPP and hoped to run as its candidate in Potong Pasir was because he wanted to repay a debt to Chiam See Tong. In the 1980s, Chiam had personally provided funds to help Raymond's father purchase an HDB flat.

I acquainted Raymond with the 4Ps and told him that, given the structural issues at work, the main thing he would need to do was to reach out systematically to residents within the SMC on a regular basis. Only when residents became personally familiar with him could he potentially surmount the lack of branding reflected in the ticket he would be running on. However, much of this hinged on whether Potong Pasir would be retained as an SMC.

In mid-March 2020, the Electoral Boundaries Review Committee released its report. On the day of the report's release, I merely caught its headlines, which included the retention of Potong Pasir as an SMC. I immediately called Raymond to congratulate him. But he sounded downbeat. The reason: while the constituency was retained in name, it was significantly altered, with the main SPP stronghold, Lorong 8, with more than 3,500 voters, carved out and absorbed into neighbouring Bishan-Toa Payoh GRC.[33] Further, the Joo Seng ward of Marine Parade GRC would be hived off and attached to Potong Pasir SMC, adding around 5,400 voters to the electoral roll.[34] All these constituted a significant re-drawing of the boundaries of Potong Pasir SMC.

At the 26 June 2018 meeting I did tell Raymond that he should spend the overwhelming amount of his time on the ground and largely eschew reaching out to residents online. However, he had a mind of his own. During the election campaign he gave two e-rallies. Both were slick and well presented. But the number of online viewers was in the low five-figures. A small percentage of those would be actual voters in Potong Pasir SMC and, the likelihood is that most of those were already Raymond's supporters. He also gave three interviews with fairly marginal alternative news websites. Even if these were mainstream portals, they would not have assisted his cause.

On the basis of spending returns filed with the Elections Department (ELD), Raymond spent $23,016 on his campaign,[35] of which around 27% was channelled to expenses for internet advertisements. (By appointment, I had visited the ELD on 17 February 2021 to inspect the election spending returns filed by candidates in six electoral divisions, including Potong Pasir SMC.) It would be difficult to conclude that

---

33 *The Report of the Electoral Boundaries Review Committee, 2020,* Presented to Parliament, 13 March 2020, Annex B, p. 8, https://www.eld.gov.sg/pdf/White_ Paper_on_the_Report_of_the_Electoral_Boundaries_Review_Committee_2020. pdf. Accessed on 20 March 2021.

34 Ibid., Annex B, p. 6.

35 "GE2020 expenses: PAP candidates spent nearly S$7 million, while opposition candidates used S$2,2 million," *CNA*, 21 August 2020, https://www.channelnewsasia. com/news/singapore/ge2020-expenses-pap-wp-candidates-voters-general-election-13042388. Accessed on 10 January 2021.

internet advertisements had even a marginal effect in moving the vote in Raymond's favour.

Significantly, another aspect of the election spending returns is worth highlighting: each candidate has to list the donors to their election campaign and the actual amounts donated. In that connection, of all the candidates' returns I had inspected at the ELD, Raymond pulled in the largest amount of individual donations. In aggregate, his campaign donations covered some 70% of his total election expenditures. The relevance of this is that during the election campaign, Raymond had touted his abilities as a fundraiser for community projects. His statements as a successful fundraiser were substantially in-line with the number of individual donors he was able to attract to support his election campaign.

On 6 July 2020, i.e., four days before Polling Day, Raymond sent me a WhatsApp message indicating that he "may be at about 45–47%" of the vote. If accurate, he could potentially prevail, or at least snag an NCMP seat. On 9 July, Cooling Off Day, I surveyed the election efforts of some of the candidates. From my observations, in Potong Pasir, Raymond was fighting a good campaign, with his election posters competing with those of his PAP opponent, Sitoh Yih Pin. But one thing was also evident: the constituency was sprawling, and it did leave me wondering whether Raymond was able to meet face-to-face in a meaningful way many of the residents of the Joo Seng ward which was absorbed into the SMC as a result of the re-drawing of boundaries effected by the Electoral Boundaries Review Committee exercise in March 2020.

On election-night, when the results for Potong Pasir SMC were announced, Raymond polled 39.33% of the valid votes cast. This varied quite a bit from the calculation he had worked on, and which he had conveyed to me on 6 July.

After the dust had settled, we met to do a post-mortem. We agreed that the lack of party branding and a re-drawing of the electoral boundaries had adversely affected his efforts. Ethnicity was also a consideration for a "few older residents". One can view this more optimistically, i.e., many younger residents, of whatever race, had warmed up to him.

The three years of ground work Raymond had put in was nothing short of valiant; he was a first-rate candidate largely let down by an unviable Party brand. He had wanted to repay the kindness which Chiam See Tong had shown to his late father. Ultimately, however, politics is a ruthless business. One must not merely have the passion for it and a desire to serve others, but also a forensic mind in focusing on what actually works in the context of the election system one is presented with.

Just before Christmas 2020, Raymond announced his departure from the SPP and politics.[36] He made a realistic decision. A vote of 39.33% was *not* a good return on some three years of political work, especially in the context of an election where the PAP was on the defensive.

The lesson of the foregoing is that the starting point for a viable campaign for elected political office is a party ticket with a strong, identifiable brand. Next comes the hard work of leveraging on that brand by doing intensive in-person outreach. The one cannot exist without the other. And, it is only the combination of the two that then puts a candidate in a favourable position. The next chapter will provide a more granular analysis of this thesis.

---

36 "SPP chairman Jose Raymond retires from politics to focus on his business", *The Straits Times*, 22 December 2020, https://www.straitstimes.com/singapore/politics/spp-chairman-jose-raymond-retires-from-politics-to-focus-on-his-business. Accessed on 20 March 2021.

CHAPTER 3

Process: The Paradox of a Virtual Election Campaign Set Against the WP's Efficacious Traditional Methods

This chapter continues from the last with the contention that a common error in the analysis of Singapore politics is to inordinately ascribe evolving political reality to privilege or change agents — personalities or the power of the people. People Power,[1] given agency by social media, and going up against an authoritarian regime is both compelling and evocative as a narrative. But, as indicated by one of the findings in this chapter, that narrative over-states Singapore's political reality.[2] Those who ascribe a transformation of the political situation to privilege or change agents tend to downplay, if not ignore altogether, a more critical variable — structure, or what can be called Process.[3] Having made that point, it should also be said that there has been one personality who had been instrumental in shaping Singapore politically. That was Lee Kuan Yew who, over the span of five decades, had become part of the structure. Thus, at GE2015 there was the "LKY effect". Lee has, however, been the exception.

---

1 A good analysis of the mixed record of People Power can be found in April Carter, "People Power Since 1980: Examining Reasons for its Spread, Success and Failure", *Themenschwerpunkt*, Vol. 31, No. 3, 2013.

2 Beyond Singapore, in more general terms, People Power seemed less efficacious during 2020–21, if we were to consider the significant reverses to democratic freedoms in Hong Kong and Myanmar.

3 This is not dissimilar to the British Political Tradition and, to that extent, I am indebted to the keen observations in the work of David Marsh, David Richards and Martin Smith, "Unequal Plurality: Towards an Asymmetric Power Model of British Politics", *Government and Opposition*, Vol. 38, No. 3, Summer 2003, especially the points made on p. 332.

Due to the COVID-19 pandemic, the weeks preceding Nomination Day, 30 June 2020, and the nine days of formal campaigning leading up to Polling Day on 10 July 2020, had reduced GE2020 to a virtual election campaign. This was because the Elections Department (ELD) laid down rules on campaigning that focused on safe management measures. These rules were set out in an ELD press release dated 8 June 2020.[4] The traditional, offline election rallies, where the Workers' Party (WP) would regularly draw crowds of 30,000 or more would, thus, not be allowed. On the other hand, the People's Action Party (PAP) has often merely drawn a sprinkling of crowds at its election rallies. Consequently, on the face of it, the adoption of safe management measures at GE2020 was disadvantageous to the WP but immaterial to the PAP. The question, however, is why did a virtual election campaign over the span of several weeks not impact the WP adversely? Some have touted the efficacy of social media as being deterministic to the outcome of GE2020.[5] This chapter provides empirical evidence which is inconsistent with that thesis.

The WP's thinking and election strategy

We start with an understanding of the WP's election strategy going into GE2020. In mid-2019, about a year before GE2020, I had a discussion with a WP member about the party's election strategy. I framed my enquiry around the fact that the party was under a cloud because of the litigation over governance issues related to the Aljunied-Hougang Town

---

4 "Press Release: Safety Measures to Ensure Safe Elections During Covid-19 Situation", Elections Department, Prime Minister's Office, 8 June 2020, https://www.eld.gov.sg/press/2020/PRESS_RELEASE_ON_SAFETY_MEASURES_TO_ENSURE_SAFE_ELECTIONS.pdf. Accessed on 10 February 2021.

5 That view was stated by a number of observers in the report "Opinion leaders, private interactions online could also have an effect", *The Straits Times*, 15 July 2020. As far as one could tell, none of those who were quoted in the report have ever done extensive scholarly research into the impact of social media on elections in general, let alone on elections in the specific context of Singapore.

Council (AHTC). The following is a summary of the main points that came up:

> *I had first contended that the only thing that the WP could do to surmount any negative public perception over the AHTC litigation was to cultivate the ground, and that was why the party had "to do so much work on the ground". The response I got was,* "That's the only thing you can do, actually."
>
> *The WP member then said that he* "saw the other day, Goh Meng Seng said he's not going to walk the ground". *I interjected, but* "you can't get into the private estates, right?"
>
> *The reply from the WP member:* "It's definitely much harder. But some MCSTs are friendly.[6] Some you can get in. But you're right, Derek."

It would be useful to disaggregate these observations and analyse them separately. First, the remark, "That's the only thing you can do, actually", relating to offline outreach efforts. Was this a rhetorical statement? Or did it reflect the WP's operational policy that placed offline campaigning as the key component to the party's election strategy? The empirical evidence to be introduced will demonstrate that offline outreach efforts reflected — and still reflects — the WP's main operational policy.

Second, it is noteworthy that a reference was made to Goh Meng Seng, leader of the People's Power Party (PPP). This was in relation to remarks Goh made in a Facebook post, which was subsequently

---

6 MCST stands for Management Corporation Strata Title, which is the managing body chosen by owners of strata-titled property units to run condominium estates.

re-published in *The Independent SG* on 19 April 2019. Goh had said the following:[7]

> *I am not going to "walk the ground", so to speak. Not going to knock on doors, shake hands and kiss babies… I am not going to play the games according to the "indoctrinated rules" set by PAP. […]*
>
> *Instead of looking at the political views, ideologies or ideals of political candidates, we have voters basically "voting blindly" according to "party branding" or whether candidates "walk the ground"! These totally misguided perception and concept of politics is the direct result of PAP's subtle brain washing.*
>
> *My "Track Record" is my consistency in providing my political views, ideas and ideals. Ideas and views which PAP would even adapt quietly without giving due credits [sic], even million dollar "elite" ministers would read and adapt in their policies.*
>
> *If you expect me to knock on doors, kiss babies, do charity work or organize events, then don't vote for me. If you only want to vote for some "big party with big brand", then I am not for you.*
>
> *But if you want an MP who will put 101% in parliamentary work, scrutinize each and every policy and laws which PAP wants to pass, then I will be an extremely good choice for you.*

Goh set out the main factors which win parliamentary elections — Party brand and Process (which includes walking the ground). But he knew that his party did not have any branding. Also, he would not walk the ground because it would be quite an exacting task for him, and he would

---

7 Quoted in "Opposition leader says it's 'illogical' to expect unelected opposition politicians to do house visits", *The Independent SG*, 19 April 2019, https://theindependent.sg/opposition-leader-says-its-illogical-to-expect-un-elected-opposition-politicians-to-do-house-visits/. Accessed on 10 January 2021.

rather not do it. Thus, Goh ran an intensive social media campaign. He was also happy to accept any invitation that came his way from alternative media sites to participate in online debates. Thus, he took part in the NUSS Pre-Election Forum 2020, livestreamed on 3 July 2020. There was a sizeable online audience for that forum, but the two main parties — the PAP and the WP — declined to participate. At GE2020, Goh garnered 28.26% of the valid votes cast, in a straight fight with the PAP candidate, Tin Pei Ling, in Macpherson single-member constituency (SMC). It was one of the lowest percentages for an alternative party/candidate contesting that election. Goh's result should be viewed in the context that he was not an entirely unknown quantity to voters. He had contested elections since 2006 where, in that year, he was a candidate for the WP in Aljunied group representation constituency (GRC). Going into GE2020 Goh had already maintained a social media presence for more than a decade.

The third point made in the discussion with the WP member was about private estates, which was partly the reason why on Nomination Day, 30 June 2020 I posted on Facebook some analysis, including the following observations on the curtailment of offline campaigning due to the COVID-19 pandemic:

A concrete manifestation of the pernicious effect of the current, what I would call muddled, ruling is that many condo estates do not allow members of the public to simply waltz in and go house-to-house to canvass for votes. Are some people just thinking that Singapore residential housing is merely a mix of HDB flats and landed properties? The Department of Statistics indicate that in 2019 condominiums & other apartments made up 16.2% of the residential housing stock.

So, this issue related to traditional election campaigning is not new or hindsight analysis on my part. I have always been aware that it is essential for an alternative party to defeat the enormous hurdle imposed by compulsory voting plus first-past-the-post (FPTP).

WP carves out wins in Aljunied GRC and Hougang SMC through house visits

At around the time of the discussion I had with the WP member, the party's volunteers, members and parliamentarians had completed at least two rounds of house visits in Aljunied GRC and Hougang SMC, i.e., where they were able to gain access to residents at their doorstep, and they were in the process of doing a third round. This was confirmed to me by a WP source. Another WP source, who had volunteered with the party since 2011 sent me an email on 28 December 2020 to say, "The results in Hougang matches the responses we got from door-to-door visit; some of the residents even recognised the new candidate as he was deeply involved in Hougang events." The new candidate was Dennis Tan who replaced Png Eng Huat. A systematic approach to reach out to residents over an election cycle through house visits provided an ability to gauge quite accurately levels of support through responses at the doorstep.[8] For definitional purposes, an "election cycle" is taken here to mean the period that starts on the day just after an election and ends on the day of the next election, i.e., generally four to five years.

The WP's preparations for GE2020 began just weeks after the 11 September 2015 general election. It was reported in October 2015 that "Since polling day last month, the Workers' Party has trained new volunteers and has started walking the ground again."[9] This was a demonstration of resilience for a party to pick itself up from an election marked by the "LKY effect", which swung decisively in favour of the ruling party. And, this was (and is) reflective of the

---

8 It should be acknowledged that not everything said at the doorstep can be taken at face value. In Chapter 2 we saw how Jose Raymond thought that, three days before the end of campaigning, he had secured 45%–47% of the vote in Potong Pasir through feedback from residents. Ultimately, he fell quite short of that estimate.

9 "One month after polling day: where are they now", *The New Paper*, 13 October 2015, https://www.tnp.sg/news/singapore-news/one-month-after-polling-day-where-are-they-now. Accessed on 12 March 2021.

WP's DNA — a fighting spirit which belies the party's credentials as a moderate political entity.

For a party that, under Low Thia Khiang and then Pritam Singh, has had a tendency to generally talk down its chances and be widely perceived as overly cautious, the statement put out by the WP on 15 March 2020, i.e., just two days after the Electoral Boundaries Review Committee (EBRC) released its report on the re-delineation of constituency boundaries, was noteworthy for doing the very opposite. The short statement ended with the following: "When the election is called, the Workers' Party will be ready and prepared for it — as we have been for the last 4 years. We will take the necessary precautions to run a fair and safe campaign."[10] In other jurisdictions, many politicians generally employ the customary phrase, "cautiously optimistic", to signal what they think of their chances. But it would be fair to characterise the WP's 15 March 2020 statement as more than that. It was bullish. It would also be fair to say that the statement was a factually accurate portrayal of the reality, i.e., that the WP had already done four years of painstaking groundwork — house-to-house visits — in its targeted constituencies in the east of Singapore, that it could go into a general election with relative confidence. And, in hindsight, the years of preparatory work were justified when, by early 2020, COVID-19 manifested itself, resulting in the ELD turning the four weeks just prior to Polling Day on 10 July 2021 into a virtual election campaign. That change to the rules of the game, warranted by a health crisis, was immaterial to the WP.

Interpersonal offline outreach, where WP members come face-to-face with constituents, take a number of forms. The weekly in-person meet-the-people sessions (MPS) is just one plank of these outreach efforts. The MPS is where, what is known as "casework" is carried out

---

10 The Workers' Party, "Election speculation amidst COVID-19", https://www2. wp.sg/election-speculation-amidst-covid-19/. Accessed on 12 March 2021.

by parliamentarians and their assistants. Singapore's MPS is equivalent to what British parliamentarians call "surgeries", where similar issues are raised by constituents. Elected representatives are often made to act as mediators,[11] amateur social workers,[12] and must also extend as much assistance as they are able to their constituents. Constituency visits, where Members of Parliament (MPs) and WP members and volunteers would go to hawker centres and other open spaces within a constituency — otherwise known as an estate walk — largely to sell the party's magazine, *The Hammer*, is another plank. But the most important of the outreach efforts are house visits. These are conducted house-to-house throughout the constituency and in one election cycle the preference is to ensure each household is visited two or three times.

Doorstepping: Deep conversations are central to a conversion strategy

Research from parliamentary elections in the United Kingdom indicates the effectiveness of politicians meeting directly, offline, with prospective voters. British academic Charles Pattie, who has conducted extensive research into election campaigning, has written: "[T]he consensus view is that constituency campaigning really does pay dividends. The harder parties campaign locally, the greater their share of the vote there, and the lower their rivals' shares."[13]

---

11 Emily Hofstetter and Elizabeth Stokoe, "Offers of Assistance in Politician-Constituent Interaction", *Discourse Studies*, Vol. 17, No. 6, December 2015, p. 725.

12 Susan Hattis Rolef, "Describing, Delimiting and Defining the Job of an MP", Conference: The Twelfth Workshop of Parliamentary Scholars and Parliamentarians, Wroxton, UK, July 2015.

13 Charles Pattie, "Hard evidence: does door-to-door campaigning work?" 16 January 2015, https://www.sheffield.ac.uk/news/nr/door-to-door-campaigning-success-comment-1.432780. Accessed on January 2021.

He has also noted:[14]

Face-to-face campaigning, where politicians and party members talk direct to the public, is shown to be more effective as a means of persuading people to vote than more remote forms of campaigning, including telephone calls, e-mails, social media interaction and leafleting.

In countries as diverse as the United States, the UK, Australia, and Canada, party canvassing at the doorstep has been linked to an increase in vote share especially for candidates/parties perceived as competitive and running in opposition to the governing party.[15] But, as one study has indicated, there is also less evidence of the effectiveness of such doorstepping techniques in some continental European countries.[16] To that extent, other countries' experience with political campaign techniques might not always have relevance to the situation in Singapore. However, in this instance, as a canvassing technique, doorstepping in fact has greater relevance and applicability for Singapore due to compulsory voting and, thus, the necessity to reach out to a significant segment of politically apathetic voters. Here, the issue turns on voter psychology, where interpersonal contact between a parliamentarian or a potential election candidate and residents, "operationalized as door-to-door appeals",[17] stimulates sympathy from

---

14 Ibid.

15 Jeffrey A. Karp, Susan A. Banducci and Shaun Bowler, "Getting Out the Vote: Party Mobilization in a Comparative Perspective", *British Journal of Political Science*, Vol. 38, No. 1, January 2008, p. 93.

16 See, Yosef Bhatti, Jens Olav Dahlgaard, Jonas Hedegaard Hansen and Kasper M. Hansen, "Is Door-to-Door Canvassing Effective in Europe? Evidence from a Meta-study Across Six European Countries", *British Journal of Political Science*, Vol. 49, No. 1, January 2019.

17 Betsy Sinclair, Margaret McConnell and Melissa R. Michelson, "Local Canvassing: The Efficacy of Grassroots Voter Mobilization", *Political Communication*, Vol. 30, No. 1, January 2013, p. 43.

residents for those who arrive at the doorstep. Materially, these efforts translate directly to votes at the ballot box. Outside of formal election campaigns these *deep conversations* in effect constitute a proxy for "deep canvassing" — a conversational technique intended to elicit emotionally significant experiences, encourage reflection on the part of residents, and where canvassers employ active listening to build trust at the doorstep.[18]

Since GE2020, WP parliamentarians have in fact employed the term "deep conversations" as they chronicle online their interactions with residents offline. By their very nature, deep conversations carried out by WP members and volunteers can only be undertaken many months before a parliamentary election. A 10-minute conversation at the doorstep means completing visits to residents in just a single block of flats over more than one evening. That and similar offline outreach efforts were likely why in a 2017 WP-released book, *Walking with Singapore*, it was stated that "every bit of ground effort requires 'blood and sweat equity' of WP members and volunteers".[19]

Conversion strategy. The face-to-face conversations in a single apartment block can then result in a so-called "neighbourhood effect", where "the weight of opinion encountered is more likely to lead to adherents of a minority view switching to the majority than vice versa".[20] In other words, the objective of deep conversations at the doorstep is that of a *conversion strategy*, where politically apathetic residents or those in the wavering middle-ground, feel enticed enough to become active,

---

18 "About Deep Canvassing", https://www.ctctogether.org/about-deep-canvassing. Accessed on 20 April 2021.

19 The Workers' Party, *Walking with Singapore*, (Singapore: Ethos Books, 2017), p. 211.

20 Ron Johnston and Charles Pattie, "Social Networks, Geography and Neighbourhood Effects", in John Scott and Peter J. Carrington, eds., *The Sage Handbook of Social Network Analysis*, (Sage Publications Ltd., 2014), https://www.researchgate.net/publication/251769111_Social_networks_geography_and_neighbourhood_effects. Accessed on 20 April 2021.

or at least passive, supporters of the politician who presented at the doorstep. This canvassing technique has been referred to as "conversion by conversation".[21] For a challenger to the PAP, there is no substitute strategy in terms of efficaciousness. Just to make the point clear: a conversion strategy is one which is executed successfully by parties in those jurisdictions which practise compulsory voting, including Australia, as scholars have pointed out.[22] Whereas, what is known as a "mobilisation strategy", is employed by parties in jurisdictions where voting is non-compulsory, thus turnout rates are uncertain and the focus of parties is on mobilising their base of identified supporters to come out to vote.[23] This is a fundamental difference that is often misunderstood. Social media is well-placed to support a mobilisation strategy; but social media is unable to give agency to a conversion strategy.

The marathon of many months of house visits leads to the final straight, which is the nine days of formal campaigning just before Polling Day. In previous elections, that final straight would have included rallies held at the WP's main stomping grounds of Serangoon Stadium and Hougang Stadium. That was not to be for the pandemic-constrained GE2020. But that final straight still saw the WP spend heavily on election materials to convert wavering voters to the WP column. Virtually all the expenditure was on print advertisements.

Election spending returns: The efficaciousness of print advertisements

The correlation between levels of expenditure by a political party on a local campaign and its outcome has been well-documented; voter

---

21 Ibid.

22 Karp, *et al.*, p. 102.

23 See, Thomas M. Holbrook and Scott D. McClurg, "The Mobilization of Core Supporters: Campaigns, Turnout, and Electoral Composition in United States Presidential Elections", *American Journal of Political Science*, Vol. 49, No. 4, October 2005.

perception of high levels of spending by an incumbent party at a constituency level plays a more instrumental role in an outcome then the outlays of a challenger party. In the words of one study:[24]

> *The empirical results demonstrate the importance of candidate spending during the campaign period and the heterogeneity of voter preferences with respect to these expenditures. Candidates that held incumbency status were found to benefit substantially compared to their challengers.*

In Aljunied GRC and Hougang SMC, the WP was the incumbent. It has also been noted, in the context of British parliamentary election campaigns, that, "To the extent that campaign spending is associated with improved vote shares, this implies that parties should see the greatest improvements in their vote in the most marginal seats, as these are where the parties will concentrate their resources."[25] And, "[t]he more competitive a constituency is for a party, the greater the boost it should receive from each extra marginal increase in its campaign effort."[26]

One commentator, writing for the online current affairs magazine *The Diplomat*, on the lessons arising from countries in the Asia-Pacific which held elections during the 2020 pandemic, observed:[27]

---

24 Marie Rekkas, "The Impact of Campaign Spending on Votes in Multiparty Elections", *The Review of Economics and Statistics*, Vol. 89, No. 3, August 2007, p. 584.

25 Charles Pattie, Todd K. Hartman and Ron Johnston, "Not All Campaigns are Created Equal: Temporal and Spatial Variability in Constituency Campaign Spending Effects in Great Britain, 1997–2015", *Political Geography*, Vol. 71, May 2019, p. 37.

26 Ibid.

27 Adhy Aman, "Elections in a Pandemic: Lessons from Asia," *The Diplomat*, 5 August 2020, https://thediplomat.com/2020/08/elections-in-a-pandemic-lessons-from-asia/. Accessed on 10 January 2021.

One can argue that the cost of campaigning in COVID-19 elections is less due to lack of rallies, reduced face-to-face interactions, and the shift to online campaigns. However, it can also be argued that the cost simply shifts from offline to online campaign activities.

For the most part, this was a fair and logical observation. But, in the case of Singapore, the picture is a mixed one. At GE2020, the observation actually did not apply to the WP. The WP's 21 candidates in six constituencies filed aggregate election expenses with the ELD amounting to $705,647.[28] Of this, the WP spent nothing on internet advertising, but it spent some $600,000 on print advertisements.[29] The print expenditure went on posters, banners, leaflets and pamphlets. The WP was to secure 10 parliamentary seats.

For the PAP, its total election spending for its 93 candidates in all 31 constituencies was $6.97 million, of which $1.8 million went towards internet advertising.[30] From all the evidence, the PAP's spending on internet advertising was not cost-effective. Much of the money was wasted. However, this is the conundrum: the PAP could not hold physical election rallies, where previously a lot of its election spending would have been devoted (and was also wasted because the PAP barely drew rally crowds of any consequence), but the party had a sizeable election budget to spend virtually up to the permissible amount — of $4 per voter — in all the constituencies. Consequently, the PAP went through the motions of utilising a large portion of that budget knowing full well that internet advertising would not move the needle in the party's favour.

---

28 "9.2 million spent by candidates on GE2020," *The Straits Times*, 21 August 2020.

29 Ibid.

30 "GE2020 expenses: PAP candidates spent nearly S$7 million, while opposition candidates used S$2.2 million," *CNA*, 21 August 2020, https://www.channelnewsasia. com/news/singapore/ge2020-expenses-pap-wp-candidates-voters-general-election-13042388. Accessed on 10 January 2021.

The third party of note, the Singapore Democratic Party (SDP), fielded 11 candidates at GE2020 across five constituencies and filed with the ELD total election expenses of $323,292, of which $138,000 went towards internet advertising.[31] Given the relatively small size of the SDP's cohort of election candidates, its budget on internet spending during a short campaign period was sizeable. It spent the equivalent of $12,545 per election candidate on internet advertising. The SDP has long placed great faith on the internet as a forum for its activities. It was one of the first parties in Singapore to establish a significant online presence, starting with a party website in the 1990s and, with the arrival of social media, it quickly embraced Twitter and Facebook, amongst other portals. However, the SDP's impressive online presence has yielded nothing for the party in terms of parliamentary seats.

By way of contrast, the party which made in-roads at GE2020, the WP, spent heavily on its offline campaign. It should, however, be said that the WP did also have a professional and sophisticated digital campaign through free-to-use online portals. In particular, the WP made heaviest, and optimum, use of Facebook where it uploaded appealing video clips on its candidates and policy positions, and its episodes of *The Hammer Show* (as a replacement for physical rallies) were also well received.

On social media statistics, Meltwater Media Intelligence measured the quantum of the various political parties' Facebook interactions over the campaign period, 30 June to 10 July 2020, and found that the WP clocked the greatest number of interactions at 296,188.[32] This was more than double the next placed party, the PAP, at 130,810 interactions.[33]

---

31 Ibid.

32 "By the numbers: Facebook interactions", *The Straits Times*, 15 July 2020. As noted in this report, "Interactions refer to likes, reactions, comments and shares on Facebook".

33 Ibid.

For context, the WP polled 279,922 votes across six electoral divisions it contested at GE2020. From this, it is logical to raise the question: how meaningful to election outcomes are statistics related to social media interactions?

Equally, how meaningful is spending by political parties in relation to election outcomes? The amounts spent and cited earlier, were based on press reports, and those reports were useful. But to get a better sense of the granularity of the expenditures by the parties required an examination of the actual election spending returns. Consequently, I went to the ELD for that purpose when the spending returns were open for inspection. The data below is a slightly deeper extension of what emerged in mainstream media reports.

In Tables 3.1 and 3.2, on the expenditures of the candidates in the WP's Aljunied and Sengkang GRC teams, I have simplified the data. Instead of a detailed breakdown, candidates' spending has been aggregated to highlight "print advertising" and what proportion it made

Table 3.1
WP Aljunied GRC election spending returns, GE2020

	TOTAL — $
TOTAL expenditure	200,940
TOTAL SPEND on Print advertising (87.66% of total expenditure)	176,150 ◄——

Table 3.2
WP Sengkang GRC election spending returns, GE2020

	Amount — $
TOTAL expenditure	132,406
TOTAL SPEND on Print advertising (84.19% of total expenditure)	111,467 ◄——

up of total election expenditure. Table 3.1 would point to why the WP team in Aljunied GRC was able to wage a campaign lamppost by lamppost, where it matched the PAP's election posters in a deliberate offline battle. And, as illustrated in Table 3.2, the WP's four-member Sengkang GRC team's election spending returns does not differ too greatly with the picture contained in Table 3.1.

Understandably, many people would be baffled as to why plenty of money went on print advertisements in a country where digital literacy is pervasive and ranks close to the top globally. The answer is optics or, what has been referred to as, *spatial visual communications*.[34] Large amounts of election spending translate directly into a high visibility campaign on the ground, where voters would immediately notice which candidate/party had resources to spend lavishly, and which did not. In short, a meaningful amount of spending, especially on print posters, is intended to provide a visual cue to give the unmistakable signal of electoral strength.[35]

More specifically, related to the WP, over a nine-day campaign, the party had to convey to *all* voters in its contested constituencies that it was fighting strongly for their votes right till the last day of official campaigning. Words would mean nothing. The party had to show materially that it was pouring in relatively large amounts of resources to reach out to apathetic voters as they travelled to the polling stations and could see for themselves the WP's campaign efforts along the roads. Those same resources would then also be intended to convert wavering

---

34 The point is elaborated at length by Delia Dumitrescu, "French Electoral Poster Campaigns in the Twenty-First Century", in Christina Holtz-Bacha and Bengt Johansson, eds., *Elections Posters Around the Globe: Political Campaigning in the Public Space*, (Springer: 2017). See, also, Delia Dumitrescu, *Spatial Visual Communications in Election Campaigns: Political Posters Strategies in Two Democracies*, Doctoral Dissertation, Ohio State University, 2009.

35 Delia Dumitrescu, "The Importance of Being Present: Election Posters as Signals of Electoral Strength, Evidence from France and Belgium", *Party Politics*, November 2011.

(middle-ground) voters to the WP's side. And, finally, the same resources would demonstrate to the WP's support base that the party did not take that support for granted but remained deserving of that support by fighting robustly through putting money into the Process. Ultimately, what all this means is being able to understand, and tap into, voter psychology.

A *Straits Times* story published on 4 July 2020, mid-way through the GE2020 campaign, was headlined "Singapore GE2020: As battle shifts online, so does election spending".[36] Insofar as the WP was concerned, the report would be at variance to the data shown in Tables 3.1 and 3.2. The report was, however, on the whole accurate insofar as the spending patterns of a few other parties were concerned at GE2020. But if the thesis is that social media was efficacious to the outcome of GE2020, then it is not fully borne out by the empirical evidence.[37]

---

36 "Singapore GE2020: As battle shifts online, so does election spending", *The Straits Times*, 4 July 2020, https://www.straitstimes.com/singapore/as-battle-shifts-online-so-does-election-spending. Accessed on 17 March 2021.

37 Even in the United Kingdom, where voting is not compulsory, there has been a significant disconnect between the direction of social media chatter and actual reality offline. As one British scholar, analysing the UK's December 2019 general election campaign, observed:

> *It has now become almost trite to point out that the political conversation on social media is not representative of the public at large. For many people this was brought into sharp focus on the day after the election, as the scale of the Conservative victory seemed to be at odds with the mood online. Social media, then, isn't a great way to take the temperature of the nation — but we should not lose sight of the fact that it is nonetheless seen as a useful way for parties to communicate with certain sections of the public.*

Richard Fletcher, "Did the Conservatives Embrace Social Media in 2019?" in Daniel Jackson, Einar Thorsen, Darren Lilleker and Nathalie Weidhase, eds., *UK Election Analysis 2019: Media, Voters and the Campaign*, (Poole, England: Centre for Comparative Politics and Media Research, Bournemouth University, December 2019), p. 80.

Still, those who have claimed that at GE2020 online campaigning complemented offline (traditional) campaigning, do make a valid point. But they cannot just leave it there. By leaving it there they give the impression that both online and offline were symmetrical and of equal weightage. Taking into account the centrality for the WP of house visits — doorstepping as a conversion strategy — and the relatively large amounts the party spent on print advertisements at GE2020, it would seem that the balance in fact weighed heavily towards a traditional, offline campaign.

Offline outreach efforts are actually the WP's comparative advantage over the PAP, and it has stepped up such efforts across its parliamentary constituencies since GE2020. Voters want to have such face-to-face interactions with their representatives. Here, a case could be made out that the WP is more-or-less trapped into the provision of what is, in effect, abnormally high levels of offline outreach. They are "abnormally high" in absolute terms, and also relative to what PAP MPs do and what is the practice of legislators in other jurisdictions.

Digital media will become critical in determining election outcomes in Singapore when the level of the WP's offline outreach drops to the same average level put in by PAP MPs. To that extent, it is noted in the scholarly literature that legislators who spend a large amount of time interacting with constituents do so because of a sense of electoral vulnerability.[38] The fact that PAP MPs are nowhere near walking the ground as intensively as their WP counterparts, would suggest that they

---

38 The same point about the sense of electoral vulnerability felt by legislators is made in the following journal articles: Taupio Raunio and Taru Ruotsalainen, "Exploring the Most Likely Case for Constituency Service: Finnish MPs and the Change Towards Personalised Representation", *Journal of Representative Democracy*, Vol. 54, No. 1, 2018, p. 50; Yasushi Hazama, "Constituency Service in Turkey: A Survey on MPs", *European Journal of Turkish Studies*, 3, 2005, Open Edition Journals, http://journals.openedition.org/ejts/471. Accessed on 15 April 2021; and, David Karlsson, "Putting Party First: Swedish MPs and Their Constituencies", *Journal of Representative Democracy*, Vol. 54, No. 1, 2018, p. 4.

do not experience an obvious sense of electoral vulnerability. That would point to an asymmetry: PAP MPs feel relatively more secure because the financial muscle of the governing party — where it can provide "targeted assistance" to segments of the population — can make up for PAP MPs' lower levels of outreach to constituents. This is not an approach unique to Singapore; it is the same for many governing parties around the world.

Let us now turn briefly to the experience of the SDP. *Channel NewsAsia* gave a breakdown of the election spending returns filed by the candidates for Bukit Batok SMC and Bukit Panjang SMC, as follows:[39]

Bukit Batok SMC

PAP, Murali Pillai: $83,295

SDP, Chee Soon Juan: $29,391

Bukit Panjang SMC

PAP, Liang Eng Hwa: $110,510

SDP, Paul Tambyah: $29,390

When these figures were published, commentary online focused on the vast amounts the PAP candidates spent relative to their SDP opponents and, despite that, the SDP's Chee Soon Juan and Paul Tambyah took 45.20% and 46.27% of the valid votes cast respectively. Undoubtedly, these were narrow victories for the PAP. A more granular breakdown of the spending, via an inspection of the returns at the

---

39 "GE2020 expenses: PAP candidates spent nearly S$7 million, while opposition candidates used S$2.2 million," *CNA*, 21 August 2020, https://www.channelnewsasia.com/news/singapore/ge2020-expenses-pap-wp-candidates-voters-general-election-13042388. Accessed on 10 January 2021.

Table 3.3
West Coast GRC election spending returns, GE2020

	Amount — $
Progress Singapore Party	
TOTAL SPEND on Print advertising	66,583 ◄
Internet advertising	0
Aggregate other expenditures	85,242
OVERALL TOTAL	151,825
People's Action Party	
TOTAL SPEND on Print advertising	201,082 ◄
Internet advertising	60,063
Aggregate other expenditures	76,715
OVERALL TOTAL	337,860

ELD, indicated that on the key metric of *print advertisements*, the PAP's Murali Pillai spent more than three times the amount Chee spent in that area, and the ratio was 6:1 by the PAP's Liang Eng Hwa over Tambyah.

Table 3.3 provides a simplified breakdown of election spending by the Progress Singapore Party (PSP) and the PAP in the five-member West Coast GRC. The PAP had flooded the GRC with its election posters, even in fairly secluded spots, but the same could not be said of the PSP. Whether this difference was consequential to the outcome is purely speculative.

What emerges from the foregoing analysis on election spending, is that in the Westminster-derived election system, if candidates wish to stand a reasonable chance to sway the outcome in their favour, they have to invest meaningful amounts in their campaign, their Party brand and in the Process. Yet, I was aware that at GE2020, at least one candidate from a minor party did not have available funds for the

$13,500 election deposit.[40] He had to borrow that amount. It is also worth noting that if one goes back to the January 2013 Punggol East by-election, the media reported that the WP's Lee Li Lian was the top-spender among four election candidates. Her campaign expenses totalled $65,227, most of which went towards three election rallies.[41] The PAP's Koh Poh Koon spent $62,991 on his campaign.[42] Assuming COVID-19 is no longer an issue by the time of the next general election, the WP's offline expenditures can only be expected to balloon because funds would be needed to organise large physical rallies.

People Power, given agency by social media, suggestive of a confrontation between the underdog and the formidable structure of elite power, and where the underdog prevails, is valorised by regular folk.[43] Ultimately, however, that narrative is at variance with the empirical evidence of elections in the Singapore context where the duality of compulsory voting and first-past-the-post sets the bar high for challengers to the incumbent. Ample materiel and manpower resources need to be poured into offline outreach efforts so as to surmount those structural hurdles.

40　That information was provided to me by the Singapore People's Party's Jose Raymond who was clued into many developments behind the scenes. To spare the particular person embarrassment I will not disclose his identity.

41　"Lee Li Lian is by-election's top spender", *AsiaOne*, https://www.asiaone.com/print/News/Latest%2BNews/Singapore/Story/A1Story20130328-411917.html. Accessed on 23 April 2021.

42　Ibid.

43　The significance of social media in giving effect to People Power is framed as a "popular mobilisation" and is set out cogently in Thomas Zeitzoff, "How Social Media is Changing Conflict", *The Journal of Conflict Resolution*, Vol. 61, No. 9, October 2017, see especially pp. 1974–1977. However, as stated unequivocally earlier in this chapter, in the context of the Singapore election system, alternative parties have to employ a "conversion strategy", not a "mobilisation strategy" to peel away at the PAP's support base. This is a key difference which throws a spotlight on the limitations of social media in Singapore elections.

Offence archaeology, and what accounted for the Sengkang GRC result

Where the internet did have an effect on GE2020 it was in the area of "offence archaeology". An editorial in the December 2018 edition of the literary journal *The New Criterion* set out the origins of this phrase:[44]

> *The term "offense archaeology" seems to have entered circulation earlier this year when the British journalist and education-industry gadfly Toby Young was appointed to a U.K. university watchdog group. Mr. Young had been a nimble and Tabasco presence on Twitter, where his politically incorrect observations won him a wide and amused following but also the consternation of the constitutionally offended. When his government appointment was announced, his articles and Twitter feed were scrutinized for impermissible remarks and attitudes, and he was pilloried and then sacked.*

At GE2020 a similar thing happened to the candidate Ivan Lim, who was expected to stand as part of the PAP team in Jurong GRC. Lim's alleged past behaviour was excavated by sleuths. They made online claims about him which were unflattering. Initially, Lim insisted on continuing as a candidate but, ultimately, he withdrew ahead of Nomination Day on 30 June 2020. Prime Minister Lee Hsien Loong acknowledged that Lim's candidacy ended as a consequence of an "internet campaign". A similar effort was made during the actual GE2020 campaign to dig up social media posts by the WP's Sengkang GRC candidate Raeesah Khan. That, however, did not adversely affect her nor the WP.

We now turn briefly to a separate line of inquiry regarding what happened at Sengkang GRC. Table 3.4 sets out four variables in favour

---

44 "Offense Archaeology", *The New Criterion*, December 2018, https://newcriterion.com/issues/2018/12/offense-archaeology. Accessed on 3 February 2021.

of the WP which out-weighed its one single negative, and the three variables in favour of the PAP. Also, here, it should be pointed out that the negative variable for the PAP, of its liberal immigration policy, affecting PMETs disproportionately, of which there were large numbers in Sengkang GRC, was not insignificant. None of the variables listed in Table 3.4 are dichotomous or unlinked.

Table 3.4
Sengkang GRC GE2020: Variables which determined the outcome

WP's Positive Variables	WP's Negative Variables
(a) Jamus Lim	(e) Raeesah Khan not popular with older Chinese voters
(b) The relative youth of the WP team	
(c) The WP brand	
(d) WP's execution on Process through a 10-year outreach effort	
PAP's Positive Variables	**PAP's Negatives Variables**
(f) The PAP brand	(i) A liberal immigration policy disproportionately affected PMETs
(g) Office-holders in the PAP GRC team	
(h) The PAP benefits structurally from a large-sized constituency, i.e., a GRC, through the law of large numbers	

SOURCE: Derek da Cunha.

The popular view which emerged from GE2020 was that the WP's Sengkang GRC victory was due to Jamus Lim. To be certain, he had electoral stardust, especially with the younger demographic in Sengkang GRC. Also, a survey by the pollster Blackbox Research, measuring online sentiment towards political personalities during the GE2020 campaign, placed Lim at the top with positive sentiment at 25.7%.[45] But it would be over-stating it to credit him entirely with the Sengkang win. As noted at the outset of this chapter, privilege or change agents are less instrumental to election outcomes in a Westminster-type election system than is often assumed. If such agents were instrumental then what would account for the fact that when WP heavyweights Low Thia Khiang, Chen Show Mao and Png Eng Huat decided not to stand for re-election, that did not appear to adversely impact the party?

Instead of privilege or change agents, Party brand and Process are far more significant. As to Process, indicated as (d.) in Table 3.4, He Ting Ru, the anchor for the WP Sengkang GRC team, made the following acknowledgment on election-night:

Finally, we could not have done this without our volunteers, without Li Lian, without Choong Yong, who've been working on the ground for more than 10 years. We would really not be here today, and we really owe a huge debt of gratitude to them.

Lee Li Lian in Punggol East and Koh Choong Yong in Sengkang West had worked the ground since just before GE2011 when both divisions were SMCs. The EBRC had subsumed the two SMCs together

---

45 Figure cited in Chong Zi Liang, "Is WP's Raeesah Khan the most disliked politician on social media in Singapore?" *Art Science Millennial*, 22 July 2020, https://artsciencemillennial.substack.com/p/is-wps-raeesah-khan-the-most-disliked?fbclid=IwAR2fubHyzDbJwb0czqYwZQ9MNiPIDJSpiK5BIz34zU5XYCZrO4n9kFy_5PU. Accessed on 20 March 2021.

with parts of a reduced Pasir Ris-Punggol GRC to form the new Sengkang GRC in advance of GE2020.[46]

The contention is that the variables in Table 3.4 have to be taken as a whole to understand the outcome in Sengkang GRC. To that extent, it should be noted that the same Blackbox Research survey which gave Jamus Lim the highest online favourability rating also gave his teammate, Raeesah Khan, the most negative sentiment rating, at 47.5%, amongst all the personalities contesting GE2020.[47]

We now turn to more conceptual issues related to Process. These last few sections of the chapter will place in better context the empirical analysis.

Compulsory voting turns out politically disengaged voters

Compulsory voting, or what is known in the scholarly literature as "compulsory voting rules" (CVR), could be said as not facilitating the democratic ideal. In a jointly authored article, the scholars Keith Jakee and Sun Guang-Zheng argued the downsides of CVR to the spirit of democracy. They noted that compelling a population to vote does not necessarily increase voter awareness of politics, let alone lead to an expansion of voter knowledge of the issues at stake at, or even the candidates contesting, an election.[48] But their conclusions have been rebutted by one of the strongest proponents of CVR, the Australian

---

46 Specifically, Polling Districts 01 to 12 of Punggol East SMC, Polling Districts 04 to 12 of Sengkang West SMC, and Polling Districts 61 to 78 of Pasir Ris-Punggol GRC would form the new Sengkang GRC. See, *The Report of the Electoral Boundaries Review Committee, 2020*, Presented to Parliament, 13 March 2020, Annex B, p. 8, https://www.eld.gov.sg/pdf/White_Paper_on_the_Report_of_the_Electoral_Boundaries_Review_Committee_2020.pdf. Accessed on 20 March 2021.

47 Ibid.

48 Keith Jakee and Sun Guang-Zheng, "Is Compulsory Voting More Democratic?" *Public Choice*, Vol. 129, No. 1/2, October 2006.

scholar Lisa Hill, who has written extensively on the subject. She has said of the work of Jakee and Sun: "The first problem here is that their argument is based on the assumption of a first-past-the-post system, which no compulsory-voting regime uses."[49] It would appear that Hill is unaware that Singapore practises both first-past-the-post (FPTP) and CVR. Amongst other observations, she has characterised CVR as having the effect of the "minimization of elite power".[50] That might be the case for Australia where, historically, electoral contestation by parties across the political spectrum has been highly competitive and where election rules do not institutionally advantage one party over another. But, for Singapore, it could be argued that CVR leads to the reverse — the maximisation of elite power.

CVR sets the bar high for entry into Parliament for challengers to the PAP. That bar becomes even more elevated when CVR occurs together with FPTP. Globally, some 97 countries out of 167 could be said to be democracies of some kind.[51] Out of those 97 countries,[52] 48 practise FPTP, but a far smaller number practise CVR.[53] And, it

---

49 Jason Brennan and Lisa Hill, *Compulsory Voting*, (New York: Cambridge University Press, 2014), p. 180. In the first half of this book, Brennan debates against CVR whereas, in the second half, Hill argues for CVR.

50 Ibid., p. 203.

51 The figures are as of end 2017, and sourced from the Pew Research Center, "Despite global concerns about democracy, more than half of countries are democratic", 14 May 2019, https://www.pewresearch.org/fact-tank/2019/05/14/more-than-half-of-countries-are-democratic/. Accessed on 5 February 2021.

52 Institute for Democracy and Electoral Assistance (IDEA), *The Global State of Democracy 2019: Addressing the Ills, Reviving the Promise*, (Stockholm: IDEA, 2019), p. 6.

53 Depending on the source one relies on, the number of countries that practise CVR is either 22 or 27. The figure is imprecise because several jurisdictions have been in transition, with a few doing away with CVR. For the source listing 22 countries see, Lauren Liebhaber, "Countries that have mandatory voting", *Stacker*, 13 September 2019, https://stacker.com/stories/3485/countries-have-mandatory-voting. Accessed on 6 February 2021. On the list of 27 countries, see, "What is Compulsory Voting?" https://www.idea.int/data-tools/data/voter-turnout/compulsory-voting. Accessed on 6 February 2021.

would appear, that only one country — Singapore — practises the combination of CVR and FPTP.

Here, it is important to reiterate the point that CVR, which results in an impressive turnout rate, does not lead to an electorate which is politically-engaged or -informed to the same degree as implied by the high rate of turnout. To that extent, the work of Shane P. Singh on CVR is significant in drawing the following inference:[54]

The bulk of empirical evidence also refutes the assertion that compulsory voting induces individuals to become politically informed. Peter Loewen et al. (2008), with an experimental study in Quebec, find no link between compulsion and political knowledge. Sarah Birch (2009, p. 67) also fails to uncover such a link with observational, cross-national data. Moreover, through an experimental analysis, Fernanda De Leon and Renata Rizzi (2012) find that Brazilian students aged 16 and 17, who are entitled to vote, but not compelled to, under Brazil's compulsory law, gather only slightly less information than their counterparts aged 18 and above, for whom voting is not optional.

He concludes:[55]

Those with substantial knowledge of politics are most equipped to organize the information necessary to cast a meaningful vote… Thus, while participation levels may inflate under compulsory rules, this rise will, in part, reflect the votes of those who are less able to navigate the vote decision process. This suggests that there is a trade-off between a country's desire to have full participation and its aim to have meaningful participation.

---

54 Shane P. Singh, "Compulsory Voting and the Voter Decision Calculus", *Political Studies*, Vol. 63, 2015, p. 551.

55 Ibid., p. 565.

Reinforcing these observations is a 2019 study of compulsory voting in Austria, which arrived at a not dissimilar conclusion: "We find that compulsory voting tends to crowd out intrinsic motivation for political participation."[56] Insofar as Singapore is concerned, the electorate is compelled to vote and, on Polling Day, some segment of that electorate is merely on auto-pilot, as it were, going to polling stations to place an **X** in the box next to the PAP symbol. Below are the four parts of a Singapore parliamentary election ballot paper.

CANDIDATE(S) PICTURE	CANDIDATE(S) NAME(S)	PARTY LOGO	BOX TO PLACE **X**

The ballot paper is actually designed to de-emphasise personalities, while emphasising party.[57] To that extent, the remarks of WP MP Gerald Giam are germane. He had said that his standing as a WP candidate in Aljunied GRC came as a surprise to him as he had been cultivating the ground in Fengshan division (which was to be re-absorbed into East Coast GRC ahead of GE2020). This is what he said: "I was fully expecting to go back to either East Coast or Fengshan. In fact, (in) the years leading up to the GE, I'd been spending a lot of time in grassroots work in Fengshan, doing house visits and food distribution, I mean, we pretty much covered the whole ward."[58]

At GE2020, in its contested constituencies, the WP had quite a number of election posters hung on lampposts simply with its hammer logo and an **X** next to it. The WP knows the election Process and is

---

56 Stefanie Gaebler, Niklas Protrafka and Felix Rosel, *Compulsory Voting and Political Participation: Empirical Evidence from Austria*, ifo Working Paper No. 315, December 2019, p. 24.

57 In a presidential election it is different, since it is personalities, and not parties, which are contesting the election.

58 Quoted in, "It's like 'night and day': Workers' Party MP Gerald Giam on being an MP versus an NCMP", *CNA*, 14 March 2021, https://www.channelnewsasia.com/news/singapore/workers-party-mp-gerald-giam-interview-ncmp-aljunied-grc-14398172. Accessed on 20 March 2021.

aware that its logo is recognisable and voters can associate with it. All this is important to surmount voter apathy. As an Institute of Policy Studies survey published in July 2021 observed:[59]

In tandem with descriptions of Singaporeans as typically politically apathetic, political discussions are not popular conversation topics with friends. Fifty-five per cent indicated only being engaged in such conversations occasionally, while 37.9 per cent indicated never talking about politics at all.

Rejected-vote incidence indicates skewing of the vote towards PAP under CVR

That elections in Singapore under CVR tend to turn heavily on Process is also manifested in the incidence of rejected votes. Here, I employ the legal definition under the Parliamentary Elections Act (PEA) of what constitutes a rejected vote/ballot or invalid ballot.[60]

Table 3.5 demonstrates a linear relationship between the incidence of rejected votes and the control variables of opposition Party brand and

---

59 Mathew Matthews, Teo Kay Key, Melvin Tay and Alicia Wang, *Lived Experiences in Singapore: Key Findings from the World Values Survey*, Bo. 18, July 2021, p. 232.

60 The PEA says that a rejected vote/ballot is one where, among others, a voter can be identified or had voted for more than one candidate or groups of candidates, or the voter had left the ballot paper unmarked, or the ballot paper was void due to uncertainty. On the other hand, for "Spoilt ballot papers", the PEA says:

A voter who has inadvertently dealt with his ballot paper in such a manner that it cannot be conveniently used as a ballot paper may, on delivering to the presiding officer the ballot paper so inadvertently dealt with, and proving the fact of the inadvertence to the satisfaction of the presiding officer, obtain another ballot paper in place of the ballot paper so delivered up (referred to in this Act as a spoilt ballot paper).

Parliamentary Elections Act, (Chapter 218), section 50, and section 45. https:// sso.agc.gov.sg/Act/PEA1954#pr50-. Accessed on 21 February 2021.

Table 3.5

Percentage of rejected votes at GE2020: Arranged from lowest to highest

	Rejected %	PAP Opponent*		Key Factor
Tier 1: Highly politically-engaged				
Punggol West SMC	0.84%	WP	38.68%	Statistical anomaly
Sengkang GRC	1.02%	WP	51.59%	Confluence of factors
Hougang SMC	1.07%	WP	60.56%	Incumbent status
Aljunied GRC	1.09%	WP	59.29%	Incumbent status
West Coast GRC	1.17%	PSP	47.75%	PSP 'A' team
East Coast GRC	1.20%	WP	46.05%	WP 'B' team
Tier 2: Politically-engaged				
Marine Parade GRC	1.36%	WP	41.69%	
Marymount SMC	1.36%	PSP	44.35%	
Chua Chu Kang GRC	1.37%	PSP	40.80%	
Pioneer SMC	1.47%	PSP / Ind	37.44%	
Hong Kah North SMC	1.48%	PSP	38.43%	
Potong Pasir SMC	1.48%	SPP	38.75%	No Party branding, redrawn boundary
Tanjong Pagar GRC	1.53%	PSP	36.34%	
Nee Soon GRC	1.55%	PSP	37.57%	

Tier 3: Diminishing levels of political engagement				
Yio Chu Kang SMC	1.67%	PSP	38.53%	
Bukit Panjang SMC	1.71%	SDP	45.48%	Out-spent by PAP
Kebun Baru SMC	1.80%	PSP	36.41%	
Holland-Bukit Timah GRC	1.83%	SDP	33.02%	
Bukit Batok SMC	1.85%	SDP	44.37%	Out-spent by PAP
Marsiling-Yew Tee GRC	1.86%	SDP	36.14%	
Tier 4: Increased political disengagement				
Yuhua SMC	1.99%	SDP	28.87%	
Jurong GRC	2.01%	RDU	24.88%	No Party branding
Sembawang GRC	2.06%	NSP	32.03%	
Pasir Ris-Punggol GRC	2.11%	PV / SDA	35.08%	No Party branding
Bishan-Toa Payoh GRC	2.14%	SPP	32.07%	

(Continued)

Table 3.5
(Continued)

MacPherson SMC	2.30%	PPP	27.61%	Disproportionate digital campaign
Tier 5: Elevated levels of political disengagement				
Tampines GRC	2.41%	NSP	32.78%	
Mountbatten SMC	2.58%	PV	25.50%	No Party branding
Ang Mo Kio GRC	2.81%	RP	27.30%	Negative optics pervasive
Jalan Besar GRC	2.90%	PV	33.64%	Disproportionate digital campaign
Radin Mas SMC	3.47%	RP	25.09%	Negative optics pervasive

SOURCE: Data obtained via an email request to the Elections Department Singapore.

*Percentage vote of PAP opponent is calculated on the basis of TOTAL votes cast, including rejected votes.

Process. Further, it is the contention here, that the incidence of rejected votes in a constituency is a symptom of a larger, less visible, dynamic at work, i.e., the extent of default-votes the PAP receives in each constituency.

What emerges from Table 3.5 is that voters across 31 electoral divisions at GE2020 were sensitive to the nature of the main opponent/challenger to the PAP. The WP's status of primary challenger to the PAP sees it dominating Tier 1. The PSP populates Tier 2. The SDP is mostly bunched in Tier 3. And, the Peoples Voice and Reform Party (RP) bring up the rear in Tier 5.[61] The incidence of rejected votes is, thus, not a random occurrence.[62]

If the percentage of rejected votes in each constituency is paired with the percentage vote received by the main PAP opponent in the constituency, as shown in Table 3.5, and if these numerical values are run through to determine a linear regression model, we get the correlation (R) equalling 0.7894, meaning that there is a strong direct relationship between the paired values.[63] Figures 3.1 and 3.2 illustrate the regression line, with the equation being:

$$y = 60:29 - 12:25 \; x$$

---

61 Any dataset containing several dozen numerical values is bound to include statistical anomalies. There is one in Table 3.5. In Punggol West SMC, the 0.84% incidence in rejected votes falls below the assumed floor of 1% and is also directly at odds with the fact that the WP candidate polled relatively poorly, garnering 38.68% of the TOTAL votes. The assumed floor of 1% rejected votes is derived from data in previous Singapore parliamentary elections. It is also worth noting that at the 2011 Singapore presidential election, rejected votes accounted for 1.76% of total votes cast.

62 As a useful point for comparison, it has also been noted that "enormous rates in the variations of invalid balloting" have occurred in the largest democracy which practises CVR, i.e., Brazil. See, Timothy J. Power and J. Timmons Roberts, "Compulsory Voting, Invalid Ballots, and Abstention in Brazil", *Political Research Quarterly*, Vol. 48, No. 4, December 1995, p. 796.

63 Thirty paired numerical values were run through a linear regression calculator. The numerical paired values for Punggol West SMC were excluded as the rejected-ballot incidence in that constituency represents an outlier. The calculator then chose 29 paired values, leaving out the pairing for Bukit Batok SMC.

Figure 3.1
Paired data of percentage opposition constituency vote with rejected vote (1)

Y-axis: percentage of opposition votes in specific constituency.

X-axis: percentage of rejected vote in specific constituency based on total votes cast.

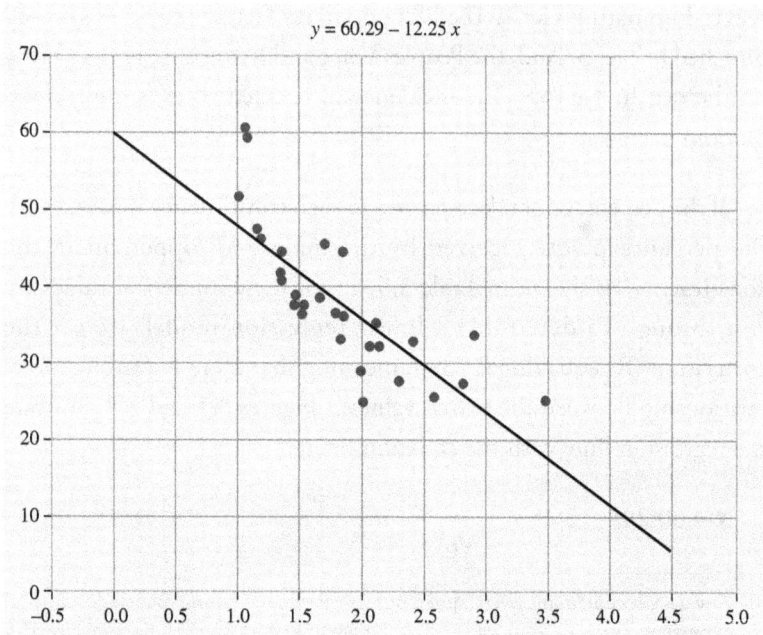

$$y = 60.29 - 12.25\,x$$

SOURCE: Graph generated by mathportal.org.

The percentage of rejected votes in specific constituencies and the percentage of votes garnered by an opposition party in specific constituencies are linearly dependent. Put in laymen's terms, the following formulations might be made:

I. Formulation related to the WP in Tier 1:

Low rejected-vote incidence ⇒ Positive WP brand + Process ⇒ Reduced PAP default-votes

Figure 3.2
Paired data of percentage opposition constituency vote with rejected vote (2)

Scatterplot, lowess, and regression line

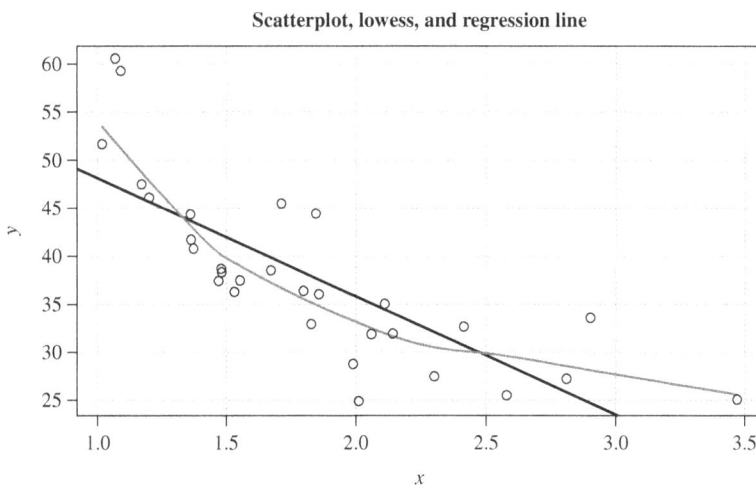

SOURCE: Graph generated by wessa.net.

II. Formulation related to the RP / PV in Tier 5:

High rejected-vote incidence ⇒ Negative Party brand + Process ⇒ Elevated PAP default-votes

Even though the WP, in Tier 1, succeeded in markedly reducing rejected votes and, thus, diminished the level of default-votes given to the PAP, the PAP continued to receive relatively high proportions of default-votes elsewhere, especially in Tiers 4 and 5. The incidence of the rejected-vote phenomenon almost trebled in Tier 5 as compared to Tier 1.

Consequently, it could be argued that there are three effects on the vote in contested constituencies by parties deemed by voters to be electorally unviable: their percentage vote lies at the bottom end of the scale; there is an observable increased incidence of rejected votes; and, the PAP is in receipt of a greater proportion of default-votes.

The literature on invalid voting is not especially substantial, but even so it varies widely on the significance that can be ascribed to the phenomenon. To that extent, the observation made by one scholar that "casting an invalid vote might also be functionally equivalent to voting for anti-establishment parties",[64] is a generalisation that might apply to many jurisdictions globally but, as has been set out above, might have little applicability to the Singapore context. It would have applicability if the incidence of rejected votes was evenly spread out across all contested constituencies. To that extent, a more accurate understanding is to refer to the "perceived value of a vote" being dependent on the viability of election candidates,[65] and when "competition intensifies" the "expected level of blank votes and null votes decrease".[66]

Taxonomy of rejected-ballot incidence

To complete the analysis, the example of Ang Mo Kio GRC is of relevance. At GE2020, the rejected-vote count for that GRC was 5,016 which, by any reasonable yardstick, is considered high, especially when the RP team there polled just 48,677 votes. It's a rejected-vote to polled-vote ratio of nearly 1:10. By way of contrast, an aggregate 6,437 rejected votes were cast across the six WP-contested electoral divisions where the WP polled an aggregate 279,922 votes, or a rejected-vote to polled-vote ratio of around 1:43. Thus, voters invalidated their votes in high numbers out of dismay that the alternative party was not up to the mark.

---

64 Mert Moral, "The Passive-Aggressive Voter: The Calculus of Casting an Invalid Vote in European Democracies", *Political Research Quarterly*, Vol. 69, No. 4, December 2016, p. 741.

65 Tiffany D. Barnes and Gabriela Rangel, "Subnational Patterns of Participation: Compulsory Voting and the Conditional Impact of Institutional Design", *Political Research Quarterly*, Vol. 71, No. 4, December 2018, p. 831.

66 Ibid., p. 835.

In absolute numbers, the 5,016 rejected votes in Ang Mo Kio GRC were the highest recorded in that general election. Out of the 5,016 rejected votes, it can be inferred that around 2,250 constituted anti-RP votes. This figure is derived by taking the 1.55% invalid votes cast in Nee Soon GRC, which is at the bottom of Tier 2, as the threshold after which voters began reacting negatively to the alternative to the PAP which they had been presented with.

The obvious component of the taxonomy of the rejected-vote incidence analysed above arises because,[67] unlike other jurisdictions, the alternative parties in Singapore tend to separate out their electoral challenges to the ruling PAP. When voters are not presented with viable alternatives to the PAP, they do not feel fully empowered. Or as has been observed, "Disempowered citizens cast an invalid vote because they feel that some elections are less important and their efficacy is low."[68]

Effectively, the parties represented in Tiers 4 and 5 are politically impotent, and are largely in receipt of protest votes — votes *against* the PAP, not votes *for* the parties. Thus, the measurement of their real levels of support is not in a straight fight with the PAP where they get the obligatory irreducible core of anti-PAP votes plus some proportion of votes from the wavering middle-ground. Their true level of support is determined when they face a proper challenge in a multi-cornered race which includes the WP. That happened at the 26 January 2013 Punggol East by-election when the RP and the Singapore Democratic Alliance garnered 1.18% and 0.56% of the total votes cast respectively. In the same way, to determine the true, and not artificial, level of support for the SDP — a party that is positioned to the left of the WP — there

---

67 Patrick Cunha Silva and Brian F. Crisp, "Ballot Spoilage as a Response to Limitations on Choice and Influence", *Party Politics*, 4 February 2021, p. 1.

68 Karel Kouba and Jakub Lysek, "What Affects Invalid Voting? A Review of Meta-Analysis", *Government and Opposition*, Vol. 54, No. 4, October 2019, p. 5.

must eventually be a three-cornered contest involving it, the PAP and the WP. Trying to keep to the pretence that the SDP and the WP are anything other than different parties with different policies and different approaches to opposition, serves little purpose. At some stage, the simplistic, and wholly false narrative of the PAP versus non-PAP binary choice must come to an end.

Ultimately, that points to a larger issue: the onus for any change to Singapore's political culture does not lie entirely with the PAP. The concept of alternative parties garnering artificial levels of support because they deliberately avoid multi-cornered fights is not much better than a ruling party whose support is partially determined as a result of turnout rates artificially boosted by compulsory voting.

CHAPTER 4

The Progress Singapore Party: Origins, Evolution and Prospects

he Progress Singapore Party (PSP), led by former People's Action Party (PAP) Member of Parliament (MP) Tan Cheng Bock (TCB), a medical practitioner by training, was founded on 28 March 2019. By the time of GE2020, it reputedly had a membership of over 1,000.[1] Notwithstanding its relatively short history, it managed to field the largest slate of election candidates. Many in the PSP had high hopes for the party. They were of the opinion that a proportion of their 24 candidates plus some from other alternative parties would, in combination, be able to deny the PAP a two-thirds parliamentary majority.[2] However, the PSP failed to make a breakthrough at GE2020. In West Coast group representation constituency (GRC), the PSP's five-member team led by TCB lost narrowly. But the PSP secured the consolation of two Non-constituency Member of Parliament (NCMP) seats. This chapter traces the PSP's origins, looks at how the portrayal of political events in the media can vary considerably from the reality, and sets out the PSP's likely prospects going into the next election.

Originating point

On the night of 8 September 2015, I had attended a Workers' Party (WP) rally at Serangoon Stadium for the 2015 general election

---

1 *The Palm*, March 2020, p. 2, https://psp.org.sg/wp-content/uploads/2020/10/The-Palm-Issue-One-March_2020.pdf. Accessed on 5 December 2020.

2 That was the opinion of the then Assistant Secretary-General of the PSP, Leong Mun Wai who, as late as May 2020, said that he hoped the combined opposition would secure one-third of the parliamentary seats. See, "I will not feel sorry if those with 'big egos' leave PSP: Tan Cheng Bock", *The Straits Times*, 22 May 2020.

(GE2015). I had arrived early — more than an hour before the start — and seated myself at the top righthand corner of the terraced concrete stand closest to the stage on the field. Part way through the rally, there was a commotion at the foot of the stand near the entrance/exit tunnel. TCB had arrived and proceeded to walk onto the field. He was accompanied by a number of individuals, who were drawing the rally crowd's attention to his presence. Some in the crowd then began chanting, "Tan Cheng Bock! Tan Cheng Bock! Tan Cheng Bock!"

TCB's presence at that WP rally during the GE2015 campaign planted the seeds to his eventual formation of the PSP. His failed presidential bid in August 2011, where he lost out fractionally to the Establishment favourite, Tony Tan, might be deemed by others as the originating point for his transformation from PAP stalwart to an opposition personality. However, it was not apparent back in 2011, or in the succeeding three years, that TCB had any further ambitions for elected public office.

In an interview with *The Sunday Times* on 20 March 2016, TCB referenced his attendance at election rallies at GE2015:[3]

I went to the PAP rallies but they didn't know how to receive me … Only old grassroots leaders who saw me came and talked with me. None of the candidates came and shook my hand. At some opposition rallies, they would be shouting my name. I said: "Hey I'm just here to watch the rally". But the way they were shouting for me I was a bit shocked.

The question arises: why would anyone who was not a candidate in an election feel that s/he ought to be received in a certain way? To be factual, TCB had been a PAP MP for some 26 years (1980–2006) for the single-member constituency of Ayer Rajah. Between 1987 and 1996

---

3 Quoted in "When I want to do something, I will do it: Dr Tan Cheng Bock", *The Sunday Times*, 20 March 2016.

he had also been a member of the PAP's Central Executive Committee (CEC), the party's highest ruling body. These are no mean achievements, but at the same time they are not extraordinary among members of the Singapore Establishment.

As an MP, TCB is remembered for convincing the government to provide free parking to its public carparks on Sundays so that families could more easily meet over the weekends.[4] This measure was introduced progressively from 1986.[5] To outsiders, the concession might seem trivial, but not to those in Singapore which carries the unenviable global reputation of being the most expensive place to own a car. In early 2011, TCB also won plaudits from many Singaporeans for his principled decision to resign from the board of a government hospital to be built in Jurong, in the west of the island, because the new hospital was to bear the name of the late property tycoon Ng Teng Fong; this followed a donation of $125 million to the hospital's construction by the Ng family. The government's own investment in the new hospital was around $1 billion. As TCB said:[6]

With this donation of $125 million the government is prepared to have the hospital renamed from Jurong General Hospital to Ng Teng Fong hospital. To me this was wrong as it looked as if any rich man could have a public institution named after him if he donates the right amount. I cannot reconcile with this and resigned from the board.

4 "Free holiday parking", *The Straits Times*, 20 March 1986.

5 However, partly as an attempt to discourage car-ownership, the government has been clawing back on the free Sunday parking privilege. In 2010, some 70% of public carparks offered free Sunday parking, but this figure shrunk to 55% by 2016. See, "Fewer public carparks offering free Sunday parking", *Today*, 6 April 2016, https://www.todayonline.com/singapore/fewer-public-carparks-offering-free-sunday-parking. Accessed on 20 December 2020.

6 "Tan Cheng Bock vs George Yeo for president?" *The Online Citizen*, 1 June 2011, https://www.theonlinecitizen.com/2011/06/01/tan-cheng-bock-vs-george-yeo-for-president/. Accessed on 2 December 2020.

TCB's profile was enhanced further when he contested the 2011 presidential election where he failed to win by a fraction of 1%. Generally, in the public mind, the post of elected president is not of great political significance because the president is deemed to have mostly a ceremonial role and limited constitutional functions.[7] Most Singaporeans perceive this to be the case and, hence, on the two occasions where there were actual presidential elections (i.e., without a walkover), there has usually been a sizeable protest vote against the candidate seen as the PAP's preferred choice. It is of significance that though most Singaporeans are of the view that the presidency appears to carry more symbolism than anything else, in reality the president could potentially play a central role politically if a certain set of circumstances were to emerge. (See Chapter 10.)

Returning to TCB's remarks about how differently he had been received at PAP and opposition rallies during GE2015, they seem to point to a particular mindset. I have it on authority that, at a senior level of the WP, there was displeasure over what TCB did. His presence at Serangoon Stadium had distracted the crowd from a WP-organised event.

In public statements, TCB had also tended to give the impression that he enjoyed public adulation and respect, and if none was accorded, he would feel slighted, and make his feelings known, even if cryptically. For instance, on 7 February 2014, TCB had posted on Facebook that in the preceding December he had received an invitation from the People's Association (PA) to a Chinese New Year's garden party at the Istana. However, on 8 January 2014, he was informed by PA Chairman and Cabinet minister, Lim Swee Say, that there was an error in the invitation list. Due to a change of policy only ex-advisers to grassroots organisations from the immediate past general election (i.e., 2011)

---

7 See, for instance, Yvonne C. L. Lee, "Under Lock and Key: The Evolving Role of the Elected President as a Fiscal Guardian", *Singapore Journal of Legal Studies*, December 2007, pp. 290–322.

would be invited.[8] As TCB described it, he did not "fit into this category" as he stood down in 2006. He then went on to say that he had attended the annual Istana event without fail since 1980 and he would miss doing so. He continued:

The warm reception usually given me by those grassroots leaders at the function, were overwhelming, more so, after the Presidential election. At times it was very touching. Last year I had to be helped to get back into my car because the crowd kept me from moving forward.

Grant it, given the minor significance of the event, the organisers should have honoured an invitation issued even though it was issued in error. That said, a Cabinet minister did telephone TCB to explain the error and apologise personally for it, and he followed up with an email of the same. Because TCB raised the matter publicly on Facebook, Lim had to make his own public statement on this storm in a teacup by apologising again for the error. He also disclosed that there were others who had been erroneously invited to the function and similarly had their invitations rescinded. While saying that he had been heartened that TCB was gracious about the error when they had spoken on the phone, he expressed surprise that TCB had now brought the matter up "publicly as an issue".[9]

It seems that the existence of real or imagined snubs appeared to recur in TCB's mind. The following year, TCB was invited by then Parliament Speaker Halimah Yacob to a lunch for past and present MPs to celebrate Singapore's Jubilee — SG50. The gathering took place in Parliament House on 29 July 2015. The next day TCB posted on Facebook a picture of himself with some of the attendees at the event.

8 "Tan Cheng Bock uninvited from Istana Chinese New Year garden party", *The Straits Times*, 7 February 2014.

9 "Lim Swee Say 'surprised' by Tan Cheng Bock publicly raising retraction of PA party invite", *Yahoo! News*, https://sg.news.yahoo.com/ex-presidential-candidate-tan-cheng-bock-uninvited-from-pa-party-033731215.html. Accessed on 3 December 2020.

He appeared happy to have been invited, though he made the following observation: "There was a noticeable absence of Cabinet Ministers and younger junior Ministers. Perhaps they were busy attending to foreign dignitaries in town or perhaps preparing for the coming GE, were some of the comments passed." Less than two weeks later there was also a suggestion from some quarters posted online that TCB might have been denied tickets to the SG50 National Day Parade. TCB himself merely posted on Facebook on 10 August 2015 a few observations:

As I watch the parade from a 64 storey high building there was something missing. High up we cannot hear the drums, the noise, the singers and songs, the cheers and sounds of the parade. Luckily, we had a TV set to help us appreciate the show better. But it was not the same. I was quite determine[ed] to watch even from a distance for I am part of the pioneer generation and SG50 celebrates this generation of builders.

The foregoing in fact constitutes trivial issues that ordinarily would not figure in political analysis. Yet, they require mentioning because TCB himself gave them an out-sized importance. Did TCB perceive slights from the Establishment? If so, did it factor in his transformation from a PAP stalwart — an independent-minded heavyweight backbench MP — to an opposition personality? It is important to be clear about one point. As sketched out in Chapter 1, in the presidential election of August 2011, TCB had positioned himself as the moderate alternative to the PAP-preferred candidate, Tony Tan. A serious analysis would conclude that this deliberate positioning allowed TCB to come to within a whisker of winning the presidency. This was due to the nature of the ground. It was moderate back in 2011, and it remained mostly the same a decade later. TCB might have been an independent-minded PAP backbencher, but he himself stated in a 28 May 1999 column in *The Straits Times* that he was a dyed-in-wool PAP-man. In his words, "I toe the party line and I am loyal to my party".[10]

---

10 "'If I think a thing is wrong, I'll tell you'", *The Straits Times*, 28 May 1999.

Since PE2011, certain episodes might have contributed to TCB's transformation politically. In his long political career, he has been a man who has undoubtedly looked out for the interest of Singaporeans. Equally, in his medical practice he was known to be kind and generous to those patients of little means. One should be in no doubt that his wanting to serve Singaporeans was what motivated him to stand for the presidency in 2011.

As a consequence of a change in criteria for nomination as a presidential candidate post-PE2011, where the 2017 version was designated a "reserved election" intended for a Malay candidate, TCB was ineligible to run for the presidency again.[11] He had on 11 March 2016 declared his intention to make another bid for the presidency despite the fact that a Constitutional Commission was in the very process of reviewing the criteria for presidential candidates.[12]

An anti-PAP coalition that did not materialise

Before TCB's establishment of the PSP, he had actually wanted to be the leader of an anti-PAP coalition. This idea emerged following the surprising victory in Malaysia of the opposition coalition Pakatan Harapan, at the 9 May 2018 general election, momentarily ending the ruling Barisan Nasional's then 61-year rule of the country. At the time

---

11 Apart from the stipulation that the 2017 presidential election be reserved for Malay candidates, the Constitutional Commission looking into revisions to the elected presidency had made a more general recommendation for those qualifying as presidential election candidates. That recommendation was that a nominee with private sector experience should have been a chief executive officer (for at least three years) of a company with "shareholders' equity at or exceeding $500 million". This was a significant variation from the previous requirement of "$100 million paid up capital", under which TCB qualified for PE2011. See, "Acting PM spoke on the release of the Constitutional Commission's report of 7 September 2016", *Prime Minister's Office*, https://www.pmo.gov.sg/Newsroom/statement-acting-pm-teo-chee-hean-release-constitutional-commissions-report. Accessed on 6 January 2021.

12 "Tan Cheng Bock will make second bid for presidency", *The Straits Times*, 11 March 2016, https://www.straitstimes.com/politics/tan-cheng-bock-will-make-second-bid-for-presidency. Accessed on 10 January 2021.

of the stunning Malaysian general election result, I wrote a fairly lengthy Facebook post (dated 10 May 2018) to draw out some lessons of the election in Malaysia for Singapore. Among other things, I made the following observation:

> *The one lesson that some diehard anti-PAP elements in Singapore would likely attempt to draw from Malaysia's GE14 — but it would be a false lesson as it is a false comparison — is that all the Singapore opposition parties should go into a coalition to take on the PAP. It is a false lesson and false comparison because all the political parties that have no parliamentary presence are simply not on the same level as the Workers' Party.*

These observations were deliberately said because, after working on Singapore electoral politics for many years, to me it was predictable how some would think, and this was intended to head-off unrealistic notions that somehow Singapore can, in electoral terms, be like Malaysia. But my public intervention was to no avail because just weeks after the Malaysian general election, speculation arose that TCB was interested in becoming head of one of the existing alternative parties, with some of the other parties taking their lead from him. This came to light when he visited the Singapore Democratic Party's (SDP's) headquarters on 28 July 2018 where he had lunch with members of several alternative parties to explore the possibility of a "united front" against the PAP. SDP chief Chee Soon Juan said, "With his experience, the SDP is confident that TCB will be able to lead the effort."[13] In turn, TCB responded: "If you want me to lead, then we must think of country first. If we go in, we go in as a team."[14] Other than the SDP, the parties represented at that lunch were all relatively minor players — the

---

13 "Opposition parties express desire to cooperate; invite Tan Cheng Bock to lead effort", *Singapore Democratic Party*, 28 July 2018, https://yoursdp.org/news/opposition_parties_express_desire_to_cooperate_invite_tan_cheng_bock_to_lead_effort. Accessed on 23 July 2020.

14 Ibid.

Democratic Progressive Party, the National Solidarity Party, the People's Power Party, the Peoples Voice (PV), the Reform Party, and the Singaporeans First (SingFirst) Party. (The last having dissolved itself just two weeks before GE2020.) On the same day that this event was held, I publicly said that, "mixing with this particular crowd — which in the pecking order of non-PAP parties rank as 3rd, 4th and 5th raters will not do anything for his [TCB's] reputation." These remarks were carried by various media,[15] and I am told by an opposition source that they stung TCB.[16] He balked at the characterisation, saying in rebuttal:[17]

I believe the men and women I met yesterday were more than willing to make way for better men and women who would stand in their place. They have guts. They have put themselves out there.

TCB's characterisation that some personalities who stand for election in opposition to the PAP "have guts" is not without merit, but he overstates the point. Politically, Singapore in the new millennium is not the Singapore of the 1970s, 1980s, or even 1990s. Being an opposition politician anytime during those decades was a dicey proposition. It is now far less so. To that extent, the situation with the SDP Chairman, Paul Tambyah, who contested GE2015 and GE2020, is noteworthy. Prior to GE2015, he had already been a high-profile physician, specialising in infectious diseases at the National University Hospital, and also teaching at the National University of Singapore's Yong Loo Lin School of Medicine. He is widely respected in his field. And, he has not been the only oppositionist who has worked in a government-affiliated

---

15 Quoted in "Tan Cheng Bock yet to decide on role in opposition coalition, says small window to effect political change", *The Straits Times*, 29 July 2018.

16 The source for this was a WP parliamentarian.

17 Quoted in "Tan...", *The Straits Times*, 29 July 2018.

organisation without concerns about job security, even if he is the most high-profile.[18]

If TCB overstated the point about having guts to stand on an opposition ticket, then subsequent events proved he was wrong about his other point — that the personalities he met at the SDP's office would be "more than willing to make way for better men and women who would stand in their place". He had hoped that the people he met from the seven minor parties, which had not won a parliamentary seat in the previous decade, would "stand down and serve from the backroom".[19] In spite of some being receptive to such an idea when he met them face-to-face, in the fullness of time none showed they were actually prepared to do so. In other words, they said one thing to his face whilst having not the slightest intention of following his advice. Thus, seven months later, the PSP came into being, and the minor parties were effectively told by the PSP that they had no role to play in the new dispensation.

An association with a member of the Lee family
With his own party established and growing in membership, throughout 2019 TCB made a conscious effort to actively court associations with the right sort of people. One such person was Lee Hsien Yang (LHY). LHY and his sister, Lee Wei Ling, have had a major public falling out

---

18 Months after GE2015, the SDP's Bryan Lim, who had contested that election, publicly announced that he had been promoted to a senior manager at a public hospital. See, "Job promotion after contesting GE for SDP's candidate Bryan Lim", *The Independent SG*, https://theindependent.sg/job-promotion-after-contesting-ge-for-sdps-candidate-bryan-lim/. Accessed on 15 January 2021. Also, the WP's Sylvia Lim had for years taught law at Temasek Polytechnic. A change in staffing policies at the polytechnic in early 2006 actually allowed her to contest the general election in that year for the WP. That change, however, was not due to her expected candidacy but, rather, the polytechnic's objective of ensuring that its employment policies were consistent with other polytechnics. See, "No need to quit TP to contest GE", *Today*, 15 March 2006.

19 Quoted in "Tan…", *The Straits Times*, 29 July 2018.

with their brother, the prime minister, since shortly after their father's death (in March 2015) and, at the time of writing (August 2021), there had been no formal end to the family feud.[20] TCB's other attempt was to establish a connection with the WP. The initial meetings with LHY actually predated the formal establishment of the PSP by several weeks.

On an otherwise quiet Sunday morning on 4 November 2018, a hawker centre in the West Coast was abuzz with excited members of the public and media. TCB, with several of his close associates, was seen having breakfast with LHY. This was at the West Coast Market and Food Centre, at Clementi West, which is a focal point of the sprawling West Coast GRC, which TCB was to contest in GE2020. The breakfast meeting was purely a photo-op, as members of the mainstream media had been tipped off to be in the area to snap pictures of the encounter. Nothing substantive was reported, with both LHY and TCB saying that they were merely having breakfast together and catching up with each other because, in the words of TCB, "we have not met for quite a while".[21] Another breakfast between the two men followed on 2 February 2019 at the Ang Mo Kio Market and Food Centre. This food centre is located in Teck Ghee, the constituency-level division of Prime Minister Lee and which is part of the larger Ang Mo Kio GRC, helmed by the prime minister. The choice of location, therefore, did not appear coincidental. Just as with the first breakfast meeting, nothing substantive appeared to emerge from this meeting. It was another photo-op for TCB to establish in the minds of the public a firm association with LHY. A week earlier, in a Facebook post on 24 January 2019, LHY had already congratulated TCB on his effort to set-up a new party because,

20 In fact, the reverse appeared to be true. See, "Lawyer Kwa Kim Li to face disciplinary proceedings over Lee Kuan Yew's will", *The Straits Times*, 21 April 2021, https://www.straitstimes.com/singapore/politics/lawyer-kwa-kim-li-to-face-disciplinary-proceedings-over-handling-of-lee-kuan-yews. Accessed on 24 April 2021.

21 "Tan Cheng Bock has breakfast with Lee Hsien Yang at West Coast hawker centre", *The Straits Times*, 5 November 2018.

in his words, TCB had "consistently put the interests of the people first. We are fortunate that he has stepped forward to serve Singapore... Cheng Bock is the leader Singapore deserves."[22]

Inevitably, with all the glare of publicity over the meetings between LHY and TCB, there was a swirl of speculation that LHY would join TCB to contest the next general election against the PAP. Only the combination of LHY and TCB standing together in a GRC team would prevail against the fortress of a PAP GRC. This was because LHY was not simply a personality but, in fact, reflected the Lee family brand. However, few were to know LHY's intentions.

Still, Australian academic Michael Barr ruminated aloud about the prospect of LHY possibly facing-off with Li Hongyi, the younger son of Prime Minister Lee, in an electoral contest.[23] As *Yahoo! News* reported in August 2019:[24]

Prof. Barr even held out the tantalising possibility of Hsien Yang taking on his nephew Li Hongyi in an electoral contest. There has [sic] been persistent rumours that Li is being groomed for higher office, alongside accusations by Hsien Yang that PM Lee wants to start a political dynasty.

---

22 Quoted in "Tan Cheng Bock meets Lee Hsien Yang for breakfast in Ang Mo Kio hawker centre", *The Straits Times Online*, 2 February 2019, https://www.straitstimes.com/politics/tan-cheng-bock-meets-lee-hsien-yang-for-breakfast-in-ang-mo-kio-hawker-centre. Accessed on 24 June 2020.

23 "Historian says 'it would be a devastating blow for Hongyi's credibility' if he faced off with Lee Hsien Yang in next GE", *The Independent SG*, 7 August 2019, http://theindependent.sg/historian-says-it-would-be-a-devastating-blow-for-hongyis-credibility-if-he-faced-off-with-lee-hsien-yang-in-next-ge/. Accessed on 24 June 2020.

24 "Early moves by the opposition before the GE is the right step: analysts", *Yahoo News Singapore*, 6 August 2019, https://sg.news.yahoo.com/early-moves-by-opposition-before-singapore-ge-is-the-right-step-analysts-031517669.html. Accessed on 24 June 2020.

In Barr's words: "If he found himself standing in the same constituency as Li Hongyi, it would be a devastating blow for Hongyi's credibility... Hsien Yang's presence would make it impossible for everyone to overlook everything that Hsien Yang and Wei Ling have been saying about Lee Hsien Loong's longer-term ambitions for his son."[25]

For almost three years, between 2017 and 2020, LHY had been making public statements heavily critical of his brother, the prime minister. These statements were largely published on his personal Facebook page. His posts generated many comments left by Singaporeans exhorting him to stand as a candidate against the PAP. LHY thanked the commenters for their encouragement but was non-committal about whether he would contest an election against the party founded by his father.

The breakfast meetings between LHY and TCB had fuelled speculation that he would be an election candidate, specifically with TCB's PSP. All this speculation reached a fever-pitch when on 24 June 2020, a day after the Singapore Parliament was dissolved for a general election, LHY joined the PSP. He was formally handed his PSP membership card by TCB who said that LHY had actually joined the party three months earlier, but due to the COVID-19 pandemic, where restrictions were imposed on meetings between individuals, he had only now been able to receive his membership card from TCB directly. TCB said of LHY:[26]

He is no ordinary person. His father is the founder of Singapore. The fact that he decided to join us is a clear indication that the current team did not follow what his dad wanted.

---

25 Ibid.

26 "Singapore PM's brother Lee Hsien Yang joins opposition party ahead of July 10 election", *South China Morning Post*, 24 June 2020, https://www.scmp.com/week-asia/politics/article/3090343/singapore-pms-brother-lee-hsien-yang-joins-opposition-party. Accessed on 6 July 2020.

When specifically asked whether he would stand as an election candidate, LHY merely said, "We will see."[27] The ambiguity about LHY's intentions continued right into Nomination Day, on 30 June 2020. Wearing PSP attire, he turned up at the nomination centre for Tanjong Pagar GRC, the constituency which his father represented for decades. Ultimately, LHY did not file papers to be nominated as a candidate, thus ending three years of speculation. Shortly after nominations had closed, LHY posted his thoughts on Facebook to explain his decision not to stand. Among other things, he said:

I have chosen not to stand for political office because I believe Singapore does not need another Lee. I am interested in politics. I am involved through speaking up, by supporting candidates and parties I believe in, by contributing my time, ideas and resources to causes I support, and by seeking an open and independent media. I do not seek power, prestige or financial rewards of political office. I hope to be a catalyst for change.

Being involved in politics can take many different forms. Amongst others it needs citizens to be aware of and contribute to the public discourse in the country, to support political parties one believes in, and to help them reach out to other voters. It is support for an independent media and for open and transparent government. It is being engaged, speaking truth to power, volunteering one's time and contributing financially or otherwise for causes that one believes in. Politics is both the right and the duty of every citizen.

Our country needs a broad and diverse parliament with members who care for its citizens and the future of our nation and hold themselves accountable to the citizens. It needs people from different walks of life who

---

27 "Singapore PM's estranged brother joins opposition party as election looms", *Reuters*, 24 June 2020, https://www.reuters.com/article/us-singapore-politics-lee/singapore-pms-estranged-brother-joins-opposition-party-as-election-looms-idUSKBN23V04A. Accessed on 24 June 2020.

can imagine, inspire and execute. We need new ideas to reinvigorate Singapore. We must have genuine discussions and rigorous debate involving a diversity of Singaporean voices as we seek to navigate the challenging waters ahead. We need leaders who listen and who are receptive to those voices and needs.

In the last few years, I have been approached by countless Singaporeans who have asked me to stand for political office. These are Singaporeans from all walks of life. I am deeply humbled. Many Singaporeans are very troubled that Singapore no longer has the leadership it needs. Sadly, the current government has failed its people. The rising anger and frustrations of the populace speaks for itself. The PAP has lost its way.

We need to take action now. Speak up and be heard. Discuss openly the issues facing our country. Read and share independent journalism. Seek transparency and accountability in government. Talk to your friends and family to help them see the need for change. Volunteer your time and resources to support the parties you believe in.

Vote fearlessly. Rescue the future of the country we love.

Politics is not just for politicians. It is for every citizen.

The rationalisation by LHY in not standing for election rings hollow when he could have simply been a passive member of the PSP West Coast GRC ticket and, if elected, also a passive MP. This would not have been dissimilar to what his late father did during the last years of his life when he was afflicted with ailments, not least a disease called sensory peripheral neuropathy, which was publicly disclosed in November 2011.[28] From October 2011 to May 2014, Lee Kuan Yew

---

28 "Singapore's Lee Kuan Yew admits to nerve illness", *BBC News*, 7 November 2011, https://www.bbc.com/news/world-asia-15615921. Accessed on 9 August 2020.

turned up for 64.6% of 82 parliamentary sittings, making him the most absent MP during that period.[29]

LHY's purpose should have been to bring into Parliament four other PSP members who would take the fight to the PAP and, with that job done, he could simply recede into the background. But this view is not shared by those who come across as (but not necessarily in reality) left-wing ideological purists who have been vocal in articulating the view that Singapore does not need another member of the Lee family to be in elected political office. They also view LHY's dispute with his brother as not an issue of national importance, but largely an intra-family falling-out. Even though I share the view that this is merely an intra-family falling-out, still, that should not have precluded LHY from standing for election, keeping in mind the key objective mentioned earlier — of bringing into Parliament four other PSP members.

A picture might not paint a thousand words: Closeness or distance to WP?

The meetings between LHY and TCB were beneficial to both sides even as each had their different motivations behind these meetings. On the other hand, TCB's meetings with WP leader Pritam Singh and his other WP colleagues were always one-sided. They were initiated by TCB, with the WP not showing much interest in them other than in extending the common courtesy of accepting invitations made by someone, whom they identified as not being hostile to the party. One such meeting was at TCB's residence on the second day of Chinese New Year in 2019. A picture, which went viral, showed TCB with Singh, and SDP leaders Chee Soon Juan and Paul Tambyah. Given the fact that the WP, under its previous leader Low Thia Khiang, was known to be very careful not to be photographed with

---

29 Howard Lee, "MPs' disappearing act", *The Online Citizen*, 16 July 2014, https://www.onlinecitizenasia.com/2014/07/16/mps-disappearing-act/. Accessed on 8 August 2020.

personalities from other alternative parties, the picture of Singh together with other opposition personalities led to speculation that an anti-PAP coalition was in the works. When asked to comment by the mainstream media on this episode, I speculated that the WP under Singh wanted to maintain links with TCB because of the latter's association with LHY.[30] As it turned out, this was wholly incorrect, as I was to subsequently find out from Singh himself. I asked him specifically about the TCB open house and how that viral picture emerged. He told me, "That was a 'Gotcha!' moment." In Singh's words: "Cheng Bock said, 'Hey, come, why don't we gather for a picture!' And, I said, I agreed." Singh noted that as there were other people around, he could not openly decline such a request.

TCB's eagerness to establish in the minds of the public that he had a personal connection with Singh and, therefore, entrée to the WP continued throughout 2019. The next event for such a possible connection to be reinforced was at the fundraising dinner for the socio-political blog, *The Online Citizen* (TOC), which was held at the Penthouse level of Singapore Land Tower in Raffles Place on 6 July 2019. On the morning of the event itself I received a tip-off from one of my sources in the alternative parties that, as representatives from all the alternative parties would be present at the fundraiser there would be an attempt to "orchestrate a photo", showing all of the opposition personalities with TCB in the centre of the picture to give the impression that he was, at least nominally, accepted as the head of some sort of anti-PAP coalition. Given what Singh had told me of how the picture at TCB's open house came about a few months earlier, I thought I would just let him know what I had heard. As it turned out, from the TOC fundraiser emerged a picture of a large group of attendees — some 40 mostly political personalities and civil society activists with TCB standing in the centre. That picture was posted by PV leader Lim Tean on his Facebook page on 6 July 2019. It garnered plenty of interest,

---

30 "Appearance of opposition leaders at Tan Cheng Bock's house creates buzz", *The Straits Times*, 8 Feb 2019.

including from some commenters who immediately noticed the absence of any representatives from the WP. A few of the comments (with their unusual grammatical construction) are reproduced below:

Lee KT, "*Why no WP*"

Daniel Loe, "*I don't see any WP members there in the photo… In my opinion, I reckon they are too opinionatic [sic] & arrogant*"

Desmond Hbk, "*None from WP?? Abit antisocial leh*"

Bg Su, "*Why no faces from WP??*"

It was pointed out by Lim Tean and others that the four WP representatives,[31] including Singh, were at the TOC fundraiser, as other pictures were to testify. But for the main event, i.e., the group picture, they were absent. Politics is about public perceptions and optics. That you wish to associate with the right sort of people, is axiomatic.

By 26 July 2019, during a PSP press conference, what had long been obvious for some time but had been left mostly unsaid, was finally spelt out by one mainstream media:[32]

It became apparent that the formerly proposed coalition among seven opposition parties, with him [TCB] taking the lead, is dead in the water, too. On Friday, Dr Tan said he has no interest in disrupting the organisational structure that is already entrenched in each political party.

---

31 Other than Pritam Singh, the other WP representatives at the TOC fundraiser were: Leon Perera, Daniel Goh, and Gerald Giam.

32 "PSP wants to be 'a credible alternative' to the PAP, but no regime change expected at next election: Tan Cheng Bock", *Today*, 26 October 2019, https://www.todayonline.com/singapore/psp-be-credible-alternative-pap-no-regime-change-expected-next-election-tan-cheng-bock. Accessed on 25 June 2020.

As the minor parties were of little interest to TCB, he renewed attempts to establish a connection with the WP. The next significant event, which was misconstrued by many members of the public, was the attendance by TCB and his senior PSP colleagues at the WP's National Day Dinner on 31 August 2019. That the PSP was the only alternative party with a significant presence at the event was again to generate considerable speculation. Pictures of TCB in the company of Singh with short captions to them were posted on several Facebook pages and various media portals.[33] The immediate public impression was that the WP had specially invited the PSP to its key annual get-together, and that the WP wished to cultivate TCB and the PSP. To find out whether that was the case, I emailed a WP source on 4 September 2019 to clarify. On the same day I received a response as follows:

On the WP National Day Dinner, TCB bought a table on his own volition. Tickets for the event are open for sale to all our residents, volunteers, supporters and the public at large. A table cost $450. Hope this clarifies.

The upshot of the foregoing is that social media had tended to give the impression — whether inadvertently or otherwise — that the WP was interested to get some sort of association with TCB in order to assist the party electorally. That was the view largely of the hardcore anti-PAP elements who were not impressed by the WP because they viewed it as being relatively timid in its opposition to the PAP. The reality, however, was quite different.

---

33 "Pritam Singh & Tan Cheng Bock socialise at Workers' Party National Day Dinner 2019 in Hougang", *Mothership SG*, 1 September 2019, https://mothership. sg/2019/09/pritam-singh-tan-cheng-bock/. Accessed on 25 June 2020; and, "'UNITY IS STRENGTH' — Singaporeans praise the bond between Tan Cheng Bock and the WP", *The Independent SG*, 4 September 2019, http://theindependent. sg/unity-is-strength-singaporeans-praise-the-bond-between-tan-cheng-bock-and-the-wp/. Accessed on 25 June 2020.

A counter-factual discussion: What if WP had endorsed TCB in PE2011?

It is a little known or discussed fact that the WP did not endorse TCB at the 2011 presidential election. The reality is that the WP did not endorse any candidate standing in PE2011. Also, of the WP's then newly elected parliamentarians following GE2011 none were to endorse, in their private capacity, TCB. On the other hand, of the four candidates standing for the presidency, Tan Jee Say, who just months earlier stood on an SDP ticket in GE2011, drew the largest number of endorsements from members of the alternative parties.

The hypothetical question that then arises is this: what if the WP had endorsed TCB in PE2011? Would TCB have won if the WP had thrown its backing behind him? Given that TCB lost by a mere 0.35% or 7,382 votes,[34] if the WP as a party had publicly endorsed him in PE2011 it is a reasonable assumption to contend that TCB would have prevailed. This is because of the goodwill and respect that the WP generated at GE2011 when it won Aljunied GRC. If the WP made a call to its supporters to back TCB in PE2011, at least a few percent of its voters who had intended to vote for Tan Jee Say would have heeded the WP's call and switched their backing to TCB.

But this hypothetical does not arise for two reasons. First, it would have been unpalatable for the WP to publicly back a candidate for PE2011 that had in a previous incarnation been a member of the PAP. Second, and more importantly, is the fact that when the elected presidency had first been mooted in the late 1980s, the WP had opposed the concept. The WP had all along said that the president should merely have a ceremonial role and be chosen by Parliament,

---

34 TCB polled 738,311 votes to Tony Tan's 745,693 votes in the 2011 presidential election.

with Parliament also being supreme in determining constitutional matters. In its 2011 manifesto (and earlier iterations), the WP said:[35]

The Office of Elected President should be abolished and the Presidency should be reverted to its former ceremonial position. The power of Parliament as the people's representatives should be unfettered.

The WP's 2020 manifesto went into greater detail in explaining the WP's opposition to the elected presidency:[36]

The President is the Head of State, a unifying figure and symbol of the nation. Our past system of having Presidents chosen by Parliament resulted in Heads of State who were held in high esteem and greatly respected by the people. The President should revert to being appointed by Parliament, and serve as a Head of State who unites Singaporeans and represents the nation. Parliament should consider, amongst other qualifications, the multiracial character of our society while choosing each President.

The President should not be tasked to safeguard the past reserves and the integrity of the public service. Instead, a separate Senate should be established and directly elected by the people to exercise all the discretionary powers currently vested in the Elected President. Parliament should be able to overturn any Senate veto with a three-quarters majority.

The WP's stand is clear. Thus, the above counter-factual would have been a non-starter even if it is of academic interest.

---

35 The Workers' Party, *Towards a First World Parliament: Manifesto 2011*, (Singapore: The Workers' Party, 2011), p. 10.

36 The Workers' Party, *Make Your Vote Count: The Workers' Party Manifesto 2020*, (Singapore: The Workers' Party, 2020), p. 33.

PSP highlights and lowlights

Within a year of its establishment, the PSP steadily took on the form of a properly run political party, with breadth and depth to it. The party organised forums for its growing membership on topics such as poverty in Singapore, and on the city-state's public housing policy and how to address the lease decay for Housing and Development Board flats. Video footage of the proceedings of these events were uploaded to online portals to reach a wider audience. These activities created buzz around the new party and kept it in the public consciousness. Attendant with these activities were changes to the party's membership structure.

On 17 January 2020, the party refreshed and strengthened its CEC; this included naming Leong Mun Wai (the Chief Executive Officer of an investment firm) as its Assistant Secretary-General, effectively the number two to TCB.[37] Not long thereafter, the PSP also opened its headquarters, located in the west of the island,[38] indicating the geographical focus of the party's electoral ambitions. The opening of the PSP's headquarters boosted the image of the party in the eyes of the public, underlining that it was a serious political player with intentions to be around for the long haul.

Still, like many a newly found political party that gravitates around a particular personality, and experiences a significant growth in its membership over a short time-span, the PSP also had its fair share of teething problems. One such problem emerged publicly in March 2020 when what appeared to be a PSP internal memo, highlighting disgruntlement among some party members, was sent to an alternative

---

37 "Progress Singapore Party shuffles leadership team", *The Straits Times Online*, 17 January 2020, https://www.straitstimes.com/politics/tan-cheng-bocks-progress-singapore-party-shuffles-leadership-team. Accessed on 29 July 2020.

38 "Tan Cheng Bock's Progress Singapore Party opens new headquarters", *Today Online*, 29 January 2020, https://www.todayonline.com/singapore/tan-cheng-bocks-progress-singapore-party-opens-new-headquarters. Accessed on 29 July 2020.

news media site.[39] The disgruntled members were complaining about the fact that the PSP was taking on the semblance of an army organisational structure. It described four divisions comprised of North, South, West, and Central. Given the fact that the PSP already had over a thousand members, it would not be surprising if its organisational structure networked its members into a seamless whole instead of leaving those members to their own devices. The issue, however, is that even with over a thousand members, on paper the PSP's electoral ambitions, where it contested widely, with the exception of the eastern half of the island, was not realistic.

In the final analysis, from all the evidence, TCB seemed confident he could pull off victories for his new party in GE2020. An incident which occurred during the election campaign itself seem to testify to this. On 6 July, TCB, accompanied by other PSP candidates and members, decided to travel to the eastern side of the island to meet his friend, Desmond Lim, of the Singapore Democratic Alliance, which had fielded a five-member team, headed by Lim himself, in the Pasir Ris-Punggol GRC. That TCB decided to take time off during a short, nine-day campaign, thereby denying himself valuable on-ground visibility in West Coast GRC, in order to visit his friend on the other side of the island, suggested a level of confidence by him that he would prevail in that GRC. What other inference can be drawn from this? It is also noteworthy that as TCB was addressing the media, he wondered aloud why another alternative party — PV — seemed to be present. Lim, who was adjacent to TCB, interjected by saying that there was a three-cornered fight there. TCB's surprised reaction: "Oh, there's a three-cornered fight? Aiyah! So sad, so sad. I didn't know because so many things happening. We are concentrating on the other side."

---

39 "Ex PSP members exposes PSP's internal conflict and unhappiness", *Sure Boh Singapore*, 6 March 2020, https://sureboh.sg/2020/03/06/breaking-ex-psp-member-exposes-psps-internal-conflict-and-unhappiness/?fbclid=IwAR21KXBPJNWQLjX NKRLHX6Z532gRxM6j8aA8KucJw_ft9VN8yty3XqWz1xo. Accessed on 20 July 2020.

In the early hours of 11 July 2020, after the results of GE2020 became clear, without any challenges lodged or disputes apparent, TCB, in a press conference, made a number of remarks. Among other things he said:

> *You all know the results. My young team didn't win a seat. But I must say, we have caused an impact in this general election. We may not have won the seats, but if you look at the level of support that is given to PSP candidates… I think the average is about 40%. That is my guess. So, with an average of 40% for a new party and going into all these new areas, I am actually quite proud of that performance. I think this is a beginning of a new chapter for PSP, and I think the movement that I've created will grow. We are not deterred by this disappointment because I think the team I have built will go further in the next elections.*

Post-GE2020

In the wake of the results of the general election, the chair of the WP, Sylvia Lim, indicated that her party would cooperate with the two individuals who would assume the post of NCMP. In an online video-conference on 12 July 2020, she said: "There will be ample opportunity, I believe, in the coming years for us to work collaboratively as much as possible with any party who should decide to take up the NCMP seats… to move the agenda forward and to play our role as constructive opposition."[40] In this instance, the two NCMPs were the PSP's Leong Mun Wai and Hazel Poa. Initially, Pritam Singh had also indicated that he would cooperate with the PSP's two NCMPs shortly after the government officially recognised him as Leader of the Opposition (LO). Given the resources he would receive in the newly created post,

---

40 "Singapore GE2020: Workers' Party ready to work with NCMPs from other opposition parties in Parliament, says Sylvia Lim", *The Straits Times*, 13 July 2020, https://www.straitstimes.com/politics/ge2020-workers-party-ready-to-work-with-ncmps-from-other-opposition-parties-in-parliament. Accessed on 29 July 2020.

he said that he would extend support to the two PSP NCMPs.[41] However, that pledge of support appeared to have been rowed back slightly when Singh gave his first speech as LO on 31 August 2020. He said:

> *The Progress Singapore Party has its own principles and ideology, that are distinct from those of the WP. Mr Leong [Mun Wai] and Ms [Hazel] Poa may propose policies and promote ideas very different from, and even in disagreement to those of the WP. It is possible that they may support government policies that we disagree with, or vice versa. However, where our positions match and are in the best interests of Singapore, I look forward to collaborating with the PSP NCMPs.*

One could speculate that, notwithstanding Singh's own inclinations to cooperate with the PSP, some of his other colleagues, including those outside the parliamentary party, were less keen.

At GE2020, the PSP had fielded a slate of candidates that on-average had relatively good qualifications, though none had that X factor — equivalent to what was reflected in the WP's Jamus Lim — that would make an instant connection with the voters. However, as was analysed in Chapter 3, such privilege or change agents are less instrumental than other factors to outcomes in a Westminster-type parliamentary election. But the lack of such personalities would be important in terms of providing direction to a party and generating buzz around it. That particular dearth in the PSP continued to be evident. At the PSP's second party conference, held on 28 March 2021, six new faces were elected to its CEC but none had the potential to ignite public interest.[42] Also, the party conference took place amidst murmurs of dissatisfaction by

---

41 "Leader of the Opposition role broadly in spirit of conventions in UK: Pritam", *The Straits Times*, 28 July 2020.

42 "Leadership reshuffle at PSP sees 6 new faces, more women", *The Straits Times*, 29 March 2021.

some members about the party's direction and leadership.[43] In the event, a few days following the party conference, TCB, already aged 80, stepped down as Secretary-General, to be succeeded by 71-year-old Francis Yuen. TCB assumed the post of Chairman.

When asked to comment on the changes within the PSP, a party spokesperson told *The Straits Times* that TCB wanted to focus his time on reaching out to other political parties as well as civil society groups, clans and other associations.[44] It is worth remembering that the attempt to establish an anti-PAP coalition with TCB as head did not materialise. And, after the PSP was set up it did not even go into a limited coalition with, say, the SDP and the PV, to fight GE2020, despite the swirl of online rumours suggesting that such a limited coalition would emerge. From this, one can only infer that, as TCB had failed to get a pact with the WP — the only first rank alternative party — he was not keen on any pact with lesser parties.

Post-GE2020, it is not clear whether formal cooperation between the PSP and the WP remains an option. One could speculate that it is likely that any significant cooperation between the two parties would come about if the PSP were to provide the WP with something that was materially significant. Short of that, it is not clear what advantage the WP would see in having an electoral pact with the PSP. Both parties do not impinge on each other's electoral footprint, with the WP focused on the east and the PSP on the west. But that convenient geographical division belies a more substantive division — one party continues to turn on the personality of one man, while the other turns on the power of its brand.

---

43 "PSP's Leong Mun Wai rejects rift rumours, as 6 new CEC members elected", *Today*, 28 March 2021, https://www.todayonline.com/singapore/unity-party-not-question-says-psps-leong-mun-wai-6-new-cec-members-elected. Accessed on 5 April 2021.

44 "Francis Yuen is new PSP chief, taking over from founder Tan Cheng Bock", *The Straits Times*, 1 April 2021.

CHAPTER 5

Civil Society Activists Make Neither Good Politicians Nor Good Political Commentators

Raeesah Khan, the Workers' Party (WP) candidate who was elected in GE2020, had been a civil society activist who, in 2016, founded the Reyna Movement, an organisation with the objective of empowering women. As it turned out, that experience — as a civil society activist — was to cause the key dramatic moment at GE2020. It was to be disclosed online, at around the half-way stage of the election campaign, that Khan had two years earlier posted online remarks alleging bias on the part of the Singapore police related to matters of race and religion. The People's Action Party (PAP) pounced on that online disclosure to attack the WP for fielding such a candidate.[1] Police reports were also filed against Khan. Some voters in Sengkang group representation constituency (GRC), where Khan contested, might have been disturbed at the disclosures but, as was examined in Chapter 3, that negative impact on the WP was offset by a confluence of other factors going in the party's favour and some moving against the PAP. Subsequent to the election, the police dropped their investigations of Khan. Instead, they issued her a "stern warning".[2] She had, effectively, dodged a bullet. The dramatic moment

---

1 "The Workers' Party's position on Sengkang candidate Ms Raeesah Khan", *People's Action Party*, 6 July 2020, https://www.pap.org.sg/news/the-workers-partys-position-on-sengkang-candidate-ms-raeesah-khan/. Accessed on 5 January 2021.

2 "WP MP Raeesah Khan given stern police warning for social media posts that promoted enmity between different groups", *The Straits Times*, 18 September 2020, https://www.straitstimes.com/singapore/wp-mp-raeesah-khan-given-stern-police-warning-for-social-media-posts-which-promoted-enmity. Accessed on 5 January 2021.

of GE2020 should not be forgotten as a mere blip. Rather, lessons should be drawn from it. For the PAP, the key lesson is that there are limits to negative campaigning. It can work sometimes, but it can also prove counter-productive. However, a bigger lesson is for the WP. At the time the disclosures about Khan were made online, some netizens sympathetic to the WP had wondered why the party did not do simple background checks on Khan's social media posts. Beyond that, there is in fact a broader, more important issue here which needs to be brought to light.

The contention in this chapter is that civil society activists do not tend to make for successful politicians, and that it is ill-advised to confuse the work of a politician with that of a civil society activist. This confusion is compounded by the fact that *civil society* is a contested concept whose boundaries are ill-defined.[3] Some theorists have argued that civil society essentially "means an ensemble of popular progressive oppositional movements not formally or necessarily affiliated with a specific political party."[4] But, here, it should be noted that the basic assumptions that the objective of civil society and its actors is the attainment of greater democracy has been shown to not always be accurate, with Thailand in 2006 being a notable case in point.[5]

---

3 See, for instance, Jussi Laine, "Debating Civil Society: Contested Conceptualizations and Development Trajectories", *International Journal of Not-for-Profit Law*, Vol. 16, No. 1, September 2014; and, Richard Mahapatra, "How much politics is too much politics for civil society", *Down To Earth*, 15 March 2019, https://www.downtoearth. org.in/blog/general-elections-2019/how-much-politics-is-too-much-politics-for-civil-society-63586. Accessed on 6 January 2021.

4 Joseph A. Buttigieg, "The Contemporary Discourse on Civil Society", *boundary 2*, Vol. 32, No. 1, Spring 2005, p. 34.

5 Eli Elinoff, "Unmaking Civil Society: Activists Schisms and Autonomous Politics in Thailand", *Contemporary Southeast Asia*, Vol. 36, No. 3, 2014, p. 365.

One scholar has attempted to frame the definitional problem surrounding civil society in the following terms:[6]

... [in a more restricted version] civil society is defined as an intermediate associational realm between the state and individuals, populated by organisations and groups that are separate from the state, enjoy autonomy in relation to the state, and are formed voluntarily by members of society to protect or advance their interests or values... Although this working definition proved useful for empirical research, it did not solve all problems. Most scholars of democratization continued to understand civil society as a homogeneous world of organizations that, although performing a social and political role, do not seek to take political power, share democratic values, and refrain from resorting to violent means to promote their values and interests. However, the real world of existing civil societies does not always reflect these characteristics...

In the context of Singapore, civil society activists have not sought political power, but have attempted to shape the nature of public discourse and to influence parties in opposition to the PAP, with possible electoral outcomes. There has been a noticeable resurgence in such thinking since GE2020. For instance, on 26 July 2020, i.e., some two weeks after GE2020, a Zoom webinar was held entitled *The Ground Speaks: Civil Society After GE2020*, which featured nine civil society activists and their reflections of activism on public policy. The holding of such a webinar so close after GE2020 and the apparent linking of the work of activists to the election might have given the impression that there was a connection between the work of activists and the election results, even though the organisers did not appear to have that intention.

---

6 Lorenzo Fioramonti, "Civil Societies and Democratization: Assumptions, Dilemmas and the South African Experience", *Theoria: A Journal of Social and Political Theory*, No. 107, August 2005, p. 67.

It is not uncommon to find the scholarly literature replete with buoyant views on civil society, such as the following:[7]

> *Civil society is decisive in the emergence of democracy, and it is also potentially important in the reduction of political, civic, and socioeconomic inequalities, and therefore, to the quality, or depth of democracy. Civil society organizations and broad movements of protest can facilitate collective action by popular groups of the poor and disenfranchised, endowing them with a greater capacity to shape institutions and policy agendas.*

To be certain, civil society activists who advocate for the disempowered, the under-privileged, the marginalised, those with disabilities, do good in their work creating a fairer and more equitable society. In Singapore, the women's group AWARE (the Association of Women for Action and Research), has been notable in its advocacy for women and in its support for gender equality.[8] Similarly, civil society organisation Maruah has attempted to engage the public in political education. Maruah has also given its feedback to the Elections Department on how to improve certain procedures.[9] The activists at the Nature Society (Singapore), NSS, have also for decades been at the forefront in advocating for environmental issues. They achieved success in a number of projects. These included forcing the government to rethink a few plans for redevelopment in favour of conservation of natural wetlands and primary forests teeming with

---

7   Michael Bernhard, Tiago Fernandes and Rui Branco, "Introduction: Civil Society and Democracy in an Era of Inequality", *Comparative Politics*, Vol. 49, No. 3, April 2017, p. 299.

8   AWARE, https://www.aware.org.sg/about/. Accessed on 4 February 2021.

9   "Letter to ELD on electoral procedures and negative campaigning", *Maruah*, 28 August 2015, https://maruah.org/2015/08/28/2022/. Accessed on 4 February 2021.

biodiversity, spawning "an era of state-NSS collaboration in nature conservation".[10]

But it is when civil society activists try to become political analysts and, beyond that, politicians, that the results are at best mixed and, in many instances, counter-productive. Some might argue that this distinction between the work of civil society activists, on the one hand, and political analysts and politicians, on the other, is artificial, and that no such divide exists. That view will be tested below.

One Singaporean scholar has observed: "The character of civil society is largely dependent on contemporary political conditions, the nature of the state, and the manner of society-state relations, thus infusing the term with a hermeneutic instability that is reflected in the broader literature."[11] That general observation can be taken as axiomatic. Narrowed down to the specific context of Singapore, if society is to varying degrees conservative in nature, then there are limitations imposed on civil society activism if that activism is viewed as a progressive force.

Another point to keep in mind is that one issue bedevilling Singapore politics is the lack of political knowledge by even the supposedly politically-engaged. The advent of social media had worsened this and, in fact, has coarsened public discourse, with a segment of the politically-engaged reliant on their diet of political news from online portals which have tended to pass off personal opinion as serious analysis.

---

10 See, Daniel P. S. Goh, "Politics of the Environment in Singapore: Lessons from a 'Strange' Case", *Asian Journal of Social Science*, Vol. 29, No. 1, 2001, p. 15.

11 Terence Chong, "Civil Society in Singapore: Popular Discourses and Concepts", *Sojourn: Journal of Social Issues in Southeast Asia*, Vol. 20, No. 2, October 2005, p. 273.

We will now proceed with a brief survey of civil society and human rights activism from abroad. The last two sections of the chapter will then focus on two Singaporean civil society activists.

Being a civil society activist sits uneasily with being a politician

Malaysia is often looked upon by some Singaporean civil society activists as a country for emulation since in that country some civil society activists have successfully transitioned to lives as politicians. But the utility of Malaysia as an example for Singapore is fraught with problems. Since Singapore left the Malaysian Federation in 1965, both countries have charted a significantly divergent course in the economic, political, and social realms.

In Malaysia, political power grows from a localised level,[12] not least because Malaysia, divided into Peninsular and East Malaysia, is a sprawling country of villages, small towns, rural and agricultural regions, and urban centres, with stark divisions between coastal and inland communities. In village or small towns across Malaysia, civil society activists work diligently for the local communities. They might have toiled as activists for years, gained a local following, before making an attempt for elected office as an assemblyman in one of the state legislatures. From the state legislature they might try to gain a seat in the Malaysian federal Parliament, the Dewan Rakyat. With minor exceptions, there is thus a fairly long, arduous and set process to follow. In addition to this formulation, other factors galvanising a critical mass have propelled political change in Malaysia, giving agency to civil society

---

12 The point has been developed in Phang Siew Nooi, "Decentralisation or Recentralisation? Trends in Local Government in Malaysia", *Commonwealth Journal of Local Governance*, Issue 1, May 2008.

activists challenging the elite-driven power structure.[13] As one observer put it in 2011:[14]

> *Democratization was being pushed by new political forces such as civil society actors, newly empowered opposition parties, and the Internet-based media. In effect,* new institutions *were being formed around* new political forces. *The pace of change is being determined by these new political forces having to challenge structural and institutional barriers representing elite-run institutions such as the dominant political parties. Often times, sites of political contention where political change emerges are situated beyond the arenas in which elite coalitions and power-sharing arrangements are being negotiated and perpetuated. It is in these new political spaces that the contours of emerging democratic space in Malaysia are being (re)delineated, often by* circumventing *conventional institutional barriers to political liberalization and democratization. The democratic space that is emerging in Malaysia today is simultaneously being shaped and contested by the political competition between status-quo and reformist forces in this society. And the boundaries of this new political space are constantly being redrawn depending on the outcomes of these political contestations. Taken together, the institutional changes discussed above have expanded the parameters of democratic space in Malaysia... [Roman font in original.]*

On the other hand, in Singapore, small and, largely monolithically urban in nature, power is heavily centralised, civil society is weak, and those actors within civil society are so few in number that the same names constantly reappear in the public discourse. There is little evidence

---

13 See, for instance, Garry Rodan, "Civil Society Activism and Political Parties in Malaysia: Differences over Local Representation", *Democratization*, Vol. 1, No. 5, 2014.

14 Surain Subramaniam, "Assessing Political Dynamics in Contemporary Malaysia: Implications for Democratic Change", *ASIANetwork Exchange*, Vol. 19, No. 1, Fall 2011, p. 49.

that the mass of Singapore voters has much appetite for a broad socio-economic and political reformist agenda in the city-state. Where there is a measure of decentralisation in Singapore, it is still through the structure of Parliament, in which the management of town councils and, therefore, municipal issues, have become inherent in the office of an elected MP since the early 1990s.

If we were to cast the issue beyond Singapore and Malaysia to personalities whose names are recognisable by educated people internationally, we again have to conclude that it is rarely possible to be a champion of human rights whilst simultaneously being a successful politician. In the United States the human rights campaigners Jesse Jackson and Al Sharpton had been relatively successful in championing human rights causes.[15] However, when they had tried to parlay their relative success as human rights advocates into a campaign for elected political office, they stumbled. Jackson had two failed bids, in 1984 and 1988, to secure the Democratic Party's nomination for US president. Similarly, Sharpton failed in his own bid for the nomination in 2004.[16]

A British example is that of the Lesbian, Gay, Bisexual and Transgender (LGBT) rights campaigner Peter Tatchell. In 1983, Tatchell was nominated by grassroots activists of the Labour Party to stand as the party's candidate in a by-election for the Bermondsey constituency. Despite the constituency being a solidly Labour stronghold, with the party having secured a 63.6% vote in the 1979 general election, Tatchell lost the seat by an enormous margin. The Labour vote collapsed to just 26.1%. At the by-election campaign, Tatchell had been subjected to

---

15 Darryl S. Tukufu, "Jesse Jackson and the Rainbow Coalition: Working Class Movement or Reform Politics?", *Humanity & Society*, Vol. 14, No. 2, 1990.

16 See, Anne Urbanowski, "Al Sharpton's 2004 Presidential Campaign: Has the Reverend Lost the Faith?", *Revue LISA/LISA e-journal* [Online], Vol. IX, No. 1, 2011, 2021. URL: http://journals.openedition.org/lisa/4153; DOI: https://doi.org/10.4000/lisa.4153. Accessed on 3 January 2021.

unsavoury election tactics from his opponents.[17] As a society, and a polity, the UK has of course moved forward as a progressive country since the 1980s; there is less of a distinction between a civil society activist and a politician. But other countries lag the UK by a few decades.

Another example one can cite is Myanmar's Aung San Suu Kyi. The relative political liberalisation in Myanmar, which saw her being elected to the lower house of the Myanmar Parliament in April 2012, also witnessed sectarian tensions, long existing between the majority Buddhists and the minority Rohingya Muslims, escalate into violence against the latter. Suu Kyi's tenure as State Counsellor (de facto head of government) was marked by what was described by senior United Nations officials as a "textbook example of ethnic cleansing" carried out by the Myanmar military (the Tatmadaw) against the Rohingya in Myanmar's Rakhine State.[18] Suu Kyi was an apologist for the Tatmadaw, to the extent of going to the International Court of Justice in the Hague to defend Myanmar from the accusation of genocide against the Rohingya.[19] One observer, writing on Suu Kyi, quoted German Philosopher Max Weber's dictum that, "Every person who wants to become a politician, and especially a professional politician, has to be aware of the ethical paradoxes and his responsibilities for what and who he can become in the context of these pressures." The observer then went on to say that in this context, "the idea of a politician like Aung San Suu Kyi also as a nonviolent activist seems like a contradiction."[20]

---

17 "Bermondsey by-election: 30 years on", *Total Politics*, 6 January 2013, https://totalpolitics.com/articles/news/bermondsey-election-30-years. Accessed on 5 January 2021.

18 "'Textbook example of ethnic cleansing': A timeline of the Rohingya crisis", *The Wire*, 21 August 2020, https://thewire.in/world/textbook-example-of-ethnic-cleansing-a-timeline-of-the-rohingya-crisis. Accessed on 10 January 2020.

19 "Aung San Suu Kyi defends Myanmar from accusations of genocide, at top UN court", *UN News*, 11 December 2019, https://news.un.org/en/story/2019/12/1053221. Accessed on 10 January 2021.

20 Mon Mon Myat, "Is Politics Aung San Suu Kyi's Vocation?", *Humanities and Social Sciences Communications*, 14 May 2019, https://www.nature.com/articles/s41599-019-0258-1. Accessed on 26 January 2021.

When the Tatmadaw launched a coup d'état on 1 February 2021, toppling Suu Kyi's National League for Democracy government, sympathy for her from the international community was in short supply.[21] As Phil Robertson of Human Rights Watch opined: "Aung San Suu Kyi rebuffed international critics by claiming she was not a human-rights activist but rather a politician. But the sad part is she hasn't been very good at either."[22]

Notwithstanding the examples in the foregoing, some Singaporean civil society activists have urged opposition politicians to take up human rights causes in a high-profile manner. A number of the key issues of the activists include their push for an end to capital and corporal punishment; a repeal of Section 377a of the Penal Code (which criminalises sex between men); concomitantly, they want full equality for LGBT individuals. They also advocate for greater rights being accorded to migrant workers. However, in spite of some personal sympathy by opposition politicians for a number of these issues, they know that anything that does not have an obvious economic dimension to it and which could resonate with the Singapore public, would be a vote loser.

Before this section is concluded, for completeness, it should be pointed out that the PAP has for long co-opted within its ranks trades union activists who have become PAP Members of Parliament

---

21 See, for example, "Aung San Suu Kyi will now find much less sympathy in the west — she only has herself to blame", *Independent*, 2 February 2021, https://www. independent.co.uk/voices/editorials/aung-san-suu-kyi-myanmar-militrary-coup-rohingya-b1795988.html. Accessed on 2 February 2021; and, Donald Kirk, "Aung San Suu Kyi disgraced herself by sucking up to the generals in Myanmar, they staged a military coup anyway", *The Daily* Beast, 1 February 2021, https://www. thedailybeast.com/aung-san-suu-kyi-disgraced-herself-sucking-up-to-the-generals-in-myanmar-they-staged-a-military-coup-anyway. Accessed on 2 February 2021.

22 Quoted in "Democracy hero? Military foil? Myanmar's leader ends up as neither", *The New York Times*, 1 February 2021, https://www.nytimes.com/2021/02/01/ world/asia/myanmar-coup-aung-san-suu-kyi.html. Accessed on 2 February 2021.

(MPs). Given that Lee Kuan Yew had from the very start of his governance of Singapore effectively tamed the trades unions, turning them into institutions that had a mostly symbiotic relationship with the ruling party,[23] trades union activists would not be considered as generally a good example of activists who transitioned to become successful politicians. Indeed, in the Gramscian notion of civil society, trades unionists are part of what is called "the superstructure" that underpins state hegemony.[24] Finally, one ought to mention the PAP MP Louis Ng. He has been a civil society activist who successfully made the transition to a politician. In fact, he continues in both roles. However, again, it is worth stressing one point: Ng is with the ruling PAP.

Alex Au: An advocate for migrant workers and a socio-political commentator

One of the most prominent of Singaporean civil society activists is Alex Au.[25] Au was one of the earliest and more serious adopters of the internet, launching his *Yawning Bread* blog back in 1996. It dealt with largely social justice issues. In the parlance that was to emerge with the rise of alternative media, Au was described as a "socio-political blogger". The most compelling blog post that Au uploaded on *Yawning Bread* was his detailed description of vote counting and being a counting agent for the Singapore Democratic Party (SDP) at GE2011.[26]

---

23 Suraendher Kumarr, "The Politics of Controlling Labour in Singapore: Continuities and Fissures in Migrant and Citizen Labour Governance", *Journal of International & Public Affairs*, Vol. 1, No. 2, 2020, https://www.jipasg.org/posts/2019/4/27/the-politics-of-controlling-labour-in-singapore-continuities-and-fissures-in-migrant-and-citizen-labour-governance. Accessed on 18 January 2021.

24 Souvik Lal Chakraborty, "Gramsci's Idea of Civil Society", *International Journal of Research in Humanities and Social Studies*, Vol. 3, Issue 6, June 2016, pp. 24–25.

25 According to a biographical reference in his own blog, Au was born in 1952.

26 "Counting agent me", *Yawning Bread*, 8 May 2011, https://yawningbread.wordpress.com/2011/05/08/counting-agent-me/. Accessed on 12 August 2020.

Au has also been a strong proponent of LGBT rights. He later enlarged his social justice focus by involving himself significantly in assisting the community of migrant workers in Singapore. As vice-president of the migrant advocacy group, Transient Workers Count Too (TWC2), Au gave voice to the large community of migrant workers when the COVID-19 pandemic made its way through Singapore's cramped migrant workers' dormitories, infecting many workers. His work for that community has been widely praised. He said at the height of the pandemic: "The Singapore government has a paternalistic, almost proprietary approach towards migrant workers — caring for them because they are of economic value. There is a subconscious blaming of the migrant workers, which is happening in other countries too."[27]

Returning to *Yawning Bread*, the blog attracted a growing following from netizens who shared Au's outlook. But Au appeared to lose interest in blogging in early 2019. At the time of writing (August 2021), Au had not posted anything for more than two years. In an interview with an online magazine in November 2008, Au stated matter-of-factly: "When it comes to social issues, I'm a leftist, but when it comes to economics, I'm right-wing."[28]

Au's comments following Lee Kuan Yew's death. In September 2015, Singapore held a general election. Around six months earlier, its founding prime minister, Lee Kuan Yew, had died. Following his death, Au gave

---

27 "Asian migrant workers locked up, dumped as coronavirus curbs eased", *Reuters*, 24 December 2020, https://www.reuters.com/article/us-health-coronavirus-migrants-trfn-idUSKBN28Y13D. Accessed on 15 January 2021.

28 Quoted by Ramesh William, "Alex Au; Gay Activist", *I-S Singapore Online*, 27 November 2008, http://is.asia-city.com/city-living/article/alex-au-gay-activist. Accessed on 5 May 2015.

a video interview with the international news organisation, AFP. It is worth reproducing those remarks here at length:[29]

Most of the people thronging to sign the condolence book or to view the lying-in- state has [sic] been over 50-years-old. So, that probably tells you quite a lot about what the newer generation of Singaporeans might think about this. Precisely because of Lee Kuan Yew's long twilight, hmm, lots of people, say, under 40 or under 45, would not have known his premiership at all. And, therefore, it would not be quite as important a factor in their lives or in their memory as for those of the older generations. So, I would think that at least half of the electorate don't have a very... aren't very moved by this event. Considering how in the last week since he passed, for every one who has had positive things to say about Lee Kuan Yew, there has been equal number of people saying... pointing out that his legacy has been as negative as it has been positive. So, I'm not sure what effect it will have on the elections.

AFP uploaded the clip onto its Facebook page. Au's remarks were not appreciated by a large number of Singaporean netizens who were still mourning the loss of Lee. The main point of contention was the assertion that, "for every one who has had positive things to say about Lee Kuan Yew, there has been equal number of people saying... pointing out that his legacy has been as negative as it has been positive." It was not clear what evidence Au relied on to make such an assertion. In any event, in the general election held just six months later (GE2015), the ruling PAP was to benefit significantly from the "LKY effect". As was stated in Chapter 1 Lee's long tenure as the strongman of Singapore,

---

29 AFP News Agency, "Many in Singapore See Negative Side to Lee's Legacy: Blogger", *YouTube*, 29 March 2015. https://www.youtube.com/watch?v=PbGwp5bjV18. Accessed on 10 November 2020.

with his evident authoritarian traits, had — even if in a small measure — bled through to a large segment of Singaporeans of adult age and across virtually all races. Through the role-modelling effect, a latent strand of authoritarianism resides in a significant number of Singaporeans.[30]

'Popular activism' to remove impediments to 'true democracy'. Shortly after GE2015, on 11 September 2015, Au, myself, and four others, were invited to be part of a panel of speakers at a forum arranged by Maruah, on an election which outcome had surprised many. At the forum, as he ended his formal presentation, Au made the following observations:[31]

> *My view is that sometimes we are too gentlemanly about it, ok. It is totally self-defeating to say, 'No, no, we cannot be seen to be confrontational. Singaporeans get scared.' So, the next slide tells you this. [The slide listed "Structural Impediments to True Democracy".]…*
>
> *And the last slide here is from Czechoslovakia, a country that has disappeared, of course. This is Prague, and that's a scene from 1989. You see… and they came out of Communism as a result of that event. They call it the Velvet Revolution, in November 1989. And the point I want to make is this: if Singaporeans rule out this kind of popular activism, then I really, really doubt that the institutional and structural changes can ever come about.*

---

30 This is not purely my analysis. A similar analysis is found in Nur Amali Ibrahim, "Everyday Authoritarianism: A Political Anthropology of Singapore", *Critical Asian Studies*, Vol. 50, No. 2, 2018.

31 "Maruah #GE2015 Post-Elections forum — Introduction & Alex Au", *YouTube*, 22 September 2015, https://www.youtube.com/watch?v=YpuPatbtgcA. Accessed on 20 December 2020.

In the Q&A session that followed the presentations by the six panel speakers, my immediate response was to what Au had proposed. These were my observations:[32]

A few quick responses, some directed to Alex. [H]e's quite certain and adamant that confrontational politics will be something which we will have to deal with in the future. I do not think that that is the case. The fact of the matter is that WP positioned itself very deliberately as being in the moderate ground and, whatever you want to say, the fact of the matter is that they have got six MPs-elect, alright. Whether they won their electoral divisions by one vote or, in the case of Aljunied GRC, by more than 2,600 votes is immaterial. What is material is the seats that you win. That's the most important point.

Even though Au introduced the virtues of the Velvet Revolution rather gently, it seemed difficult to allow it to go unchallenged. I could have also pointed out then, that the Velvet Revolution was a product of broader developments in Eastern Europe and the more emollient attitude of Mikhail Gorbachev, leader of the Soviet Union, towards internal developments in the then Communist Eastern Bloc.[33] The Velvet Revolution, starting on 17 November 1989, in fact followed from the fall of the Berlin Wall eight days earlier. Context is important when advocating for major political change.

---

32 "Maruah #GE2015 Post-Elections forum — Q & A", *YouTube*, 23 September 2015, https://www.youtube.com/watch?v=Q2ngpQdwlUI&t=4778s. Accessed on 20 December 2020.

33 For perspectives on the Velvet Revolution, see Steven Saxonberg, "The 'Velvet Revolution' and the Limits of Rational Choice Models", *Czech Sociological Review*, Vol. 7, No. 1, Spring 1999; and, Andre Glucksman, "The Velvet Philosophical Revolution", *City Journal*, Winter 2010, https://www.city-journal.org/html/velvet-philosophical-revolution-13255.html. Accessed on 22 December 2020.

GE2020, where the WP achieved a second breakthrough, and cemented its position as effectively the only opposition game in town, would have come as a disappointment to Au. Reading the entries in his blog, it is clear that he is not enamoured of the WP, for two reasons. First, the WP does not support the repeal of 377a, for which he has long campaigned.[34] In Au's words: "The Workers' Party will not step forward to support repeal of Section 377a or the discriminatory censorship of gay representation in media, surely the first steps that have to be taken to tear down institutionalised discrimination and societal homophobia."[35] He further accused the WP of "not standing up for equality, non-discrimination and a more progressive society".[36] Second, the WP's moderate style of opposition to the PAP would, in Au's view, not remove the structural impediments to what he calls "true democracy". The next civil society activist shares similar views.

Thum Ping Tjin: Historian, activist, and opponent of the Workers' Party's moderation

The news website, *Rice Media*, launched in 2017, provides a take on social and political issues. On 8 September 2018 it ran a story with the headline, "Who's Afraid of PJ Thum?"[37] This was a tweak on Edward Albee's play *Who's Afraid of Virginia Woolf?* The *Rice Media* story was a paean on Thum Ping Tjin, an Oxford-trained historian

---

34 See, "When you should vote PAP", *Yawning Bread*, 16 March 2011, https://yawningbread.wordpress.com/2011/03/16/when-you-should-vote-pap/. Accessed on 18 December 2020.

35 "Workers' Party, data privacy, and the elephant in the room", *Yawning Bread*, 13 March 2011, https://yawningbread.wordpress.com/2011/03/13/workers-party-data-privacy-and-the-elephant-in-the-room/. Accessed on 18 December 2020.

36 Ibid.

37 "Who's afraid of PJ Thum?" *Rice Media*, 8 September 2018, https://www.ricemedia.co/current-affairs-opinion-whos-afraid-pj-thum/. Accessed on 5 January 2021.

who has broadened his interests to include civil society activism and commentary on contemporary electoral politics. He also runs the website *New Naratif*, which proclaims itself as "openly subjective".[38] The *Rice Media* story carried no byline, but there was evident upset by the author or authors that members of the Singapore Establishment had come down hard on Thum because the Singaporean historian/ civil society activist had on 30 August 2018 met with then Malaysian Prime Minister Mahathir bin Mohamad at the Malaysian federal administrative capital of Putrajaya. In a Facebook post on the same day Thum wrote:

> *I met with Malaysian Prime Minister Dr Mahathir today. I urged him to take leadership in Southeast Asia for the promotion of democracy, human rights, freedom of expression, and freedom of information. I also expressed hope for closer relations between the people of Malaysia and Singapore, and presented him a copy of "Living with Myths in Singapore".*

On the face of it, some don't find anything particularly offensive about this post or of Thum meeting with Mahathir. They would consider those who took offence to the meeting as over-reacting. But some Singaporeans have viewed Mahathir as a stumbling block to Malaysia and Singapore having harmonious relations. Equally, the meeting between Thum and Mahathir came just five months after Thum appeared as a representor before the Singapore Parliament's Select Committee on Deliberate Online Falsehoods, on 30 March 2018. In that capacity, Thum was questioned for some six hours by Minister for Law and Home Affairs, K. Shanmugam, over his written submission to the Select Committee. The initial part of that questioning revealed discrepancies

---

38 "About — New Naratif", *New Naratif*, https://newnaratif.com/about-us/. Accessed on 6 January 2021.

in Thum's publicly declared credentials.[39] But the bulk of the questioning had to do with Operation Coldstore, an operation carried out on 2 February 1963 by Singapore's Special Branch (the precursor of the Internal Security Department), and the Field Police, which rounded-up dozens of leftist elements in Singapore. Those who are not historians — such as myself — are really in no position to comment on this historical event of almost six decades ago.[40] But that really is not the

---

39 In September 2018, the Select Committee published its report. A small part of that report dealt with Thum's credentials and is reflected in this media story, "Thum Ping Tjin had 'clearly lied' about credentials, no weight given to his views: Select Committee", *CNA*, 20 September 2018, https://www.channelnewsasia.com/news/singapore/thum-ping-tjin-lied-academic-credentials-select-committee-10739894. Accessed on 21 December 2020. In response, Thum said on 22 September 2018: "I completely disagree with the Report of the Select Committee's allegation that I 'clearly lied' and misrepresented my academic credentials. I will respond more fully in due course." ("Thum Ping Tjin refutes Select Committee's assertion that he lied about academic credentials", *Yahoo! News*, 22 September 2018, https://sg.news.yahoo.com/thum-ping-tjin-refutes-fake-news-committees-assertion-lied-academic-credentials-055406525.html. Accessed on 15 December 2020.) At the time of writing (August 2021), Thum had yet to "respond more fully". In any event, I had independently investigated the matter through correspondence with academics and senior officials at the University of Oxford. My discoveries do not differ much with the findings of the Select Committee's report.

40 Relative to Thum, most people do not even have a fraction of one percent of knowledge on 1950s–1960s Singapore, and would readily say that he is an expert on that period. Indeed, shortly after the Select Committee hearings when *The Straits Times* journalist Elgin Toh contacted me to comment on Operation Coldstore for a major feature article, I declined because it would have been presumptuous of me to comment on something in which I had no scholarly expertise. The piece by Toh was to run as, "Why Coldstore is a hot topic", *The Straits Times*, 6 May 2018. For avoidance of doubt, Thum, as a historian, should be extended latitude in how he interprets history based on the evidence he presents, including declassified documents from the UK archives, even if there are some reservations about the methodology he employs. However, it might be a little ill-advised for anyone to move beyond the parameters of academia to publicly campaign on an issue, especially when there is no firm consensus on it from other scholars. But Thum takes a contrary view, as noted by one observer: "Thum has participated in a number of forums on history and civil society. He sees this as a duty and dismisses the notion that an academic can be strictly 'apolitical'. 'Academics are participants in the world. We are citizens, we have a role to play. And it is our responsibility to make the world better.'" In "Thum Ping Tjin — The 'Blacklisted' Historian", *The Naysayers Book Club*, https://naysayers.sg/thum-ping-tjin/. Accessed on 11 January 2021.

point. The point is that Thum's central thesis in his written submission was that "politicians of Singapore's People's Action Party" have been a clear source of "fake news" in the period "from 1963 to 1987".[41] The period he cited pre-dated the advent of social media by decades, yet he made that his central thesis in a submission to a Select Committee on Deliberate Online Falsehoods. From its very name the Select Committee's terms of reference should be quite obvious.

A claim about the SDP, and another about Chiam See Tong. Most Singaporeans have no recollection or understanding of the events of the 1960s. However, a large segment of Singaporeans who were in their 20s and older during the 1990s do still remember the events of that decade, when a moderate SDP under Chiam See Tong, emerged out of GE1991 with three parliamentary seats, the highest in decades. That otherwise significant milestone was to prove short-lived. The issue turns on the question: did the SDP's electoral chances get ruined by others who took the organisation into a confrontational direction in relation to the ruling party? Chiam left the SDP shortly before GE1997. In that election he was to retain his Potong Pasir seat under the newly formed Singapore People's Party (SPP), while the two remaining SDP seats were recaptured by the PAP. GE1997 was to underline the fact that only moderate opposition can prevail against the PAP,[42] and is something which remained durable into GE2020. That, however, is not Thum's position. He has moved beyond being a historian on 1950s/1960s Singapore to being a commentator on contemporary Singapore electoral politics.

As part of a series of broadcast interviews with politicians conducted for *The Online Citizen* for GE2020, Thum did one such interview with

---

41 Parliament of Singapore, Thum Ping Tjin, Written Representation 83, Submission to the Select Committee on Deliberate Online Falsehoods, 26 February 2018.

42 Derek da Cunha, *The Price of Victory: The 1997 Singapore General Election and Beyond*, (Singapore: Institute of Southeast Asian Studies, 1997), p. 58.

SPP candidate Jose Raymond, where Thum made the following observations:[43]

> *If you look at what non-PAP parties have been able to achieve, it's been very much about accountability and asking questions and bringing publicity. The SDP has pointed out that the PAP has stolen a whole bunch of their policies. But then they [the PAP] portrayed them as the PAP's policies and did not give any credit there, and there was no attempt to collaborate. So, a criticism might be, well that sounds great, well let's collaborate, let's all work together, but in the real world we know the PAP is not gonna want to collaborate. At best, they're going to steal your ideas. At worst, they're going to take every opportunity to try and humiliate you, like they did Mr Chiam.*

There are two separate parts to these observations. The first is the claim that the PAP has stolen policies from the SDP, which Thum takes as a statement of fact because that has been alleged by the SDP itself.[44] The second is the claim that the PAP had humiliated Chiam. As to the first, the analogy one could use to describe the SDP's Chee Soon Juan is of a person who has been throwing darts at a political dart board regularly for the past quarter-of-a-century. With that amount of dart-throwing, inevitably he is going hit the bull's eye a few times, but he has also hit the wall, the ceiling, the floor, even his own foot. He has been jailed and fined for criminal offences, and sued for defamation; and, the SDP's policy on reduced defence expenditures, for example,

---

43 "TOC GE2020 Livestream — 2 July 2020 Jose Raymond", *YouTube*, 2 July 2020, https://www.youtube.com/watch?v=AlBJp8mciKo&t=3284s. Accessed on 10 December 2020.

44 See, for instance, "SDP again claims PAP stole their idea", *The Independent*, 28 July 2017, https://theindependent.sg/sdp-again-claims-pap-stole-their-idea-this-time/. Accessed on 5 February 2021.

does not gain favour with many voters.[45] In late April 2020, the SDP put out a campaign slogan called "Four Yes, One No" (4Y1N). The third "yes", as described in the SDP's website, reads:[46]

> *SDP will push to provide retirees over 65 with a monthly income of $500. Under the SDP Retirement Income Scheme for the Elderly (RISE), the bottom 80% of retirees, many of whom depend on their working children for financial support and especially those who do not have working children, will receive $500 every month.*
>
> *The Household Expenditure Survey shows that the average retiree household receives nearly $500 as income from their working children. With retrenchments and pay cuts expected to rise as a result of Covid-19, working adults will find it even harder to provide for their own children and take care of their retired parents at the same time. By providing $500 for the average retiree, RISE will also reduce the financial pressure of younger working generations.*

It was noticeable that when the SDP launched its main manifesto, *The Way Forward*, seven months earlier, in late September 2019, there was no mention of this pledge in the 157-page document (a document which only exists in print form).[47] It is possible that people other than

---

45 The SDP's Paul Tambyah has presented the SDP's policy on defence spending in the following terms "[A] strong military is not the same as excessive and unsustainable defence spending." See, "Strong defence needed, but not excessive spending", *The Straits Times*, 6 February 2016.

46 "SDP launches 4Y1N campaign for GE in response to COVID-19 pandemic", *Singapore Democratic Party*, 28 April 2020, https://yoursdp.org/news/sdp-launches-4y1n-campaign-for-ge-in-response-to-covid-19-pandemic/. Accessed on 28 December 2020.

47 "SDP launches printed manifesto with updated healthcare, education policies", *CNA*, 29 September 2019. https://www.channelnewsasia.com/news/singapore/sdp-printed-manifesto-policies-updated-healthcare-education-11951948. Accessed on 15 December 2021.

those associated with the SDP might have also argued for a not dissimilar proposal.[48] That, in fact, would not be an uncommon occurrence.

As for the claim Thum made that the PAP had humiliated Chiam, it is not clear on what basis he made it. It is a claim that goes against the accepted narrative. In fact, it is a claim which is 180 degrees at variance from the available evidence. All opposition MPs encounter a difficult time because of the bureaucratic hurdles they need to surmount. But that is very different from making a claim that they had been humiliated. There was only one occasion where Chiam was humiliated, and that was *before* he became an MP when, at the 1984 general election, Lee Kuan Yew compared Chiam's GCE O-Level results with that of his opponent, Mah Bow Tan. After Chiam entered Parliament, the PAP generally treated him with respect because they could see that he was a good, hard-working constituency MP, well-liked by many of his constituents. In fact, if anything, Chiam had embarrassed the PAP when he was the only MP to get to his feet in a Parliament sitting on 10 March 1992 to object to a racist joke by PAP backbencher, Choo Wee Khiang.[49]

It could be argued that Thum's remarks about Chiam having been humiliated by the PAP were not casual, but deliberate, observations, intended to revise the political history of the 1990s. The reality of that decade is that a more strident and confrontational SDP under Chee Soon Juan ruined the party and its electoral prospects for a generation, while the moderate Chiam was re-elected by voters and continued to serve the residents of Potong Pasir single-member constituency (SMC). There is a clear continuum between the troubling political developments of the 1990s and the subsequent three decades. Consequently, Singaporeans forget those events at their own peril.

---

48 As a policy proposal for the PAP, I had written in *Breakthrough* that the government should provide a life annuity that acts as a monthly pension for Singaporeans from the age of 65. I had suggested $300 a month as the pension amount. Derek da Cunha, *Breakthrough: Roadmap for Singapore's Political Future*, (Singapore: Institute for Policy Studies and Straits Times Press, 2012), pp. 239–240.

49 da Cunha, *The Price of Victory...*, op. cit., pp. 28–29.

The WP is assailed for the slightest of reasons. On 25 June 2016, the WP put out a statement on the decision by British voters in the referendum of 23 June 2016 to have the UK leave the European Union (Brexit). The result of the Brexit vote sent political tremors across the globe. Responsible political parties around the world needed to absorb the meaning of the vote and attempt to head off similar tendencies by local electorates through understanding their grievances. The WP statement, signed by its then Assistant Secretary-General, Pritam Singh, made the following points:[50]

Brexit is not only about the United Kingdom and the European Union. It is a sobering reminder about the shortcomings and limits of globalisation, the scale of immigration, how quickly the poison of racism and xenophobia can shape the public discourse, the perceptions and prospects of locals losing good jobs to foreigners, the extent of change people can stomach, the importance of a strong social compact, amongst so much more. It is also about aspirations, and a sense of what home was, is and should be.

Singapore is not alien to such emotions. We had a sense of what mattered to Singaporeans especially in the years from 2004–2010, when home started to feel so different because of the pace of change, an emotion that came to the fore again after the release of the Government's Population White Paper in 2013. In 2008, former Prime Minister Lee Kuan Yew opined that the ideal population size for Singapore was 5 to 5.5m people. In 2014, a former CEO of the HDB argued for a population of 10m after 2030. The significance of these numbers go far, far beyond the obvious. Economics and trade considerations are paramount for developed countries, but as Brexit showed, many other things matter as well.

---

50 The Workers' Party, "The Workers' Party's Perspective on Brexit", 26 June 2016, https://www.wp.sg/the-workers-partys-perspective-on-brexit/?fbclid=IwAR3Bue TQesDuR-R5yWo6DwkJQMvDQ9rhqZnbXsA2ia0UpjWa60xSfDZKvq4. Accessed on 12 December 2020.

Change is constant. But it needs to be carefully managed. For a very small, multi-racial and sovereign nation, the pressures and fissures created by globalisation necessitate that change is stewarded very carefully so that a strong consensus emerges across society. Our engagement with globalisation and our competitiveness need to be balanced with inclusivity, social harmony and rootedness in order for a strong consensus to emerge. That would require a clear disassociation with demagogues and a permanent commitment to address globalisation's shortcomings. Because Singapore is not just a city. It is a country. It is all we have. It is our home.

Most people would find this statement not particularly controversial. Thum, however, took issue with it. Starting off by saying that the WP statement was "well meaning", he immediately then said it drew "incomplete conclusions from #Brexit." The last part of Thum's post read:

If the Worker's [sic] Party wishes to avoid Singaporean xenophobia of the sort that drove Brexit, it must fight for the alternative to the conservative and neoliberal status quo. That means formulating a coherent and comprehensive policy platform with a wide appeal that reconnects with disaffected citizens. It means fighting for reform of the system, arguing for ideas, and mobilising people to achieve one's ends, rather than implicitly accepting the existence of undemocratic institutions and rules which work against the people's stated preferences. It means fighting and campaigning to win elections, not merely to be the best loser. If the Worker's [sic] Party cannot do these things, it will remain irrelevant to Singaporean voters.

It is fair to say that many ordinary people would not understand the meaning of the "neoliberal status quo". Even among scholars, there is no consensus definition of what "neoliberalism" means.[51] However, Thum has invoked the term not infrequently. So, it's not clear how that would work if the WP is pushed towards a path of "arguing for ideas, and mobilising people to achieve one's ends".

In the lead-up to GE2020, Thum had been actively involved in interviewing politicians for *The Online Citizen*. But following the outcome of the election, where the WP came away with positive results, Thum was quiet for a protracted period. The WP's moderate politics as a prescription for parliamentary opposition in Singapore had proved effective when it was endorsed by the majority of the voters in Aljunied GRC, Hougang SMC, and Sengkang GRC. Thum, however, remained undeterred.

At a Progress Singapore Party (PSP) fundraiser on 1 October 2020 where he was invited as the keynote speaker, Thum spent five minutes of his speech assailing the WP. To summarise those five minutes: Thum upbraided WP chief Pritam Singh for not supporting the repeal of 377a; he derided WP MP Jamus Lim's proposal for a minimum wage because "it's technical, it's limited, it's about tweaking, making the policy correct"; and, he said that the "Workers' Party is not part of the solution, they're part of the problem". What the PSP leaders might have thought of this criticism of the WP is not entirely clear.[52]

---

51 See, for instance, Julie Rowlands and Shawn Rawolle, "Neoliberalism is Not a Theory of Everything: A Bourdeain Analysis of *Illusio* in Educational Research", *Critical Studies in Education*, Vol. 54, No. 13, 2013; Rajesh Venugopal, "Neoliberalism as Concept", *Economy and Society*, Vol. 44, No. 2, 2015; and, Ben Fine and Alfredo Saad-Filho, "Thirteen Things You Need to Know About Neoliberalism", *Critical Sociology*, Vol. 43, No. 4–5, 2017.

52 If one were to go online to search for the clip of Thum's PSP fundraiser speech there are two versions to be found. One version uploaded to the *New Naratif*'s YouTube channel carries the full remarks, including the criticism of the WP, whereas in a clip uploaded by the PSP the segment of Thum's speech on the WP has been carefully edited out.

By sheer coincidence, a few hours earlier on the same day that Thum spoke at the PSP fundraiser, I had given a presentation at an Institute of Policy Studies webinar on GE2020. It is worth reprising a small part of that speech:[53]

> *A British parliamentary saying goes as follows: "The opposition occupies the benches in front of you, but the enemy sits behind you." For the WP, the PAP is the opposition, but the real enemy constitutes a number of radicals in the hardcore anti-PAP element who are infected with the virus of delusion. One should remember that three decades ago Mr Chiam See Tong built up a politically moderate SDP only to see others in the party move it to a confrontational direction, destroying opposition chances for a generation. Already in this election, one activist claimed that Mr Chiam, when he was an MP, had been humiliated by the PAP. This was clearly an attempt to revise recent political history. This would have escaped most people's attention; but it came across as an attempt to create a false new narrative about the 1990s.*

Is that the answer to the question by *Rice Media*, "Who's afraid of PJ Thum?", which was posed earlier on? If it is, then it shows up the deception of the superficial PAP versus non-PAP binary choice which is constantly purveyed in online discourse. Another question to be asked is whether it is reasonable to think in terms of a possible continuum between the political events of Singapore during the 1990s and that which panned out in the subsequent two decades and will pan out in the third decade of the new millennium? Are there any lessons of

---

53 Derek da Cunha, "Conceptualising Political Power in Singapore Following the Pandemic, and Amidst the Virus of Delusion." Text of Presentation Delivered at the IPS Online Forum on GE2020, 1 October 2020, https://lkyspp.nus.edu.sg/docs/default-source/ips/dr-derek-da-cunha_ips-post-ge2020-online-forum-presentation-011020.pdf?sfvrsn=4dd34a0a_2. Accessed on 21 December 2020.

relevance, especially if one thinks in terms of political phenomena occurring in cycles?

Inferences to be drawn

Civil society activists might not in fact have much public support across a large part of Singapore society, even as they appeal to a narrow but vocal group of followers who are able to magnify their presence online. Though that might be true, the activists themselves cannot be ignored completely nor considered irrelevant. This is because they are given platforms — and, therefore, a figuratively large megaphone — to propagate their views. That has, in fact, been the case with the personalities referenced in the foregoing.

Having said that, civil society activists play a useful role in raising issues seldom publicly ventilated. Every society has a place for those who fight and advocate for the weak, the marginalised, the discriminated. This is as long as activists are aware that there are limitations to what they can achieve. Where the main point of contention arises is when dogmatic or ideological perspectives are articulated and passed off as fact and objective analysis. It seems that in the eyes of the activists, if other people do not subscribe to the values they espouse, then they are somehow considered deficient. If Singaporeans, particularly following Lee Kuan Yew's death, have become increasingly tired of one aspect of the PAP government, it is its tendency towards self-satisfaction, self-adulation, and self-reverence. Consequently, it is not clear that Singaporeans would then accept the same behaviour from those at the other end of the socio-political spectrum.

Decades ago, an Irish writer, in reviewing the work of the intellectual Aldous Huxley, was to observe, "He is at once the truly clever person and *the stupid person's idea of the clever person*; he is expected to be relentless, to administer intellectual shocks."[54] [Italics added.] The Digital Age seems tailor-made for those passing off personal opinions as serious analysis to their starstruck followers, whose idea of the clever person is someone who delivers bare assertions — i.e., evidence-free accounts — on socio-political phenomena confidently and eloquently.

Also, those who might wish to draw from history, to argue that in the 1950s Singapore was replete with activists who were to become politicians, might well be drawing on something taken out-of-context. The sovereign power in the Singapore of the 1950s was the United Kingdom. In the context of the colonial master beginning the process of departing the scene, where a vacuum was to emerge, there were any number of individuals who were out to enrich themselves from the spoils left behind by the colonialists. The politics of what was to become an independent Singapore thus started from a blank sheet where most political practitioners did not have prior practical experience with elected politics. It is therefore difficult for today's politicians to learn anything useful from a bygone era. In today's world, where high productivity and multi-tasking are expected of individuals, the electorate is exacting in what it looks out for in a politician. It should not be forgotten that the theme running through this chapter and others in this book remains a simple but abiding principle: that a politician should generally reflect what the broad swathe of the ground can accept and would be willing to accept. A politician should not attempt to run well ahead of the ground when the ground is not ready for such a move.

---

54 "Elizabeth Bowen on Huxley", in Donald Watt, ed., *Aldous Huxley*, (New York: Routledge, 1975), p. 275. Bowen's full remarks were:

Mr. Huxley has been the alarming young man for a long time, a sort of perpetual clever nephew who can be relied on to flutter the lunch party. Whatever will he say next? How does he think of those things? He has been deplored once or twice, but feeling is in his favor: he is steadily read. He is at once the truly clever person and the stupid person's idea of the clever person; he is expected to be relentless, to administer intellectual shocks.

Coming full circle, what was Raeesah Khan's experience during the one year following her election as an MP? She devoted much of her time to meeting with her constituents. She has also followed through on her interest as a civil society activist by delivering a substantive speech, as an adjournment motion in Parliament on 6 July 2021, on the subject of "Sexuality Education in Schools as the First Line of Defence Against Sexual Violence".[55] Two weeks later, Khan was interviewed by the online video portal *Something Private*, which bills itself as "A platform for Southeast Asian Women by Southeast Asian Women". The discission focused on issues of racism and sexual education.

Finally, at a parliamentary debate on 3 August 2021, on the motion, "Empowering Women", Khan brought up an anecdote alleging that, three years earlier, when she had accompanied a rape survivor to a police station, the police had mishandled the case. When asked to substantiate her remarks so that the incident could be properly investigated, she was unable or unwilling to do so. She said: "[I]t was three years ago and I do not wish to re-traumatise the person that I accompanied. But I have to say that these anecdotes are not isolated."[56] She also said that she had been unsuccessful in getting in touch with the victim.

Even ardent WP members, posting online, expressed some surprise that a serious matter had been brought up to Parliament but had not been substantiated. It ought to be said that the issues of interest to Khan have been ably advocated for by the civil society organisation AWARE, which has been at the forefront in raising public consciousness about matters related to gender equality and sexual violence. Politically, for a WP MP, one of just 10, to have a preoccupation with these same issues,

---

55 Parliament of Singapore, Matter Raised on Adjournment Motion, Raeesah Khan, *Sexuality Education in Schools as the First Line of Defence Against Sexual Violence*, https://sprs.parl.gov.sg/search/sprs3topic?reportid=matter-adj-1680. Accessed on 20 July 2021.

56 Quoted in "WP MP's allegations of police mishandling of sexual assault case are serious, Desmond Tan", *The Straits Times*, 3 August 2021.

might have the inadvertent effect of typecasting that MP as a social justice warrior. That might amount to a slight misalignment with how the WP of Low Thia Khiang and Pritam Singh had re-anchored the party to the political centre-ground. Some might say that this will not adversely impact the WP and that it is in fact no bad thing for one member of the parliamentary party to be more progressive in leanings. To be certain, that is a valid school of thought. How that will pan out electorally remains to be seen.

CHAPTER 6

The WP's Winning Formula: Parallels with the UK's
New Labour and the Median Voter Theorem

ne of the main criticisms levelled at the Workers' Party (WP)
under the leadership of Low Thia Khiang and, subsequently,
Pritam Singh, has been that the party assumed a too moderate,
if not timid, stance in its opposition to the People's Action Party (PAP).
This criticism was made more acute because it was contrasted with the
stance adopted by the previous WP Secretary-General, J.B. Jeyaretnam,
who was an implacable opponent of the PAP and had been lionised by
hardcore opposition supporters. From the early 2000s, and especially
after the WP breakthrough at GE2011, unflattering things were said
about the WP in online discussions. These included allegations that the
WP was merely the "PAP B team", or that the WP was "PAP-lite". These
smears were the product of fringe elements who amplified their voice
online. Shortly after GE2011, when a journalist approached Low to
question whether the WP's moderate approach to opposition would be
continued, he replied saying, words to the effect, that he was aware of
online criticism of the party but that the voters liked the WP's brand
of opposition. Low was not wrong; he was merely reflecting ground
sentiment. Singh has provided a continuum to Low's approach to
opposition. In fact, Singh can be said to be a protégé of Low. Singh's
thinking on the role of a parliamentary opposition, especially in terms
of what works for the WP politically and how the party can make a
meaningful contribution to Singapore, is a direct manifestation of Low's
political philosophy.

This chapter will examine the WP's challenges and prospects after
its second breakthrough at GE2020. But before delving into that, it is
worthwhile attempting to understand whether there is something

innately unusual about the WP's political positioning in relation to the ruling party. Here, the UK's Labour Party is a useful basis for comparative assessment and analysis. This is because left-of-centre parties tend to have similar experiences in their opposition to right-of-centre parties or conservative forces. It is commonly accepted that the latter have achieved some unity of purpose by being able to keep their eye firmly on the prize — power. Whereas, those on the left tend to be more divided. As observed by one writer:[1]

The organic unity of the right is bound by the common urge for private profit that lures every individual to the siren's song of easy money that drives him/her to join the cut-throat competition to scramble up the ladder of upward mobility to make good. The agenda of the left on the other hand is addressed to the need for collective action (instead of individual efforts for self-achievement) to bring about equality in society. But it is here that the constituency is fragmented by conflicting and divergent interests — perpetually changing — stemming from differences in class positions and socio-religious origins of their components...

It should be stated that this chapter is not an exercise in *whataboutism*. Instead, it is an exercise in laying bare certain phenomena related to political parties, their ideologies, and their approach to contesting elections, that are universal. To that extent, the situation with the WP in the framework of the Singapore political landscape post-2001 is not unique. The chapter points out inaccurate perceptions held by some Singaporeans on a number of specific issues of political significance, which continues to be perpetuated as wholly false narratives. To that extent, context is important before engaging in an analysis of how the WP can consolidate and expand on its GE2020 gains.

---

1 Sumanta Banerjee, "Why is the Left More Divided than the Right?" *Economic and Political Weekly*, Vol. 48, No. 38, 21 September 2013, p. 16.

Labour had cycles with left-wing radicalism and moderation

No exact or direct parallels can be drawn between the UK Labour Party and the WP. In contrast to the WP, the Labour Party is mammoth in historical terms, in its strength (membership and material resources), and the fact that it has been in government quite a number of times since its founding in February 1900. On the other hand, the WP has never even come close to being in government. Yet, there is one uncanny parallel between the two: it revolves around where and how a political party should position itself in relation to the electorate. The UK Conservative Party, just like the PAP, has been considered the natural party of government. This was particularly so for much of the 60 years from the end of World War I till 1979. That six-decade period was punctuated by just a few Labour governments. And, for the 18 years from 1979 till 1997, Labour was consigned to the political wilderness. The popularity of the Conservatives under Margaret Thatcher during the 1980s was only part of the reason for this; Labour being racked with internal squabbling centred on entrism by left-wing elements who were identified as a Trotskyist Militant Tendency, entrenched Labour further in the political wilderness.[2] By the late 1980s, after much effort, Labour was to rid itself of left-wing elements. But it had to take the tenure of three Labour leaders — Neil Kinnock, John Smith, and Tony Blair — to move the party more towards the centre-ground of British politics before Labour was to become electable again, with its landslide victory at the May 1997 general election. The party had been transformed to New Labour. As with Labour, a similar metamorphosis occurred with the WP. Not long after Jeyaretnam was succeeded by Low as leader of the WP in 2001, some implacable anti-PAP elements inhabiting the online world, unhappy at Low's shift of the party from being a hard-line to a moderate opponent of the PAP, characterised the approach as "WP Baru" or New WP.

2 Eric Shaw, "The Labour Party and the Militant Tendency", *Parliamentary Affairs*, Vol. 42, No. 2, April 1989, p. 180.

In economic policy, New Labour was to endorse the market mechanism and promote partnership with the private sector, and though "there remained a social democratic element, albeit watered down" in Labour's platform, "it was based on redistribution and interventionism".[3] In a nutshell, Blair's New Labour was viewed as adopting Thatcher's neoliberal economic policies.[4] In fact, Thatcher herself in 2002 (i.e., 12 years after she had left office), when asked what was her greatest achievement, replied: "Tony Blair and New Labour. We forced our opponents to change their minds."[5] Even before Blair became prime minister in 1997, his detractors were already deriding New Labour as "Tory-lite".[6] The New Labour project came to an end with the defeat of the government of Gordon Brown at the 2010 general election. Under the leadership of Ed Miliband, Labour was to lose the 2015 general election. Two years later, at the 2017 election, Labour, under Jeremy Corbyn, was defeated again but Corbyn surprised his critics by doing better than expected. Consequently, he was to lead Labour into the 2019 election. This time the party suffered its worst defeat since 1935. That denouement was attributed primarily to Corbyn, who had variously been described as "far-left", "hard-left" or "ultra-leftist".[7] In other words,

---

3 Mark Wickham-Jones, "Signalling Credibility: Electoral Strategy and New Labour in Britain", *Political Science Quarterly*, Vol. 120, No. 4, (Winter), 2005, p. 671.

4 See Sonja Cecar, *Blatcherism: How Much Thatcherism is in Blairism*, (VDM Verlag Dr. Mueller, 2007); and, Amir Ali, *South Asian Islam and British Multiculturalism*, (London: Routledge, 2016), p. 46.

5 Quoted in Oleg Komlik, "Thatcher's greatest achievement", *Economic Sociology & Political Economy*, 19 March 2018, https://economicsociology.org/2018/03/19/thatcherisms-greatest-achievement/. Accessed on 10 January 2021.

6 "British Labour Party wins landslide, Major concedes", *The Baltimore Sun*, 2 May 1997.

7 Andrea Whittle, "Making Sense of the Rise and Fall of Jeremy Corbyn: Towards an Ambiguity-Centred Perspective on Leadership", *Leadership*, 2020, Vol. 17, No. 4, first published online 23 November 2020, Issue published 1 August 2021, pp. 13–14, 19; and, John McTernan, "Labour is Not a Socialist Party — and It Has Never Been", *Prospect*, 11 March 2016, https://www.prospectmagazine.co.uk/politics/labour-is-not-a-socialist-party. Accessed on 10 January 2021.

it took two years — between 2017 and 2019 — for the voters to be fully acquainted with Corbyn. He had been an echo of what Labour was in the 1980s. A younger generation, who had joined the party and was enamoured of Corbyn, simply did not know about that earlier history nor was that generation interested in knowing about it. The more centrist Keir Starmer succeeded Corbyn as Labour leader. And, it did not take long for him to face the charge from hard-left elements of being Tory-lite.[8]

Lessons for the WP from Labour's experience

The foregoing, distilling the UK Labour Party's grappling with ideological issues, has its lessons for the WP. Internally, after the departure of Jeyaretnam from the WP in 2001, the party membership and the party's supporters had embraced the pragmatic approach to opposition adopted by Low. That, however, was to lead to online vitriolic attacks against the party. All the attacks, including the smearing of the party as the "PAP B team", "PAP-lite", or the "wayang party",[9] did not originate from the PAP. Their provenance was largely from those who adhered to a radical alternative to the PAP. They appeared to be represented by those who either held personal grievances against the Establishment or expressed fealty to the previous leader (Jeyaretnam). To these individuals, voters who had merely moderate opposition leanings were dismissed as "pretend opposition supporters".

---

8 See, for example, "Labour meltdown: 'Pathetic' Keir Starmer dubbed 'Tory-lite' in furious online backlash", *Express*, 1 May 2020, https://www.express.co.uk/news/uk/1275928/Labour-Party-news-Keir-Starmer-update-coronavirus-UK-lockdown. Accessed on 10 January 2020; and, "Keir Starmer's 'new management' will cost Labour minority votes. Does he care?" *The Guardian*, 27 September 2020, https://www.theguardian.com/commentisfree/2020/sep/27/keir-starmer-labour-minority-votes-red-wall-tory. Accessed on 10 January 2021.

9 In Singlish, "wayang" refers to someone acting or being fake.

The smearing of the WP as PAP-lite was to appear with increasing frequency in the two years prior to GE2020, and was largely manifested as comments left to threads on Facebook posts and news stories, giving them quite a reach. The record on this issue needs to be set straight because it is wholly incorrect for anyone to suggest that it was Minister Vivian Balakrishnan who had first levelled that charge when he had an exchange with the WP's Jamus Lim at the GE2020 campaign debate, telecast live on 1 July 2020. In fact, at the time of the WP's 60th anniversary celebrations in 2017, *The Straits Times* had already reported that "by taking a moderate stance, the WP has been dismissed by some opposition supporters as being 'PAP-lite'."[10] References to the WP as PAP-lite go back even earlier and can be found on blogs not known to be ideologically sympathetic to the PAP.[11] Thus, from the evidence, the term "PAP-lite" was invented by radical elements on the leftward side of the political spectrum. They also included individuals who were on the margins of Singapore society. These individuals possessed an internet connection and social media accounts, which they employed to post online comments railing at anyone who was either not in the same situation as themselves or did not empathise fully with them.

The foregoing reflects the point that has been made elsewhere in this book — that the so-called "opposition" is not monolithic. The hardcore anti-WP elements have argued that it was pointless to vote for the WP, as their allegation was that the WP represented a "fake opposition".

10　"It's time for the Workers' Party to be more than a check and balance", *The Straits Times*, 29 October 2017, https://www.straitstimes.com/politics/its-time-to-be-more-than-a-check-and-balance. Accessed on 10 January 2021.

11　See, for instance, the comment left by Fnhh to the story "General election 2015: Huge win for PAP signals stasis", *Yawning Bread*, 12 September 2015, https://yawningbread.wordpress.com/2015/09/12/general-election-2015-huge-win-for-pap-signals-stasis/. Accessed on 10 January 2021; and, the comment by sushi88, to the thread "General Election 2015", 4 September 2015, *Kiasu Parents*, https://www.kiasuparents.com/kiasu/forum/viewtopic.php?t=83218&start=5100. Accessed on 10 January 2021.

As with the UK Labour Party watering down and jettisoning altogether, previous policy positions to become more electable,[12] so too was the approach of the WP after Jeyaretnam's tenure as Secretary-General of the party. In an interview with the media in October 2007, Low set out his views as an elected servant of the people:[13]

The term opposition is a legacy of the Western parliamentary system, and I have never believed that an opposition party should oppose for the sake of opposing or to shoot one's mouth off.

Politics should be about responsible politics. The opposition should be a watchdog, not a mad dog. That should be the path for a political party.

At the time, Low's reference to "a mad dog" was taken by some netizens as an allusion to either Jeyaretnam or the Singapore Democratic Party's (SDP's) Chee Soon Juan, or both.[14] However, it is unclear whether Low was making such a reference. In any event, his remarks foreshadowed a significant change in approach by the WP. The party was to contest GE2011 by assuming a watchdog role when the party said during the election that it wanted to be a "co-driver" to the PAP. Without lofty ambitions, but in a limited way, and by providing a slate of candidates

---

12 That is set out cogently in Michael Temple, "New Labour's Third Way: Pragmatism and Governance", *The British Journal of Politics and International Relations*, Vol. 2, No. 3, 2000. See, also, Eugenio Bagiani, "Review Essay: Ideology and the Making of New Labours", *International Labor and Working-Class History*, No. 56, (Fall 1999), p. 103.

13 "WP chief: 377A debate shows more openness", *AsiaOne*, 31 October 2007, https://www.asiaone.com/print/News/AsiaOne%2BNews/Singapore/Story/A1Story20071031-33469.html. Accessed on 10 January 2021.

14 Gopalan Nair, a former WP member and ardent supporter of J. B. Jeyaretnam, who now lives in exile in the United States, had suggested that the "mad dog" reference might be in relation to the SDP. See, "Singapore. Low Thia Khiang is a let down for the cause of democracy", *Singapore Dissident*, 31 October 2007, http://singaporedissident.blogspot.com/2007/10/singapore-low-thia-khiang-is-let-down.html. Accessed on 10 January 2021.

which would appeal to voters, all that was enough for the WP to make a breakthrough by taking a group representation constituency (GRC), Aljunied, from the PAP at that election.

At GE2015, the WP came up with the slogan of a "Rational, Responsible and Respectable" party. There is no fourth R — no Radical. The WP has no radical agenda.[15] The party hoped to consolidate and expand its parliamentary presence. But it could not surmount a bigger challenge at GE2015. That election became mostly about the legacy of Lee Kuan Yew, who had died some six months earlier, on 23 March, resulting in the PAP benefiting at the polls from an "LKY effect".[16] Undaunted, the WP continued to refer to itself and its approach to opposition as "rational, responsible and respectable" as it moved towards the next parliamentary general election.[17] The employment of this phrase was reiterated by the WP during the actual GE2020 campaign itself.[18] The WP's brand of opposition, undergirded by a party willing to do hard work to grind out, house-by-house, support for itself brought it positive results with a second GRC falling into the party's column.

---

15 Derek da Cunha, "Conceptualising Political Power in Singapore Following the Pandemic Election, and Amidst the Virus of Delusion". Text of Presentation Delivered at the IPS Online Forum on GE2020, 1 October 2020, https://lkyspp.nus.edu.sg/docs/default-source/ips/dr-derek-da-cunha_ips-post-ge2020-online-forum-presentation-011020.pdf?sfvrsn=4dd34a0a_2

16 "PAP won GE2015 before campaign began: Polling firm Blackbox Research", *The Straits Times*, 5 February 2016, https://www.straitstimes.com/politics/pap-won-ge2015-before-campaign-began-polling-firm-blackbox-research. Accessed on 19 February 2021.

17 "WP will remain rational and responsible, says new chief Pritam Singh", *Today*, 8 April 2018, https://www.todayonline.com/singapore/pritam-singh-takes-over-low-thia-khiang-new-wp-secretary-general. Accessed on 19 February 2021.

18 See "GE2020: Votes for the Workers' Party will count in 3 ways, says Pritam Singh", *CNA*, 2 July 2020, https://www.channelnewsasia.com/news/singapore/ge2020-votes-for-workers-party-will-count-in-3-ways-pritam-singh-12895018. Accessed on 19 February 2021.

It is not possible to quantify the hardcore anti-PAP elements who have smeared the WP as PAP-lite or other derogatory terms, with those elements insinuating that the party was not fully committed in its opposition to the PAP. Any figure would be a mere guess. But even if that hardcore anti-PAP element amounted to a relatively small segment of the electorate, it magnified itself online to assume a disproportionate voice.

Most Singaporean voters who are considered sympathetic to the notion that Singapore needs a check and balance on the PAP's powers, and would look to the WP as serving that role, would consider the hardcore anti-WP elements irrational. In fact, if one were to view the issue in purely ideological terms, there is rationality to these anti-PAP/anti-WP elements.[19] These elements subscribe to the views espoused by some civil society activists (in Chapter 5) that the WP, under Low and Singh, not merely kept in place, but in fact shored-up, what the activists said were anti-democratic structures in Singapore. Both Low and Singh have been aware of this criticism which, potentially, could move votes against the WP. However, they have also been aware that the WP's positioning close to the centre-ground allows the party to gain more votes than it might lose.

J.B. Jeyaretnam would have dismissed the WP's gains with derision

It would be accurate to say that J.B. Jeyaretnam (JBJ) had been the symbol of opposition to the PAP during the 1980s and 1990s. Notwithstanding his acrimonious departure from the WP in 2001, many members of the party had tended to maintain a dignified and respectful attitude towards him in recognition of his impact as an

---

19 This is stating the matter by way of explanation and is in no way sympathising with that ideological approach.

opposition icon in Singapore.[20] They would not publicly utter any criticism of him.[21] But JBJ never reciprocated and continued to criticise the party with which he had been so closely associated.

In *Breakthrough*, JBJ was quoted at length about his intentions in 2007 to establish a new party, which was to become the Reform Party. He was strident in saying that his new party would have as its main "objective a complete change in the way this country is run. No tinkering!"[22] And, that any Singaporean who "is happy with the current system in Singapore" should not approach him but "Go and see Mr Chiam See Tong or Low Thia Khiang who are happy with the system."[23] Subsequent to the publication of the book, another set of remarks by JBJ was stumbled upon. This was a video interview, possibly the very last one JBJ gave, conducted by Hugo Restall (HR), the Editor of the *Far Eastern Economic Review*. The following are key extracts:[24]

HR: Can you tell me a little about the platform of your new party? How does this differ from the Workers' Party that you were associated with for so long?

JBJ: Well, it differs substantially. Even when I was in the Workers' Party, after I was first elected to Parliament in 1981, I then voiced my complete dissatisfaction with the way Singapore was being run or managed by the

---

20 At the time of writing, in August 2021, this has not changed.

21 For political reasons, members of the WP might not publicly agree with this section of the chapter even if privately they acknowledge that it is an honest account of what has transpired over the years.

22 Quoted in Derek da Cunha, *Breakthrough: Roadmap for Singapore's Political Future*, (Singapore: Institute of Policy Studies and Straits Times Press, 2012), p. 100.

23 Ibid.

24 The actual date of this interview is uncertain, but it took place in 2008, likely just weeks before JBJ's passing on 30 September of that year. See, "JBJ Interview", Interview between JBJ and FEER Editor Hugo Restall in 2008, YouTube, 19 March 2009, https://www.youtube.com/watch?v=djutoHKXxRg&t=15s. Accessed on 12 March 2021.

PAP. And, I said the system had to go, and a new system had to come into place. And that's why Lee [Kuan Yew] said I had to be destroyed, more than once. But, er, the Workers' Party, the other members of the Council, particularly two or three of them, weren't very happy about, you know, my stance. And, for other reasons as well, I quit the Workers' Party.

HR: How were they unhappy with your stance?

JBJ: Well, even today, you know, they take the attitude that the system is alright. The present system. For me, it isn't alright. They take the [attitude] that all is needed is a bit of little improvement here and there… [T]o me it's got to be a clean operation.

HR: So, they are more like the docile opposition Parliament members who are often praised by the PAP?

JBJ: That's right, yes! (Chuckles.) You said it! That's why Lee has said they will accept Low Thia Khiang and Chiam See Tong. And, I think, he has said once or twice that they are not against the system, whereas Jeyaretnam is, and that's why Jeyaretnam has to be destroyed. So, after I came out of bankruptcy, I decided to form a new party.

Putting aside the fact that Restall had goaded JBJ into a particular answer, those netizens who keep claiming that JBJ would have been proud of the WP's breakthroughs at GE2011 and GE2020 appear to have a tenuous grasp on reality. But there has been a noticeable tendency towards this kind of mythologising of political history in Singapore. Low Thia Khiang, who had been widely considered one of the most hard-working constituency Members of Parliament (MPs), was subjected to JBJ's derisive laughter as JBJ insisted that there should be a thorough overhaul to "the system" which, in JBJ's view, Low was happy with. In JBJ's parlance, "it's got to be a clean operation". Apparently, the "clean operation" to the system would not include JBJ's second son, Philip, who had quite a number of years earlier already become a prominent member of the Singapore Establishment. Among the younger Jeyaretnam's achievements was his elevation in the ranks of Singapore's legal fraternity where, in 2003, he was appointed a Senior Counsel and, between 2004 and 2007, was president of the Law Society. He was also to have other Establishment appointments that predated his father's death by a few years.[25] JBJ had nothing negative to say about his son's conscious decision to actively involve himself with the Establishment.

A second part of JBJ's interview with Restall is worth noting. When asked about what he thought of the campaign of civil disobedience launched by the SDP's Chee against the government (which Chee quietly abandoned, or suspended, in 2009), he answered:[26]

> *I myself am not against it. But, I said, I didn't think the time has yet come for that. Before you can effectively, you know, launch a disobedience you've got to educate the people. You've got to get them ready to participate in it. And that is just not possible today in Singapore because of the fear that grips Singaporeans. They say, yes alright, if we come and participate in this*

---

25 In a media interview in 2009, about a year after his father's death, Philip Jeyaretnam, when told that some Singaporeans believed that he (Philip) had been co-opted by the Establishment replied: "The reason for this reaction stems from an identification of the state with a particular political party. And that is wrong. The breakthrough which Singapore needs to make is to have an establishment which encompasses the full range of political opinions within the constitutional set-up of Singapore." Quoted in "The rise and rise of Philip Jeyaretnam", *The Straits Times*, 4 December 2009. The problem with this response, and the thinking behind it, is that the public's conflation of the state and the PAP has partly been due to decades of continuous rule by the PAP and what has been perceived by some as the blurring of lines between the two by Lee Kuan Yew. It is a conflation held by many, not least among those in intellectual circles. See, for instance, the article by Terence Chong, "Embodying Society's Best: Hegel and the Singapore State", *Journal of Contemporary Asia*, Vol. 36, No. 3, 2006. And, as asserted by another writer, "Under his [Lee Kuan Yew's] tutelage, it is true that party and government machinery have been interlocked to a remarkable degree..." James Minchin, *No Man is an Island: A Study of Lee Kuan Yew*, (Sydney: Allen & Unwin, 1986), p. 1.

26 "JBJ Interview", op. cit.

civil disobedience, what is going to happen to us? Aren't we all going to be arrested and carted off to the courts, and then put into prison? So, hmm, that is the main stumbling block to launching any civil disobedience campaign in Singapore. We've got to educate the people, and this is what, as I said twice over the press conferences, you know, we've got to educate Singaporeans of what they're able to do, you see. A lot of them are completely ignorant or oblivious of what they as citizens can do in Singapore. You see, I get the message all the time, "We can't do anything. We can't do anything." I say, "That's nonsense." I mean, if the people can't do anything then what's going happen to the country?

The hectoring tone barely disguised the circular reasoning. JBJ said Singaporeans were fearful to participate in something like civil disobedience but he still saw a place for it. All that was required was for Singaporeans to be educated, and not left "ignorant or oblivious". There was no explanation as to how Singaporeans could become educated. Much of JBJ's statements during the time he was a politician tended to be of such a nature. He placed great store on form. As an illustration, the initial request he made when he entered Parliament after the October 1981 Anson by-election was that — as the first opposition MP in the House in many years — he should sit by himself on the opposition benches, holding forth against the PAP, whose MPs would all have to crowd on the government benches.[27] The reply he got was that he would get a seat in the House, but not a special seat. Underlying this tendency to grandstand was the notion that, in his rhetoric and conduct, JBJ felt that he was somehow the benchmark of what amounted to a true opponent of the PAP. Anyone whom he deemed as not being in-line with his combative philosophy and demeanour towards the PAP and the broader Establishment was somehow deficient.

---

27 This would mirror the format of the UK's House of Commons.

A person who engaged in combative politics against the might of the PAP would have gotten a sharp response visited on him/her. And so that proved to be the case for JBJ over a three-decade timespan. Apart from dealing with lawsuits from PAP leaders, JBJ was also referred to Parliament's Committee of Privileges on four occasions for saying things out of turn.[28] In one of those occasions he was fined $25,000 for the offence of contempt of the Committee of Privileges and of Parliament.[29] This illustrates a simple point: that the notion of parliamentary privilege and immunity is not, as some seem to believe, the broad shield by which a parliamentarian can hide behind to do and say things without consequences.[30] In fact, the notion of unfettered parliamentary privilege and immunity, which some in Singapore tend to believe in, is a chimera.[31] Yet, there are still Singaporean netizens who would consider the SDP's Chee and the Peoples Voice Lim Tean

---

28 "When politicians cross the line", *The Straits Times*, 11 March 2018, https://www. straitstimes.com/politics/when-politicians-cross-the-line. Accessed on 12 March 2021.

29 *Committee of Privileges* (Second Report) (Paper Parl. 4 of 1987), *Official Reports — Parliamentary Debates (Hansard)*, https://sprs.parl.gov.sg/search/topic?reportid=007_19870127_S0003_T0006. Accessed on 12 March 2021.

30 In a consultation paper presented to the UK House of Commons in April 2012, it was observed: "Parliamentary privilege is an often misunderstood concept. It is not helped by its name; the connotations of the word 'privilege' are unfortunate, as it is associated with special treatment for individuals. The term 'parliamentary privilege' might superficially imply, to those not familiar with it, that there are special rights or protections for parliamentarians, perhaps even to the extent that MPs and peers are 'above the law'." It goes on to state that, "Parliamentary privilege is part of the law, rather than something which puts MPs or peers above the law." *Parliamentary Privilege*, Presented to Parliament by the Leader of the House of Commons and Lord Privy Seal by Command of Her Majesty, April 2012, https://assets.publishing. service.gov.uk/government/uploads/system/uploads/attachment_data/file/79390/consultation.pdf. Accessed on 12 March 2021.

31 The ambit of parliamentary privilege and immunity continues to be debated in the UK. A 2013 report by a Joint Committee of the House of Lords and House of Commons suggested that parliamentary privilege and immunity tended to evolve and, therefore, it disagreed with the notion of "codifying parliamentary privilege as a whole". House of Lords and House of Commons, *Parliamentary Privilege: Report of Session 2013–2014*, p. 69, https://publications.parliament.uk/pa/jt201314/jtselect/jtprivi/30/30.pdf. Accessed on 12 March 2012.

as worthy successors to JBJ in Parliament. Why? Because both are known for their sharp rhetoric and apparent fearlessness. To netizens, Chee and Lim would somehow terrify the PAP because they would ask the tough and embarrassing questions.

It can be said that JBJ's hard-line, unvarnished approach to opposition was, ultimately, to be discredited by the voters themselves. Under his 30-year watch as Secretary-General of the WP (1971–2001), the party secured just one fully elected seat in Parliament at any one time. On the other hand, under Low's leadership, the WP took a decade (2001–2011) to secure six fully elected parliamentary seats. At GE2020, the WP, with its credentials for moderation established, grew that number to 10.

Notwithstanding the above realities, one still sees netizens posting comments that they "miss him", in reference to JBJ. It seems that what they miss, from another era, is JBJ's fiery rhetoric and standing up to Lee Kuan Yew, which had given some momentary psychological relief from their own circumstances. Many of those who keep saying that they "miss him" were not personally acquainted with him.[32] They only knew him at a distance — in witnessing his fiery speeches at election rallies or having passed by him at Raffles Place or in front of Centrepoint Shopping Centre where he could regularly be found hawking his book,

---

32 I first met JBJ on 13 September 1991 when he, I, Tan Cheng Bock and Chiam See Tong were panel speakers at a National University of Singapore Society forum on the general election held two weeks earlier, on 31 August 1991. At that forum I had praised both Tan and Chiam as "voices of decency and rationality in Singapore politics today". My remarks appeared to offend JBJ because he had been excluded from them. After the forum, the then *Asiaweek* and later *Straits Times* correspondent Roger Mitton and I exchanged notes. I told him that JBJ was furious at my remarks, but Mitton told me not to worry as the audience knew that the remarks were constructed in that way because Tan and Chiam were elected MPs, and JBJ was at that stage out of Parliament. Throughout the 1990s I would regularly bump into JBJ at diplomatic functions where he would cut an isolated figure. As such, I would go up to him to keep him company and we would have conversations centred on the politics of the day.

The Hatchet Man of Singapore, while he thundered,[33] "Make it right for Singapore!"

It would be appropriate to quote from what JBJ's son, Philip, had publicly said of his late father's approach to politics. This was from an interview in August 2019:[34]

[T]hat was the life he chose. And in a way he relished the battle because he believed in what he was doing. And so actually that's a life which is well lived. He lived a hard but I think very fulfilling life... He never just coasted, he never rested, right? He was always trying to achieve something he believed in.

And I think I've imbibed some of that from him. I think we are here to do our best within the limited time that we have, to do things that we find purposeful.

The WP post-JBJ is not a party that turns on the vision of one person. The WP under the leadership of Low and, subsequently, Singh, has been a party based on constructive politics — taking into account a realistic understanding of the structural challenges facing any opponent of the governing party. Those challenges then prod the party leadership to formulate the appropriate tone and approach to opposition. Further, much of the WP's policies, as reflected in its 2020 election manifesto, are derived from feedback given to the party by ordinary Singaporeans. In other words, today's WP, which operates by having its parliamentarians maintain a near-continuous presence on the ground, is guided largely by what most Singaporeans are prepared to accept.

33 J.B. Jeyaretnam, *The Hatchet Man of Singapore*, (Singapore: Jeya Publishers, 2003).

34 Quoted in "Lunch with Sumiko: Philip Jeyaretnam on work, public service, politics and life with his late father", *The Sunday Times*, 4 August 2019, https://www. straitstimes.com/singapore/a-life-in-chapters. Accessed on 12 March 2021.

Will the WP view political power like a priceless Ming vase?

If longevity is the yardstick of success, then the New Labour project under Blair was the most successful of all the UK's Labour governments, stretching for 13 years, from 1997 to 2010. But if success is defined as a lasting positive impact on millions of ordinary people, then Clement Attlee's post-war Labour government which introduced the National Health Service, would be accorded that accolade. Given the fact that the WP is not in any position to form a government in the near term, realistically what it can hope to achieve is to have longevity as the primary parliamentary opposition. And, through growing its presence in Parliament, the WP can temper PAP policies, compelling the ruling party to be more responsive to the concerns from the ground. In other words, by proxy, the WP can gain ownership of the government's policies. Through growing its parliamentary presence, the WP can exert enough pressure on the ruling party to force it to make policy compromises that benefit materially an increasingly larger pool of Singaporeans.

And, a major contention here, is that centripetal forces within the Singapore electorate over the span of at least two decades have been exerting an influence in prompting the WP to re-position itself in the political spectrum. This then turns on the concept of the Median Voter Theorem, which will be analysed shortly.

At a broader level, it could be said that the WP's attitude to political power is not dissimilar to that held by Blair. According to his mentor, Liberal Democrat peer Roy Jenkins, Blair's attitude to political power was akin to a "museum curator carrying a priceless Ming vase across a slippery floor, desperate not to drop it".[35] In more down-to-earth terms what this means is being cautious in keeping a focus on the main issues

---

35 Paraphrased in Andrew Adonis, "Tony Blair and Europe: Shattering the Ming Vase", *Prospect*, 11 November 2017, https://www.prospectmagazine.co.uk/politics/tony-blair-and-europe-shattering-the-ming-vase. Accessed on 16 January 2021.

that affect the majority of the voting public. It means not being embroiled with what would be considered as matters of marginal concern to most voters. This cautious approach operates at two levels: at the level of macro policy; and, at the level of constituency outreach. The optics would be of significance at the macro policy level, whereas at the constituency outreach level both the optics and substance matter.

The efficaciousness of the Median Voter Theorem

Voters in the middle-ground, which also includes moderate PAP voters, are key to the WP's success. That then throws a spotlight on the Median Voter Theorem. The theorem demonstrates how a dominant political party, including in a state with an authoritarian-leaning regime, would feel pressured by opponents who are increasingly popular with the electorate, to move away from perceived policy extremes and towards the centre.[36] As implied by the word "median", the theorem is focused on voters whose political inclinations are fairly centrist and not anchored to any noticeable degree away from the political centre. Consequently, the median voter is elevated in significance when the political landscape assumes a competitiveness not previously apparent between two political parties. In that connection, the observation has been made that "… higher electoral competitiveness incentivizes incumbent governments to *moderate* their policy positions so that they better align with that of the median voter and thus appeal to a larger portion of the electorate."[37] [Italics in the original.]

---

36 See, for instance, Charles K. Rowley, "The Relevance of the Median Voter Theorem", *Journal of Institutional and Theoretical Economics*, March 1984; and, Torben Iversen and Max Goplerud, "Redistribution Without a Median Voter: Models of Multidimensional Politics", *Annual Review of Political Science*, Vol. 21, 2018.

37 Axel Cronert and Pär Nyman, "Electoral Opportunism: Disentangling Myopia and Moderation", American Political Science Association, 9 February 2021, *APSA Preprints*. doi: 10.33774/apsa-2021-s7h95, p. 5.

By extension, it could be said that, through its political positioning, the WP reflects the median voters as a collective and would, in and of itself, be considered the median party in the Singapore Parliament. Evidence for this appeared to emerge at a marathon parliamentary debate on 14 September 2021 on the issue of jobs for Singaporeans; Singapore's foreign talent policy; and, the country's free trade agreements, specifically the Comprehensive Economic Cooperation Agreement with India. At the end of that debate, the bloc of WP MPs voted against two motions, one by the government and, the other, by the Progress Singapore Party,[38] because the WP's amendments to both motions, which would have provided more nuance and, thus, be in-line with WP policy, could not be carried. This might be said to be the clearest manifestation of the WP as the median party in Parliament, reinforcing a symbiosis between the median voter and the WP's positioning towards the centre-ground. As set out in one scholarly article:[39]

If the parliamentary median is the choice of the median elector, the link is made between majority electoral preferences and what goes on in the legislature, where the median party has a controlling influence... That influence should show up in a close relationship between the parliamentary median party policy positions and the government policy positions.

A case can be made out that, as a consequence of the WP's breakthrough in taking a GRC at GE2011, the PAP government was compelled to extend more generous social welfare and other benefits to voters post-GE2011. Inter alia, these benefits included the Pioneer

---

38 "Robust debate in Parliament over foreign competition in job market", *The Straits Times*, 15 September 2021.

39 Michael D. McDonald, Silvia M. Mendes and Ian Budge, "What are Elections for? Conferring the Median Mandate", *British Journal of Political Science*, Vol. 34, No. 1, January 2004, p. 2.

Generation Package, introduced in 2014, which was presented to the electorate in terms of honouring the contribution to Singapore of those citizens born before 1950.[40]

The WP's Jamus Lim posted a comment on the Median Voter Theorem on his Facebook page on 23 January 2021 in the context of an interaction he and his volunteers had with constituents:

One couple we spoke to thanked us for speaking up on behalf of Singaporeans. They shared their belief that the presence of an opposition in parliament makes a difference to the policies that the government rolls out.

As someone who has studied the issue from an academic perspective, I couldn't agree more. This point — that in the presence of two parties, the policies proposed tend to converge close to the middle — is known as the Median Voter Theorem, and it is supported by a large body of research, both in terms of political science theory, as well as empirical evidence from around the world.

And from a practical perspective, we do observe a certain responsiveness by the government to the points we raise in Parliament, if they deem our arguments of merit. Since we believe we make our case on behalf of important — and perhaps neglected — segments of society, we ultimately see this as a positive development, both for our country and our democracy.

The Median Voter Theorem and, the contention, that it has had practical effect in Singapore, politically since GE2011 following the WP's first GRC breakthrough, would support the notion that displacing the PAP government is not the only available option to achieving political objectives. This is from the point of view of both the WP and a sizeable segment of the Singapore electorate. It could be argued that

---

40 They had to become Singapore citizens before 31 December 1986 to qualify for the Package.

much of the electorate accepts the basic framework of governance in Singapore, but that it wants that framework tweaked and to have policies modified so that they would be more responsive to the concerns of ordinary folk. The inescapable inference to be drawn is that "… to the extent that democracy is about aggregating exogenous preferences into a collective decision, anything that brings policy closer to the median voter would almost by definition be a desirable feature."[41] The median voter in Singapore is given agency by virtue of the fact that the WP facilitates proximity voting (referenced in Chapter 1) — i.e., the WP is viewed as the most proximate and acceptable choice to many voters.

The WP ecosystem: How the party gains support at the localised level

Any expansion of political influence tends to start from the ground with constituency outreach efforts. In that connection, the WP has methodically been growing its own ecosystem in a part of the eastern half of the island. Aljunied GRC and Hougang single-member constituency (SMC) had formed the bedrock of this ecosystem since 2011. Punggol East, when it was an SMC was, briefly, between 2013 and 2015, part of that ecosystem as well, before it was re-captured by the PAP at GE2015. Punggol East is now back in that ecosystem but in the guise of the larger Sengkang GRC. The three constituencies of Aljunied, Hougang, and Sengkang are now informally part of an enlarged WP ecosystem.

What exactly is a WP ecosystem? The ecosystem is reflected in the practice of politics which the WP subscribes to and has generated a positive reception at the ground level. It involves connecting the party directly to residents in the WP's geographical footprint. The core of this footprint are the constituencies held by the WP. This began at GE1991 when Low won Hougang SMC. He engaged in retail politics by making

---

41 Cronert and Nyman, "Electoral Opportunism", op. cit.

a direct connection to voters through his regular meet-the-people sessions (MPS), his visits to homes in Hougang, and his walkabouts throughout common areas in the constituency. These collective physical outreach efforts were expanded when at GE2011, i.e., some 20 years after the Hougang victory, the WP took Aljunied GRC. Consequently, the WP upscaled its outreach efforts through a more institutional framework. This began with the creation of the Aljunied Constituency Committee (AJCC). As stated in the book *Walking with Singapore*, commemorating the WP's 60th anniversary:[42]

The Aljunied Constituency Committee (AJCC) was established in June 2011 to assist the MPs in organising community events and activities that bring residents together and to act as a feedback arm for residents to relay their needs and concerns about municipal and national issues. AJCC would organise regular constituency-level events such as tea sessions, talks, and fitness sessions, to give residents face-time with their MPs and to interact amongst themselves. Together with the Hougang Constituency Committee (HGCC), AJCC would also plan large-scale dinners to celebrate festivals such as Chinese New Year, Deepavali, and Hari Raya.

... AJCC is led by the five elected MPs of Aljunied GRC and self-funded with contributions from the MPs and donors.

In the WP ecosystem, its MPs are often viewed by many of their constituents as friends. This is in contrast to PAP MPs whom residents tend to approach rather guardedly because they are viewed as "the authority". This is not an uncommon perception. The human touch is thus the keystone to the WP ecosystem: it is manifested in the intersection of house visits, MPS, regular food distribution to needy families in constituencies within jurisdiction, the reaching out to various

---

42 The Workers' Party, *Walking with Singapore*, (Singapore: Ethos Books, 2017), p. 158.

religious and clan groups, and even taking residents on day-trips to Malaysia. All this has created a bonding between many of the constituents and the WP MPs. This bonding, an intangible variable, is a priceless asset for the WP, and one in which the PAP might not be able to compete with. To be clear, it represents an emotional connection between the WP and an increasing number of voters. It contrasts with a public perception of the PAP as mostly technocratic.

Beyond the human touch, which requires a continuous presence on the ground by WP MPs, members and volunteers, constituents desire practical assistance for some basic needs. As an example, given that there are a number of WP MPs who are trained as lawyers, providing free legal advice has been one form of practical assistance. For instance, in November 2019, the party provided certified documents for Lasting Power of Attorney, free of charge, to residents of Hougang SMC and Aljunied GRC.[43]

But probably, the most significant and consistent practical assistance the WP has provided is in the area of food distribution. It is worth noting how it came about, as described in *Walking with Singapore*:[44]

The food distribution programme for needy families was started in the rental blocks in Fengshan. We started in Fengshan, then we extended it to East Coast as well. We have a programme we call Blue Cycle. This is a WPCF [Workers' Party Community Fund] programme where we take household items that certain families want to donate, like fridges and fans, and give them to poor and needy families. We also have a Kiddy Wheelie programme where we loan out books on a personal T-loan to families with

---

43 "Workers' Party MPs provide free legal services to Aljunied-Hougang residents", *The Independent*, 26 November 2019, https://theindependent.sg/workers-party-mps-provide-free-legal-services-to-aljunied-hougang-residents/. Accessed on 9 February 2021.

44 *Walking with Singapore*, op. cit., p. 209.

young children. We deliver these books to the homes and we are also working
on a couple of other programmes as well. So many touch points in East
Coast and Fengshan every week since at least December 2015 till now.

The distribution of food, electrical and other items, has been regularised largely through the generosity of WP supporters. The programme reflects two things. First, that politicians must demonstrate that they are able to alleviate rudimentary problems — the lack of food and necessities for basic living — experienced by people on the ground. Second, the fact that despite headline figures that regularly laud Singapore as a relatively affluent society, there are not insignificant pockets of grinding poverty across the island-republic largely hidden in the ubiquity and uniformity of blocks of Housing and Development Board flats.

Optimally sizing the challenge to the PAP and targeting new constituencies

The WP's objective at the election to follow GE2020 would be to put together another challenge to the PAP that is optimally sized. It's challenge at GE2020 — of four GRCs and two SMCs contested for a total of 21 candidates — was sized optimally. Given the understandably enhanced expectations of the WP by many voters, the party would feel the pressure to increase its number of candidates. A meaningful enlargement in its slate of candidates would satisfy part of the anti-PAP ground in accepting that the WP is serious in challenging the PAP robustly and is not simply satisfied with a relatively small presence in Parliament. A meaningful increase in the number of WP candidates will also justify why the party will continue to strike out on its own and sees no necessity in having links with other alternative parties.

As made plain through much of this book, as a consequence of GE2020 the gap between the WP and the other alternative parties has become so large that much of the voting public could work on the assumption that those other parties will have little chance to get elected. In other words, GE2020 could also be viewed as the high-water mark for some of the other alternative parties. The voting public could then view a WP challenge, involving an enlarged slate of candidates, as effectively a by-election, with the objective of sending the entire cohort of WP candidates to Parliament. At some stage, perhaps during the election campaign itself, the WP has to make that argument. It cannot continue to want to avoid offending the other alternative parties when the electoral realities have become obvious to many voters. The main question is whether the WP can in fact find more suitable and committed election candidates? Assuming that the answer to that question is in the affirmative, the WP's electoral efforts will continue to be focused on the eastern part of Singapore.

Marine Parade GRC and East Coast GRC have continued to be difficult challenges for the party to surmount. But the surprise announcement on 8 April 2021 that Heng Swee Keat, who helmed East Coast GRC for the PAP, had ruled himself out of the running to be prime minister, suddenly put East Coast GRC firmly back into play for the WP.

Also, since GE2020, the WP might already be thinking, if not actively planning, about contesting in constituencies considered fertile ground. Of course, nothing is guaranteed. But it is worth focusing on the concept of the "spillover effect". This is where a party contests in constituencies adjacent to its strongholds so that its strength could spillover into those constituencies. To that extent, there could be several possibilities for the WP. These include Jalan Besar GRC, Tampines GRC, and Potong Pasir SMC. In particular, the relatively densely populated Tampines GRC, with its demographics which appears to be a combination of that found in Aljunied GRC (on-average an older demographic) and Sengkang GRC (on-average a relatively younger demographic), might be the best prospect for the WP.

Some other alternative parties that previously contested in the suggested target constituencies would of course cry foul. But electoral and, more broadly, political realities have changed so remarkably since GE2020, that though these other parties can complain and even threaten to play a spoiler's role, the WP is likely to ignore them and proceed with contesting in the target constituencies. It should be remembered that the WP did not dissuade any other alternative party from engaging in a multi-cornered fight with it at the Punggol East by-election of 26 January 2013. That by-election saw a four-cornered fight.

Of course, much of the foregoing assumes that the next report of the Electoral Boundaries Review Committee (EBRC) will not shift boundaries so radically that make the constituencies referenced unrecognisable from GE2020. However, even assuming radical changes to electoral boundaries, this might not in fact impact the WP's election efforts too materially given, that in the minds of voters, the eastern half of Singapore constitutes the WP's well-established geographical footprint. This truism is testified by the WP taking Sengkang GRC, a GRC that emerged only at GE2020 due to a significant redrawing of electoral boundaries. The electoral boundaries might have been redrawn but they still fell directly within the WP's geographical footprint.

For completeness, one final point should be made: the assumption — and long-standing convention — that opposition-held constituencies would be left untouched by the EBRC, might no longer hold. That is one possibility that cannot be ruled out.

CHAPTER 7

WP's Potential Pitfalls: Burnout, Celebrity Status, and an NCMP Scheme which Created an Intra-Party Class Structure

The painstaking effort to have in-person meetings on a regular basis with constituents while simultaneously being expected to contribute to policy initiatives and make interventions in Parliament, sums up much of the work of Workers' Party (WP) Members of Parliament (Mps). As analysed in Chapter 3, in terms of offline outreach, People's Action Party (PAP) MPs clock-up only a fraction of the work-rate put in by their WP counterparts. This chapter outlines a number of pitfalls facing the WP. One pitfall for the party is the very real likelihood that a number of its MPs experience burnout. The pace of house-to-house visits so early in the new Parliament testifies to a reality. It turns on the WP's awareness that such visits are the only way to fend off PAP attempts to re-capture seats lost to the WP.

The hard-working WP MP Png Eng Huat did not stand for re-election at GE2020. Officially, the party said he was stepping down to facilitate party renewal — an injection of fresh blood into party ranks. Unofficially, I had heard from one source that Png had become "tired". Both accounts are not mutually exclusive. Png had been an MP for just eight years (when he was elected at the Hougang by-election of May 2012), and it was surprising that he had called it quits after a relatively short stint. But it would not be entirely surprising if one or more of the WP MPs elected at GE2020 experience the same strain as a consequence of the demands of the job and decide not to stand for re-election.

Celebrity status sits incongruously with a politician's role as a servant of the people

Another potential issue for the WP is if one or two of its MPs start to believe that they are celebrities — with legions of followers — and not simply servants of the people. The WP's parliamentarians post regular updates on social media platforms detailing their work in Parliament and in constituencies under their jurisdiction. Dennis Tan and Leon Perera regularly post on Facebook short snippets with accompanying pictures of their constituency outreach efforts. This exercise serves as a transparent and public record of their work on the ground. And that is one purpose of a politician's social media accounts — to provide a running record of activities conducted. Jamus Lim has also made regular online postings. Reflective of the intellectual that he is, he has provided far more detail in his postings, which catalogues the amount of effort he puts into his work as an MP. All of that is appreciated by supporters who want to keep apprised of what their MPs have been doing.

However, there have also been occasional lapses. These were highlighted by the businessman and former Nominated MP (NMP) Calvin Cheng, who is known to be heavily pro-PAP. He made online observations asserting that Lim and Raeesah Khan were "celebrity MPs" because their Facebook status updates tended to indicate their upper-middle class status. This was in terms of their taste and ability to afford things out of reach of most ordinary people. On 13 November 2020, Cheng made two Facebook postings on the matter. He observed of Lim:[1]

> WORKERS' Party celebrity MP shares with his fans the joys of Italian sweetbread panettone, with a designer espresso, lovingly shot with his latest iPhone 12. A well-deserved treat after his tireless fighting for the proletariat. I am looking forward to my kaya toast and kopi siu dai tomorrow morning.
>
> Good night to all you bourgeoise folks!

---

1 "Calvin Cheng points to social status of WP MPs Raeesah Khan and Jamus Lim", *The Independent.sg*, 19 November 2020, https://theindependent.sg/calvin-cheng-points-to-social-status-of-wp-mps-raeesah-khan-and-jamus-lim/. Accessed on 10 February 2021.

On Khan, Cheng mused:

Happy Birthday to Sengkang MP Raeesah Khan.

It's wonderful she got to spend her birthday amongst the heartlanders at Compassvale as well as her 3-storey bungalow home in Eunos.

The best of both worlds! Truly blessed!

The postings are self-explanatory. Cheng is known to be over-the-top in his observations online but in this instance, he did point out an issue of some political consequence. That issue is not so much the elevated status and means of the two WP MPs, as many PAP MPs are also relatively affluent. Rather, it is simply that, in politics, if one styles oneself as advocating for the less privileged, it is best not to flaunt so publicly one's own privileged background. To do so would be incongruous. As one scholar explains: "The study of how ethnicity, class, and other of the so-called background characteristics affect political behaviour is important and highly relevant to (but no substitute for) the study of personality and politics. To the extent that a characteristic becomes part of an actor's personal make-up, it is no longer 'background' — it is an element of the psyche."[2]

Equally important, commentary accompanied by pictures posted online by parliamentarians should either be about policy matters or the showcasing of the lives of ordinary people, the challenges they face and their lived experience. In that regard, WP chief Pritam Singh has in fact set the standard for online postings. His social media postings often laud and give importance to the marginalised. It has to be stressed that the traditional bedrock of the WP's support base constitutes the working classes and a disproportionate number of ethnic minorities. Singh and his colleagues have since GE2015 been diligently expanding that

---

2 Fred I. Greenstein, "Can Personality and Politics be Studied Systematically?" *Political Psychology*, Vol. 13, No. 1, March 1992, p. 116.

traditional bedrock of support by knitting together a coalition of voters across most demographics. (See Chapter 8.)

MPs can display their human side by posting an occasional picture on a festive or celebratory occasion with a family member. But regularly bringing in family members, especially children, to a politician's official online portal should not be the norm and, in fact, is not good practice; there is a reason why, with minor exceptions, PAP MPs generally do not engage in such a practice.[3] If voters perceive a pattern of an MP being self-indulgent with what he says and does, they could have a less favourable opinion about the MP. However, that is not a view shared by everyone. Two Australian academics make the following contention:[4]

Showcasing, or at least referencing, family members in public fora by means of interviews, press statements, and photographs has provided politicians with the ideal vehicle through which to perform their everyday humanity, and thereby their identification with the wider public. A certain image of a politician's private, domestic life, a spouse and their children, has increasingly become a tool for political gain. And in the digital era, the role of a politician's spouse has moved from occasional waving on election night to the permanent circulation of images and footage online.

The reader can decide on what is appropriate. Perhaps the ideal is to meet somewhere in-between the two views. Here, it is worth noting that Singapore Democratic Party (SDP) chief Chee Soon Juan had in

3 A notable exception in recent times was the Minister of State Tan Kiat How. He became a father and posted pictures and a video clip of his son. See, "Becoming a dad is scary, frustrating & worth every moment: 4 S'pore politicians on fatherhood", *Mothership SG*, 20 June 2021, https://mothership.sg/2021/06/fathers-day-politicians/. Accessed on 22 June 2021.

4 Jay Daniel Thompson and Rob Cover, "Should politicians' family members be off-limits for public criticism?" *ABC Religion & Ethics*, 27 April 2021, https://www.abc.net.au/religion/should-politicians-families-be-off-limits-from-criticism/13318474. Accessed on 15 May 2021.

the past been heavily criticised for bringing his then underaged children into his political work. This had included his children helping him sell his books. It is not tenable to subject Chee to criticism while then remaining silent when other politicians do more-or-less the same thing. Of course, in the case of Chee, the critics' key issue was that he had focused on his family members in order to elicit sympathy from the voters. In a short biographical sketch, "Singapore's 'Martyr,' Chee Soon Juan", published in the *Far Eastern Economic Review* in 2006, it was observed:[5]

> *Perhaps it's in his genes. One of Chee's daughters is old enough that she had to be told that her father was going to prison. She stood up in her class and announced, "My papa is in jail, but he didn't do anything wrong. People have just been unfair to him."*

Family members should not be made to suffer in any way for whatever the public might feel about a politician. Here, understandably, there would be sympathy for Chee's family who have stood by him over many years. Whether public sympathy for Chee's family might have translated into a level of support for him at the polls is hard to say, but cannot be discounted.

Lionising politicians can set one up for disappointment

Another, related issue — with potential political downside — has been the hagiographic urge by staunch WP supporters to hold aloft personalities like Singh, Lim and Nicole Seah. The last had anchored the WP's East Coast GRC team and is a favourite of anti-PAP netizens. It seems almost inevitable that those who lionise political personalities to such an extent

---

5 Hugo Restall, "Singapore's 'Martyr,' Chee Soon Juan", *Far Eastern Economic Review*, July/August 2006, https://ccnmtl.columbia.edu/projects/caseconsortium/casestudies/1/casestudy/files/feer/p024.pdf. Accessed on 15 May 2021.

will at some stage feel disappointed that their heroes never fully lived up to the lofty expectations. Chen Show Mao — a WP MP between 2011 and 2020 — is a case in point. Great hopes were placed on Chen. He had sterling paper qualifications, with degrees from Harvard, Oxford and Stanford. He was also a Rhodes scholar. He made a name for himself internationally as a corporate legal heavyweight. That he stood on a party ticket in opposition to the ruling PAP instantly made him, in the eyes of many voters, the axiological embodiment of all that was positive and possible. However, once in Parliament, Chen was to disappoint. He made no memorable or eloquent speeches. Perhaps due to burnout and/or boredom together with his failed 2016 bid to take over the leadership of the WP from Low Thia Khiang,[6] Chen decided not to seek re-election at GE2020. Also, it ought to be remembered that Chen offered some mildly encouraging words of support to the SDP's Chee when the latter contested the Bukit Batok by-election in May 2016. Chen's tentative intervention on that occasion was not in-keeping with his party's line.

Chen had used social media sporadically, and the cryptic nature of some of his Facebook postings tended to baffle netizens. This tendency for opacity made his 2016 leadership challenge surprising. On that failed challenge I had posted this brief remark on my Facebook page on 29 May 2016 (the very day of the challenge): "Mr Chen reminds me of a UK politician in the 1990s whom someone once referred to as 'meekly ambitious'." I was then asked whom I was referring to, and replied: "The person was Douglas Hurd, a polite, non-abrasive Tory who, to the surprise of many, threw his hat in the ring as a candidate to replace Margaret Thatcher as leader of the party (and PM)."

With hindsight, it can be contended that the WP had a close call in seeing off Chen's meekly ambitious attempt to replace Low as leader. Two years later, Low's protégé, Pritam Singh, was elected leader

6 "Low Thia Khiang beats Chen Show Mao in Workers' Party polls to retain secretary-general post", *The Straits Times*, 20 May 2016, https://www.straitstimes.com/politics/low-thia-khiang-beats-chen-show-mao-in-workers-party-polls-to-retain-secretary-general-post. Accessed on 10 January 2021.

unopposed and the WP's fortunes were to take off. To his credit, Chen did not express any rancour with his party colleagues when he stepped aside from parliamentary life.[7] His disappointing performance in Parliament might be ascribed as one reason why the WP lost majority support at GE2015 in the Paya Lebar division of Aljunied GRC. That was the division which Chen had overseen. It would seem that, in the space of four years, the voters had rapidly cooled to him.

Chen's is a cautionary tale for those who say that people who are highly credentialed would either make good politicians or would be committed to becoming a good politician. In Singapore, highly credentialed people are not in short supply. But to be a good politician within the WP's frame of reference involves the duality of committing to a physically exhausting regimen of work for outreach to constituents, on the one hand, and preparatory work to make meaningful interventions in Parliament, on the other. On that basis, many highly credentialed people simply would not pass muster. Since GE2020, sources have indicated that the WP had received quite a number of expressions of interest by highly qualified individuals — including from academia, the legal profession, and government-linked corporations — to join its ranks. Those prospective members were told that they would be put through their paces. If they can take to the mundane physical outreach work that they will have to engage in over a protracted period then they could be considered as possible parliamentary election candidates. But the party offers no guarantees of candidacy at the next election. To that extent, it does not follow that those with sterling academic credentials or have reached the peak in their own profession, would necessarily possess high energy levels — an innate quality for the considerable physical work required within the WP ecosystem — nor could it be assumed that they would be good parliamentary performers.

It is of course trite to acknowledge that the public mood is fickle by nature. The Singapore electorate has, over the decade since 2011, shown

---

7 He did not seek re-election but remained a member of the WP.

itself to be volatile. Writing in 1979, one commentator made the point that "the presence or absence of heroes in the public realm depends rather more on matters of feeling than of fact."[8] Even for a person of such a stature as Lee Kuan Yew, five years after his death, the hagiographic spell that once held many Singaporeans in thrall of him is slowly being lifted.

On the other hand, it should be said that Singh's stature was enhanced during the GE2020 campaign. In a moment of crisis for the WP, when Raeesah Khan was being assailed for indelicate Facebook postings published in 2018, Singh offered a calm and proportionate response that was generally appreciated by voters.[9] He took the pressure with ease. In an instance of threat to the WP, Singh explained in an indirect but logical way the attractiveness of the WP brand to voters. Rather than being defensive, Singh's approach illustrated why the WP brand, moulded by both him and Low Thia Khiang, was shown to have Teflon-like properties, where mud flung by opponents does not tend to stick.

Leader of the Opposition

As official Leader of the Opposition, in his very first debate with Prime Minister Lee Hsien Loong, on 2 September 2020, Singh had the better of the exchange. The matter turned on whether voters were "free riders" because the WP's election strategy seemingly involved exhorting voters to send WP candidates to Parliament in the knowledge that the voters would also have the PAP as the government and its grassroots advisers

8 Scott Edwards, "Political Heroes and Political Education", *The North American Review*, Vol. 264, No. 1, Spring 1979, p. 13.

9 "Singapore GE2020: WP's Raeesah Khan apologises for posts which allegedly promoted enmity between different groups", *The Straits Times*, 5 July 2020 (revised on 1 September 2020), https://www.straitstimes.com/politics/singapore-ge2020-wps-raeesah-khan-apologises-for-posts-which-allegedly-promoted-enmity. Accessed on 10 January 2021.

attending to the needs of those same constituents. Given its significance, it is useful to set down part of that exchange:[10]

Mr Pritam Singh: I thank the Prime Minister for the responses. Just two points. The first one about the free rider. I do not think the residents in Aljunied, Hougang for 30 years now and even Sengkang as a result of the results of the last election, would appreciate being called free riders. They are not free riders.

The residents of Aljunied, I can speak more authoritatively for Aljunied residents because I am a sitting Member there.

We are not just doing nothing having been voted in. We are not just letting the other guy, the government of the day do something. We have got to do what we have to do. We have got to run the Town Council which is why Mr Lee Kuan Yew conceived of the Town Councils in the first place. Because if you want to move forward in the system as an Opposition Member of Parliament, you have got to prove your worth in the Town Council. And we have had growing pains. I am not going to deny that.

But if we were bungling things up, I would not be here today. My team would not be here today. We have tried our best in the circumstances that we are in. The Sengkang team is not going to have an easy time. First term, it is always going to be tough. But the voters of these constituencies put their faith in us because they know an Opposition in Parliament is ultimately good for Singapore.

And it is not just — and if I can suggest this — it is not just the NCMP version of the Opposition, with full respect to everyone who was an NCMP in this Parliament and those that came before. But it is when you have elected Opposition MPs, the Government listens harder. And that means

---

10 *President's Address: Debate on President's Address, Official Reports — Parliamentary Debates (Hansard)*, 2 September 2020, https://sprs.parl.gov.sg/search/sprs3topic?reportid=president-address-1461. Accessed on 15 May 2021.

something to people. That is my view. I am sure the PAP may have a different take on it. But that is my perspective. And that is why it is important for there to be elected Opposition MPs.

The Prime Minister alluded to a dishonest sort of packaging of what I am suggesting. The bigger moral imperative that I have and it is a huge burden — and I felt this burden before the last elections — was whether the people who are standing as Workers' Party candidates could follow through. That is the heaviest decision. That is the heaviest burden that I have. And if you choose someone who is not committed, not vested, that is the biggest pain for me as the leader of one party that aspires to represent Singaporeans in Parliament.

So, I will have to do what is good and what is right by Singapore. Looking for the best people. Do I want to contest all the seats, more seats, slowly grow? A lot of it depends on the quality of people that come and are attracted by the Workers' Party and our platform. If Singaporeans are attracted to it, then sure there is a prospect of growth. But it is not growth for growth's sake. I am not desperate for power, Prime Minister. But we have got to get good people if we want to bring this country forward. The PAP has been doing that as the Prime Minister has alluded to.

At this point in our growth, we have to grow our roots as a loyal Opposition. After more than 50 years of Independence, this is the first time the Government has recognised the Office of the Leader of the Opposition. We have many, many more miles to go. But we are not chasing a destination. We intend to do right by Singapore.

Mr Lee Hsien Loong: *I appreciate Mr Pritam's explanations. I am in no way undervaluing his motivations, his passion, his desire to do right by Singapore, his wish to have a high-quality Opposition built up in Singapore. I understand that. I think it is good for Singapore that you have honest* *people in the Opposition, people who believe in what they are trying to do, people who will stand up and fight for their ideals. And from time to time, agree very strongly with the Government. I think that is entirely reasonably.*

I think it is also good that you have Opposition who take their Town Council responsibilities seriously, who look after their constituencies assiduously and conscientiously and do their best for their voters and give the voters a reason to vote for them. I think it is entirely reasonable.

But I would say however, if you stand and you tell people, "Vote for me, I will be a better MP than the other one, the PAP MP", I think that is entirely reasonable. But if you say, "Vote for me; somebody else will vote for the PAP and therefore the PAP will be the government", that, the economists will call a free rider. It means that you are taking advantage of somebody else who is doing the duty of electing a government for the nation. And you are not doing your part expressing your true views and preference as a voter whom you want to be the next government. And if everybody takes that attitude, then you are going to end up with a government which you do not want. Because the argument which he makes is that he is very careful, he only chooses candidates he can trust to be Workers' Party candidates. I think I give him that. It is the right and responsible attitude to take. But I think other Opposition parties may say they have been trying to get good candidates too. And they could make the same argument as you have, that it is good to have an Opposition in Singapore, "Vote for us. Somebody else will look after the government of Singapore".

The first portion of PM Lee's response amounted to a concession that the WP's approach to opposition is to the benefit of Singapore. If any politician is able to secure such a concession from their opponent, then that is no small victory. And, in all likelihood, Singh would have prepared well for this first major clash with the prime minister by considering what would likely be the two or three lines of attack his protagonist would employ. In consequence, his response came across as effortless when, in reality, it was likely the product of plenty of preparation.

Politics has its metaphorical hills and valleys for its practitioners. As a general rule, a politician who emerges from an election having done relatively well for herself/himself and her/his party would tend to get a short honeymoon of three to four months with the voters before her/his favourability ratings plateaued and then dipped. More than a year after GE2020, Singh has, remarkably, been able to maintain a relatively high level of popularity for both himself and the WP. This is reflected by how he and the party have been covered in the mainstream media. Perhaps the best illustration of this was the interview Singh gave for *The Sunday Times'* main feature, Lunch with Sumiko, published on 17 January 2021. Though guarded in his statements, what he said in that interview gave insights into his political philosophy, provided a hint of the WP's strengths, and also indicated why the PAP has found it difficult to trip-up the WP.

Singh subscribes to being grounded and calm, and neither being happy nor sad at events "because things come in cycles".[11] Further, the WP, he says, adheres to a universal rule of party politics, that its members "never run down or criticise our running mates no matter what other people may feel about it."[12] In that connection, the following point was also quite telling: "He admits that, internally, it is difficult to make everyone sing from the same song sheet as motivations for joining the opposition vary. Some are more angsty, some have a longer

---

11 "Lunch with Sumiko: WP chief Pritam Singh on the need to keep calm and stay grounded", *The Sunday Times*, 17 January 2021, https://www.straitstimes.com/singapore/politics/lunch-with-sumiko-keep-calm-and-stay-grounded. Accessed on 15 May 2021.

12 Ibid.

vision and an open mind, and others are more hasty for change."[13] From this, it is not unreasonable to speculate that perhaps one or two of the new cohort of WP MPs have had the impulse of wanting to achieve a significant amount politically and quickly. It would, therefore, not be a surprise if the combination of burnout and unmet expectations led one or more not to seek re-election. No one knows this for certain, but it is being flagged here as a possibility, especially as Png and Chen, each having served just under a decade as MP, decided to either call it quits or timeout on their parliamentary life. If it is timeout, then we can take it that both needed a break and could at some point return to frontline politics if they feel they have been re-energised and/or the circumstances are more propitious. And, the same could apply to Low Thia Khiang.[14]

It could be said that politics appears to be in Low's blood. Even after not seeking re-election at GE2020, Low has helped the WP substantively, especially with meet-the-people sessions (MPS) by offering to cover for any WP MP who might be on a leave of absence and cannot personally run an MPS. It should also be noted, that Low remains highly popular within the WP. Even though he did not seek re-election as an MP at GE2020, he retained a seat on the WP's Central Executive Committee (CEC) at the party's biennial election on 27 December 2020. With his Chinese-educated background, Low's continued prominence within the

---

13 Ibid.

14 It should be pointed out that politicians wanting, and succeeding, in returning to frontline politics after stepping down from that role is not uncommon. The most notable example would be Malaysia's Mahathir bin Mohamad. Also, David Cameron quit as UK prime minister following the UK's 2016 referendum vote to leave the European Union — Brexit — only to seemingly become bored two years later, and had expressed a desire to return to Parliament in the hopes of becoming Foreign Secretary. See, "David Cameron 'wants to return to frontline politics as Foreign Secretary' because he is 'bored s...less'", *The Mirror*, 1 November 2018, https://www.mirror.co.uk/news/politics/breaking-david-cameron-wants-return-13520913. Accessed on 15 May 2021.

WP will help the party retain support among the Chinese-educated/ speaking ground.

If both Png (who was also re-elected to the CEC at the December 2020 internal party election) and Low were to stand again on the WP ticket at the general election that would follow GE2020, they would undoubtedly give a significant boost to morale within the WP's ranks. And, morale tends to be half the battle.

Singh had also indicated in the interview that card-carrying members of the party numbered in the hundreds but, more significantly, "It is the volunteers and the movement that we call it which gives us a certain heft."[15] In quantitative terms the WP has a rank-and-file that is proportionate to the party's parliamentary strength. However, the real strength is the quality of the "movement". The WP went into GE2020 as a strongly motivated force.

The AHTC litigation

One of Singh's first challenges as WP leader was in handling the litigation over Aljunied-Hougang Town Council (AHTC). This litigation involved claims against a number of individuals, including Singh, WP chair Sylvia Lim, and former WP chief Low, together with some other unelected members of the party. In total, around $33.7 million was being claimed as a result of what the plaintiffs, AHTC and Pasir Ris-Punggol Town Council (PRPTC), alleged were governance failures — conflicts of interest, and a lack of safeguards — which resulted in over-payments to AHTC's former manging agent, FM Solutions & Services.[16] When he took over as head of the WP, Singh's first order of business was to

---

15 Ibid.

16 "AHTC alleges that all payments totalling $33 million made to ex-managing agent are void", *The Straits Times*, 27 July 2017, https://www.straitstimes.com/politics/ ahtc-alleges-that-all-payments-totalling-33-million-made-to-ex-managing-agent- are-void. Accessed on 15 February 2021.

raise funds from the public for legal fees so as to mount a defence of the AHTC lawsuit. The party engaged one of Singapore's leading law firms, Tan Rajah & Cheah. Legal heavyweight, Chelva Rajah, SC, led the defence. Following a call for donations, within the space of less than three days in late October 2018, more than $1 million was raised from over 6,100 individual donors.[17]

In a 329-page judgment on the AHTC litigation dated 11 October 2019, Justice Ramesh Kannan established liability on the part of the defendants for breaching their "fiduciary duties" and/or "duty of skill and care". He also indicated that the quantum of monies the plaintiffs could reasonably expect to recover would have to be determined at the next phase of this two-phase trial.[18] However, both the plaintiffs and defendants appealed the initial judgment and, as of August 2021, it was still being considered by the Court of Appeal. The upshot of this protracted case is that prior to GE2020 it weighed heavily on the WP even though the relative success of its crowdfunding effort in October 2018 provided the party with temporary relief. Due to various considerations, not least because the case was still sub judice, it would not be appropriate to examine aspects of it. However, it is sufficient to say that, as the efficaciousness of WP's crowdfunding effort had indicated, the millstone around the WP's neck imposed by the AHTC litigation appears to be less apparent.

---

17 "In Good Faith: Appeal for Support", https://ingoodfaith.blog/2018/10/24/appeal-for-support/. Accessed on 10 January 2021.

18 *In the High Court of the Republic of Singapore, [201] SGHC 241*, Suit Nos 668 and 716 of 2017, https://www.supremecourt.gov.sg/docs/default-source/module-document/judgement/191011---ahtc-2019-sghc-241-pdf.pdf. Accessed on 15 February 2021. For a press report on the judgment, see, "AHTC case: Workers' Party leaders put political interests above that of town council and residents, says judge", *The Straits Times*, 11 October 2019, https://www.straitstimes.com/politics/ahtc-case-wps-pritam-singh-sylvia-lim-and-low-thia-khiang-found-liable-for-damages-suffered. Accessed on 15 February 2021.

The party has of course learnt from the entire AHTC episode to ensure that whatever missteps it had made are not repeated. The setting up of the Sengkang Town Council, chaired by WP MP He Ting Ru, appeared to have fully taken on board the need to move swiftly with a handover to WP management of the new Town Council with attendant contracts for municipal services, and it ensured that the process was transparent.[19] Details of the initial stages of the handover process were posted online by He. The efforts she and her fellow Sengkang MPs in that exercise served to close off any room for potential misunderstandings to emerge. The WP can thus focus on an equally important matter — conceptualising the extent, and the manner, it should fight the next general election.

The NCMP scheme had implicitly created a class structure within the WP

In all that it does, the WP has to emphasise one fact: that its opposition is principled, not opportunistic. Logically, the WP cannot be in favour of something because the party gains short-term benefit from it. Back in the 1980s, the PAP had laid the trap of the Non-constituency Member of Parliament (NCMP) scheme which, in the past, the WP had embraced because the first-past-the-post election system had set such a high bar for challengers to the PAP to gain entry into Parliament. Now that the WP has demonstrated that it can win seats outright from the PAP, as a matter of party policy and principle, the WP should oppose the NCMP scheme. The existence of the NCMP scheme had in fact previously created a strange phenomenon within the party, as elucidated below.

At an Institute of Policy Studies conference in 2015, an NMP in the batch appointed on 26 August 2014, made pointed remarks to me

---

19 "'New Sengkang Town Council to run on its own', WP's He Ting Ru to be chairman", *The Straits Times*, 19 July 2020 (updated 1 September 2020), https://www.straitstimes.com/politics/new-sengkang-town-council-to-be-run-on-its-own-wps-he-ting-ru-to-be-chairman. Accessed on 15 February 2021.

about the WP. He said that from what he observed of WP parliamentarians, both inside and outside the chamber of Parliament, there was an "obvious class structure" within the party. He asserted that WP fully elected MPs tended to mix mostly amongst themselves, and there would not be much mixing with the NCMPs. (Arising out of the results of GE2011 there were two WP NCMPs.) At the time, I considered the remark interesting but did not give it much thought. Hence, I did not ask the NMP to elaborate any further. However, sometime thereafter, I bumped into a PAP MP and took the opportunity to ask him whether he had a similar impression of the WP. He said that he did not disagree with the observation made by the NMP.

The issue of the significance, or otherwise, of NCMPs, arose just after GE2015. This was when Lee Li Lian, who had been elected an MP in the Punggol East by-election on 26 January 2013, was not re-elected at GE2015 but, by virtue of being one of the best placed losers, was offered an NCMP seat. She, however, declined. The WP then proposed that Daniel Goh, a candidate from the WP's East Coast GRC team, be the party's replacement for the NCMP seat rejected by Lee.[20] In accordance with statute, NCMP seats are decided on the basis of the exact percentage of votes an opposition candidate or candidates secured in an electoral division. An opposition party can only decide which candidate or candidates from its best losing GRC team it wished to become an NCMP. (Under the Constitution, only a maximum of two NCMPs can come from a single GRC team.) An opposition party cannot choose its preferred candidate for NCMP from across the electoral divisions it contested.[21] In consequence, the WP had to file a

20 "WP files motion that the NCMP offered to Lee Li Lian declared vacant; wants Daniel Goh to take it up", *The Straits Times*, 18 January 2016, https://www.straitstimes.com/politics/wp-files-motion-to-have-ncmp-seat-offered-to-lee-li-lian-declared-vacant-wants-daniel-goh. Accessed on 12 March 2021.

21 From this it should be even more apparent that an opposition party offered an NCMP seat cannot then decline and offer the seat to another opposition party. However, that has not stopped some Singaporeans from going online to urge something which is a non-starter.

motion to get Parliament to vote to allow Goh to assume the vacant NCMP seat.

The curious thing is that the WP had, on principle, opposed the basic premise of the NCMP scheme but it still wanted one of its candidates to take up the seat which Lee had declined. This apparent contradiction was accentuated as, at the time of the first Parliament sitting following GE2015, the government indicated its intentions to increase the maximum number of NCMPs from nine to 12. This was to make the WP's opposition to the fundamental concept of NCMPs even more pronounced. The stepped-up number of NCMPs was to become effective at the subsequent general election (i.e., in 2020). This proposed increase in the maximum number of NCMPs would, in the PAP government's view, ensure that there would always be a minimum of 12 opposition parliamentarians, which it viewed would be sufficient to satisfy that segment of Singaporeans who wished for alternative voices in Parliament but without displacing the ruling party. Underlying this policy was the presumption that the PAP was the natural party of government. At the same time as the proposal to increase the number of NCMPs, the government decided to immediately give NCMPs the same voting rights as MPs. Previously, NCMPs could not vote on constitutional amendments, supply or supplementary bills, money bills or on motions of no-confidence in the government. Thus, from 2016, there would be an enhancement in the status of NCMPs. But this enhanced status did not apply to an NCMP's allowance. That allowance remained at 15% of that for a fully elected MP. This variance in compensation signified the different levels of responsibilities. The commonly held view, especially in materialistic Singapore, is that money defines status. As of early 2021, an MP's annual allowance was $192,500, or around $16,000 a month. Contrast that to an NCMP's annual allowance of $28,900, or around $2,408 a month. This difference in monetary compensation between MPs and NCMPs implicitly created a two-class system not just within Parliament but also within the opposition party — the WP — which had both MPs and NCMPs.

WP chair, Sylvia Lim, in a speech to Parliament in support of the motion to allow the NCMP seat vacated by Lee to be taken by Goh, simultaneously decried the NCMP scheme in the following terms:[22]

Do we want a system where opposition MPs only come to Parliament to debate? If opposition parties do not manage constituencies, they would not be able to demonstrate that they, too, were up to the task of representing their constituents, building vibrant communities and yes, running the Town Councils. Should the ruling party decay or become corrupt, it would be too late to look around for any other party with ground experience, as there may well be none.

…, even as we move this motion [to have the NCMP seat filled by Daniel Goh], we are under no illusion that NCMPs can replace the check and bargaining power the people have with elected opposition MPs in Parliament.

At the time of this controversy, then WP chief Low, was even more dismissive of NCMPs. He said:[23]

NCMP is just like duckweed on the water of a pond. You don't have roots, unlike elected MPs where you have a constituency. You run [the] town council. You get close in touch with your residents. You can sink roots there.

Intellectually, it would be difficult to disagree with Low's observations. He himself would not have accepted an NCMP seat.

---

22 "Motion on NCMP Seat — Speech by Sylvia Lim", *The Workers' Party*, https://www2.wp.sg/motion-on-ncmp-seat-speech-by-sylvia-lim/. Accessed on 6 January 2020.

23 "WP chief Low Thia Khiang's 'duckweed' analogy takes root in Parliament debate: 6 things about the humble plant", *The Straits Times*, 30 January 2016, https://www.straitstimes.com/politics/wp-chief-low-thia-khiangs-duckweed-analogy-takes-root-in-parliament-debate-6-things-about. Accessed on 12 March 2021.

Equally, Sylvia Lim had also said that if, after being elected an MP, she was defeated in an election but offered an NCMP seat, she would do the same as Lee Li Lian, i.e., decline the seat. However, the PAP and its large group of online supporters, assailed Lee for turning down the NCMP seat. Commenting on this on my Facebook page on 18 September 2015, I said the following:

There appears to be much hullabaloo about WP's Ms Lee Li Lian not accepting the NCMP position. To me, given her considerations, she decided not to take the easy way out.

Make no mistake of the fact that she could have just as easily accepted the position, taken the $2k+ monthly allowance (NCMPs get 15% of a fully elect MP's salary), and merely did the very minimum in Parliament.

Many others in the minor opposition parties would have accepted the position in a heartbeat. Those same others are naturally envious and frustrated that they could not even get close to being in the top 10 of best opposition losers. That is their particular problem.

Also, we all know that in the last Parliament, one PAP MP made no speeches at all, and another made just one speech within those four years.

Beyond that, Ms Lee has demonstrated that, in her politics, she subscribes to minimum standards. I attach a screenshot of her FB [Facebook] status update of March 21 of this year.[24] It speaks for itself.

Her conduct is admirable and contrasts markedly with that of another personality from a different opposition party who has not given a second thought to using minors for his and his party's political advancement.

---

24 The screenshot I referred to was of Lee in a selfie with 16-year-old Darwase, a resident of Punggol East. Lee had said in her accompanying post that Darwase wanted to be a WP volunteer, but she suggested that, given his age, he should focus on his studies. She diplomatically pointed out that, "At this moment, our youngest volunteer is 21 years old." I contend that Lee had placed her motherly instincts ahead of personal political benefit. That is to her great credit.

Lee was fully aware that moving from being an MP to NCMP meant a significant drop in her standing politically, with which she might have found difficulty in reconciling personally, let alone with those whom she came into contact. She also knew that there were practical limitations to the role of an NCMP. Though her party colleagues, who were MPs, would be polite, she might have felt that the class divide that suddenly emerged with a change in her parliamentary status would manifest itself in some ways. She had decided to avoid all that.

In an interview published in the mainstream media on 14 March 2021, Gerald Giam, who had been an NCMP at the time the NMP made the remark about an "obvious class structure", but who was elected as part of the WP's Aljunied GRC team at GE2020, seemed to give weight to the notion of the large gulf between being an NCMP and an MP. He said that it's "almost like night and day because when you are elected an MP, people expect you to solve their problems."[25] In other words, on that latter point, much of the voting public do not have much expectations of an NCMP.

Given the foregoing, if the WP ever found itself again in a situation where it was the only party from the alternative camp that got candidates elected to Parliament but fell short of 12, which is the maximum number of NCMPs allowed, should it accept any NCMP seats just to reach the threshold of a minimum of 12 opposition voices in Parliament? Intellectually, the answer should be in the negative. By way of illustration, if the WP retained all of its 10 MP seats arising out of GE2020 and also had candidates in other electoral divisions as best losers, giving those candidates the right to fill the remaining two seats as NCMPs, the WP's Central Executive Committee should reject the offer of NCMP seats. The WP cannot continue to have it both ways by, on principle, opposing

---

25 Quoted in, "It's like 'night and day': Workers' Party MP Gerald Giam on being an MP versus an NCMP", *CNA*, 14 March 2021, https://www.channelnewsasia.com/news/singapore/workers-party-mp-gerald-giam-interview-ncmp-aljunied-grc-14398172. Accessed on 20 March 2021.

the NCMP scheme and then gamely allowing its election candidates to accept the position. At an intellectual level this would be an untenable position to adopt even if, politically, WP supporters would likely be in favour of the party continuing to accept NCMP seats.

The only situation where the WP could be justified in still accepting NCMP seats, even as it decries the scheme, is if there was a total wipe-out of the party at a general election, and no candidates were elected from other alternative parties. In that situation, a case could be made out that it would be the responsible thing for the party to maintain a parliamentary presence to question PAP policies, instead of giving the PAP free rein to do what it liked without official protest. In such a situation, many Singaporeans would expect that the WP to fulfil its role as a parliamentary opposition.

By a quirk of fate, at GE2020 the WP was not placed in a position where its stated opposition to the NCMP scheme would have been put to the test yet again and, likely, found wanting. The Progress Singapore Party's West Coast GRC team became best losers with its 48.32% of the valid votes cast. It thus provided two NCMPs to make-up 12 opposition parliamentarians. That figure, of 12, which emerged out of an amendment, passed in Parliament, to the NCMP scheme in 2016, can be said to constitute PAP planning parameters for the number of opposition voices in order to give the impression that it — the PAP government — remains in control of events. Whether the PAP will still remain in control of events in the medium term, is another narrative in its own right.

CHAPTER 8

The WP Views the PAP as the Opposition:
But are Some Opposition Parties the WP's Enemies?

ingapore's first-past-the-post (FPTP) election system, based on a simple plurality of votes, has accentuated the angst of those opposition supporters who would prefer a Workers' Party (WP) as an implacable, not moderate, opponent to the People's Action Party (PAP) because the stark reality of those supporters' small numbers ensures that, as a consequence of FPTP, they have difficulty in gaining any presence in Parliament for their kind of opposition. However, irrespective of their small numbers they can still play the role of a spoiler, potentially hampering the WP. On the other hand, an electoral system based on proportional representation (PR) would hold out the prospect of minor parties, representing heavily anti-PAP elements, attaining a semblance of a parliamentary presence which they would then be good at magnifying by constantly advocating for the kinds of policies that keep the media attention firmly on them.

A system of PR, where seats in a legislature more accurately reflect the percentage of votes gained by a party can have two markedly different effects: one, is that it encourages parties towards consensus and coalition building; and two, it can also potentially open up cleavages along ethnic, religious and other fault lines.[1] Ironically, the two outcomes might not

---

1 As one scholar has noted, "[I]n a vote-weighted [i.e., PR] model, voters' strategies are predicated on… a compromise which provides them with incentives to vote for extremist parties." Indridi H. Indridason, "Proportional Representation, Majoritarian Legislatures, and Coalition Voting", *American Journal of Political Science*, Vol. 55, No. 4, October 2011, p. 958. See also Eliezer Ben-Rafael, "The Faces of Religiosity in Israel: Cleavages or Continuum?" *Israel Studies*, Vol. 13, No. 3, Fall 2008, p. 97; and, Burt L. Monroe and Amanda G. Rose, "Electoral Systems and Unimagined Consequences: Partisan Effects of Districted Proportional Representation", *American Journal of Political Science*, Vol. 46, No. 1, January 2002.

be mutually exclusive.[2] Singapore's system of FPTP, derived from the Westminster model, makes it a majoritarian, not consensus democracy. Consequently, this inevitably leads to political power being disproportionately concentrated in the party that is the best organised, has enormous resources and numbers within its rank-and-file, and can execute on the electoral process with efficiency while leveraging on incumbency status. As set out in Chapter 1, the so-called "opposition" to the PAP is heavily fragmented where, in Table 1.2, main voting bloc D, comprising the irreducible core of anti-PAP voters can be sub-divided into two sub-blocs — those who, due to their economic situation, are implacable opponents of the PAP and are prepared to embrace nativism; and, those who are ideologically liberal or progressive.

Due to these realities, significant barriers exist preventing the WP from cooperating with other alternative parties. It could be argued that it would be an error for the WP, as a goodwill gesture, to provide even a small measure of support to liberal or progressive-leaning parties. This is because, by their very nature, such ideologically-anchored parties will not be satisfied with anything other than a fully realised liberal agenda. In other words, after gaining initial support, such parties will keep pushing their agenda even if it was at the expense of the party that gave them initial support.

Barriers to WP cooperating with the SDP

At GE2020, both the Singapore Democratic Party's (SDP's) Chee Soon Juan and Chairman, Paul Tambyah, garnered 45.2% and 46.27% of the valid votes cast in Bukit Batok and Bukit Panjang single-member constituencies (SMCs) respectively. The results of both candidates surprised on the upside. On that basis, supporters of the SDP raised

---

2 The dichotomy is analysed by Cho Seok-Ju, "Voting Equilibria Under Proportional Representation", *The American Political Science Review*, Vol. 108, No. 2, May 2014, p. 294.

their hopes that both personalities, and the SDP as a party in general, would do well at the subsequent election. Implicit in these hopes was that the WP would not merely show the way but would be prepared to cooperate with the SDP in helping the party return to Parliament since it was last there in 1996. However, in conversations with WP members, the consistent impression that has been conveyed is that there is little scope for the WP cooperating with the SDP. In a discussion in 2019, WP chief Pritam Singh made the following remarks:[3]

There's a good reason why we've avoided any invitations from the SDP. [The SDP] had sent us an invitation about discussions for a coalition. They invited Tian Chua from the PKR, and asked us to come down for a general discussion. I won't touch them with a ten-foot pole.

The PKR referred to is Malaysia's Parti Keadilan Rakyat (People's Justice Party) headed by Anwar Ibrahim. Tian Chua has been a prominent member of the PKR, a component of the Pakatan Harapan coalition. Tian visited Singapore in July 2018 and gave a talk at the SDP's headquarters on 7 July about the PKR's experience with coalition politics. According to the SDP, the talk was attended by "[a]ll the opposition parties except the Workers' Party".[4] Three weeks later, on 28 July 2018, the SDP held a discussion with a number of alternative parties and asked Tan Cheng Bock (who had then not yet set up his own party) to lead an anti-PAP coalition.[5] The WP was not present at that discussion. It continued to decline invitations from the SDP.

3 Discussion with Pritam Singh, 10 June 2019.

4 "SDP brings opposition parties together to hear Pakatan Harapan experience", *Singapore Democratic Party*, 7 July 2018, https://yoursdp.org/news/sdp_brings_ opposition_parties_together_to_hear_pakatan_harapan_experience/. Accessed on 10 January 2021.

5 "Opposition parties express desire to cooperate; Invite Tan Cheng Bock to lead effort", *Singapore Democratic Party*, 28 July 2018, https://yoursdp.org/news/opposition_ parties_express_desire_to_cooperate_invite_tan_cheng_bock_to_lead_effort/. Accessed on 10 January 2021.

There has been a long desire by the SDP under Chee to establish some cooperative arrangement with the WP, but there has been firm resistance to the idea from the latter. Posting on Facebook on 13 September 2015, i.e., shortly after the disastrous results of GE2015 for the alternative parties, Chee said to SDP supporters: "One thing that many of you have pointed out is that the SDP and WP should work closer together to present a more coordinated opposition strategy and message at the next GE. Given the outcome of the polls, I think so too."[6]

Notwithstanding the desire by the SDP to get politically closer to the WP, one of the main barriers to that arrangement has been the SDP's politics, which are to the left of the WP. That political positioning is not the only difference. There is also a strong perception among some Singaporeans that the SDP's approach to opposition is partly motivated by personal grievances harboured by some of its members against the government. This is in contrast with the WP which, notwithstanding the litigation it has been embroiled in related to the Aljunied-Hougang Town Council, has tended to project an image of professionalism, not one grounded in personal grievance.

Another barrier to SDP-WP cooperation has been the SDP's history of either implicitly or explicitly denigrating the WP publicly. For instance, when the International Bar Association held a symposium in Singapore in 2007, WP chair Sylvia Lim, who was a speaker at the symposium, argued that Singaporeans were more than capable of handling domestic legal issues on their own, including that of the rule of law, and that they did not require support from the international community. Her remarks drew the ire of SDP members present at the symposium; they were to take to the SDP's online portal to denounce

---

6 "SDP to explore working closer together with WP next time out: Chee", *Today*, 14 September 2015, https://www.todayonline.com/ge2015/chee-soon-juan-raise-possibility-working-together-wp?fbclid=IwAR3PTEwU1ihSwlgPoMVrhyX-HZFd GJSy4wNyztawFPf8kZ6DUkBpgSxkOes. Accessed on 10 January 2021.

Lim, not one but twice. The first post, dated 21 October 2007, launched excoriating criticism of the WP, saying:[7]

[Lim] Parrot[ed] what the PAP so disingenuously advocates.

Appeasing the PAP so that we can be an acceptable opposition is not to "draw a balance" as Ms Lim claims. It is rather an unfortunate tactic that will be conveniently exploited by the PAP.

The SDP said it before and we say it again: Singapore's Opposition cannot stand up for the people on bended knees.

The SDP continued to assail the WP the next day, with a second post signed by its then Assistant Secretary-General, John Tan, who contrasted the remarks by Lim with her fellow panel speaker, prominent Malaysian lawyer and human rights campaigner Ambiga Sreenivasan. Tan said:[8]

Ms Ambiga had earlier said that fundamental values of judicial independence, press freedom, independence of law societies do not belong to the West only but to us in Asia, too.

As an aside, the courageous Malaysian lawyer is presently under investigation by the Malaysian police for defying the illegal assembly law and conducting a march together with her fellow lawyers in protest of [sic] interference of the judicial process by the government.

---

7 "SDP disappointed with WP's IBA comments", *Singapore Democratic Party*, 21 October 2007, https://yoursdp.org/news/sdp_disappointed_with_wp_s_iba_comments/. Accessed on 10 January 2021.

8 "Observations at the IBA Symposium", *Singapore Democratic Party*, 22 October 2007, https://yoursdp.org/publ/perspectives-observations_at_the_iba_symposium-2-1-0-938/. Accessed on 10 January 2021.

I came away with this disturbing observation that among our three Singaporean speakers (a cabinet minister, an academician, and an oppositionist) there was one common view — that there were no serious problems with the rule of law in Singapore and that there is no repression here.

This is most unfortunate.

If the SDP had reservations about the stand taken by another alternative party, perhaps it should have considered the ramifications of making those reservations known so publicly. To openly criticise the WP and then later expect to have a cooperative relationship with it might have been a little optimistic. In any event, it seems that the SDP has always hoped to have a cooperative relationship with the WP purely on terms laid down by the SDP. In that regard, in the run-up to the Punggol East by-election of 26 January 2013, the SDP was keen on throwing its hat in the ring even though the constituency had previously been contested by the WP and, electorally, was part of the WP's geographical footprint. Realising that the WP would not give way to the SDP and therefore spawn a multi-cornered fight with the PAP, the SDP proposed the WP to make way for an SDP candidate who would be a "unity candidate" in a joint campaign; if the SDP won the by-election, the SDP would let the WP run the town council.[9] Unless one was in a dystopian reality, any reasonable person would immediately conclude that this was not merely an unserious proposal but was also pointedly intended to insult the WP. SDP chief Chee said of the proposal: "A successful unity candidate would mean another seat in Parliament for the opposition. It would lay the ground for bigger

---

9 "SDP proposes joint campaign with WP in Punggol East by-election", *CNA*, 11 January 2013, https://www.channelnewsasia.com/news/singapore/sdp-proposes-joint-campaign-with-wp-in-punggol-east-by-election-8343624. Accessed on 10 January 2021.

opposition representation in the next general election."[10] These remarks might accurately be characterised as either self-serving or inconsistent. Chee had been part of the group within the SDP which had wanted to expel the moderate oppositionist Chiam See Tong from the party back in 1993 which, under the Singapore Constitution, would have meant Chiam losing his Member of Parliament's (MP's) seat and the opposition's parliamentary presence being immediately reduced by 25%.[11] In other words, back in the early 1990s, Chee did not accept the notion of a PAP versus non-PAP binary that he was suggesting in 2013. Still, it is worthwhile considering the hypothetical situation of the SDP having a presence in Parliament alongside the WP.

A counter-factual of the SDP and the WP in Parliament arising out of GE2020

Employing evidence-based behaviour analysis, what would have happened if at GE2020 either Chee or Tambyah had secured just enough votes to become a best loser, succeeding in snaring one of two Non-constituency Member of Parliament (NCMP) seats available after the WP had won 10 parliamentary seats outright? What would have been the SDP's priorities in Parliament? Would the party persistently raise civil liberties and human rights issues? For instance, would an SDP NCMP speak on the rule of law, the need to do away with the Internal Security Act (ISA) and for restorative justice for ex-ISA detainees (of which a number have been members of the SDP since Chee assumed the party's helm), and such like? These are pertinent questions.

---

10 Ibid.

11 Chiam, in a suit brought before the High Court, had challenged the legality of his expulsion from the SDP. The Court ruled his expulsion unlawful. Chiam, therefore, retained his party membership and, consequently, his seat in Parliament. A detailed examination of this episode, which highlighted the chasm between moderate and hardcore opposition in Singapore during the 1990s, can be found in the work by Loke Hoe Yeong, *The First Wave: JBJ, Chiam & The Opposition in Singapore*, (Singapore: Epigram, 2019).

Based on historical antecedents since the early 1990s, it would be surprising if the SDP did not place human rights front and centre of its parliamentary agenda. It is a party that persistently looks backwards at what it considers as human rights abuses committed by the PAP government which require redress. Even as this chapter was being written in late May 2021, there was an online commentary by SDP Central Executive Committee member Bryan Lim about a book he had read and was recommending — *1987: Singapore's Marxist Conspiracy 30 Years On.*[12] He said that the edited volume had told the "truth from these honourable men & women".[13] And, as noted in Appendix 2, Paul Tambyah had in 2015 made several high-profile public interventions on behalf of teenage blogger Amos Yee following the state's prosecution of the latter for an expletive-laden video that included ridiculing the Christian faith. Tambyah's interventions were not in-line with broad public sentiment at the time.

Returning to the counter-factual, if PAP parliamentarians responded robustly to an SDP NCMP's speeches as the NCMP waxed lyrically about alleged PAP government abuses, and if the WP's cohort of 10 MPs kept a silence, what would have been the response? The response would likely have been ardent SDP supporters taking to social media and, instead of condemning the PAP's attempt to push back the SDP's parliamentary agenda would, instead, concentrate their online anger on the WP for not providing covering support for the SDP NCMP. Effectively, what one would have in Parliament, in terms of the opposition, is the tail wagging the dog. Wasn't the WP being told that it would merely be reduced to playing a supporting role to the SDP when Chee had proposed collaborating with the WP at the Punggol

---

12 Chng Suan Tze, Low Yit Leng and Teo Soh Lung, eds., *1987: Singapore's Marxist Conspiracy 30 Years On*, (Singapore: Ethos Books, 2017).

13 "SDP's Bryan Lim reads Singapore's Marxist Conspiracy, urges people to 'find out the truth'", *The IndependentSG*, 26 May 2021, https://theindependent.sg/sdps-bryan-lim-reads-singapores-marxist-conspiracy-urges-people-to-find-out-the-truth/. Accessed on 27 May 2021.

East by-election, with a winning SDP candidate sitting in Parliament while the WP would do the work of Town Council management?

Many netizens, who support the notion of collaboration across the alternative parties, would not think through the issue to its logical conclusion. But what has been described is not far-fetched. It is based on the available empirical evidence of how each party conducts itself and approaches the idea of elected political office. Many netizens appear to view things in immediate terms, in terms of a more strident voice in Parliament.

Before ending this section, it is worth noting that in 1996 when the SDP made a representation to the Select Committee on Verification of Heath Care Subsidy of Government Polyclinics and Public Hospitals, its written submission included the statement that, "Between 1970 and 1990, the Government's share of total health expenditure fell from 40% to 5% with the sharpest from within the last 10 years."[14] This was erroneous. Consequently, the four SDP representors were referred to Parliament's Committee of Privileges. The Committee imposed the following fines: $25,000 on Chee; $13,000 on Wong Hong Toy; $8,000 on S. Kunalen; and, $5,000 on Kwan Yue Keng.[15] The WP's Low Thia Khiang, who was a member of the Committee of Privileges, had proposed amendments to the sanctions, as follows: $5,000 for Chee, $2,500 for Wong, $1,000 for Kunalen, and that Kwan be merely reprimanded.[16] Low, not for want of trying, was of course out-voted. (To use parliamentary jargon, his amendments were "negatived".) This event happened before the social media era but, nonetheless, at the time it was discussed by politically-engaged Singaporeans. The hardcore

---

14 Eighth Parliament of Singapore, *Report of the Select Committee on Verification of Health Care Subsidy of Government Polyclinics and Public Hospitals*, Presented to Parliament on 30ᵗʰ September 1996, p. viii.

15 Eighth Parliament of Singapore, *Report of the Committee of Privileges: Complaints Against Representors from the Singapore Democratic Party*, Presented to Parliament on 22ⁿᵈ November 1996, p. xxiii.

16 Ibid., Appendix D, p. D6.

anti-PAP types, instead of viewing Low's effort for what it was — a well-meaning attempt to soften the blow on the SDP representors — took the reverse tact. They criticised him for agreeing with the basic PAP premise that the representors had consciously misled Parliament and, therefore, deserved to be punished. This is another example of Voltaire's injunction "The perfect is the enemy of the good." The 1996 episode highlights the real possibility of how things could pan out if, together with the WP, there was another party to the left of the WP in Parliament, and that party adopted a truculent and combative approach to the PAP and expected the WP to fully sign off on that approach.

What of the PSP as a possible partner of the WP?

The surface impression is that the Progress Singapore Party (PSP) and the WP are quite similar in political terms and so, logically, one could expect some collaboration, if not a tacit alliance between the two parties going into the election that will follow GE2020. The surface impression is, however, at a variance to the reality. Chapter 4 had sketched out how PSP chief Tan Cheng Bock (TCB) had attempted to court the WP. At best, his attempts yielded mixed results. In advance of GE2020, there were a number of stumbling blocks to a formal arrangement between the PSP and the WP. One was the WP's inability to identify who would be the candidates standing on the PSP ticket. In a discussion with Singh in 2019 he had mentioned this concern. The WP's view was that the PSP could not run simply on the personality of TCB. If the PSP was unable to draw star candidates to its ranks, then it did not make much sense for the WP to establish any formal connection with the PSP. Another, related, concern was TCB's thinking that he could go well beyond just establishing some formal connection with the WP. In Singh's words, "He [TCB] wanted to be the glue that brought WP and SDP together." Singh told TCB categorically that such a thing would not happen. It did not occur to TCB that there were significant differences between the WP and the SDP, and the fact that the SDP under Chee carried a lot of baggage. The PSP and the WP did not pursue any further the subject of collaboration between them other than the PSP's unilateral decision not to encroach on the constituencies the WP was targeting for GE2020.

Post-GE2020, there could be some room for both parties to collaborate, but limited to Parliament, if the issues were to have an economic dimension which would be of interest to a large segment of Singaporeans. To that extent, both the WP and the PSP support the idea of a minimum wage, although the PSP's proposal is for a minimum living wage.[17] Other issues that could be a focus for cooperation would include: making it easier for Singaporeans to tap their Central Provident Fund (CPF) monies, increasing subsidies for healthcare, and addressing the issue of Housing and Development Board (HDB) lease decay. On these, the WP and the PSP will likely find some unity of purpose, even if their existing policy approaches to addressing these issues diverge in terms of the details. But beyond issues of an economic dimension, more substantive differences exist between the parties. One relates to the elected presidency. The PSP, in its GE2020 manifesto, had stated that it wanted to "expand presidential oversight over more key public appointments". On the other hand, the WP has been consistent in wanting the elected presidency scrapped altogether and a reversion to the role of a ceremonial president.

A more serious difference between the parties turns on Section 377a of the penal code, criminalising sex between men. Just days before

---

17 "GE2020: PSP launches manifesto calling for minimum living wage, Sers for all flats", *Today*, 29 June 2020, https://www.todayonline.com/singapore/ge2020-psp-launches-manifesto-calling-minimum-living-wage-sers-all-flats. Accessed on 6 January 2021.

GE2020, the PSP made known that it supported the repeal of S377a. It said:[18]

> *We have received many queries from the public regarding Progress Singapore Party's stance on Penal Code S377a.*
>
> *The party's stance is that we would not object to a repeal of Section 377a in order to eliminate the criminalisation of homosexuality.*
>
> *However, the current debate over S377a goes beyond the criminal aspect. It has become a proxy combat zone for other issues like the sanctity of traditional family structures. These structures are long-standing human institutions that should be allowed to remain undisturbed before S377a is repealed.*
>
> *However, we will not be doing a deep dive into the different parameters involved at this point.*

This statement, and in fact the issue over 377a, did not get much notice during the GE2020 campaign, unlike GE2011 where it proved problematic for the SDP. On the other hand, the WP's stance on 377a had long been telegraphed. The WP had taken the decision not to support the repeal of 377a because there was no consensus within the party for doing so. That was the WP's official line. And, the last statement the WP made public on this was when Singh spoke to students at the National University of Singapore on 3 April 2019.[19]

The repeal of 377a had been supported by Lee Hsien Yang, and to what extent he, as a prominent PSP member, had any influence on PSP

---

18 "GE2020: PSP supports the repeal of 377A in principle", *Yahoo! News*, 8 July 2020, https://sg.news.yahoo.com/ge-2020-psp-supports-repeal-of-377-a-in-principle-171514775.html. Accessed on 6 January 2021.

19 "Workers' Party will not call for repeal of section 377a, as there is no consensus among its leaders: Pritam Singh", *The Straits Times*, 8 April 2019, https://www.straitstimes.com/singapore/workers-party-will-not-call-for-repeal-of-section-377a-as-there-is-no-consensus-among-its. Accessed on 6 January 2021.

policy in that regard is not clear. It ought to be pointed out that during the presidential election campaign of August 2011, when asked about 377a, TCB gave an answer that some might have found puzzling. He said: "As a doctor I've seen patients of mine also with this type of lifestyle. It's a lifestyle choice. So, I've no difficulty in accepting this lifestyle choice."[20] It's unclear whether Lee Hsien Yang views the matter as a "lifestyle choice" or, indeed, whether Lesbian, Gay, Bisexual and Transgender (LGBT) rights activists would have been comfortable with TCB characterising homosexuality as a "lifestyle choice" even as he supported a repeal of 377a.

In the months following GE2020 there was one issue that emerged where there was also a difference in policy between the WP and the PSP. This involved the government's efforts to stem the COVID-19 outbreak through contact-tracing. The matter emerged when the digital system TraceTogether was rolled out by the government to facilitate contact-tracing of persons who might have been in physical proximity with an infected person. The government had earlier made an undertaking that the system, manifested as either a smartphone app or a physical token device, would only be used for the one purpose it was created for — tracing persons who had been in proximity to someone infected with COVID-19. Subsequently, however, the government disclosed that under Section 20 of the Criminal Procedure Code (CPC), the police would be able to use information from TraceTogether in criminal investigations. The government's backtracking on an earlier promise to restrict use of TraceTogether for just COVID-19 contact-tracing triggered some public backlash.[21] This led to a concession by the government that the police could only follow-up on information

---

20 "TOC Face to Face 2 18 August 2011 Part 2", YouTube, 21 August 2011, https://www.youtube.com/watch?v=I9hh_Wzy6lo. Accessed on 18 February 2021.

21 "Some TraceTogether users upset with Govt's revelation on police access to data, say they'll use it less", *Today*, 7 January 2021, https://www.todayonline.com/singapore/some-tracetogether-users-upset-govts-revelation-police-access-data-say-theyll-use-it-less. Accessed on 7 January 2021.

collected by TraceTogether for seven types of serious criminal offences.[22] An urgent Bill was moved in Parliament so that this tight restriction on use of TraceTogether data would be set into law. The WP expressed its reservations that data collected by TraceTogether could be used in police investigations, but the party said that it would support the Bill. Singh, noting that the Bill would see a "significant reduction" in the wide ambit of the CPC said that "a Singaporean's right to privacy is better protected with this Bill than without it."[23] Some netizens were disappointed with the WP's stand on the matter and, unsurprisingly, reverted to form by accusing the WP of not playing its role as the opposition but, instead, being "PAP-lite". On the other hand, the PSP was adamant that it could not support the Bill. NCMP Leong Mun Wai, noting that the PSP fully supported the government's efforts at combatting the COVID-19 pandemic, nonetheless said that public trust in political institutions would be eroded if the Bill was passed into law. In his words: "[T]he PSP is not objecting to this Bill for the sake of objecting. We have thought of supporting it with some changes but to trade off public trust in public health measures which must be of utmost priority in a pandemic crisis, for public safety is too much for us."[24]

Though the WP's and the PSP's positions on TraceTogether data collection were divergent, intellectually and politically both positions made sense for each of the two parties. For the WP, there was a simple realisation, that whatever the party said, the Bill would still be pushed

---

22 "Bill to restrict use of TraceTogether to serious crimes seeks to assure public their data will be safeguarded: Vivian", *The Straits Times*, 3 February 2021.

23 "Workers' Party supports Bill on use of TraceTogether data, but asks how critical info is for criminal probe", *The Straits Times*, 2 February 2021, https://www.straitstimes.com/singapore/politics/wp-prepared-to-support-bill-that-restricts-use-of-contact-tracing-data-says. Accessed on 3 February 2021.

24 "NCMP Leong Mun Wai TraceTogether speech in Parliament 2 Feb 2021", *Progress Singapore Party*, 2 February 2021, https://psp.org.sg/ncmp-leong-mun-wai-tracetogether-speech-in-parliament-2nd-feb-2021/. Accessed on 3 February 2021.

through the PAP-dominated Parliament. The WP made its reservations known but, ultimately, it was aware that, politically, in the situation of a heath crisis the optics would look better for the party if it placed national interest ahead of, what might come across to some as, narrow partisan point-scoring. On the other hand, the PSP's position also made sense for the PSP, because being a far smaller entity in Parliament, in order for its voice to be heard it had to differentiate itself from the crowd. True enough, in its opposition to the Bill the PSP got its media publicity.[25] At the early stage of a new Parliament, the differences in policy positions between the WP and the PSP have become increasingly stark, as will be elaborated later.

The lesson from Malaysia's Pakatan Harapan coalition is not merely how the different parties gravitated together to form a coalition-of-convenience against the Barisan Nasional government, defeating the latter at the May 2018 general election,[26] but also how relatively quickly the coalition fell apart due to policy differences and individual ambitions amongst its key players. The same cannot be ruled out in any attempt at coalition-building between the WP and some other alternative party. Those political personalities outside the WP who urge the formation of a coalition might well be the very ones who then fracture that coalition when they conclude that they cannot move the WP towards their own political vision for Singapore. Whatever guarantees that they give to the WP in advance would be worth nothing because that is the nature of politics. This point about real barriers to the WP collaborating with other alternative parties needs to be explained further because, as an issue, it simply will not go away.

---

25 "PSP opposes Bill, asks Govt to 'keep its original promise' on data", *The Straits Times*, 3 February 2021.

26 What can be described as a fairly accurate, but in hindsight romanticised, version of the Pakatan Harapan's victory can be found in Kee Thuan Chye, *The People's Victory: How Malaysians Saved Their Country*, (Marshall Cavendish Editions, 2019).

Are the WP's differences with other alternative parties greater than with the PAP?

By mid-March 2021, some eight months after GE2020, talk began to re-emerge online about the alternative parties needing to collaborate so as to put up a united front against the PAP. In response to one netizen, Peoples Voice (PV) leader Lim Tean, who is never short on sharp rhetoric, posted on his Facebook page on 13 March 2021, the following: "Opposition without wanting to be the government is a total waste of time. An opposition that is worth its salt and wants to do good for the People must be working towards being the government." These remarks constituted barely disguised criticism of the WP. Yet, should the WP take lectures from Lim? He and his PV fell well below of securing victory in constituencies the PV contested at GE2020. Lim himself had helmed the PV team in Jalan Besar group representation constituency (GRC) that took 34.64% of the valid votes cast against a PAP team led by arguably the most unpopular Cabinet minister in that election, Josephine Teo. Also, a five-member PV team went into an ill-advised three-cornered fight, that included the Singapore Democratic Alliance, in Pasir Ris-Punggol GRC. The PV team garnered just 12.17% of the valid votes cast and, in the process, lost election deposits amounting to $67,500.[27] Since GE2020, PV members have conducted themselves in such a manner that has given the impression that these results either never happened or that the results are somehow irrelevant.

Relative to other politicians, post-GE2020, Lim continued to hold in thrall a relatively large number of Singaporean Facebook users, appealing directly to their feelings. Those users appear to be disproportionately of the older, baby-boomer, generation, many of whom had also avidly attended events at Hong Lim Park where Lim was a speaker, and where they applauded him for his fiery rhetoric aimed at the PAP. Lim's online following is mostly restricted to the irreducible core of anti-PAP voters (see Chapter 1). It does not get much beyond

---

27 The threshold for retaining an election deposit in Singapore parliamentary elections is 12.5% or one-eighth of the valid votes cast.

that. Reacting to Lim's Facebook post of 13 March 2021, a person with the handle Jordan Tan, left the following comment as a set of questions:

Why are Opposition parties so splintered and such a disparate lot? Why not set aside all the personal political aspirations and form a coalition to REMOVE the PAP once and for all? What differences do Opposition parties have with each other, that is [sic] equal or greater than your differences with the PAP?

These questions call out for answers. In providing answers, it is first worth noting that there are a number of issues of totemic significance across the alternative parties. By way of illustration, it would be sufficient to mention just four: the decay of HDB flat leases; the large population of foreign nationals (colloquially termed "foreign talent") living and working in Singapore and, related to that, its impact on the employment of Singaporeans; retirement adequacy and the matter of Singaporeans' CPF savings; and, the emergence of a culture war that, in recurrent media headlines, has focused on LGBT rights. Each of these will be taken in turn.

HDB lease decay. Many of the alternative parties are likely to find common cause on the matter of HDB lease decay. Most are likely to suggest that the government resolve it through a one-off extension to the leases of first-generation flats with attendant government subsidies for their refurbishment. Alternatively, the HDB could phase-in a re-housing of those living in aging HDB blocks. In other words, instead of the Selective En bloc Redevelopment Scheme (SERS), the government might have to concede to a wholescale redevelopment of blocks of HDB flats which have aged to the extent of falling into disrepair. A wholescale redevelopment of such blocks of flats would not include the same generous SERS compensation package to existing owners who have little choice but to re-locate. That, nevertheless, might be one of the politically viable solutions for the PAP in dealing with HDB lease decay.

CPF savings and retirement adequacy. On the issue of retirement adequacy and the utilisation of CPF savings, across the alternative parties there are evident policy differences. The WP takes the approach of allowing for, what might be described as a *moderately expanded* utilisation by Singaporeans of their CPF savings. This approach by the WP contrasts markedly with some other alternative parties which either tend to place the onus on the government to fund Singaporeans in their retirement and/or allow for a far higher ceiling on the amounts that Singaporeans can withdraw from their CPF savings. (This includes a withdrawal of savings in their entirety at age 55.) Much of the Singaporean voting public is aware of the difference between what is desirable and what is possible. Most, being reasonable and pragmatic, will opt for the latter, which is what the WP puts on the table.

Foreign nationals and a pandemic spawning racial incidents. On the substantial pool of foreign nationals in Singapore, the PSP and the PV have taken an increasingly populist line, prompting some Singaporeans to make parallels with anti-foreigner sentiment in other countries. The stance of the PSP and the PV is significantly at variance from that adopted by the WP, which is far more nuanced in any discussion of the issue. The WP mostly focuses on advocating for employment for Singaporeans. The WP shies away from direct criticism of foreign nationals.[28] The principle behind this approach underscores what would be apparent to any sitting MP — that in the electoral division being overseen, perhaps up to 40% of the residents might be non-Singaporeans.[29] Many of these non-Singaporeans are, to varying degrees, integrated with the community of Singaporeans.[30]

---

28 At the Punggol East by-election in January 2013, it was observable that the WP campaign was unwilling to engage in direct discussion about the issue of foreigners in Singapore. At the time, I recall having a conversation with a senior journalist at *The Straits Times*, and he said that he also noticed that the WP tended to merely "dance around the issue".

29 Such has been the demographic change of Singapore since the early 2000s.

30 Here, it ought to be pointed out that, as a generalisation, Western expatriates do tend to lead separate lives from most Singaporeans, and that their contact with Singaporeans is largely of a transactional nature. There are, of course, exceptions to this generalisation.

Consequently, MPs regularly get appeals from residents to assist on immigration-related matters.[31] MPs might, therefore, find themselves in the invidious position of, on the one hand, writing appeal letters on behalf of Singaporean constituents who have a family member or relative who's a non-Singaporean and, on the other, being pressured by other Singaporeans to speak out in Parliament against the population of foreign nationals in Singapore. Political parties that hold actual constituency seats — namely, the PAP and the WP — are fully aware of this existential reality and tend to tread carefully so that they don't place themselves in a no-win situation.

On the other hand, the PSP, through its NCMP Leong Mun Wai, has spoken out multiple times on the issue of Singaporeans being disadvantaged by the population of non-Singaporeans. The issue he has raised is important but whether he has shown much finesse in raising it is another matter. This is what Leong said in his maiden speech to Parliament on 1 September 2021:[32]

It is disconcerting to have many of our countrymen live outside Singapore in Johor and Batam while we are housing more than two million foreigners on our island at the same time. Surely, more consideration can be given to Singaporeans who are citizens of our sovereign city-state. We are not being xenophobic or nativist because we have a long tradition of accepting foreigners into our society. In fact, many of us have fond memories of the old foreign talents who have trained and helped us to "eat other people's lunch" and "not to take away our lunch".

31 This is not any different from the experience of many British MPs conducting their routine surgeries.

32 *Debate on President's Address*, 1 September 2021, *Official Reports — Parliamentary Debates (Hansard)*, https://sprs.parl.gov.sg/search/sprs3topic?reportid=president-address-1452. Accessed on 20 March 2021.

He went on to make the following observations:[33]

The Government, however, had introduced a different brand of foreign talent to us from the turn of the millennium. As a high-profile manifestation of that policy, Mr John Olds was appointed the CEO of DBS Bank in August 1998. At that time, I remembered a senior Japanese banker had called me and commented, "Leong-san, it's like having a foreigner to run Mitsubishi Bank in Japan. It is unthinkable!".

Mr Speaker, Sir, in my heart, I had supported the appointment of John Olds in 1998. However, I am deeply disappointed now because 22 years later after his appointment, DBS is still without a homegrown CEO.

Leong's second set of remarks, in effect referencing Piyush Gupta, the Chief Executive Officer (CEO) of DBS Bank were controversial. Gupta had been born in India. When he was appointed CEO of DBS in September 2009, he was a Singapore permanent resident but, according to a *Reuters* report at the time, he was in the process of applying for Singapore citizenship.[34] So, factually, Gupta was not "homegrown". However, Singaporeans' concern with the issue of the population of foreigners in their midst has not really focused on those who secure positions at the very top of the professions. In fact, if one goes back to the period pre-2000, most Singaporeans equated the concept of "foreign talent" with precisely those from around the world who were the best and brightest in their fields and could add value to companies by being at their apex. The problem which increasing numbers of Singaporeans have had with the PAP government's foreign talent policy at the turn of the millennium has been that foreign nationals have been competing with Singaporeans, and displacing them, in mid-level positions — i.e.,

---

33 Ibid.

34 "Newsmaker — DBS taps Citi banker Piyush Gupta for Asia push", *Reuters*, 1 September 2021, https://www.reuters.com/article/idINIndia-42139520090901. Accessed on 20 March 2021.

as PMETs. Leong's oblique reference to Gupta did not go down well with the government. The then Minister for Communications and Information, S. Iswaran, was to respond to Leong's remarks by contrasting them with the approach taken by the WP to the issue of foreign nationals. He said:[35]

We have painstakingly built an open and inclusive economy — that is able to create opportunities for Singaporeans by welcoming competitive enterprises and talent. It is a precious asset that we must not squander.

I was therefore reassured when the Leader of the Opposition [Pritam Singh] recognised in his speech that the presence of foreign workers, and I quote, "gives Singapore a vitality that keeps us economically relevant and also provides jobs and opportunities to our fellow Singaporeans". I think this is an important signal and a good starting point.

In contrast, I was troubled when Non-Constituency Member of Parliament Leong Mun Wai lamented that we do not have a homegrown CEO for DBS. By all means, let us passionately argue the case to do more for Singaporeans. But, as Parliamentarians, let us also be careful about what our words convey; in this case, the message we send to those who — to paraphrase Mr S Rajaratnam — have chosen out of conviction to become citizens of Singapore.

Undeterred, Leong countered:[36]

In terms of why I want to keep to my statement is because when I gave the speech, when people listened to the speech, including the new citizens and

---

35 Debate on President's Address, 4 September 2021, *Official Reports — Parliamentary Debates (Hansard)*, https://sprs.parl.gov.sg/search/sprs3topic?reportid=president-address-1478. Accessed on 20 March 2021.

36 Ibid.

foreigners in Singapore, they would have appreciated that I said it was over a period of 22 years. Why did the Government not put in certain safeguards in the process or certain other rules to ensure that we have the skills transfer. Localisation is not the word anymore, but at least to ensure that Singaporeans will be groomed to take over the job.

By way of rebuttal, Iswaran said: "I just want to go back to a point I made in my speech. As Parliamentarians, we must be not just the Voice of the People… Do not take that lightly. Because what we say cannot be unsaid."[37]

The PSP had deliberately positioned itself to take on a populist line, emphasising the importance of Singaporean-ness. A sizeable proportion of the PSP membership comprises PMETs, and Leong had become the face of the party's efforts to raise their concerns in Parliament over the issue of the foreigner influx. In a Budget debate in March 2021, those concerns seemed to move into the unlikely direction of "foreign food", when Leong asserted: "I am a bit worried that in the future, we may have a scenario whereby our hawker centres are no longer serving local food, but more and more foreign food. So is that a scenario that is acceptable if that happens?"[38]

The emphasis on things "foreign" by Leong and the PSP was to come to a head when Law and Home Affairs Minister K. Shanmugam gave a reply in Parliament on 11 May 2021 to a question in relation to a number of racial incidents in Singapore spawned by the COVID-19 pandemic and, in which, those of Indian ethnicity seemed

---

37 Ibid.

38 Budget: Committee of Supply — Head L (Ministry of Sustainability and the Environment), 4 March 2021, *Official Reports — Parliamentary Debates (Hansard)*, https://sprs.parl.gov.sg/search/sprs3topic?reportid=budget-1620. Accessed on 21 March 2021.

to have been scapegoated. Part of Shanmugam's answer was framed in terms of highlighting agitation by certain opposition parties against the India-Singapore Comprehensive Economic Cooperation Agreement (CECA), which had been signed in 2005, and which allows for relatively liberal movement of people ("natural persons") between the two countries.[39] The agreement, however, does not grant Indian citizens the automatic right to employment or permanent residency status in Singapore.[40] But some Singaporeans have increasingly perceived Indian nationals as disproportionately securing jobs in relatively desirable fields such as banking and finance, and Information Technology and, in the process, either displacing Singaporeans from these fields or making it harder for Singaporeans to gain employment in them.[41] Equally important, as an acronym, CECA, has in the minds of an increasing number of Singaporeans become synonymous with Indian nationals and, in many instances, simply Indians. Consequently, it has assumed racist overtones, fomenting anti-Indian sentiment which by June 2021 began to move from cyberspace to the real world as manifested in a number of incidents.

In his short parliamentary statement, Shanmugam, referred to growing populism and of parties "encouraging racism and xenophobia and dog whistling".[42] He went on to say:[43]

---

39 *India-Singapore Comprehensive Economic Cooperation Agreement*, http://www. commonlii.org/sg/other/treaties/2005/1/INSFTA-Agreement.html. Accessed on 12 May 2021.

40 Ibid.

41 National Service obligations, including annual in-camp training, are often cited by Singaporeans as one factor that counts against them in the jobs market.

42 Ministry of Home Affairs, *Oral Reply to Clarification Questions on Recent Racial Incidents Connected to the Pandemic, by Mr K Shanmugam, Minister for Home Affairs and Minister for Law*, 11 May 2021, https://www.mha.gov.sg/mediaroom/ parliamentary/oral-reply-to-clarification-questions-on-recent-racial-incidents-connected-to-the-pandemic-by-mr-k-shanmugam-minister-for-home-affairs-and-minister-for-law/. Accessed on 13 May 2021.

43 Ibid.

> *There have been several canards about CECA, promoted by a whispering*
> *campaign. If anyone here believes that CECA is a problem, put it up for*
> *a Motion, debate it openly and let's hear whether Singaporeans benefit*
> *or lose from it. I am looking at you, Mr Leong. I invite you to put up a*
> *Motion to debate CECA. You know that most of what is said about*
> *CECA is false.*

In response, Leong said that his party would be interested to take up the challenge at some stage, but he also stated unequivocally that he and the PSP were not being xenophobic and "definitely racism has no place" in their "overall thinking".[44] For his part, the WP chief and Leader of the Opposition, Pritam Singh, said his party agreed with Shanmugam's statement, making clear that, "There is no place for racism in Singapore — no ifs, no buts."[45]

Shanmugam's statement and the responses highlighted an obvious difference in emphasis between the PSP and the WP over foreign talent. The one year which elapsed since GE2020 indicated that that difference had grown to become a wedge issue between the two parties. Even within the PSP, there was increasing disquiet among some members that the party had engaged in "cheap politics".[46] As one PSP member told *Today* in a report published on 16 July 2021, "Taking a very antagonistic stance might ruin trade relations... [W]hen (political party members) come out and ask for numbers of jobs that have been

---

44 Quoted in "Racism and xenophobic behaviour will become normalised if S'pore is not careful, warns Shanmugam", *The Straits Times*, 11 May 2021, https://www. straitstimes.com/singapore/racism-and-xenophobic-behaviour-will-become-normalised-if-spore-is-not-careful-warns. Accessed on 13 May 2021.

45 Ibid.

46 Quoted in "Some party members concerned with 'racial undertones' of NCMP Leong Mun Wai's Ceca speeches; closed door meeting to be held", *Today*, 16 July 2021, https://www.todayonline.com/singapore/some-psp-members-concerned-racial-undertones-ncmp-leong-mun-wais-ceca-speeches-closed-door. Accessed on 18 July 2021.

lost and replaced by CECA Indians, you are targeting the Indian community."[47] In response, the PSP leadership put out a statement saying that the party's stance on CECA was not about Indians.[48] But the party's public stance is inconsistent with that of some of its supporters who have posted on Facebook racially-charged comments about CECA.

The clearest indication of the division between the WP and the PSP over the issue of CECA surfaced when the WP was compelled to vote against a PSP motion tabled on 14 September 2021 because it appeared heavily focused on CECA. The PSP motion read:[49]

FOREIGN TALENT POLICY: That this Parliament calls upon the Government to take urgent and concrete action to address the widespread anxiety among Singaporeans on jobs and livelihoods caused by the foreign talent policy and the provisions on Movement of Natural Persons in some free trade agreements like the Comprehensive Economic Cooperation Agreement.

All nine WP members present in Parliament voted against the PSP motion. The WP MPs also voted against the government's own motion which, among other things, included the statement that, "[T]his House… deplores attempts to spread misinformation about free trade agreements like the Singapore-India Comprehensive Economic Cooperation Agreement (CECA), stir racism and xenophobia, and cause

---

47 Ibid.

48 "Progress Singapore Party rejects claims that its stance on CECA is about Indians", *The Straits Times*, 19 July 2021, https://www.straitstimes.com/singapore/politics/progress-singapore-party-rejects-claims-that-its-stance-on-ceca-is-about-race. Accessed on 19 July 2021.

49 Fourteenth Parliament of Singapore, *First Session, Order Paper, No. 38*, 14 September 2021. Accessed on 17 September 2021.

fear and anxiety amongst Singaporeans."[50] The WP stated publicly that it had opposed both motions because the amendments it had proposed in Parliament to the motions calling for "better information disclosure to improve employment policies could not be carried". The WP statement and stance, posted on its official Facebook page, was applauded by the party's supporters, but it ought to be recorded that there was also a smattering of netizens who said, variously, that they were "sad", "disappointed" and "disgusted" that the party did not see fit to support the PSP motion.

LGBT rights. As had been touched on earlier in this chapter, the PSP and the SDP support the repeal of 377A but the WP's stand is clear — for the time being it supports the retention of 377A. Officially, the party's publicly declared position is that its leadership is divided on that matter. In fact, there is an obvious reality on the ground: the staunchest supporters of the WP in the party's old strongholds of Hougang SMC and Aljunied GRC, are the most adamant in wanting the retention of 377A, as indicated from feedback which the party has occasionally received. An anecdote might be sufficient to illustrate the point. In May 2019, Lee Hsien Yang and his immediate family visited South Africa where his younger son, Li Huanwu, was to marry his boyfriend, Heng Yiru.[51] (South Africa had been chosen as it had legalised same-sex marriage in 2006.) Pictures were posted online of the couple and immediate family members of the two.[52] The reaction online was overwhelmingly positive. Not long thereafter, a WP parliamentarian

---

50 Ibid.

51 "Lee Hsien Yang's 2nd son, Li Huanwu, marries boyfriend in South Africa", *Mothership*, 24 May 2019.

52 "Li Huanwu, grandson of Singapore founding father Lee Kuan Yew, marries boyfriend, Heng Yiru — and Chinese social media users cheer them on", *South China Morning Post*, 25 May 2019, https://www.scmp.com/news/asia/southeast-asia/article/3011806/li-huanwu-grandson-singapore-founding-father-lee-kuan-yew. Accessed on 8 August 2020. The report tended to highlight a disconnect between online and offline sentiment on a polarising issue.

on house visits in Aljunied GRC told me that one of the first remarks made by residents to him was in relation to this event in South Africa. As he put it, the reaction from the ground was less positive and unprompted. The remarks from residents turned on "What is that?"

The disconnect across personalities from other opposition parties

Returning to the Facebook user Jordan Tan, even before the questions he left on Lim Tean's post on 13 March 2021, he had earlier, on 8 March 2021, left a comment on a Facebook post by Singh. The WP chief had posted about the party's interventions in Parliament in the previous two weeks during the various debates following the Budget announcement. Tan left a comment asking the following: "I was wondering if there have been any cooperation and synergy between WP and other Opposition parties, and their… leaders such as Tan CB, Kenneth Jeya, Lim Tean and Chee SJ [Soon Juan]?" Two other Facebook users replied to Tan, indicating in the negative.

Chapter 2 had noted the observation made by some that the SDP had "rebranded". But that chapter suggested that any perceived rebranding appeared to be cosmetic in nature. The SDP revolves around one personality — Chee. The PSP also revolves around the personality of TCB. The PV is not dissimilar — it revolves around Lim Tean. As for Kenneth Jeyaretnam, when it was disclosed that, in late April 2020, the WP's Low Thia Khiang had suffered a bad fall and had to be hospitalised, his Reform Party (RP) put out the following statement: "This fall bears a troubling resemblance to the circumstances in which Danny Loh, who was managing agent of Aljunied Town Council passed away. We wonder whether stress caused by Gov [government] investigations had been a factor."[53] The RP statement was in direct

---

53 "Reform Party draws flak for statement on Low Thia Khiang's hospitalisation", *AsiaOne*, 4 May 2020, https://www.asiaone.com/singapore/reform-party-draws-flak-statement-low-thia-khiangs-hospitalisation. Accessed on 15 February 2021.

contrast to the many expressions of goodwill towards, and concern for, Low made by senior PAP politicians.

Still, there are observers who keep ignoring the empirical evidence and continue to speak in ambiguous terms about the need for greater "opposition" to the PAP. The reality is that the WP is in fact in the advantageous position of being in Singapore's political centre-ground. Across the alternative parties, to the WP's left is the SDP; and, to the WP's right are parties such as the PSP and PV. Beyond policy, the differences in temperament of personalities are significant and, thus, cannot be ignored.

WP knits together a coalition of voters

It is worth noting that during the GE2020 campaign, the WP's Singh had made remarks that were the closest to saying outright that there was a clear distinction between the WP and the other alternatives. In a Party Political Broadcast on 2 July 2020, he said:[54]

> *The PAP will form the next Government. That is a certainty. Even in 2011, when Singaporeans were openly unhappy, the PAP won 81 out of 87 seats, even though it won only 60 per cent of the vote. If you live where the Workers' Party is contesting, the PAP does not need your vote to form Government. But we need your votes.*

Looking at the construction of these remarks, it could be interpreted that Singh was suggesting, without being explicit, that the other alternative parties were not electable (thus, "The PAP will form the next Government.") Consequently, voters in all the six WP-contested constituencies could vote for the WP without worrying that the PAP

---

54 "GE2020: WP Speaks in Party Political Broadcast on Jul 2", YouTube, 2 July 2020, https://www.youtube.com/watch?v=mLljv5OaGs4. Accessed on 16 February 2021.

would be defeated as the government. If one looked back to when Singh was first elected an MP, in 2011, there has been a consistency in his thinking about certain matters. This is particularly so in relation to the WP having formal dealings with other alternative parties. For instance, at a July 2011 Institute of Policy Studies forum, where he was a participant, Singh was asked whether the opposition would be ready to form a government. He side-stepped the question and, instead, suggested that the WP did not rule out the possibility of forming a "unity government" with the PAP, should the latter fall short of a parliamentary majority in a general election. This is what he said:[55]

> It may be the case in the future that the PAP only wins 30 seats and they have to form a coalition government, and realise that there is only a finite number of individual parties they want to work with.
>
> Let's not rule out the prospects of the PAP forced into coalition politics. And coalition governments don't mean that things don't happen... (there) could be unity government... There is a huge political space for us to actually think about, insofar as how politics in Singapore... is going forward.

These remarks caused an outcry amongst hardened anti-PAP netizens, who could not stomach the fact that the WP would actually be contemplating forming a "unity government" with, what those netizens would consider, their implacable enemy. Consequently, within 24 hours, Singh was compelled to retract his remarks, saying that they were merely "theoretical",[56] and that, "The party [the WP] has never discussed the idea of coalition at all."[57] However, Singh's original remarks

---

55 Quoted in "Pritam retracts coalition suggestion", *The Straits Times*, 10 July 2011.

56 Ibid.

57 Quoted in "MP Pritam Singh clarifies coalition government comment", *The New Paper*, 10 July 2011.

highlight a reality: the WP will mirror the nature and expectations of the broad electorate. The party has held this position since GE2011, but it is not political for it to articulate that position so openly.

Instead of any notion of being part of a coalition of parties arrayed against the PAP, the WP's focus has been on knitting together a coalition of voters across most demographics. This coalition of voters is the direct result of careful positioning in the political spectrum by the WP as a moderate alternative to the PAP. As stated in an earlier chapter, this positioning allows for proximity voting by a large segment of the electorate; they vote the party and its brand that closely approximates what they can support.

Main voting bloc B, of moderate PAP voters in Table 1.2 (Chapter 1), which the WP successfully induced a portion of to its side in Aljunied GRC at GE2020, would be a focus of much of the WP's outreach efforts. Unlike the hardcore of PAP voters, moderate PAP voters are not averse to seeing merely tweaks or minor modifications — not a wholesale change — to the way Singapore is governed. This was analysed in Chapter 6 in terms of the Median Voter Theorem. The WP is the only party which moderate PAP voters might feel both comfortable with and which could at least pressure the PAP towards a more centrist direction politically. And, one year after GE2020, the PAP's support within its moderate base of voters looked shaky in the face of a WP that retained high levels of popularity.

Logic would dictate that in fact the only segment of voters still available for the WP to bring over to its side is the bloc of moderate PAP voters. At GE2020, in terms of valid votes cast, in Marine Parade GRC, the WP was 7.74% adrift from victory; and, it was 3.87% adrift in East Coast GRC. In those constituencies, the WP had tapped out most of the other segments of voters. The only remaining segment for the party to mine are moderate PAP voters.

In his 2021 New Year's Day message,[58] Singh, speaking as WP leader, made clear that his priority was a "mission to build a moderate and fair Party that seeks to provide a trusted alternative to voters, and act as a balancing force to our political system." As long as moderate PAP voters keep perceiving the WP to be, in both word and deed, the duality of a moderate and trusted alternative to the PAP, then that segment of voters can see themselves being enticed over to the WP.

There are, however, two questions. Will the PAP staunch any further haemorrhaging of its vote towards the WP? And, in fact, does the PAP have the resolve to do so? Answers to these questions are attempted in the next two chapters.

---

58 "WP will continue to champion policy alternatives in new year, says Pritam Singh", *The Straits Times*, 1 January 2021, https://www.straitstimes.com/singapore/politics/wp-will-continue-to-champion-policy-alternatives-in-new-year-says-pritam-singh. Accessed on 17 February 2021.

CHAPTER 9

PAP Succession: Public Image and Reality, and Whether There is a Resolve to Claw Back Lost Support

The previous three chapters demonstrated the centrality of the Workers' Party (WP) to the narrative developed in this book. This was not least in terms of why any association the WP might have with the other alternative parties, or if the WP pursued a mostly progressive agenda, would dim the party's electoral prospects. The other entity by which the WP's prospects should be judged against is, of course, its main opponent — the People's Action Party (PAP). This is one of two chapters that fills the remainder of the narrative.

The events which coalesced around GE2020, and the actual results of that election, cannot be viewed in isolation. Instead, today's events can only be understood in relation to political history stretching back three decades. To merely take a snapshot of the events of 2020 and attempt to divine answers from them is to subject a complex subject to parochial and cursory treatment that is seemingly a reflection of the Digital Age. To that extent, readers are asked for their indulgence as reference is made to personalities and issues from the recent past, so that proper perspective is established and the political continuum is fully understood. The popular view in the public imagination generally deviates from a more textured reality. That reality underscores the difficulty for substantial change to occur in Singapore's political realm.

A successor will neither be a hawk nor a dove, but a product of the PAP system

One issue which is a preoccupation with the mainstream media and a number of online commentators, centres on political succession. Who will succeed

Lee Hsien Loong (LHL) as prime minister? This is not an issue that interests me terribly, as my analysis has long been that whoever becomes prime minister (PM) will merely be a product of the PAP system and continue a type of austere governance to which Singaporeans have long been accustomed.[1] However, it would be remiss not to say something on the matter, given that it appears to excite others. The political succession issue has been framed in the conventional Singapore technocratic narrative about the fourth-generation (4G) PAP leaders — i.e., those who hold full Cabinet ministerial rank. Heng Swee Keat, who entered politics at GE2011, rose quite rapidly through the ranks, holding key portfolios, to eventually get promoted on 1 May 2019 to deputy prime minister (DPM). Consequently, that promotion led Heng to be widely viewed as the presumptive PM. This was notwithstanding the fact that three years earlier, during a Cabinet meeting, he had suffered a serious stroke. He was to recover quite miraculously from that medical episode, but questions lingered about whether he could take on the stresses of the high-pressured role of PM. The stroke has not appeared to impair Heng's faculties. Here, it should be remembered that LHL himself had been stricken with intermediate grade malignant lymphoma in October 1992. After going through chemotherapy, LHL's cancer went into remission in April 1993. He continued to maintain a high work-rate as DPM and, later, PM. The same could have been said of Heng. However, unexpectedly, on 8 April 2021 (the "8 April announcement"), Singaporeans were to learn that Heng was taking himself out of the running for PM. In his letter to LHL, Heng said, among other things, that:[2]

The next prime minister should have a sufficiently long runway — to master the demands of leading our nation; formulate and see through our longer-term strategies for the country; and win the confidence and support

---

1 This, again, throws a spotlight on privilege agents being less significant than structural or systemic issues, as was analysed in Chapter 3.

2 Prime Minister's Office, Singapore, *Letter from DPM Heng to PM Lee*, 8 April 2021, https://www.pmo.gov.sg/-/media/PMO/Newsroom/Files/Media-Release/20210408---Letter-from-DPM-Heng-to-PM-Lee-pdf.pdf?la=en. Accessed on 20 April 2021.

of Singaporeans to build this shared future together. This long-term orientation of successive PAP governments and the support of our people have been critical to Singapore's success.

This year, I am 60. As the [COVID-19] crisis will be prolonged, I would be close to the mid-60s when the crisis is over. The 60s are still a very productive time of life. But when I consider the ages at which our first three prime ministers took on the job, I would have too short a runway should I become the next prime minister then. We need a leader who will not only rebuild Singapore post-COVID-19, but also lead the next phase of our nation-building effort.

When I had a stroke in 2016, you and Cabinet colleagues were unstinting with your support. With the great work of my medical team, and the care and encouragement of my family, friends and fellow Singaporeans, I was able to recover fully. Having worked with you, ESM Goh Chok Tong and MM Lee Kuan Yew, I know that the top job imposes exceptional demands on the office-holder. In a very different post-Covid-19 world, the demands will be even more exacting. While I am in good health today, it is in the best interests of the nation, for someone who is younger to tackle the huge challenges ahead.

After careful deliberation and discussion with my family, I have decided to step aside as leader of the 4G team, so that a younger leader who will have a longer runway can take over. It will be for the 4G team to choose this person, and I stand ready to support the next leader.

Heng's decision to no longer want to be considered for the top political job did not really come as a surprise to me. As far back as 2018 I had thought that was a real possibility and this was one reason why I declined to give quotes to journalists whenever they contacted me during 2018–2019 to get my take on the 4G leadership.[3] My reason was that

---

3 When, over lunch, on 5 September 2019 I had remarked to three journalists from *The Straits Times* that it was not at all cut-and-dry that Heng would become PM, they dismissed the very thought. In their view, there was no question that Heng would be the next PM.

Heng, having spent much of his working life as a bureaucrat, was never really able to shake off the heavy air of bureaucracy that seemed to surround him. Consequently, he could never come across as a natural politician. That has been my basic thesis. Thus, I was right, but likely for the wrong reason.

However, the 8 April announcement led many journalists and other observers to work themselves into a frenzy. They seemed to think that the announcement would have considerable ramifications politically and in other dimensions. Some online chatter by those never short of criticism of the PAP was of the view that the announcement had all to do with the 53.39% votes cast for the PAP team headed by Heng in East Coast group representation constituency (GRC). To these critics, the 7,769 votes that separated the PAP and WP teams, was not a good winning margin for a prime minister-in-waiting. It would require 3,885 voters to switch sides for the WP to win East Coast GRC by one vote. A serious analysis would conclude that that would not be an easy feat to achieve. A vote of 53.39% amounts to a conclusive margin of victory. For some perspective, the WP won Sengkang GRC with 52.12% of the vote. That was also a conclusive result.

But Australian scholar Michael Barr provided a markedly different take. Shortly after GE2020, he argued that the significant drop in the PAP's popular vote nationally had much to do with Heng. He said:[4]

> *Heng was… in charge of the PAP's national campaign, so he bears heavy responsibility for the flop. It is a sign of the state of self-delusion, both in cabinet and among what passes for Singapore's political commentariat, that a recurring theme of the election-night coverage was that 'this is not a referendum on Heng Swee Keat'. It was.*

4 Michael Barr, "Singapore government in denial", *East Asia Forum*, 12 July 2020, https://www.eastasiaforum.org/2020/07/12/singapore-government-in-denial/. Accessed on 6 January 2021.

This view, stated with such certainty and confidence, is inconsistent with the empirical evidence set out in Chapters 2 and 3. For Singaporeans, economic rationality drives much of what they do, including how they vote in elections. And, due to an election held in the eye of a pandemic, where there were job losses and a decline in personal wealth, some Singaporeans most adversely affected and who had previously been PAP voters, decided to move away from the party.

The 8 April announcement by Heng sent some observers into a tizzy. They brought up the old trope about the PAP being riven with major splits, something which has been talked about at irregular intervals for decades, but which consistently has proved a false dawn. During the GE2015 campaign, in a broadcast involving the portal *Inconvenient Questions*, where I was a panel speaker, I had publicly dismissed the notion of there being such splits. My view does not differ much from one scholar who in an article published in 2020 had noted that "the PAP will remain cohesive, as it is still the best and safest route for ambitious politicians to gain access to power in the foreseeable future."[5] On the 8 April announcement, while a few bloggers have tended to indicate that wishful thinking could be a political strategy, the actual leading indicator of broad public sentiment, i.e., the local stock market, in its first reaction, appeared to shrug off the announcement as a non-event. For most of the morning of 9 April 2021, the Straits Times Index (STI) slipped in and out of positive territory by 1–2 points. It closed the day at 3,184.54, down 1.86 points or 0.1%.

The mainstream media had all along considered Chan Chun Sing, a former army major-general, and possibly Ong Ye Kung, a former civil servant and trades unionist, as contenders for the top job, if a possible alternative to Heng was ever required. Following the 8 April announcement, a third person, Lawrence Wong, was viewed as another

---

5 Netina Tan, "Minimal Factionalism in Singapore's People's Action Party", *Journal of Current Southeast Asian Affairs*, Vol. 39, No. 1, 2020, p. 136.

contender for PM; this was due to his prominence as joint head of the Multi-ministry Task Force combatting the COVID-19 pandemic through much of 2020 and into 2021. It was felt by many people that Wong had done a good job. In a Cabinet reshuffle following the 8 April announcement, the PM decided to assign Wong the important Finance ministry portfolio. This seemed to indicate that Wong was the frontrunner to be PM. Of the likely contenders for PM, Chan has, in the public perception, often been viewed as relatively conservative and this has been partly attributed to his military background. On the other hand, Ong has been perceived as more down-to-earth; he was part of the PAP's Aljunied team that was defeated by the WP at GE2011 and, consequently, this has been viewed by many as a plus point for him, in terms of a broad political experience. As for Wong, he has projected a steady pair of hands, but also comes across as someone straining not to put a foot wrong. That latter characterisation might be due to a feeling that he is over-correcting his demeanour as a result of the blunt statement he put out on 24 March 2017 when he was National Development Minister. Then, he had said that only a small percentage of Housing and Development Board (HDB) flats were eligible for the Selective En bloc Redevelopment Scheme but, "For the vast majority of HDB flats, the leases will eventually run out, and the flats will be returned to HDB, who will in turn have to surrender the land to the State."[6] As argued in Chapter 2, this statement had unintentionally weaponised the issue of HDB lease decay against Wong's own party.

As is the fluid nature of politics, even in the context of Singapore, known for its certainty and disinclination to provide surprises, who is up or down in the political stakes is a calculation that is often implicitly made by lay people and commentators alike. To that extent, it is

6 Quoted in "Not all old HDB flats are eligible for en bloc: Lawrence Wong", *Today*, 24 March 2017, https://www.todayonline.com/singapore/not-all-old-hdb-are-eligible-en-bloc-lawrence-wong. Accessed on 20 April 2021.

worthwhile mentioning Tan See Leng, who stood as a PAP candidate at GE2020 for Marine Parade GRC. Following the results of that election, Tan was promptly made a Cabinet minister. He was then to come into the public consciousness in parliamentary debates in July and September 2021. Those debates turned on the increasingly vexed issue of Singaporeans being displaced from their jobs; the country's foreign talent policy; and, free trade agreements (FTAs) Singapore had concluded with a number of countries, most notably with India, which critics claimed had contributed to the triple effects of some Singaporeans losing their jobs to an influx of Indian nationals, wage suppression, and an increasing incidence of under-employment. Tan provided a robust defence of government policies, making out the case that FTAs could not be considered the main cause of unemployment and under-employment by Singaporeans. His calm demeanour, ability to think on his feet, and a rich, sonorous voice which conveyed a sense of reassurance, indicated that he had some of the qualities necessary for the top job. Only his relative political inexperience, of having been elected at GE2020, would be considered a minus, but even that could be set aside given how quickly he has been able to look and sound like a seasoned politician.

The popular view is usually at variance to the reality

Apart from differences in personalities, the issue of whether a person is a "hawk" or a "dove" within the PAP might in fact be a false dichotomy. The PAP system, as conceived and developed by Lee Kuan Yew, is inherently conservative, austere and paternalistic by nature. In the past, it was said that those who had liberalising or modernising tendencies would join the PAP and try to reform it from within, to make the party and the leadership from which the government was drawn, more emollient and empathetic to the ground. Delving into the historical record going back some three decades reveals a pattern whereby the public impression of a PAP personality is one that does not quite fit into an image that emerges from a detailed excavation of the evidence. The evidence throws up a picture that is more complex and does not fit in the binary of hawk or dove. To some extent, these are uncomfortable issues, but they need to be reviewed if there is to be a better understanding of developments within the PAP post-GE2020.

Take for example, George Yeo, a former brigadier-general, who entered politics on the PAP ticket in 1988. He was widely viewed as having liberalising instincts who could conceivably reform the PAP from within. As it turned out, Yeo did not change the PAP in any way whatsoever. Instead, over two decades, the PAP had changed him. Yeo was part of the PAP team in Aljunied GRC that was defeated by the WP at GE2011. Even some ordinarily staunch opponents of the PAP felt that Yeo was one of the nicer individuals within the PAP and it was both a pity and ironic that he had to exit politics through defeat at an election. However, all this is part of the general surface impressions that is replete both online and offline. In point of fact, a nice-guy image belied a personality that was in lock-step with party philosophy. For instance, Yeo, as Trade and Industry Minister, had argued for the entry of casinos into Singapore, an idea which had been staunchly opposed by many Singaporeans, on moral and religious grounds, but to no avail. And, earlier, as Minister for Information and the Arts, he adopted a subtle, more sophisticated, policy to government censorship by introducing the concept of "OB markers" (out-of-bound markers), which were undefined and, therefore, placed the onus on individuals to self-censor even otherwise innocuous statements. (He first employed the term OB markers in 1991.) As one scholar observed, "OB markers are intended to limit political engagement, civic action, and participation, and anything else remotely linked to domestic politics in Singapore."[7] What is a sophisticated policy intended to achieve the political objective of hegemony by a political party is viewed by less sophisticated minds

---

7 Terence Lee, "Gestural Politics: Civil Society in 'New' Singapore", *Sojourn: Journal of Social Issues in Southeast Asia*, Vol. 20, No. 2, October 2005, p. 144.

as something which is benign and, thus, acceptable. Then, in 1995, Yeo exhorted Singaporeans to:[8]

Remember your place in society before you engage in political debate. Debate cannot generate into a free-for-all where no distinction is made between the senior and junior party. You must make distinctions — what is high, what is low, what is above, what is below, and then within this, we can have a debate, we can have a distinction... people should not take on those in authority as "equals".

These utterances fall within the Gramscian theory of subordination and hegemony, where people are not merely ruled by force alone but also ideas.[9] Notwithstanding all this, Yeo's popularity with Singaporeans, especially those of a younger age, seemed to centre on his willingness to engage with them on issues directly. During the 1990s, Yeo would write letters to be published in his own name, and not that of his press secretary, in the "forum" page of *The Straits Times*. This was an unusual step for a Cabinet minister; it gave a powerful impression of Yeo more than willing to interact with ordinary Singaporeans. It was that, and other similar gestures, that created an impression of a person who, within the PAP context, was relatively liberal.

Since politics is very much about optics, it's not surprising that anyone who comes across as affable, has good social skills, is not abrasive, and appears to be receptive to different points of view, would be seen in a positive light by many people. And, so, it proved with Tharman Shanmugaratnam. He entered Parliament as part of the PAP's 2001 intake. With a sharp mind, and a command of financial matters, in the space of

---

8 Quoted in Leonel Lim, *Knowledge, Control and Critical Thinking in Singapore: State Ideology and the Politics of Pedagogic Recontextualization*, (New York: Routledge, 2016), p. 174.

9 Thomas R. Bates, "Gramsci and the Theory of Hegemony", *Journal of the History of Ideas*, Vol. 36, No. 2, April–June 1975, p. 351.

a decade he rose to become DPM. After GE2020, he relinquished the DPM post to assume the titles of senior minister and Coordinating Minister for Social Policies. He has been well-regarded by many Singaporeans. But because Shanmugaratnam is not of Chinese ethnicity, in a city-state whose demographic is three-quarters ethnic Chinese, he has been ruled out as a potential PM. He himself has said he is not interested in being PM even though he is rated highly by many Chinese Singaporeans.

Shanmugaratnam has great public relations skills, talks a good game, always demonstrates empathy but, if hypothetically, he were to become PM, would he be able to deliver on a broad agenda somewhat in-line with what his admirers would expect — i.e., more progressive, less elite-driven?

In an episode that led up to the GE2020 campaign, some might say Shanmugaratnam seemed unable to diverge from his party's line. This related to the PAP candidate Ivan Lim, who was supposed to be part of Shanmugaratnam's PAP team for Jurong GRC. Due to an internet campaign which questioned Lim's suitability as an election candidate, he withdrew his candidacy. Almost immediately, both LHL and DPM Heng said that the PAP would launch an investigation over the circumstances surrounding this matter. More than a year after GE2020, there was still no word on any investigation. Shanmugaratnam himself had remained silent throughout. In fact, on election-night itself when his team was confirmed as the winner of the contest in Jurong GRC, Shanmugaratnam did not seem to mind that Lim was part of the team accepting victory in a Facebook livestream. That decision spawned some public criticism of Shanmugaratnam. In a comment he left to his own Facebook post of 12 July 2021, he provided the following rationalisation:

Some have asked why Ivan Lim was in the PAP Jurong GRC team's FacebookLive session after the election results were announced. Allow me to explain. As a prospective candidate until he stepped aside shortly before Nomination Day, he had worked very hard on the ground — as I mentioned in my opening speech. He is naturally not part of the team of MPs. But I wanted to acknowledge the contribution he has made, and have him add his own thanks to residents in addition to those of the five MPs. I felt it was right, and hope you understand my approach on such matters.

Putting aside Shanmugaratnam, some three decades earlier, another non-ethnic Chinese PAP-man who had been touted as prime ministerial material by no less than Lee Kuan Yew himself, Suppiah Dhanabalan, had also been ruled out because of his ethnicity. In a tribute to Lee shortly following his death, Dhanabalan wrote:[10]

I resigned from Cabinet (in 1992) because I had a great difference of view over the use of the Internal Security Act in the 1987 arrests. (In 1987, 22 people — many linked to the Catholic Church — were arrested and detained without trial under the ISA for alleged involvement in a "Marxist conspiracy".)

Lee Kuan Yew thought that mine was a Christian view, because he knew I was a Christian. But it was not a hard-headed political view. We had a difference and the whole Cabinet knew.

The way he saw it depended on his experience, and he had some very traumatic experiences with the communists and how they infiltrated legitimate organisations to get what they wanted. I was looking at it from my point of view, without the experiences he had.

I wouldn't venture to say whether he was right or I was right. So, it was not that he was ruthless, but that he saw dangers where I didn't. Whether it was real or not remains to be seen.

---

10 "Remembering Lee Kuan Yew: A leader who was ruthless in demanding honesty", *The Straits Times*, 24 March 2015, https://www.straitstimes.com/singapore/remembering-lee-kuan-yew-a-leader-who-was-ruthless-in-demanding-honesty. Accessed on 10 February 2021.

When he was a Cabinet minister, Dhanabalan was straightforward, if robust, in his views. In the same condolence letter, Dhanabalan, also made the following observation:[11]

> *To call Lee Kuan Yew my friend would not be quite right. More accurately, we were colleagues. I don't think he had many friends, because he was so focused on doing what was good for the nation, and that would require him sometimes to act against his friends. If he was too friendly with anyone, that could colour his decision, so he was very careful.*

This candour would have escaped most people's attention but it is of some significance. Dhanabalan never went for expedient, politically correct or populist views. He was once described by the *Far Eastern Economic Review* as a man of "tough-minded integrity".[12] The view that Lee did not have many friends tends to chime with what at least two prominent British academics have said. The historian C. Northcote Parkinson, "who met Lee in the 1950s during the latter's periodic visits to Singapore's university, observed him cutting students down and doubted that he was a man even capable of friendship."[13] The British political scientist, and close associate of many Singapore Establishment figures, Michael Leifer (who passed away in 2001), once told me that the second most prominent member of the founding generation of PAP leaders, Goh Keng Swee,[14] did not consider Lee a friend, and Leifer was quite adamant about that. The issue arose in a discussion I had with Leifer where I remarked that Goh and Lee appeared to be firm friends.

---

11 Ibid.

12 This was after it was announced Dhanabalan would be made Minister for National Development, succeeding Teh Cheang Wan, who had committed suicide on 14 December 1986 over serious allegations of corruption.

13 James Minchin, *No Man is an Island: A Study of Lee Kuan Yew*, (Sydney: Allen & Unwin, 1986), p. 25.

14 This was due to their common connection with the London School of Economics.

He instantly took issue with that by saying, "They are not friends, but they respect each other."[15] I retorted, "Are you sure about that?" He replied, "Very sure."[16] But the contrary view — that Goh and Lee were firm friends — has become the accepted conventional wisdom.[17] It is one based on a not unfair assumption: how could Goh and Lee, for so long close political associates, not be life-long friends, and how could anyone suggest otherwise? Or it could in fact be based on rather thin evidence.[18] Where exactly does the truth lie? And does it matter? Whether it actually matters may be determined only in the fullness of time.

15 Discussion with Michael Leifer. This was a discussion with Leifer where we exchanged views and analysis over a manuscript he was putting together on Singapore's foreign policy. This manuscript was to be published as *Singapore's Foreign Policy: Coping with Vulnerability*, (London: Routledge, 2000). Leifer was widely regarded as an objective scholar on the politics and international relations of Southeast Asia. Consequently, there would be no reason for him to concoct the observation that Goh and Lee were "not friends", even as he said that they respected each other. Leifer's objectivity and widespread respect as a scholar was acknowledged in my tribute, "In Memoriam: Michael Leifer, 1933–2001", *Contemporary Southeast Asia*, Vol. 23, No. 1, April 2001.

16 Ibid.

17 Lee said in his eulogy delivered at Goh's funeral that they had become "close friends" during their student days in London (1949–50). However, he made no further reference to their being friends in their later years. Lee's eulogy could be described as a checklist of Goh's achievements and importance as a major figure in the development of Singapore. But the eulogy seemed to lack warmth. (Full video footage of the eulogy can be found online.) Prime Minister's Office, "Eulogy by Minister Mentor Lee Kuan Yew at the State Funeral Service for the Late Dr Goh Keng Swee at the Singapore Conference Hall, Sunday 23 May 2010", https://www.pmo.gov.sg/Newsroom/eulogy-minister-mentor-lee-kuan-yew-state-funeral-service-late-dr-goh-keng-swee. Accessed on 15 March 2021.

18 It is noteworthy that in a chapter on Goh Keng Swee for the book *Lee's Lieutenants*, the authors mentioned that when Goh left the political scene in 1984, Lee sent him a letter and signed off as "Harry", and that Goh in his reply addressed Lee as "Dear Harry". Apparently, there is significance in this, or at least some readers would have drawn their own inference, otherwise why would the authors highlight what would ordinarily be considered something fairly inconsequential. Relying on such thin evidence, akin to Kremlinology, has become a habit in Singapore, and the inferences drawn are often incorrect. Tilak Doshi and Peter Coclanis, "The Economic Architect: Goh Keng Swee", in Kevin Y.L. Tan and Lam Peng Er, eds., *Lee's Lieutenants*, (Singapore: Straits Times Press, Revised Edition 2018), p. 138.

For balance, it should be pointed out that Lee did have an obvious friendship for another central PAP personality, S. Rajaratnam.[19] Even after Rajaratnam had left politics he would regularly meet with Lee at the Istana for lunch.[20]

Some might say that Goh could have been a better PM than Lee. Goh was not so obviously insecure. He was a tough task-master, being methodical in his thinking on how to attain objectives. He did not have liberal inclinations, and was in fact not ideological at all. The idea that Goh and Lee might implicitly have been competitors could be posited as a possible reason why there was mutual respect, but an arm's length distance, between them. On the other hand, Rajaratnam was simply viewed by Lee as his most loyal and trusted confidante.

Returning to Dhanabalan, whatever portfolio he held, whether foreign affairs or national development, he provided a steady hand. On a matter of principle — related to the arrest of individuals in an episode that came to be known as Operation Spectrum — he was to eventually resign from Cabinet and leave politics. This was a major step because the PAP's philosophy has, at least from 1965, and even after Lee's death, been steeped in Lee's own philosophy. Those who join, and remain within, the PAP, know, or ought to know, that they have joined not merely a political party but a system of governance. When he was once told that to Singaporeans he appeared "to be to some degree dictatorial",[21] Lee did not disagree with that notion. Instead, he said: "I don't think I

---

19 In his eulogy delivered at Rajaratnam's funeral on 25 February 2006, Lee spoke of their "enduring bond". Singapore Government Media Release, "Minister Mentor's Eulogy for Mr S. Rajaratnam", https://www.nas.gov.sg/archivesonline/data/pdfdoc/20060225995.htm. Accessed on 15 March 2021.

20 It was said that Lee and Rajaratnam never really made much, if any, conversation during their lunches. Instead, Lee found comfort in the presence of a long-time friend.

21 Han Fook Kwang, Warren Fernandez and Sumiko Tan, *Lee Kuan Yew: The Man and His Ideas*, (Singapore: Straits Times Press, 1998), p. 444.

worry too much about what people think. And when you say people here, you mean the people in the news media, people in academia, the so-called liberals with a small l. I think I can put up with them."[22] Unless the PAP makes a conscious effort to move away decisively from an austere, paternalistic and autocratic form of governance that has become its nature, it is difficult to conceive of any who remain in the party as coming across as "doves" or reformers.

A successor who has the ability to stem a resurgent WP

The relevance of the narrative thus far centres on one point: like any political party, the PAP has leading personalities whose interactions with each other and whose public image differ either to some extent, or markedly, to the actual reality. The only difference between the PAP and other parties is that it and its leading personalities have been able to shield differences or disagreements within their number from public notice with the objective of projecting an image of cohesiveness. This has been emblematic of the party Lee had created and the importance he placed on personal privacy and Establishment secrecy.

Whoever the 4G leaders choose as PM, that person must be viewed as not only credible to Singaporeans but also to those outside the country. It could be argued that the smaller a country, the more important is the personality and capabilities of its leader in defining that country and elevating its stature, so that it can punch above its weight internationally. Lee Kuan Yew and LHL were able to achieve that for Singapore. Jacinda Ardern has been able to achieve that for New Zealand. She is well-regarded, having responded with skill, sensitivity and decisiveness at two defining moments — a major act of terrorism on New Zealand soil

---

22 Ibid.

in March 2019 and the COVID-19 pandemic.[23] She gave New Zealand, an otherwise relatively small and geographically remote country, an outsized international profile, earning the respect of much of the global community.

On a more domestic level, whoever succeeds LHL as PM, whether it be Chan Chun Sing, Ong Ye Kung, Lawrence Wong, or someone else, might in fact not matter substantively. The PAP's organisation, and its emphasis on machine politics — the turning out of in excess of 90% of the electorate where substantial numbers of voters would place an X in the box next to the PAP logo — would be sufficient to make up for uninspiring leadership among those in contention to become the fourth PM of Singapore.

Still, on the margins, prime ministerial leadership might matter for the PAP if one takes into account the fact that a year after the WP's relative success at GE2020, the WP retained a high level of popularity amongst the electorate and well beyond the constituencies directly under its watch. Thus, it might be useful for the PAP if the person anointed, or chosen as presumptive PM, is not perceived by middle-ground voters as having negatives. This is simply because the combination of a popular WP, on the one hand, and a presumptive head of the PAP who is deemed less-than-popular, on the other, could well translate into further parliamentary gains for the WP. So, electorally, it would make sense for the PAP to emplace a leader whom voters believe could deliver for them and, thus, stem further gains by the WP. It should be said that this particular issue facing the PAP — of how its leader could, on the margins, affect its electoral performance — was never apparent when either Goh

---

23 See, for instance, "New Zealand Shooting: The world is praising Jacinda Ardern's response to terrorist attack", *The Independent*, 20 March 2019, https://www.independent.co.uk/news/world/australasia/new-zealand-shooting-jacinda-ardern-video-reaction-world-praise-a8832186.html. Accessed on 8 February 2021; and, "New Zealand's Jacinda Ardern wins big after world-leading COVID-19 response", *NBC News*, 20 October 2020, https://www.nbcnews.com/news/world/new-zealand-s-jacinda-ardern-wins-big-after-world-leading-n1243972. Accessed on 8 February 2021.

Chok Tong or LHL assumed the prime ministership in 1990 and 2004 respectively. Both had faced organised political opposition that was feeble. Arising out of GE2020, the PAP is in a different ball game. The party is experiencing some measure of pressure. But does it have the ability to not merely hold the line electorally, but in fact recover some lost ground suffered at GE2020? A more fundamental question might actually be whether the PAP in fact has the resolve to move towards recovering lost ground?

Four key issues the PAP needs addressing in clawing back support

GE2015 had advantaged the PAP by taking place at an opportune moment for the ruling party, following shortly after the death of Lee Kuan Yew. In almost an inversion, GE2020 had disadvantaged the PAP by taking place during the COVID-19 pandemic. Consequently, if one was to rule out unique circumstances, the PAP ought to claw back part of the support it lost at GE2020. It can regain some percentage of the drop in its popular vote even if it might not take back seats lost to the WP, and might even lose more seats to the WP. The preceding three chapters had analysed why the WP would be well placed to consolidate, and enhance, its parliamentary presence. Incumbency will assist the PAP at the national level in clawing back votes it lost. And, incumbency at the localised level, i.e., concentrated in the east of Singapore, will assist the WP in maintaining, if not growing, its parliamentary presence.

So, what must the PAP do to claw back lost support? The usual practice of many students of politics is to draw up a laundry list of issues a party must address to win support nationally. If one believes that economic motivation drives much of voter behaviour,[24] then there are four key issues

---

24 See, for instance, Michael S. Lewis-Beck, "Economic Determinants of Electoral Outcomes", *Annual Review of Political Science*, Vol. 3, June 2000, https://www.annualreviews.org/doi/full/10.1146/annurev.polisci.3.1.183. Accessed on 10 February 2021.

the PAP confronts and which it needs to address concretely to not just staunch but reverse the haemorrhage of support to the opposition:

- the decay of leases on HDB flats;
- the loss of jobs by Singaporeans, especially PMETs in their 40s, to foreign nationals due to Singapore's relatively liberal immigration policy;
- the rising cost of living and the realisation that there is a significant segment of Singaporeans of at least 60 years of age who have no viable retirement plan that provides them with a regular income stream (other than monthly pay-outs from their Central Provident Fund savings, which could be a paltry amount); and,
- the grievances nursed by those who live in private housing who for years have felt neglected by government policies which have heavily been channelled to those living in public flats; these grievances were compounded significantly during the COVID-19 pandemic.

Just touching on HDB lease decay, almost as a foil to prevent HDB lease decay being the dominant narrative connected to Singapore property, towards the end of 2020 and the early part of 2021, a flurry of news reports of HDB flats in prime areas hitting and surpassing the $1 million mark in the resale market became commonplace.[25] To put things in perspective, the 82 HDB flats that sold for over $1 million in the resale market in 2020 made up 0.35% of all HDB resale transactions.[26] A property analyst who did research measuring price

---

25 "13 HDB resale flats sold for at least $1m each last month", *The New Paper*, 5 February 2021, https://www.tnp.sg/news/singapore/13-hdb-resale-flats-sold-least-1m-each-last-month. Accessed on 30 March 2021; "A record 23 HDB resale flats sold for over S$1 million in February: SRX data", *Today*, 4 March 2021, https://www.todayonline.com/singapore/23-hdb-resale-flats-sold-over-s1-million-february-new-record-srx-data. Accessed on 30 March 2021; and, "82 HDB resale flats sold for at least S$1m in 2020: SRX", *The Business Times*, 8 January 2021, https://www.businesstimes.com.sg/real-estate/82-hdb-resale-flats-sold-for-at-least-s1m-in-2020-srx-0. Accessed on 30 March 2021.

26 "Record 82 HDB resale flats sold for $1m last year", *The New Paper*, 8 January 2021, https://www.tnp.sg/news/singapore/record-82-hdb-resale-flats-sold-1-million-last-year. Accessed on 30 March 2021.

levels across several localities was less impressed with the million-dollar transactions and concluded that newer BTO (Build-to-Order) flats at higher floors in prime areas were actually having the effect of accelerating a price decline in older flats, which amounted to the bulk of the stock of HDB flats.[27]

The above is not an exhaustive list of issues that the PAP government faces and needs addressing. But they are the key issues which, if adequately addressed, will see a rebound in the PAP's popular vote. The ruthlessness of politics is such that a party that is truly interested in power — and not just in mollifying disparate and narrow segments of voters — should merely focus on a few key issues it knows impacts most acutely the largest proportion of voters. It is the concept of utilitarianism. Propounded by English philosopher Jeremy Bentham, and later by John Stuart Mill, in its essence, utilitarianism means actions ought to be taken to achieve the greatest amount of good for the greatest number of people.[28] In other words, where electoral outcomes are concerned, a proper political party, desiring power, can ignore issues which could be described as *on the margins*. The above four issues are not on the margins but are central to large numbers of Singaporeans. Even the ballpark figure of close to 20% of Singaporeans who live in private housing cannot be ignored, simply because at one time in the not-too-distant past, a part of those Singaporeans used to be ardent PAP supporters. As

---

27 Kyle Leung, "Million-dollar HDB flats are hiding a worrying resale price trend. Here's the proof", *99.co*, 12 December 2020, https://www.99.co/blog/singapore/million-dollar-hdb-flats-are-hiding-a-worrying-resale-price-trend-heres-proof/. Accessed on 30 March 2021.

28 For perspectives on the usefulness of the concept, see, variously, Jonathan Riley, "Utilitarian Ethics and Democratic Government", *Ethics*, Vol. 100, No. 2, January 1990; Antoinette Baujard, "Utilitarianism and Anti-Utilitarianism", 2013, halshs-00906899, https://halshs.archives-ouvertes.fr/halshs-00906899/document. Accessed on 7 February 2021; Dan Usher, *Utilitarianism, Voting and the Redistribution of Income*, Queen's Economics Department Working Paper No. 1385, 15 June 2017; and, Julian Savulescu, Ingmar Persson and Dominic Wilkinson, "Utilitarianism and the Pandemic", *Bioethics*, Vol. 34, No. 6, July 2020, https://www.ncbi.nlm.nih.gov/pmc/articles/PMC7276855/. Accessed on 8 February 2021.

was analysed in *Breakthrough*, that group began to drift away from the PAP in GE2011.[29] That drift accelerated at GE2020.

The ability and resolve of the government to move on at least one of the four issues mentioned above, i.e., related to PMETs, was actually swiftly demonstrated on two occasions in the months that followed GE2020. On 27 August 2020, the Ministry of Manpower (MOM) announced that the minimum qualifying monthly salaries for foreigners intending to work in Singapore on S Passes and Employment Passes would be increased.[30] In the case of an Employment Pass, the minimum qualifying salary for new applicants would increase by $600 from $$3,900 to $4,500 from 1 September 2020.[31] The quantum of increase was not inconsequential and, theoretically, would impact on the overall size of the foreign workforce in jobs above the level of those in the lowly-paid migrant community. On 3 March 2021, MOM announced another measure whose effect would curtail further the overall employment numbers of foreign nationals. This related to so-called Dependant's Pass (DP) holders, i.e., spouses of those who were on S and Employment Passes allowed to work as a DP holder as long as they secured a letter of consent from an employer. MOM was to impose a significant change to policy: from 1 May 2021 all such individuals would have to apply for S or Employment Passes, unless they were business owners who created employment for Singaporeans.[32] Both measures

---

29 Derek da Cunha, *Breakthrough: Roadmap for Singapore's Political Future*, (Singapore: Institute for Policy Studies and Straits Times Press, 2012), p. 48.

30 "Minimum qualifying salary to rise by S$600 for Employment Passes and S$100 for S Passes, higher requirement for financial services", *CNA*, 27 August 2020, https://www.channelnewsasia.com/news/singapore/mom-employment-pass-s-pass-minimum-qualifying-salary-fair-hiring-13059356?cid=h3_referral_inarticlelinks_24082018_cna. Accessed on 30 March 2021.

31 Ibid.

32 "Dependant's pass holders who want to work have to apply for work passes from May", *CNA*, 3 March 2021, https://www.channelnewsasia.com/news/singapore/dependant-pass-holders-have-to-apply-work-passes-may-14321444. Accessed on 30 March 2021.

could be said as attempts by the government to mollify Singaporean PMETs and those Singaporeans seeking employment in that mid-tier of the job spectrum. But the government would have to move much more on this issue of job security for Singaporeans, and it would have to address concretely the other issues mentioned if it is to claw back lost electoral support.

Singaporeans accept globalisation, but not the version that emerged after 2000

One way the government will *not* entice voters back to support the PAP is by putting out the kind of statement made by PM Lee Hsien Loong (LHL) when he gave an interview on 14 March 2021 to the BBC's Karisma Vaswani (KV) for the programme Talking Business Asia. Below is the key part of the exchange:[33]

KV: *[G]lobalisation, even in your own country, has not always benefited everyone. Many people have felt left out here. Do we need a new economic model?*

LHL: *Globalisation has benefited everybody in Singapore. You may not feel it so, but if we did not have the multinationals here, if we did not have the international trade that we have, if we were not open as we are, I have no doubt all of us would be worse off. But what has generated tensions is when the interface is so stark, people see the competition directly — because they are in a global market now. But at the same time, they understand that our way forward cannot be to close ourselves up, because if we do that, we are all going to be worse off.*

33 Prime Minister's Office, *PM Lee Hsien Loong's interview with BBC for Talking Business Asia*, 14 March 2021, https://www.pmo.gov.sg/Newsroom/PM-interview-with-BBC-for-Talking-Business-Asia. Accessed on 30 March 2021.

Many Singaporeans have a great respect for LHL But they are unlikely to be pleased with his remarks, especially the idea that all Singaporeans have benefited from globalisation, even though they might not feel it which, to them, would come across as somewhat patronising. LHL's other remarks also amounted to little more than a strawman argument. Globalisation and its connection with Singapore's relatively liberal immigration policies became a political issue after LHL assumed the prime ministership in 2004 where there was a noticeable influx of foreign nationals into the country which put pressure on housing, other infrastructure, and the jobs market for Singaporeans. Apart from marginal, radical elements who are driven by xenophobia or cannot find anything worthy about their country, most Singaporeans understand, and fully accept, the need to embrace globalisation and that Singapore should remain a welcoming place for foreign talent. That has always been the case going back to the early years of Singapore's independence. Major multinational corporations (MNCs) have had a strong presence in Singapore since the 1970s. The scale and the impact of that MNC presence were set out in a 1985 journal article:[34]

A good deal of the economic growth in Singapore has been achieved as a result of foreign direct investment... In this respect Singapore is vastly different from Asia's other New Industralizing Countries (NICs)... Singapore has nurtured those industries favoured by its multinational corporation investors (such as petroleum products, electronics and shipbuilding/repairs), rather than textiles, clothing and plastics. By 1978, in Singapore, multinational corporations accounted for 52 per cent of employment, 63 per cent of value added, 71 per cent of total output, and 84 per cent of manufactured exports... Most of the investment is from Japanese and United States companies.

34 Kevin Grice and David Drakakis-Smith, "The Role of the State in Shaping Development: Two Decades of Growth in Singapore", *Transactions of the British Institute of Geographers*, Vol. 10, No. 3, 1985, p. 348.

Consequently, Singapore's embrace of MNCs and globalisation is nothing new. It is not a 21ˢᵗ century phenomenon. The embrace of globalisation, which brought MNCs to Singapore in a big way during the 1970s, constituted a major asset for Singapore and Singaporeans.[35] Few Singaporeans ever complained; in fact, many took pride at the MNC presence. Therefore, the choice for most Singaporeans has never been the binary of either opening up or closing off the country to the rest of the world, as suggested by LHL. Instead, many Singaporeans mostly want a reversion to the situation prior to the 2000s where, with some exceptions (such as filling vacancies in the nursing profession), foreign nationals largely filled occupations at the two ends of the employment market. At the bottom end are the low-skilled migrant workers, employed as cleaners, domestic helpers, and in the construction and ship-building industries, for example. At the other end, are the individuals who are at the top of their professions, heading major companies and organisations in Singapore, thus enhancing the value of those companies and organisations and, by doing so, enhancing the overall value of Singapore. What has happened with Singapore's experience with globalisation during the first two decades of the new millennium was that a conscious policy decision was taken to liberalise immigration to allow employment in the mid-tier of the jobs market, of largely PMETs, thus placing enormous pressure on many Singaporeans employed in that tier or looking for employment there. Data from the United Nations indicated that in 2019 nearly one million Malaysians were living in Singapore.[36] It is noticeable that this group has not come in for scrutiny, or criticism, from certain alternative parties who have instead focused on the Comprehensive Economic Cooperation

35 For further elaboration on the establishment of MNCs in Singapore, see, Lee Soo Ann, *Singapore: From Place to Nation*, (Singapore: Prentice Hall, 2007), especially the chapter on "Manufacturing and MNCs", pp. 153–168.

36 "UN data shows Malaysians make up biggest migrant group in Singapore at 44pc", *The Malay Mail*, 29 January 2020, https://www.malaymail.com/news/malaysia/2020/01/19/un-data-shows-malaysians-make-up-biggest-migrant-group-in-singapore-at-44pc/1829498. Accessed on 30 March 2021.

Agreement (CECA) with India, with those parties claiming that CECA has led to an influx of Indian migrants into Singapore.

Compounding the problem related to a relatively liberal immigration policy, has been the National Service obligations, including annual in-camp training for reservists (i.e., "operationally ready NSmen"), which physically fit Singaporean males are required by law to perform. Logically, quite a number of employers would rather hire foreign nationals who can work throughout the year as they do not have such an obligation which would disrupt the continuity of work. Thus, this disadvantages Singaporeans in terms of job opportunities. There is no comparable example of another *country* anywhere in the world which has this extraordinary situation of the vast scale of a foreign presence in the local workforce whilst simultaneously a sizeable segment of citizens is, effectively, disadvantaged as a consequence of statutory obligations to contribute to national security.[37] For context: at the turn of the

---

37 Other countries, such as Israel and South Korea, also rely heavily on a citizens' armed force for national defence, with similar annual in-camp training programmes for reservist personnel. However, none have the combination of such a programme together with an enormous pool of foreign nationals in the workforce, which has the effect of placing direct pressure on citizens' competing in the jobs market. It is also worth pointing out that a 2018 *Jerusalem Post* article made the following observations:

> *Successfully circumventing mandatory military enlistment is becoming an increasingly widespread occurrence in Israel. The enlistment rate among Israelis who are obligated to serve has plummeted from 75% to less than 50% in only 20 years. While Israeli law allows the military to punish draft-evaders with jail time, the reality is that most cases are simply ignored. Hence, compulsory military enlistment in Israel is but an old myth. In reality, 35% of the Israeli population carries the burden, while the remaining 65% find ways to avoid military service without having to suffer any consequences.*

"The myth of compulsory military service in Israel", *The Jerusalem Post*, 18 October 2018, https://www.jpost.com/opinion/the-myth-of-compulsory-military-service-in-israel-569779. Accessed on 1 April 2021.

millennium, foreigners comprised some 25% of the population of Singapore; this ballooned to around 38% some 20 years later.[38] Even the figure of 25% had already been described in a 2002 book in these terms: "Singapore now has the highest proportion of immigrants of any country in the world."[39]

It is a testimony to the efficacy of half-a-century of the PAP's socialisation process that has normalised in the minds of many Singaporeans something which in virtually any other country would never be considered normal nor accepted. How malleable Singaporeans have been might have to do with their provenance. Lee Kuan Yew always looked at race and culture to provide explanations why certain groups of humans behaved in a particular way. Perhaps Singaporeans' malleability had largely had to do with what Lee once told China's strongman Deng Xiaoping. He said that most Singaporeans "were descendants of illiterate, landless peasants from Fujian and Guangdong while they [the nationals of the People's Republic of China] had the progeny of the scholars, mandarins and literati…"[40] A Singaporean scholar has provided a different explanation:[41]

---

38 On the proportion for 2020 see, "Singapore's population declines to 5.69 million, with fewer foreigners", *CNA*, 24 September 2020, https://www.channelnewsasia.com/news/singapore/singapore-population-declines-non-residents-citizens-pr-13141862#:~:text=NUMBER%20OF%20FOREIGNERS%20FALLS,million%20as%20of%20June%202020.&text=This%20was%20%E2%80%809Clargely%20due%20to,permit%20holders%2C%20said%20the%20report. Accessed on 2 April 2021.

39 Diane K. Mauzy and R.S. Milne, *Singapore Politics Under the People's Action Party*, (London: Routledge, 2002), p. 191.

40 Lee Kuan Yew, *From Third World to First*, (Singapore: Times Media Private Limited, 2000), p. 662.

41 Loh Kah Seng, "Within the Singapore Story: Use and Narrative of History in Singapore", *Crossroads: An Interdisciplinary Journal of Southeast Asian Studies*, Vol. 12, No. 2, 1998, p. 17.

> *... the Singapore Story is more than an account of the past; rather it is a complex bundle of predetermined axioms and arguments on Singapore's history, geography, economics, sociology, and politics. While it does allow a range of possible perspectives, all of these nonetheless focus on the basic concept of "vulnerability." The persistent admonition that the nation is racially explosive discourages the public from dismissing dubious ideas as PAP propaganda since to do so would be, in effect, to threaten one's own economic future. The Singapore Story thus predetermines how Singaporeans perceive and interpret the reality they experience, and to the extent that they regard the regime's ideas uncritically as "common-sense" truisms, they partake in the government's ongoing hegemony.*

The results of GE2020 do, however, suggest a slight change in the collective mindset of Singaporeans, where at polling stations some decided to register displeasure at, what they considered, the inherent unfairness that had long been apparent. The government has the full ability to address this matter substantively and swiftly. But judging by LHL's BBC interview remarks, given just eight months after GE2020, the government might in fact not be willing to go in the direction suggested. Reinforcing that view one can point to the remarks by DPM Heng given on 17 May 2021 at a virtual press conference to share recommendations of the Emerging Stronger Taskforce (a group set-up to chart how Singapore could emerge economically stronger from the COVID-19 crisis). Heng had said that the term "Singapore core" should not be narrowly defined to include just Singaporeans but should include others who have made a "commitment to Singapore, the commitment to the well-being of Singapore and Singaporeans."[42] These remarks are unlikely to go down well with, let alone ameliorate the real concerns of, a large segment of voters who, of course, are Singaporeans. Those

---

42 Quoted in "Emerging Stronger Taskforce: Avoid narrow definition of 'Singapore core', says DPM Heng", *The Straits Times*, 17 May 2021, https://www.straitstimes. com/singapore/emerging-stronger-taskforce-avoid-narrow-definition-of-singapore-core-says-dpm-heng. Accessed on 19 May 2021.

voters would perceive the government as being tone-deaf to the message Singaporeans had sent at GE2020.

A fairly rudimentary question arises: even if the PAP government decides to merely tinker with policy adjustments to the above four crucial issues flagged, will it ever face a serious risk of losing power? The next chapter attempts to answer that question through setting out one plausible hypothesis. It is merely a hypothesis, not an ironclad factual narrative.

CHAPTER 10

Has the Elected Presidency Become Pivotal to the PAP's System of Governance Irrespective of Parliamentary Election Outcome?

his chapter will analyse the extent to which the Elected Presidency has become pivotal to the People's Action Party's (PAP's) system of governance. Can that system of governance survive even if the PAP, as a party, is defeated in a parliamentary general election? This is a germane question only because Lee Kuan Yew himself had publicly ruminated on whether a hypothetical PAP defeat at the polls would make a material difference to the way Singapore is run. He had spoken at length on the safeguards he had put in place. The question is also germane because other countries have seen the power-elite retain governance even as they have lost popularity amongst the citizenry. Much of the discussion that follows is hypothetical and purely of academic interest. We start with the notion of the Deep State.

Just like the concept of "neoliberalism", the Deep State has come into increasing usage in political discourse. It has become part of the lexicon of the social sciences as the world moved into the 21st century. In its conventional, and accepted, meaning, the Deep State constitutes some sort of shadowy government that controls the levers of power in a country, dominates its wealth for the benefit of those co-opted into its ranks, and decides the cultural, economic, political, and security destiny of the country independent of the government of the day, whether that government is elected or otherwise.[1] These elements which make up the political-ontological nature of the Deep State focus on a

---

1 Patrick H. O'Neil, "The Deep State: An Emerging Concept in Comparative Politics", *Political Institutions: Non-Democratic Regimes eJournal*, November 2017, http://ssrn.com/abstract=2313375. Accessed on 4 February 2021.

simple concept — those who are at the centre of the Deep State serve certain identified entrenched power interests while diminishing that of others. To some, this might come across as a conspiracy theory but, in reality, the Deep State exists in parts of the world.[2]

The Deep State was popularised in fiction by novelist John le Carré,[3] but shortly thereafter it was re-popularised as fact in a 2014 essay, and later in a book,[4] by Mike Lofgren, a former US Congressional staff member. Lofgren contended that the United States exhibited all the symptoms of the Deep State. Beyond the US, some countries in the Middle East, specifically Egypt and Turkey,[5] have focused academic interest on the Deep State.[6]

---

2 Ludvig Beckman, "Popular Sovereignty Facing the Deep State. The Rule of Recognition and the Powers of the People", *Critical Review of International Social and Political Philosophy*, 2019, https://www.tandfonline.com/doi/pdf/10.1080/136 98230.2019.1644583. Accessed on 5 February 2021.

3 John le Carré, *A Delicate Truth*, (London: Penguin Books, 2013).

4 Mike Lofgren, *The Deep State: The Fall of the Constitution and the Rise of a Shadow Government*, (New York: Viking, 2016).

5 See, for instance, Bill Park, "Turkey's Deep State", *The RUSI Journal*, Vol. 153, No. 5, 26 November 2008, https://www.tandfonline.com/doi/pdf/10.1080/0307 1840802521937. Accessed on 5 February 2021; Mehtap Sooyler, *The Turkish Deep State: State Consolidation, Civil-Military Relations, and Democracy*, (London: Routledge, 2017); Marijn Clevers and Zina Nimeh, *Pharaohs of the Deep State: Social Capital in an Obstinate Regime*, United Nations University Working Papers Series, #2015–056; and, Issandr El Amrani, "Sightings of the Egyptian Deep State", *Middle East Report Online*, 1 January 2012, https://merip.org/2012/01/sightings-of-the-egyptian-deep-state/. Accessed on 5 February 2021.

6 The Deep State also exists in parts of Southeast Asia, most notably, in Myanmar and in Thailand. In the case of Myanmar, the bureaucracy and the military (the Tatmadaw) represent the key elements of the Deep State. For Thailand, the bureaucracy, the military, and the monarchy, are the inter-woven threads that make up the fabric of the Deep State. On Thailand as a Deep State, see Eugenie Merieau, "Thailand's Deep State, Royal Power and the Constitutional Court (1997–2015)", *Journal of Contemporary Asia*, Vol. 26, No. 3, 2016. On Myanmar as a Deep State, a 2017 podcast offers the best insights. Maureen Aung-Thwin, "Democracy and the Deep State in Myanmar", Carnegie Council for Ethics in International Affairs, 25 April 2017, https://www.carnegiecouncil.org/studio/multimedia/20170425-aung-thwin-democracy-deep-state-myanmar. Accessed on 7 February 2021.

Has the Elected Presidency Become Pivotal to the PAP's System of Governance?

279

By the definitional parameters outlined above, Singapore is *not* a Deep State. The elected government, formed by the same political party since 1959, operates openly even as it has steadily appropriated greater powers to itself. In the sophisticated realm of governance in Singapore there is both rule of law and rule by law. Both co-exist, with rule by law enabled via the super-majorities secured by the ruling PAP in successive elections over the span of six decades.

Decades of PAP socialisation

In terms of a broader definition, it could be argued that more than 60 years of PAP socialisation of almost every aspect of life in Singapore has implicitly created something that is more sophisticated than the Deep State. The PAP is ubiquitous. Its tentacles reach far and wide across the island-republic. The foundational elements of PAP dominance are embodied in the Establishment. These elements include, among others: major corporate interests closely aligned to the state, i.e., through government-linked corporations (GLC); the mainstream media, which is regulated through the Newspaper and Printing Presses Act; a "natural aristocracy" — so described by Prime Minister Lee Hsien Loong in 2015 — of mainly handpicked current and former bureaucrats;[7] and, the sprawling security and intelligence apparatus. On a day-to-day basis, these elements — which, as organisations and individuals, are funded extravagantly — merely play a supporting role to the government. The boards of directors and trustees of conglomerates, statutory boards, government-affiliated organisations, and other entities which consciously have decided to closely associate themselves with the PAP government, tend to see the same names of individuals reappearing time and again. In other words, it is a relatively small and trusted cadre of individuals — the *natural aristocracy* — who have had consistently good academic credentials, are competent and deemed to be politically reliable.

---

7 "PM tackles questions on S'pore system, freedom of speech at IPS conference", *Today*, 3 July 2015, https://www.todayonline.com/singapore/cases-against-bloggers-dominate-dialogue-pm. Accessed on 3 February 2021.

For avoidance of doubt, in the best traditions adopted from Singapore's former colonial master, the British, the Singapore civil service, even at senior levels, exercises impartiality when carrying out its duties, which are generally routine and mundane in nature. These duties are executed legally, but at the behest of a government that has appropriated, via passage through Parliament, laws that are favourable to the continued existence of the same government.

Founding prime minister, Lee Kuan Yew had spoken of measures which he had put in place to prevent a radical change to how Singapore would be run even if the PAP was somehow displaced as the government at a general election. He had focused on the powers of the Elected Presidency, primarily in preventing a government from imprudently spending the country's financial reserves which had been built up by successive PAP governments. In 2006, Lee went one step further with the following observation: "Without the elected president and if there is a freak result, within two or three years, the army would have to come in and stop it."[8] He further maintained: "Please do not assume that you can change governments. Young people don't understand this."[9] Lee's reference to the army — even in the hypothetical context of there not being an elected president — was unnecessary, and no person who truly adheres to democratic norms and practices would ever have countenanced such an idea, let alone broached it in public. Lee merely believed in the procedural aspects of democracy, the primary one being the holding of parliamentary general elections every four or five years.

With reference to Lee raising the theoretical spectre of intervention by the military in the event of the PAP's defeat in a general election, it

---

8 "Lee Kuan Yew defends PAP's political dominance", *Reuters*, 16 September 2006.

9 Quoted in "Singapore tries to imagine a future without its founder, Lee Kuan Yew", *The Washington Post*, 18 March 2015, https://www.washingtonpost.com/world/singapore-tries-to-imagine-a-future-without-lee-kuan-yew/2015/03/18/b12acc7c-cbe7-11e4-8730-4f473416e759_story.html. Accessed on 3 February 2021.

Has the Elected Presidency Become Pivotal to the PAP's System of Governance?

281

is worth noting that through a carefully planned process, handpicked members of the senior ranks of the Singapore Armed Forces (SAF), retiring usually in their 40s, would then be appointed to key positions in GLCs, statutory boards, the civil service, or they would be fielded as parliamentary election candidates by the PAP. The assimilation of the SAF into civilian life is not a recent phenomenon. It has always existed because the SAF was established as a heavily conscript and, therefore, citizens' armed force. What became more apparent from the late 1980s onwards was the migration of senior officers — with spectacular academic backgrounds as "SAF scholars" — to key positions in civilian life. That SAF scholars had sterling academic credentials has never been in doubt. The real issue, however, has been the carrying over from military to civilian life of a culture that was misaligned to the new organisation, with implications for staff morale. It is axiomatic that military culture is at variance to the culture found in the private sector, quasi-government organisations, or even in the civil service.

As testimony to the cohesiveness of the Singapore Establishment, no Establishment figure has ever really spoken out publicly about the perniciousness of the shuffling of *natural aristocrats* across organisations as though organisational culture, customs, conventions, and the morale of staff, do not matter whatsoever. No value appears to be ascribed by the powers-that-be to such abstractions as "corporate culture" or "staff morale". Perhaps, more significant, is the Establishment's groupthink and instinctiveness in knowing what to say and what not to say, even in private conversation.

Given that it was Lee himself who broached the hypothetical of an SAF intervention in the event of the defeat of the PAP at the polls (and even in that scenario only within two or three years of such a defeat), one might begin to entertain the possibility that the micro-manager, Lee, had constructed layer upon layer of safety-valves to ensure that his project — Singapore — would never change radically long after he had left the scene.

With the PAP enjoying enormous institutional and structural advantages that have been methodically put in place over more than half-a-century, it is simply not credible, nor to the benefit, of those in opposition to the PAP to be disparate — in terms of parties, ideology, policy differences, and overall outlook. To begin facing the challenge of reversing the process of PAP socialisation of most aspects of Singapore life requires a unity of purpose and a tightly-woven unified bloc. A loose conglomeration of alternative parties fails to reach the standard suggested here. In fact, in electoral terms, it will likely to lead Singapore back to the days where there was just a handful of fully elected non-PAP MPs. Consequently, it is only the Workers' Party (WP), as currently constituted, that stands an outside chance of being a government-in-waiting, and has to be patient in slowly growing its parliamentary presence until it reaches a tipping point. The WP's assets are its disciplined rank-and-file; a large corps of dedicated volunteers and supporters willing to provide manpower and materiel support to the party; its rigorous efforts at grassroots outreach which have even been envied by the PAP; and, its laser-like focus on the real and substantive — not imagined and narrow — issues that affect the majority of Singaporeans.

Before proceeding any further, it is worthwhile asking the question: does the PAP exist to serve the interest of all Singaporeans, or does it exist — as other political parties do in many other countries — merely to promote the interest of those aligned to or associated with a group in power and their underlings? In other words, on the latter, is the PAP merely a cause unto itself? Prior to the 2000s, few Singaporeans would ask such a question because the PAP, as with Lee himself, had long become synonymous with Singapore. But as the first two decades of the new millennium progressed, that is a question that is increasingly being asked by Singaporeans because more and more of them perceive a disconnect between the PAP as a governing party and as a system of governance, on the one hand, and broader Singapore society, on the other.

Has the Elected Presidency Become Pivotal to the PAP's System of Governance?

283

Measured by both population and geographical size, Singapore is a small country. Yet, there are political positions and layers of bureaucracy not seen in countries of similar size. In terms of political posts, for instance that of "senior minister" was created after the 1984 general election, with the first recipient being S. Rajaratnam, who was to hold it for just a few years. The post could be said as establishing a precedent to allow Lee to assume it after he stepped down as prime minister in 1990. Lee held the post for almost 14 years, between 2004 and 2011, before assuming the even more elevated title of "Minister Mentor". Singapore has also had periods where there were no less than two deputy prime ministers simultaneously. Even in the United Kingdom, from where Singapore derives its political system, but is a country many times larger than the republic, there is no automatic political post of deputy prime minister. Some UK governments have had the post but some have not seen the need for it. One has to question whether for such a small country like Singapore there really is a need for levels of political hierarchy that incur not insignificant cost to the taxpayer?

The political bureaucracy also exists lower down the hierarchy. WP chief Pritam Singh was to highlight one such layer of bureaucracy when he delivered a speech to Parliament on 24 February 2021 in response to the government's annual budget announcement. Singh raised the issue of Community Development Councils (CDCs). CDCs were established in 1997, with the island divided geographically into five CDCs, each headed by a mayor. The mayors are PAP Members of Parliament (MPs) appointed by the prime minister. Most Singaporeans are unfamiliar with what CDCs do, let alone aware of the name of the mayor overseeing the CDC in which they are resident. But both the alternative media and social media had just before GE2020 and thereafter been making a few references to CDCs.

CDCs are an unknown quantity to Singaporeans, yet CDC mayors earn salaries in one year well beyond the reach most Singaporeans could ever earn during their lifetime. The 2012 White Paper on *Salaries for a*

Capable and Committed Government specifies a mayor's annual salary as $660,000.[10] That remuneration does not include another $192,500, which is an MP's annual allowance.[11] In his speech, Singh made the following points:[12]

> *... CDCs have come into the spotlight after GE2020 because many Singaporeans are of the view that the salaries of Mayors are outrageous, principally because they are not perceived to be commensurate with a Mayor's roles and functions. Other Singaporeans are of the view that the CDCs functions can be carried out by existing entities or by Ministries and statutory boards including other organisations under the PA [People's Association], particularly since the social footprint of each CDC is uneven and can differ greatly compared to another. Yet others simply don't know what the CDCs do. Effectively, the need for mayors continues to be widely questioned and it would appear that there is scope for a serious review of the necessity of having full-time mayors.*

Singh's view was that CDCs seemed to do so little of note, such as distributing vouchers to households to use at neighbourhood shops. Consequently, to him, the government was "trying to find some way to make the CDCs relevant in view of their relative absence in the public

---

10 *White Paper: Salaries for a Capable and Committed Government*, 10 January 2012, p. 32, https://government.report/Resources/Whitepapers/d2ea0290-bb0d-4fad-9e89-de958914dfc_white-paper-salaries-for-a-capable-and-committed-govt.pdf. Accessed on 25 February 2021.

11 It should be pointed out that an MP is not a political appointment; hence, an MP can receive an MP's allowance and a salary from another job. But a mayor cannot receive a mayor's salary and another salary as a political appointment holder in the government. Examples of political appointment holders include: Parliamentary Secretary, Minister of State, Senior Minister of State, and Minister.

12 The Workers' Party, "Budget Speech 2021 – Speech by LO Pritam Singh", 24 February 2021, https://www.wp.sg/budget-speech-2021-speech-by-lo-pritam-singh/. Accessed on 25 February 2021.

Has the Elected Presidency Become Pivotal to the PAP's System of Governance?

285

mindshare."[13] Singh gave a shrewd political speech. The reality is that, up to the moment he spoke about CDCs, mayors and their enormous financial compensation, few Singaporeans would have even been aware of any of it. He had, therefore, placed this issue front and centre and, in so doing, put the government on the defensive. The very next day, a CDC mayor, Denise Phua, gave a response to the speech. She said:[14]

> *Mr Singh's accusation that the Government is trying to find some way for the CDCs to be relevant by asking them to manage the CDC vouchers scheme, is belittling the CDCs and our partners.*
>
> *There is nothing to be ashamed about making sure one is always relevant.*
>
> *We organise the resources, communicate the scheme, and get as many merchants as possible to sign up and make full use of this well-intended help scheme.*
>
> *The value of the CDC structure… is its relative agility and ability to respond and develop programmes in the district faster than a bigger government machinery.*

As compared to the responsibilities of elected mayors in major cities around the world, who control vast budgets to oversee policing, heath care, municipal functions, among others, the unelected mayors of Singapore's CDCs do not have anything approximating those responsibilities, yet they command financial compensation several times that of mayors elsewhere. All this reality would otherwise be a source of embarrassment but, in PAP-dominated Singapore, Establishment figures only appear to feel embarrassed

---

13 Ibid.

14 Quoted in "Budget debate: Mayor Denise Phua rebuts Pritam Singh on relevance of CDCs and mayors", *The Straits Times*, 25 February 2021, https://www.straitstimes.com/singapore/politics/budget-debate-mayor-denise-phua-rebuts-pritam-singh-on-relevance-of-cdcs-and. Accessed on 26 February 2021.

if criticised by their peers.[15] The views of those outside that circle do not really count. The case for having an intermediate layer of bureaucracy between the central government and the local population makes sense for much larger countries but, by contrast, in relatively minuscule Singapore such an intermediate layer, in the form of CDCs, is superfluous when many functions can already be carried out efficiently by social service organisations under various government departments. Seemingly superfluous bureaucratic layers therefore reinforce the circuitry of power and privilege enjoyed by a self-selecting elite.

Lee's soliloquy on the Elected Presidency

Returning to Lee's 2006 reference to military intervention, where perhaps he was merely floating an idea to get people thinking, not much was immediately said about it. Neither was Lee himself to dwell on the topic. It was only to be some three years later, in 2009, at a conference,[16] that the novelist, Catherine Lim, quizzed Lee. She asked, "In the event of a very serious threat of a freak election, would you do the unthinkable and, that is, send in the army?" Lee gave a lengthy response:

> *Let me put it simply like this: first, we maintain the system which gives any opposition the opportunity to displace us peacefully. And we allow the system — we have not interfered with the civil service, we've not interfered*

---

15 The former senior civil servant, Ngiam Tong Dow, gave some mildly forthright remarks for a volume of essays in Simon S.C. Tay (ed.), *A Mandarin and the Making of Public Policy: Reflections by Ngiam Tong Dow*, (Singapore: NUS Press, 2006). However, even such an occasional murmur of difference within Establishment ranks in Singapore tends not to last. In 2013, Ngiam recanted on interview comments he had publicly given that, in his view, Cabinet ministers were afraid to speak up in Cabinet due to their high salaries. See "Ngiam Tong Dow says his recent comments on ministers unfair and illogical", *The Straits Times*, 11 October 2013, https://www.straitstimes.com/singapore/ngiam-tong-dow-says-his-recent-comments-on-ministers-unfair-and-illogical. Accessed on 26 February 2021.

16 This was at the 5th anniversary conference of the National University of Singapore's Lee Kuan Yew School of Public Policy, held on 2 September 2009.

Has the Elected Presidency Become Pivotal to the PAP's System of Governance?

287

with the judiciary, we've not interfered with the parliamentary procedures, the police, and so on. And if you can win an election, so be it. And, at some time, some place, we will not be able to find a team which can equal an opposition team, and that day we deserve to be out. If we become corrupt, we become inefficient, we can't deliver, we're out. Now, what if we have a freak election? As we may well have because many voters now tell you openly, 'You know my family, three of us voted for you but two of us voted against you just to let you know we want an opposition voice and we don't want you to be so overwhelming'. So, in that situation you may have a freak result. I say, alright, that worries me.

So, we have set in place a president with blocking powers, so that any opposition that comes in will find first he cannot touch the reserves, otherwise you can promise the sky and spend the money, and all our hard-earned savings will go in five years. Second, you cannot change the top officials without the president's consent. The first three or four officials, commanders, police and so on, you cannot change them. And if they retire, and you want to appoint a new one, the president must approve. And all the government funds, and raiding of the funds, even under our control now, the PAP, must be approved by the president who has a Council of Presidential Advisers, who are very well versed, experienced economists, businessmen, who will advise the president, yes or no.

Now, why should we do that if we expect to overturn an election? We expect that if we're voted out, to stay out, and hope that within one term that new government, incompetent, unable to deliver, will be out. And there's enough core competencies and the funds to enable a fresh PAP Government to revive the system. Why do you think we put in all these safeguards? I spent 15 years thinking up these safeguards, and finally persuaded my younger colleagues that we needed this because they can't guarantee that each time they'll produce a better team than the opposition, just because they've done that in the past. I don't see any problem at the next election,

probably the election after that. But if we don't find a good team in the
election after that, and the opposition gets a good team together, we are at
risk. That's the way it is.

It has already been noted elsewhere in this book that the WP opposes the Elected Presidency. The WP has been consistent in its opposition to the post of an Elected Presidency since the idea was first mooted in the late 1980s. In that regard, there is nothing to stop the WP from going directly to the people, i.e., in calling a referendum, to seek to overturn or by-pass the president's constitutional powers. Of course, Lee's 15 years of thinking up safeguards also meant that he considered such a scenario occurring, and his solution: the over-turning or by-passing of the president's powers at a referendum would only be possible if two-thirds of voters supported such a measure. That is a high enough threshold that it seems inconceivable a referendum measure would pass. In effect, for a referendum measure to pass involving the curtailment, over-turning or by-passing of the powers of an elected president, it would mean that the core PAP vote within the electorate would have to fall to below 33%.[17]

As envisioned by Lee, the Elected Presidency has become pivotal in ensuring the continuance or, at worst if the PAP is voted out, the revival of the system of governance he put in place over five decades. Given the constitutional responsibilities, the president, supported by a Council of Presidential Advisers (CPA) — all of whom being PAP government appointees — could potentially make things difficult for an entity that displaced the PAP. This is because they deemed the new government too radical in terms of fiscal policies and in wanting to replace key personnel at the helm of civil service departments, statutory boards, and

---

17 Main voting bloc A, in Table 1.2, Chapter 1, quantifying the hardcore of the PAP vote, puts it at 35%.

Has the Elected Presidency Become Pivotal to the PAP's System of Governance?

289

other organisations with links to the PAP. To that extent, constitutional law expert Kevin Tan, has made the observation:[18]

The sort of person that [sic] fills the post of Elected President is the very epitome of a PAP leader or at least the way they perceive the jun zhi to be: good at money management, paternalistic, like the good father who has the power to say no when things go wrong, very successful, has managed large corporations, person of high moral standing.

Again, it's a bit of a dilemma because unless you have a very widescale constitutional consciousness among the people, they are not going to bat an eyelid where transgressions occur.

Tan's remarks were made back in 1997. This was two decades before a female and one-time trades unionist, Halimah Yacob, assumed the presidency in a "reserved election" for Malay candidates.

Since the establishment of the Elected Presidency, none of the holders of the post appear to have to-date blocked a request from the PAP government to dip into past reserves. Also, from what has been available from the public domain, there has been no evidence that any appointee to a government department or statutory board has ever been delayed, let alone blocked, by the president. But would the same occur in the unlikely event of there being a non-PAP government? On that point, why wouldn't a new government wish to use a broom to sweep away what would, in effect, be *natural aristocrats* — perceived to be closely aligned to the PAP — holding senior government and quasi-government positions? As already noted, in-line with the British civil service tradition, civil servants in Singapore could be expected to behave in a non-partisan manner, serving the new government loyally and would not be a disruptive presence. But even in the United Kingdom there have been

---

18 Quoted in "Why more power should be given to Singaporeans", *The Straits Times*, 28 February 1997.

attempts by governments to get around the senior ranks of the civil service in Whitehall either because of deep-seated bureaucratic inertia or the perception that the senior echelons of the civil service were not broadly supportive of government policy. That latter was dramatised by the UK's referendum decision to leave the European Union (Brexit), a policy supported strongly by the right of the Conservative Party — which, at the time of Brexit, was in government — but was said to be opposed by much of the civil service, which mostly wanted to remain in the EU. It was the juxtaposition of Brexiteers versus Remainers. And, Boris Johnson, when he was foreign secretary, had directly alleged that the UK Treasury was "the heart of remain".[19] Even well before the election of a Conservative government in 2010 after a 13-year hiatus, the New Labour government of Tony Blair had attempted to by-pass perceived obstructionism in the civil service by appointing increasing numbers of special advisers (SpAds) — political appointees working directly with Cabinet ministers and with the prime minister's office at No. 10.[20] The number of SpAds more than doubled under Tony Blair from that of his predecessor, John Major.[21]

In the case of Singapore, if the elected president, on the advice of the CPA, does not cooperate fully with a new government in allowing that government to carry out its own policy programme and fulfil manifesto commitments — which might involve an enormous financial outlay — the new government's work would be hampered. In other words, the new government would be "unable to deliver". To quote Lee

---

19 David Donaldson, "Brexiteers trigger unlikely civil service renaissance", *The Mandarin*, 15 October 2018, https://www.themandarin.com.au/99943-brexit-triggers-unlikely-civil-service-renaissance/. Accessed on 7 February 2021.

20 "Blair pins down civil service reform", *The Guardian*, 22 September 1999, https://www.theguardian.com/politics/1999/sep/22/labour.labour1997to99. Accessed on 7 February 2021.

21 Simon King, "Regulating the Behaviour of Ministers, Special Advisers and Civil Servants", June 2003, https://www.ucl.ac.uk/constitution-unit/sites/constitution-unit/files/102.pdf. Accessed on 7 February 2021.

Has the Elected Presidency Become Pivotal to the PAP's System of Governance?

291

at length: "We expect that if we're voted out, to stay out, and hope that within one term that new government, incompetent, unable to deliver, will be out."

As much as the PAP has tried to conflate itself with Singapore, intellectually and factually, it would be incorrect to treat the two as synonymous. Also, a single person — the elected president — deciding on the need for safeguards for the well-being of the country seems at variance to the will of the people as reflected in a democratic parliamentary election. The same point, cast through a different lens, is made by Kevin Tan:[22]

[T]he elected president adds a unique twist to the classic idea of the separation of powers doctrine. We are accustomed to constitutional set-ups where either the legislature or the judiciary provide checks and controls on the executive. However, under the elected president scheme one executive provides checks on the other.

It is appropriate to mention that, with the minor exception of once having praised the constituency work of the WP's Low Thia Khiang in Hougang single-member constituency, Lee's consistent political narrative over many decades had been that those in opposition to the PAP, and who could potentially displace the PAP as the government would, as a matter of course, be incompetent, inefficient, corrupt, and would soon enough lead Singapore to ruin. He had never really suggested publicly — even if he might have entertained the possibility privately — that a political entity which displaced the PAP could actually be benevolent for Singapore and provide good governance. And, as he posited in public, such an entity would only get into power by virtue of a "freak election" result. In other words, the result would not truly

---

22 Kevin Tan, "The Presidency in Singapore: Constitutional Developments", in Kevin Y.L. Tan and Lam Peng Er (eds.), *Managing Political Change in Singapore: The Elected Presidency*, (London: Routledge, 1997), p. 70.

be the conscious decision of the people to vote out the PAP. Instead, it would happen by accident because too many voters suddenly thought along the same lines of merely wanting to fire a shot across the PAP's bow and nothing more but, in so doing, the mass of shots riddled the PAP ship-of-state and sank it politically. As a consequence, to follow Lee's train of thought, in time to come the voters would realise how reckless they were and how ruinous the new government was, prompting them to swiftly re-float the PAP, bringing it back to power.

At a more micro-level, this line of thinking by Lee was also at work during GE2011 where he cautioned the voters of Aljunied group representation constituency (GRC) that if they voted in the team of candidates from the WP, they (the voters) would have five years to "repent". Two general elections (or nine years) later, the voters of Aljunied GRC had not repented, notwithstanding significant litigation the WP had been embroiled over governance issues related to the Aljunied-Hougang Town Council (AHTC) and all the negative headlines that AHTC was to generate for the WP. In fact, at GE2020, the majority of voters in the adjacent GRC of Sengkang thought it a good idea to vote into Parliament another WP GRC team.

More than five years after his death, even as his legacy of authoritarian traits live on in a segment of Singaporeans, Lee's mesmerising spell over Singaporeans is slowly but surely being lifted. His remarks about Housing and Development Board (HDB) flats continuing to increase in value as long as the economy kept on growing have proven a fallacy in the face of the reality of HDB lease decay. And, his offspring, once providing a picture-perfect snapshot of the harmonious and well-adjusted family steeped in "Asian values", has also fractured with the falling-out between Prime Minister Lee Hsien Loong and his two siblings.

The PAP's cult of the offensive in elections

Dire warnings of the political consequences of casting votes for the alternative to the PAP might have worked in the past for the ruling party

Has the Elected Presidency Become Pivotal to the PAP's System of Governance?

293

but, as GE2020 demonstrated, increasing numbers of Singaporeans feel far more acutely the dire threat to their livelihoods and economic well-being arising out of PAP policies. If practical-minded Singaporeans were presented with either the choice of defeat of the PAP, on the one hand, or a major threat to their livelihoods and economic well-being, on the other, the option for them would be all too obvious. At GE2011 and GE2020, economic motivation was a key driving force for many Singaporeans as they walked into polling stations. In Sengkang GRC in GE2020, a few other issues gravitated together to push the WP over the finish-line.

Economic motivation is represented in the four key policy areas the PAP has to address, as was highlighted in the previous chapter. The PAP has to address those policy areas concretely if the party is to dissipate disaffection by the voters. The PAP's ability — as the government — to achieve that objective exists. The question is whether the PAP has any resolve to do so?

If past practice is any guide, as a government, the PAP does not adopt a single approach to attaining its electoral outcomes. Instead, it has always employed a combination of inducement, the bringing to the consciousness of the electorate the risks of electing the alternative, divide-and-rule, and hardball election tactics. These are taken in combination by the PAP's juggernaut election machine which then attempts to steam-roll the opposition in almost a cult of the offensive which was much favoured by Lee. That has been the PAP's playbook. This multi-track approach might have served the party well in a bygone era but, it could be argued that, other than inducement, the others have now lost their efficacy. Yet, a year after GE2020, with a few exceptions Singapore's political culture, formed in the 1960s, has remained mostly intact.[23] More to the point, although the election cycle is in its early

---

23 One of those exceptions was the government agreeing to the livestreaming of parliamentary sessions as a concession to the opposition, and another was the establishment of the office of Leader of the Opposition, with some resources for the new post.

stage (August 2021), there is no evidence of a change to the PAP's multi-track approach to its dyed-in-wool election strategy.

Foot-dragging or delays in the provision of municipal services and community improvement projects, or being placed lower down in the queue for the various upgrading programmes for ageing HDB blocks of flats for precincts which voted opposition, have proven less effective than they had been a generation earlier. This was to be illustrated when, in a Facebook post on 15 October 2019, WP chief Singh highlighted the issue of a simple barrier-free-access (BFA) proposed for construction in the Bedok Reservoir Road within the jurisdiction of AHTC. In his words:

First mooted by residents to the Aljunied-Hougang Town Council in late 2012, it was finally handed over to the Town Council by the People's Association this afternoon, seven years after it was first proposed. While the TC continues to wait for all the documentation and additional pipe diversion works to be completed, we have received approval to open the BFA for resident use. It will be open tomorrow.

Each year, the Government makes available about $40m to all Town Councils for community improvement upgrading projects. But all MPs must go through their Grassroots Advisers to raise projects for consideration. In opposition wards like Aljunied and Hougang, the losing PAP candidates are the Grassroots Advisers.

Through such upgrading projects, losing PAP candidates are made relevant for residents and can be said to campaign for votes well before the General Elections because they are embedded as leaders in various grassroots organisations that approve the dispensation of large sums of taxpayer dollars. I spoke about why the PAP has adopted such political double standards at a rally during the 2015 elections.

Has the Elected Presidency Become Pivotal to the PAP's System of Governance?

295

He went on to say:

A simple BFA ramp that could have been built in months, took years to complete. How many senior citizens, immobile, and yet others recovering from episodes such as debilitating strokes could have benefited from this facility earlier, but for how the PAP determines the People's Association operates in opposition wards? Other proposals by opposition MPs for the community are commonly ignored by the People's Association.

This will not do, no matter who is in Government and who is the opposition. Singapore and Singaporeans deserve better.

There was a reply to this post by the PAP grassroots adviser for the area who refuted Singh's remarks, but there was a swift rebuttal by Singh. There is no necessity to get into that exchange here.[24] Ultimately, there was a widespread feeling that public sentiment was on the side of the WP. That sentiment did not look favourably on why, in otherwise efficient Singapore, an uncomplicated project like a walkway ramp could take seven years to be completed. The Singapore public is aware that politics is a partisan business. But the public is also sensitive to the fact that when it comes to the elderly and those with disabilities, there should not even be a perception that a community project might have been delayed for partisan reasons.

As the WP and the PAP do their calculations, so the voters also do their own calculations with respect to the upgrading of HDB flats. To most thinking voters, it simply does not seem practical nor logical for the PAP to withhold upgrading for blocks of HDB flats in precincts

---

24 The exchange was reported in "Workers' Party chief, Pritam Singh, PAP grassroots adviser spar over allegation of 'double standards'", *The Straits Times*, 21 October 2021, https://www.straitstimes.com/politics/wp-chief-pritam-singh-pap-grassroots-adviser-spar-over-allegation-of-double-standards. Accessed on 8 February 2021.

that have given majority support to an alternative party, since those flats could quickly turn into high-rise slums. The idea, and the optics, of high-rise slums are not in keeping with Singapore's ethos of being clean and green.

Also, increasingly, Singaporean voters appear less impressed about risks associated with a so-called "freak election", resulting in the defeat of the PAP. This is because the view that is in the ascendant is that the displacement of the PAP as the government would not spawn chaos or economic ruin. Singaporeans have looked up north, to Malaysia, their closest neighbour, and seen that when the long-standing Barisan Nasional government — a government that had been in power for a similar length of time as the PAP — was defeated at the May 2018 general election, it did not trigger chaos and ruin for Malaysia. In fact, Malaysia's economy grew at a rate faster than Singapore's during the two years 2018 and 2019. Malaysia's economy grew at 5.5% in 2018 and 4.4% in 2019 versus 3.2% and 0.7% respectively for the Singapore economy.[25]

The final point relates to the PAP's hardball election tactics. Those tactics, involving the PAP launching personal attacks on members of the opposition, also appear to have lost their potency. And, insofar as the WP is concerned, they have become counter-productive. This was demonstrated at GE2020 when the WP's Raeesah Khan was assailed by the PAP and its supporters for having made inappropriate Facebook posts

---

25 Department of Statistics Malaysia: Official Portal, "Gross Domestic Income 2019", https://www.dosm.gov.my/v1/index.php?r=column/cthemeByCat&cat=266&bul_id=dmtScmJyMk9pQWRnNW5PZER6bDNJUT09&menu_id=TE5CRUZCblh4ZTZMODZIbmk2aWRRQT09. Accessed on 8 February 2021; Ministry of Trade and Industry Singapore, "Economic Survey of Singapore 2018", https://www.mti.gov.sg/-/media/MTI/Resources/Economic-Survey-of-Singapore/2018/Economic-Survey-of-Singapore-2018/FullReport_AES2018.pdf. Accessed on 8 February 20221.; and, Ministry of Trade and Industry Singapore, "Economic Survey of Singapore 2019", https://www.mti.gov.sg/-/media/MTI/Resources/Economic-Survey-of-Singapore/2019/Economic-Survey-of-Singapore-2019/FullReport_AES2019.pdf. Accessed on 8 February 2021.

Has the Elected Presidency Become Pivotal to the PAP's System of Governance?

297

touching on race and questioning the impartiality of the Singapore police in carrying out law enforcement duties. Some constituents in Sengkang GRC agreed that she was not suitable to be an MP. But a larger number of constituents thought the attacks on a young female candidate were even less appropriate. There's an ethical and political calculation to negative election campaigning. And, there is ample scholarly literature analysing the efficaciousness of, what is in effect, mudslinging tactics during election time.[26] As one article has observed, "The decision to attack is a political calculation, based on the presumption that its execution will damage the intended target more than it will jeopardize the status of the candidate[s] sponsoring the attack."[27] Whether PAP election strategists actually did any calculations before the party jumped onto the bandwagon to attack Khan's character, is unknown. In other words, it might be inaccurate to contend that the PAP miscalculated, when in actual fact it might never have done any calculations at all but merely made an assumption that negative campaigning works based on historical antecedents. Whatever the case may be, on balance, the employment by the PAP of negative election tactics is unlikely to be effective against a WP that has attempted to ensure that it conducts its opposition — inside and outside Parliament — with relative dignity, eschewing boisterous politics.[28] Being seen to take the moral high ground has resulted in the WP being relatively Teflon-like to the PAP attack machine.

---

26 See, for instance, Martin Haselmayer, "Negative Campaigning and Its Consequences: A Review and a Look Ahead", *French Politics*, Vol. 17, 2019; Eric Beerbohm, "The Ethics of Electioneering", *The Journal of Political Philosophy*, 2015, Vol. 24, No. 4; Lee Sigelman and Mark Kugler, "Why is Research on the Effects of Negative Campaigning so Inconclusive? Understanding Citizens' Perceptions of Negativity", *The Journal of Politics*, Vol. 65, No. 1, 2003; and, Stergios Skaperdas and Bernard Grofman, "Modelling Negative Campaigning", *American Political Science Review*, Vol. 89, No. 1, March 1995.

27 Richard R. Lau and Ivy Brown Rovner, "Negative Campaigning", *Annual Review of Political Science*, 2009, Vol. 12, p. 292.

28 Hardball election tactics could, however, work if the PAP employed them against opponents in other alternative parties who are far less dignified than the WP and, in the minds of many voters, simply brought such tactics onto themselves.

SUMMARY
Key Concepts and Issues of Material Significance

G iven that each of the 10 chapters in this book was conceptually conceived, with each concept and theme standing on its own, attempting to draw threads from all the chapters to form a common unified theme might be too ambitious a task, nor would it do justice to the analysis in each of the chapters. Consequently, in lieu of a conclusion to this book, it might be more appropriate to highlight — in summarised form — some of the key concepts and issues of material significance it has covered.

All the inferences drawn from the analysis of various issues have been based on the empirical evidence. The empirical evidence suggests the following:

- That the political polarity in Singapore is between authoritarian-leaning and centrist-leaning forces. The left-right axis, which captures the political reality in many other jurisdictions, does not have much relevance in Singapore, even if progressive/liberal ideological elements tend to magnify their voice online by appearing to be larger and more influential than they are.

- Progressives/liberals populate the smaller of two sub-blocs represented in D — the Irreducible core of anti-PAP voters — which is part of the voting blocs in Table 1.2 formulated in Chapter 1. That table effectively sets out the lay of the political landscape in Singapore.

- A case could be made out that in order to expand its parliamentary numbers, the Workers' Party (WP) has to continue positioning itself to facilitate proximity voting by those in voting bloc B — Moderate PAP voters. The electoral arithmetic is such that for the WP, its path to victory is through B. If the WP deviates markedly from the political positioning it adopted at GE2020 — for example, if it moved to appeal to voters who desire a more strident opposition to the PAP — the numbers do not add-up for the WP to prevail at the ballot box.

- One way to grasp a proper understanding of electoral politics in Singapore is to view the subject through the lens of the 4Ps — Policies, Personalities, Process and Party branding. To that extent, it is difficult for Personalities — characterised as privilege or change agents — to have an outsized influence in a general election. This is because the Singapore parliamentary election system is derived from the Westminster model, where parties are emphasised and personalities tend to recede to the background.

- For a challenger to the ruling party, Process and Party branding are far more essential than anything else. Yet, these two variables are often underappreciated by both lay-people and many political commentators alike.

- Process is heavily dictated by the electoral system whose twin aspects are first-past-the-post (FPTP) and compulsory voting rules (CVR). This duality sets the bar high for any challenger to the incumbent party. In order to surmount that bar, a challenger is forced into a resource-intensive effort of cultivating the ground over many months, if not years.

- Under CVR, where voter turnout is in excess of 90%, a conversion, instead of mobilisation, strategy is required. A conversion strategy is given effect offline through in-person meetings with voters at the doorstep. This is described as "conversion by conversation".

- Voters are sensitive to observable differences — in terms of policies and personalities — projected across the alternative parties. If voters deem the alternative to the PAP as deficient in some way, many will be disinclined to vote against the PAP, even if voters have been impacted negatively by what they consider as failed PAP policies. This speaks to the generally conservative — with a small "c" — nature of many Singaporean voters.

- As long as Singapore continues with CVR, social media cannot have a decisive impact on an election campaign. Traditional and resource-intensive methods that include the retail politics of house-visits (doorstepping) and, during the election campaign proper, heavy expenditure on print advertisements, are essential to visibly demonstrate to voters a party's electoral strength and the extent of its desire to represent voters in Parliament. Election candidates and parties have to invest meaningful amounts of time and money not only in the process but in their own candidacy and their party in order to stand a realistic chance of prevailing in an election. Contrary to popular belief, these efforts cannot be done either cheaply nor remotely.
- Other than the WP, the Progress Singapore Party and possibly the Singapore Democratic Party, the other alternative parties do not provide a viable challenge to the PAP. Their continued contestation of parliamentary elections might be rationalised by them as an effort at not giving the PAP a walkover and hence, forestalling the disenfranchisement of voters. Though such a rationale is compelling, a greater case can be made out that, as minor players in the political scene, these alternative parties actually disempower voters at the ballot box. This is manifested in the increasing incidence of invalid ballots when voters are presented with an alternative to the PAP they know is not competitive.
- The work of a civil society activist cannot be conflated with that of an elected politician or someone who aspires to elected political office. This is especially apparent in the Singapore context where there is no observable clamour by the voting public for non-material issues, i.e., related to civil liberties and human rights.
- Many middle-ground voters do not subscribe to a PAP versus non-PAP binary. To such voters that is a false choice. On the other hand, many middle-ground voters accept that there is a PAP versus WP binary. The varying incidence of invalid voting which divides the alternative parties into five tiers (Table 3.5, Chapter 3), provides empirical evidence to underpin this inference.

- The minor parties have no real strategy to make themselves more competitive electorally other than beseeching the WP to assist them in that endeavour.
- The WP's significant advantage is in its brand, reflecting political moderation. At a more basic level it is manifested in the party's distinctive hammer logo which many voters can identify with and which they take as representing the foil to the PAP's lightning symbol.
- The WP has been able to optimise its moderate credentials through knitting together a coalition of voters across most demographics. A case could thus be made out that if the WP began associating, either informally or formally, with some of the alternative parties then, in the perception of a not insignificant segment of the voting public, it would begin to dilute its main asset — its brand — and, consequently, diminish its electoral support.
- GE2020 cannot be viewed as an ordinary general election. The COVID-19 pandemic, and the negative impact it had on livelihoods disadvantaged the PAP. Yet, even in that extraordinary situation voters were mostly prepared to opt only for the proximate alternative to the PAP — the WP — where it was available.
- Economic motivation will remain the key factor determining how Singaporean voters exercise their choice at the ballot box in the near term.
- A case can be made out that the WP constitutes the median party in the Singapore Parliament. The WP gives effect to the Median Voter Theorem, by prompting the ruling party to edge towards the political centre. In concrete terms, this is manifested by the government being compelled to be more responsive — and, thus, generous — to the concerns of the ground.

Concluding observations

As was set out at the start of this book, many Singaporeans who might have sub-consciously role-modelled themselves after Lee Kuan Yew, will have to break decisively from his austere, conservative legacy if Singapore's political culture is to evolve to one where the interests of the elites are relegated in favour of the interests of ordinary people. Singapore's political culture will evolve meaningfully only when the ruling PAP gets a clear message from the voters that they are ready for such a psychological change. GE2020 did not provide a clear-cut message in that respect. Its message was more tentative and equivocal.

Given that the WP is widely viewed as the main challenger to the PAP, only an enhancement of the WP's parliamentary numbers to at least double that it had attained at GE2020, will give evidence that Singaporeans were ready to embrace change in both their psychological outlook and political culture. Just as the WP can only move as fast as its core support base allows, so too the PAP — as the governing party — will only move to reflect changed political realities when it loses seats in a parliamentary general election far greater than that it suffered at GE2020.

APPENDIX 1

Results of the 2020 Singapore Parliamentary
General Election Based on VALID Votes Cast

Constituency/Party/Candidates(s)	Total Votes	Percentage
Aljunied GRC		
PAP	57,330	40.05%
Chan Hui Yuh		
Chua Eng Leong		
Victor Lye Thiam Fatt		
Shamsul Kamar Bin Mohamed Razali		
Alex Yeo Sheng Chye		
WP	85,815	59.95%
Gerald Giam Yean Song		
Sylvia Lim		
Muhamad Faisal Bin Abdul Manap		
Leon Perera		
Pritam Singh		
Ang Mo Kio GRC		
PAP	124,597	71.91%
Darryl David		
Gan Thiam Poh		
Lee Hsien Loong		

(Continued)

(Continued)

Constituency/Party/Candidates(s)	Total Votes	Percentage
Nadia Ahmad Samdin		
Ng Ling Ling		
RP	48,677	28.09%
Kenneth Andrew Jeyaretnam		
Noraini Bte Yunus		
Soh Guan Soon		
Yeo Yao Hui, Charles		
Zhu Laicheng		
Bishan-Toa Payoh GRC		
PAP	62,983	67.23%
Chee Hong Tat		
Chong Kee Hiong		
Ng Eng Hen		
Saktiandi Bin Supaat		
SPP	30,696	32.77%
Steve Chia		
Melvyn Chiu		
Williamson Lee		
Osman Sulaiman		
Bukit Batok SMC		
SDP	12,787	45.20%
Chee Soon Juan		
PAP	15,500	54.80%
Murali Pillai		
Bukit Panjang SMC		
PAP	18,085	53.73%
Liang Eng Hwa		

(Continued)

Constituency/Party/Candidates(s)	Total Votes	Percentage
SDP	15,576	46.27%
Paul Ananth Tambyah		
Chua Chu Kang GRC		
PSP	42,012	41.36%
Abdul Rahman Bin Mohamad		
Choo Shaun Ming		
Tan Meng Wah		
Yuen Kin Pheng		
PAP	59,554	58.64%
Gan Kim Yong		
Low Yen Ling		
Don Wee		
Zhulkarnian Abdul Rahim		
East Coast GRC		
WP	53,375	46.61%
Abdul Shariff Aboo Kassim		
Foo Seck Guan		
Dylan Ng		
Nicole Seah		
Terence Tan Li-Chern		
PAP	61,144	53.39%
Cheryl Chan Wei Ling		
Heng Swee Keat		
Mohd. Maliki Bin Osman		
Tan Kiat How		
Tan Soon Neo Jessica		

(Continued)

(Continued)

Constituency/Party/Candidates(s)	Total Votes	Percentage
Holland-Bukit Timah GRC		
SDP	36,100	33.64%
Min Cheong		
James Gomez		
Alfred Tan		
Tan Jee Say		
PAP	71,218	66.36%
Edward Chia Bing Hui		
Christopher de Souza		
Sim Ann		
Vivian Balakrishnan		
Hong Kah North SMC		
PAP	16,347	60.99%
Amy Khor Lean Suan		
PSP	10,457	39.01%
Gigene Wong		
Hougang SMC		
PAP	9,791	38.79%
Lee Hong Chuang		
WP	15,451	61.21%
Dennis Tan Lip Fong		
Jalan Besar GRC		
PV	34,261	34.64%
Michael Fang Amin		
Leong Sze Hian		

(Continued)

Constituency/Party/Candidates(s)	Total Votes	Percentage
Lim Tean		
Nor Azlan Bin Sulaiman		
PAP	64,631	65.36%
Heng Chee How		
Denise Phua Lay Peng		
Josephine Teo		
Wan Rizal Wan Zakariah		
Jurong GRC		
PAP	91,846	74.61%
Huang Wei Zhong Shawn		
Rahayu Binte Mahzam		
Tan Wu Meng		
Tharman Shanmugaratnam		
Xie Yao Quan		
RDU	31,260	25.39%
Michelle Lee Juen		
Liyana Dhamirah		
Ravi Philemon		
Nicholas Tang		
Alec Tok		
Kebun Baru SMC		
PSP	7,842	37.08%
Kumaran Pillai		
PAP	13,309	62.92%
Kwek Hian Chuan		

(Continued)

(Continued)

Constituency/Party/Candidates(s)	Total Votes	Percentage
MacPherson SMC		
PPP	7,489	28.26%
Goh Meng Seng		
PAP	19,009	71.74%
Tin Pei Ling		
Marine Parade GRC		
WP	55,047	42.26%
Azhar Latip		
Fadli Fawzi		
Nathaniel Koh		
Ron Tan Jun Yen		
Yee Jenn Jong		
PAP	75,203	57.74%
Mohd. Fahmi Aliman		
Seah Kian Peng		
Tan Chuan-Jin		
Tan See Leng		
Edwin Tong Chun Fai		
Marsiling-Yew Tee GRC		
SDP	40,690	36.82%
Damanhuri Bin Abas		
Khung Wai Yeen		
Lim Boon Heng		
Benjamin Pwee		
PAP	69,813	63.18%
Hany Soh Hui Bin		
Lawrence Wong		

(Continued)

Constituency/Party/Candidates(s)	Total Votes	Percentage
Alex Yam Ziming		
Zaqy Mohamad		
Marymount SMC		
PSP	9,943	44.96%
Ang Yong Guan		
PAP	12,173	55.04%
Gan Siow Huang		
Mountbatten SMC		
PAP	16,285	73.82%
Lim Biow Chuan		
PV	5,775	26.18%
Sivakumaran Chellappa		
Nee Soon GRC		
PSP	53,181	38.10%
Bowyer Bradley Peter		
Kalayarasu Manickam		
Muhammad Taufik Bin Supan		
S. Nallakaruppan		
Tay Chye Seng		
PAP	86,308	61.90%
Derrick Goh Soon Hee		
K. Shanmugam		
Muhammad Faishal Ibrahim		
Ng Kok Kwang, Louis		
Carrie Tan Huimin		

(Continued)

(Continued)

Constituency/Party/Candidates(s)	Total Votes	Percentage
Pasir Ris-Punggol GRC		
SDA	37,237	23.67%
Abu Bin Mohamed		
Harminder Pal Singh		
Kuswadi Bin Atnawi		
Lim Bak Chuan Desmond		
Kelvin Ong Soon Huat		
PV	19,147	12.17%
Goh Keow Wah		
Lim Kay Cheow		
Mohamed Nassir Ismail		
Prabu Ramachandran		
Vigneswari VR		
PAP	100,932	64.16%
Janil Puthucheary		
Sharael Taha		
Desmond Tan		
Teo Chee Hean		
Yeo Wan Ling		
Pioneer SMC		
Ind	655	2.78%
Cheang Peng Wah		
PSP	8,289	35.22%
Lim Cher Hong		
PAP	14,593	62.00%
Patrick Tay Teck Guan		

(Continued)

Constituency/Party/Candidates(s)	Total Votes	Percentage
Potong Pasir SMC		
SPP	7,302	39.33%
Jose Raymond		
PAP	11,264	60.67%
Sitoh Yih Pin		
Punggol West SMC		
PAP	15,655	60.98%
Sun Xueling		
WP	10,017	39.02%
Tan Chen Chen		
Radin Mas SMC		
RP	5,922	25.99%
Kumar Appavoo		
PAP	16,864	74.01%
Melvin Yong Yik Chye		
Sembawang GRC		
PAP	94,176	67.29%
Lim Wee Kiak		
Mariam Jaafar		
Ong Ye Kung		
Poh Li San		
Vikram Nair		
NSP	45,778	32.71%
Ng Chung Hon		
Sathin s/o Ravindran		

(Continued)

(Continued)

Constituency/Party/Candidates(s)	Total Votes	Percentage
Sebastian Teo		
Yadzeth Bin Hairis		
Yeo Tiong Boon		
Sengkang GRC		
PAP	55,319	47.88%
Amrin Amin		
Lam Pin Min		
Lye Hoong Yip Raymond		
Ng Chee Meng		
WP	60,217	52.12%
Chua Kheng Wee		
He Ting Ru		
Jamus Jerome Lim		
Raeesah Begum Binte Farid Khan		
Tampines GRC		
PAP	94,668	66.41%
Baey Yam Keng		
Cheng Li Hui		
Desmond Choo Pey Ching		
Koh Poh Koon		
Masagos Zulkifli		
NSP	47,875	33.59%
Choong Hon Heng		
Fong Chin Leong		
Mohd. Ridzwan Bin Mohammad		

(Continued)

Constituency/Party/Candidates(s)	Total Votes	Percentage
Vincent Ng Kian Guan		
Yeo Ren-Yuan		
Tanjong Pagar GRC		
PSP	45,807	36.90%
A'bas Bin Kasmani		
Chua Teck Leong, Michael		
Harish Pillay		
Low Wei Ling		
Soon Jun Wei, Terence		
PAP	78,330	63.10%
Chan Chun Sing		
Eric Chua Swee Leong		
Indranee Thurai Rajah		
Joan Pereira		
Alvin Tan Sheng Hui		
West Coast GRC		
PAP	71,658	51.68%
Ang Wei Neng		
Foo Mee Har		
Desmond Lee Ti-Seng		
Rachel Ong Sin Yen		
S. Iswaran		
PSP	66,996	48.32%
Khoo Poh Tiong Jeffrey		
Leong Mun Wai		

(Continued)

(Continued)

Constituency/Party/Candidates(s)	Total Votes	Percentage
N. Loganathan		
Hazel Poa		
Tan Cheng Bock		
Yio Chu Kang SMC		
PSP	9,519	39.18%
Kayla Low		
PAP	14,775	60.82%
Yip Hon Weng		
Yuhua SMC		
PAP	14,131	70.54%
Grace Fu Hai Yien		
SDP	5,901	29.46%
Robin Low		

SOURCE: Elections Department Singapore.

APPENDIX 2

The Amos Yee Episode: Its Impact on GE2015, and Why Fringe Elements Constitute a Greater Threat to the WP than the PAP

Other than the "LKY effect", another issue which depressed the vote for the alternative parties and, conversely, inflated the PAP's vote, at GE2015 was the so-called "Amos Yee episode". In the days following the death of Lee Kuan Yew on 23 March 2015, a teenage blogger, Amos Yee, uploaded an expletive-laden video to YouTube titled *Lee Kuan Yew is Finally Dead!* In the video, Yee, who was then 17 years of age, attacked Lee, his followers, and the Christian faith. The video, coming so soon after Lee's passing, caused uproar among many Singaporeans. But Yee also had supporters, from civil society, academia, the arts community and personalities from two alternative parties. All of them were ostensibly more concerned about his welfare given that two dozen or so police reports were filed against Yee, which led to his arrest.[1] Yee was successfully prosecuted for wounding religious feelings and spent two short stints in custody, in 2015 and 2016.[2]

Dignity and personal honour are neither exclusively Eastern nor Western concepts. They are values which transcend race, religion and nationality, and they were held by many of those who were upset over

---

1 "Amos Yee, who made insensitive remarks on Christianity, arrested", *The Straits Times*, 30 March 2015, https://www.straitstimes.com/singapore/courts-crime/amos-yee-who-made-insensitive-remarks-on-christianity-in-video-arrested. Accessed on 20 March 2021.

2 "Teen blogger Amos Yee gets 6 weeks' jail and $2000 fine for wounding religious feelings", *The Straits Times*, 30 September 2016, https://www.straitstimes.com/singapore/courts-crime/teen-blogger-amos-yee-gets-six-weeks-jail-and-2000-fine-for-wounding. Accessed on 20 March 2021.

Yee and his antics. In the event, the state's penalties handed down to Yee cannot, objectively, be viewed as excessive but had just about the right deterrence effect on other teenagers who might have gone similarly wayward. But some Singaporeans felt that the penalties and even state intervention were unnecessary. Indeed, on 4 July 2015, a letter addressed to Prime Minister Lee Hsien Loong and signed by 77 individuals asked that the state "discharge its prosecutorial function with caution, sensitivity and generosity".[3]

Cherian George, a Hong Kong-based Singaporean scholar, had written at length about the Yee episode and said, among other things, that "Singaporeans' baying for vengeance was ultimately less excusable than the antics of a psychologically troubled child."[4] In the eye of the controversy, the prominent artist Alfian Sa'at decided to have dinner with Yee and his parents and quickly made public his own thoughts on the Yee episode. He expressed upset at "the way the media [had been] painting [Yee] — with insinuations that he might fall within the autism spectrum", but he said that he had told Yee he demurred about bringing in religion into a rant about Lee Kuan Yew.[5] However, he agreed with Yee's criticism of Lee, and he made clear that, "Amos Yee, as a teenager, is as normal as they come".[6]

The civil society activist Kirsten Han, in an exchange with me at a forum organised by the British High Commission for International

---

3 "Open letter over state's treatment of Amos Yee sent to PM", *The Straits Times*, 5 July 2015, https://www.straitstimes.com/singapore/open-letter-over-states-treatment-of-amos-yee-sent-to-pm. Accessed on 20 March 2021.

4 Cherian George, *Singapore, Incomplete: Reflections on a First World Nation's Arrested Political Development*, (Singapore: Woodsville News, 2017), p. 42.

5 Alfian Sa'at, "Comment: A conversation with Amos Yee and family", *Yahoo! News*, 11 May 2015, https://sg.news.yahoo.com/blogs/singaporescene/comment--a-conversation-with-amos-yee-and-family-090836714.html. Accessed on 20 March 2021.

6 Ibid.

Democracy Day on 15 September 2015,[7] had a simple solution to the Amos Yee episode, when I remarked that it was untrue that Christians were not offended by his video. She said, breezily, that if one did not wish to be offended by Yee's YouTube video then simply do not view it. I replied, with words to the effect, that the video did not get five to eight views but more like between 500,000 and 800,000 views and, consequently, it was difficult to ignore.

The blogger Roy Ngerng, who was a candidate for the Reform Party (RP) at GE2015, and who has been inclined towards the theatrical, had also stood by Yee in a highly public display of support.[8] Further, Singapore Democratic Party (SDP) member and physician Paul Tambyah spoke out robustly against the state's reaction to Yee. He made several interventions, including as part of a question he posed to Prime Minister Lee Hsien Loong at a conference on 2 July 2015 commemorating Singapore's 50 years of independence.[9] Tambyah also delivered a speech during a candlelight vigil for Yee at Speakers' Corner, Hong Lim Park, on 11 May 2015.[10]

---

7   Han, myself, and Simon Long (of *The Economist*) were three speakers at the forum held at the British High Commissioner's residence, Eden Hall. There was an audience of around 100.

8   "My heart goes out to Amos Yee, my friend — Roy Ngerng", *Malay Mail*, 2 May 2015, https://www.malaymail.com/news/what-you-think/2015/05/02/my-heart-goes-out-to-amos-yee-my-friend-roy-ngerng/888925. Accessed on 20 March 2021.

9   This was the SG50 conference organised by the Institute of Policy Studies. Tambyah had the privilege of asking the prime minister the very first question during the Q&A, and he focused his prepared question (he was reading from a piece of paper) on civil liberties and human rights.

10 In his speech, Tambyah described himself "as a member of Singapore's civil society". Chapter 5 sets out why one should not conflate a civil society activist with a politician, and why it's generally difficult to transition from being a civil society activist to making a success as a politician. Tambyah, however, might be an exception. Indeed, for the simple fact that Singaporeans generally place great store on status, Tambyah — at the top of his profession as an infectious disease expert — could well get elected.

Melodrama continued to revolve around the Yee episode. Yee had been scheduled to be enlisted for National Service in December 2016 but, a few months earlier, fled to the United States, where he sought political asylum. The leader of the RP, Kenneth Jeyaretnam who, already in 2015 had thrown his support behind Yee,[11] flew to the US to back the asylum bid because he felt Yee was being persecuted and harassed by the Singapore government.[12] Yee succeeded in gaining asylum. Subsequently, he was to spend his time in the US publicly advocating for paedophilia in a (now removed) YouTube channel; he had also operated a pro-paedophilia online message board.[13] Further, Yee was a guest in an episode of right-wing talk show host Jeff Lee Peterson's The Fallen State, where he categorically set out his rationale for supporting paedophilia.[14] In November 2020, Yee was indicted by a grand jury in an Illinois court for solicitation and possession of child pornography. At the time of writing — August 2021 — that case had yet to run its course.

The US-based Singaporean civil society activist Melissa Chen, who had initially assisted Yee in his asylum request, was to publicly acknowledge that she had erred. She was to denounce Yee as early as December 2018 after discovering his tendencies, saying: "The obvious problem on hindsight is that the desire to see him as a figure, as some sort of figure, that could take the shape of our own cause, admittedly

---

11 "Amos Yee back in prison for 3 weeks; to be assessed for reformative training", *The Straits Times*, 2 June 2015, https://www.straitstimes.com/singapore/courts-crime/amos-yee-back-in-prison-for-3-weeks-to-be-assessed-for-reformative-training. Accessed on 20 March 2021.

12 "US judge to rule on Singaporean blogger's asylum request", *Reuters*, 8 March 2017, https://www.reuters.com/article/cnews-us-usa-singapore-blogger-idCAKBN 16F02A. Accessed on 21 March 2021.

13 "'Internet troll' Amos Yee charged with child porn", *Chicago Sun Times*, 16 October 2020, https://chicago.suntimes.com/crime/2020/10/16/21519739/internet-troll-amos-yee-charged-with-child-porn. Accessed on 21 March 2021.

14 "Amos Yee on the Next Battleground of the Left (Excerpt 3 of 3)", YouTube, 20 March 2018, https://www.youtube.com/watch?v=7rZv0uKPuLk&t=55s. Accessed on 21 March 2021.

led to developing blind spots and biases."[15] Amongst those who had backed Yee in 2015, Chen's recantation constituted a notable exception.

Even without the surfacing of later tendencies towards paedophilia on Yee's part, it is necessary to be clear about one point. Many Singaporeans were firmly of the view that there was much wrong about Yee's 2015 YouTube video: the timing, an excoriating attack on a just deceased person; the extreme vulgarity; and, the wanton denigration of a religion employed to attack that deceased person. And, Yee's age — 17 years — does not amount to a mitigating factor, and neither does a possible psychological disorder.[16]

Some who supported Yee believed in what they had said publicly, i.e., state intervention was unnecessary as Singapore society was more than capable of handling, and coping with, Yee's behaviour. In other words, they did so because they believed they were well-meaning. Others relished in the Yee episode as it gave vent to their long-held antipathy towards Lee Kuan Yew, in particular, and the Singapore state, in general.

Whatever it might have been, to the general public quite a number of civil society activists and their allies were discredited by the Yee episode. The Workers' Party (WP) had remained untainted by that episode. The party had kept its hands clean by not advocating for Yee. However, because the episode happened so soon after Lee's death and just before GE2015, the WP appeared to suffer from a second-order

---

15 Quoted in "Lady who helped Amos Yee get asylum in US now wants him deported from US", *Mothership SG*, 10 December 2018, https://mothership.sg/2018/12/amos-yee-melissa-chen-deport/. Accessed on 20 March 2021.

16 As one consensus view that cuts across most legal jurisdictions, has put it: "Although there is some argument to the contrary, within the criminal justice system, there has been a strong push to exclude personality disorders, specifically ASPD [Anti-Social Personality Disorders], from the types of mental illnesses potentially significant enough to warrant exculpation of fault or consideration of decreased criminal responsibility." Sally M. Johnson, "Personality Disorders at the Interface of Psychiatry and the Law: Legal Use and Clinical Classification", *Dialogues in Clinical Neuroscience*, Vol. 15, No. 2, June 2013, p. 208.

effect at that election by being seen in the eyes of part of the electorate as an indistinguishable element of this amorphous thing called "the opposition". Thus, a responsible and moderate opposition party fell victim, not to the PAP, but to fringe elements who adopted a posture of absolute opposition to an authoritarian-leaning government without a care for any unintended political consequences. In a nutshell, they merely facilitated the consolidation of that government's power. Given short memories, it is unlikely that the central lesson here would have been learnt by many. Indeed, a fringe element, pushing a niche agenda, will continue to cause far more problems for the WP than the PAP.

APPENDIX 3

Results of the 2020 Singapore Parliamentary General Election Vote-Percentages Calculated on the Basis of TOTAL Votes Cast, Including Rejected Votes

		Overseas Votes	Local Votes	Total	Total (%)
Aljunied GRC	PAP	86	57,244	57,330	39.61%
	WP	212	85,803	85,815	59.29%
	Rejected	0	1,582	1,582	1.09%
	TOTAL	298	144,629	144,727	
Ang Mo Kio GRC	PAP	167	124,430	124,597	69.88%
	RP	77	48,600	48,677	27.39%
	Rejected	7	5,009	5,016	2.81%
	TOTAL	251	178,039	178,290	
Bishan-Toa Payoh GRC	PAP	130	62,853	62,983	65.79%
	SPP	102	30,594	30,696	32.07%
	Rejected	6	2,043	2,049	2.14%
	TOTAL	238	95,490	95,728	
Bukit Batok SMC	SDP	23	12,764	12,787	44.37%
	PAP	24	15,476	15,500	53.78%
	Rejected	0	533	533	1.85%
	TOTAL	47	28,773	28,820	
Bukit Panjang SMC	PAP	15	18.070	18,085	52.81%
	SDP	20	15,556	15,576	45.48%
	Rejected	0	586	586	1.71%
	TOTAL	35	34,212	34,247	

(Continued)

(Continued)

		Overseas Votes	Local Votes	Total	Total (%)
Chua Chu Kang GRC	PSP	70	41,942	42,012	40.80%
	PAP	92	59,462	59,554	57.83%
	Rejected	0	1,410	1,410	1.37%
	TOTAL	162	102,810	102,976	
East Coast GRC	WP	147	53,228	53,375	46.05%
	PAP	135	61,009	61,144	52.75%
	Rejected	0	1,393	1,393	1.20%
	TOTAL	282	125,630	115,912	
Holland-Bukit Timah GRC	SDP	126	35,972	36,100	33.02%
	PAP	255	70,963	71,218	65.15%
	Rejected	6	1,993	1,999	1.83%
	TOTAL	383	108,928	109,317	
Hong Kah North SMC	PAP	14	16,333	16,347	60.08%
	PSP	5	10,452	10,457	38.43%
	Rejected	0	403	403	1.48%
	TOTAL	19	27,188	27,207	
Hougang SMC	PAP	15	9,776	9,791	38.38%
	WP	35	15,416	15,451	60.56%
	Rejected	0	272	272	1.07%
	TOTAL	50	25,464	25,514	
Jalan Besar GRC	PV	76	34,185	34,261	33.64%
	PAP	109	64,522	64,631	63.46%
	Rejected	5	2,943	2,948	2.90%
	TOTAL	190	101,650	101,840	
Jurong GRC	PAP	154	91,692	91,846	73.11%
	RDU	69	31,191	31,260	24.88%
	Rejected	2	2,517	2,519	2.01%
	TOTAL	223	125,400	125,625	

(Continued)

		Overseas Votes	Local Votes	Total	Total (%)
Kebun Baru SMC	PSP	30	7,812	7,842	36.41%
	PAP	25	13,284	13,309	61.79%
	Rejected	0	387	387	1.80%
	TOTAL	55	21,483	21,538	
MacPherson SMC	PPP	12	7,477	7,489	27.61%
	PAP	26	18,983	19,009	70.08%
	Rejected	0	625	625	2.30%
	TOTAL	38	27,085	27,123	
Marine Parade GRC	WP	197	54,850	55,047	41.69%
	PAP	210	74,993	75,203	56.96%
	Rejected	2	1,787	1,789	1.36%
	TOTAL	409	131,630	132,039	
Marsiling-Yew Tee GRC	SDP	49	40,641	40,690	36.14%
	PAP	91	69,722	69,813	62.00%
	Rejected	0	2,097	2,097	1.86%
	TOTAL	140	112,460	112,600	
Marymount SMC	PSP	25	9,918	9,943	44.35%
	PAP	30	12,143	12,173	54.29%
	Rejected	0	305	305	1.36%
	TOTAL	55	22,366	22,421	
Mountbatten SMC	PAP	58	16,227	16,285	71.9%
	PV	27	5,748	5,775	25.5%
	Rejected	5	584	589	2.6%
	TOTAL	90	22,559	22,649	
Nee Soon GRC	PSP	61	53,070	53,131	37.51%
	PAP	89	86,219	86,308	60.94%
	Rejected	1	2,199	2,200	1.55%
	TOTAL	151	141,488	141,639	

(Continued)

(Continued)

		Overseas Votes	Local Votes	Total	Total (%)
Pasir Ris-Punggol GRC	SDA	58	37,179	37,237	23.17%
	PV	20	19,127	19,147	11.91%
	PAP	160	100,772	100,932	62.80%
	Rejected	3	3,392	3,395	2.11%
	TOTAL	241	160,470	160,711	
Pioneer SMC	IND01	1	654	655	2.74%
	PSP	4	8,285	8,289	34.70%
	PAP	22	14,571	14,593	61.09%
	Rejected	0	350	350	1.47%
	TOTAL	27	23,860	23,887	
Potong Pasir SMC	SPP	27	7,275	7,302	38.75%
	PAP	32	11,232	11,264	59.77%
	Rejected	1	278	279	1.48%
	TOTAL	60	18,785	18,845	
Punggol West SMC	PAP	18	15,637	15,655	60.45%
	WP	5	10,012	10.017	38.68%
	Rejected	1	216	217	0.84%
	TOTAL	24	25,865	25,899	
Radin Mas SMC	RP	17	5,905	5,922	25.09%
	PAP	30	16,834	16,864	71.45%
	Rejected	1	817	818	3.47%
	TOTAL	48	23,556	23,604	
Sembawang GRC	PAP	108	94,068	94,176	65.90%
	NSP	51	45,727	45,778	32.03%
	Rejected	1	2,947	2,948	2.06%
	TOTAL	160	142,742	142,902	
Sengkang GRC	PAP	105	55,214	55,319	47.39%
	WP	81	60,136	60,217	51.59%
	Rejected	0	1,194	1,194	1.02%
	TOTAL	186	116,544	116,730	

(Continued)

		Overseas Votes	Local Votes	Total	Total (%)
Tampines GRC	PAP	107	94,561	94,668	64.81%
	NSP	56	47,819	47,875	32.78%
	Rejected	5	3,516	3,521	2.41%
	TOTAL	168	145,896	146,064	
Tanjong Pagar GRC	PSP	198	45,609	45,807	36.34%
	PAP	251	78,079	78,330	62.13%
	Rejected	3	1,930	1,933	1.53%
	TOTAL	452	125,618	126,070	
West Coast GRC	PAP	113	71,545	71,658	51.07%
	PSP	125	66,871	66,996	47.75%
	Rejected	1	1,645	1,646	1.17%
	TOTAL	239	140,061	140,300	
Yio Chu Kang SMC	PSP	19	9,500	9,519	38.53%
	PAP	19	14,756	14,775	59.80%
	Rejected	0	413	413	1.67%
	TOTAL	38	24,669	24,707	
Yuhua SMC	PAP	20	14,111	14,131	69.14%
	SDP	7	5,894	5,901	28.87%
	Rejected	0	406	406	1.99%
	TOTAL	27	20,411	20,438	

SOURCE: Elections Department Singapore, via email request. Data received on 26 February 2021.

SELECT BIBLIOGRAPHY*

Books and Manuscripts

Amir Ali, *South Asian Islam and British Multiculturalism*. London, Routledge, 2016.

Brennan, Jason and Lisa Hill, *Compulsory Voting*. New York, Cambridge University Press, 2014.

Cecar, Sonja, *Blatcherism: How Much Thatcherism is in Blairism*. VDM Verlag Dr. Mueller, 2007.

Chng Suan Tze, Low Yit Leng and Teo Soh Lung, eds., *1987: Singapore's Marxist Conspiracy 30 Years On*. Singapore, Ethos Books, 2017.

Chua Beng Huat, *Communitarian Democracy in Singapore*. London, Routledge, 1997.

Clery, Elizabeth, John Curtice and Roger Harding (eds.), *British Social Attitudes 34*. London: NatCen Social Research 2017.

da Cunha, Derek, *The Price of Victory: The 1997 Singapore General Election and Beyond*. Singapore, Institute of Southeast Asian Studies, 1997.

da Cunha, Derek, *Singapore Places its Bets: Casinos, Foreign Talent and Remaking a City-state*. Singapore, Straits Times Press, 2010.

da Cunha, Derek, *Breakthrough: Roadmap for Singapore's Political Future*. Singapore, Institute for Policy Studies and Straits Times Press, 2012.

---

* This bibliography only includes works directly cited in the text and footnotes.

George, Cherian, *Singapore, Incomplete: Reflections on a First World Nation's Arrested Political Development.* Singapore, Woodsville News, 2017.

Han Fook Kwang, Warren Fernandez and Sumiko Tan, *Lee Kuan Yew: The Man and His Ideas.* Singapore, Straits Times Press, 1998.

Holtz-Bacha, Christina and Bengt Johansson, eds., *Elections Posters Around the Globe: Political Campaigning in the Public Space.* Springer, 2017.

Jackson, Daniel, Einar Thorsen, Darren Lilleker and Nathalie Weidhase, eds., *UK Election Analysis 2019: Media, Voters and the Campaign.* Poole, England, Centre for Comparative Politics and Media Research, Bournemouth University, December 2019.

Jeyaretnam, J.B., *The Hatchet Man of Singapore.* Singapore, Jeya Publishers, 2003.

Kee Thuan Chye, *The People's Victory: How Malaysians Saved Their Country.* Marshall Cavendish Editions, 2019.

le Carré, John, *A Delicate Truth.* London, Penguin Books, 2013.

Lee Kuan Yew, *From Third World to First.* Singapore: Times Media Private Limited, 2000.

Lee Soo Ann, *Singapore: From Place to Nation.* Singapore, Prentice Hall, 2007.

Leifer, Michael, *Singapore's Foreign Policy: Coping with Vulnerability.* London, Routledge, 2000.

Lim, Leonel, *Knowledge, Control and Critical Thinking in Singapore: State Ideology and the Politics of Pedagogic Recontextualization.* New York, Routledge, 2016.

Lofgren, Mike, *The Deep State: The Fall of the Constitution and the Rise of a Shadow Government.* New York, Viking, 2016.

Loke Hoe Yeong, *The First Wave: JBJ, Chiam & the Opposition in Singapore.* Singapore, Epigram, 2019.

Mauzy, Diane K. and R.S. Milne, *Singapore Politics Under the People's Action Party.* London, Routledge, 2002.

Minchin, James, *No Man is an Island: A Study of Lee Kuan Yew.* Sydney, Allen & Unwin, 1986.

Morelock, J. (ed.), *Critical Theory and Authoritarian Populism.* London, University of Westminster Press, 2018.

O'Brien, Mark and Donnacha O Beachain, eds., *Political Communication in the Republic of Ireland.* Liverpool, Liverpool University Press, New Edition, 2014.

Rodan, Garry, *The Political Economy of Singapore's Industrialisation: National State and International Capital.* Basingstoke, Macmillan, 1989.

Rodan, Garry, *Transparency and Authoritarian Rule in Southeast Asia: Singapore and Malaysia.* London, Routledge, 2004.

Scott, John and Peter J. Carrington, eds., *The Sage Handbook of Social Network Analysis.* Sage Publications Ltd., 2014.

Solijonov, Abdurashid, *Voter Turnout Trends Around the World.* Stockholm, International Institute for Democracy and Electoral Assistance, 2016.

Sooyler, Mehtap, *The Turkish Deep State: State Consolidation, Civil-Military Relations, and Democracy.* London, Routledge, 2017.

BREAKTHROUGH 2.0
332

Statistics Singapore, *Population Trends 2020*, https://www.singstat.gov.sg/-/media/files/publications/population/population2020.pdf

Tamney, Joseph B., *The Struggle Over Singapore's Soul: Western Modernization and Asian*. New York, Walter de Guyter, 1996.

Tan, Kevin Y.L. and Lam Peng Er, eds., *Managing Political Change in Singapore: The Elected Presidency*. London, Routledge, 1997.

Tan, Kevin Y.L. and Lam Peng Er, eds., *Lee's Lieutenants*. Singapore, Straits Times Press, Revised Edition, 2018.

Tay, Simon S.C. (ed.), *A Mandarin and the Making of Public Policy: Reflections by Ngiam Tong Dow*. Singapore, NUS Press, 2006.

The Workers' Party, *Towards a First World Parliament: Manifesto 2011*. Singapore, The Workers' Party, 2011

The Workers' Party, *Walking with Singapore*. Singapore, Ethos Books, 2017.

The Workers' Party, *Make Your Vote Count: The Workers' Party Manifesto 2020*. Singapore, The Workers' Party, 2020.

Watt, Donald, ed., *Aldous Huxley*. New York, Routledge, 1975.

Welsh, Bridget, James Chin, Arun Mahizhnan and Tan Tarn How (eds.), *Impressions of the Goh Chok Tong Years in Singapore*. Singapore, NUS Press, 2009.

Zakaria, Fareed, *The Future of Freedom: Illiberal Democracy at Home and Abroad*. New York, W.W. Norton, 2003.

Journal Articles, Working Papers and Conference Papers
Arceneaux, Kevin and David W. Nickerson, "Who is Mobilized to Vote? A Re-Analysis of 11 Field Experiments", *American Journal of Political Science*, Vol. 53, No. 1, January 2009.

Bagiani, Eugenio, "Review Essay: Ideology and the Making of New Labours", *International Labor and Working-Class History*, No. 56, Fall 1999.

Baldassarri, Delia and Amir Goldberg, "Neither Ideologues nor Agnostics: Alternative Voters' Belief Systems in an Age of Partisan Politics", *American Journal of Sociology*, Vol. 120, No. 1, July 2014.

Banerjee, Sumanta, "Why is the Left More Divided than the Right?" *Economic and Political Weekly*, Vol. 48, No. 38, 21 September, 2013.

Barnes, Tiffany D and Gabriela Rangel, "Subnational Patterns of Participation: Compulsory Voting and the Conditional Impact of Institutional Design", *Political Research Quarterly*, Vol. 71, No. 4, December 2018.

Bates, Thomas R., "Gramsci and the Theory of Hegemony", *Journal of the History of Ideas*, Vol. 36, No. 2, April–June 1975.

Beckman, Ludvig, "Popular Sovereignty Facing the Deep State. The Rule of Recognition and the Powers of the People", *Critical Review of International Social and Political Philosophy*, 2019, https://www.tandfonline.com/doi/pdf/10.1080/13698230.2019.1644583.

Beerbohm, Eric, "The Ethics of Electioneering", *The Journal of Political Philosophy*, Vol. 24, No. 4, 2015.

Ben-Rafael, Eliezer, "The Faces of Religiosity in Israel: Cleavages or Continuum?" *Israel Studies*, Vol. 13, No. 3, Fall 2008.

Bernhard, Michael, Tiago Fernandes and Rui Branco, "Introduction: Civil Society and Democracy in an Era of Inequality", *Comparative Politics*, Vol. 49, No. 3, April 2017.

Bhatti, Yosef, Jens Olav Dahlgaard, Jonas Hedegaard Hansen and Kasper M. Hansen, "Is Door-to-Door Canvassing Effective in Europe? Evidence from a Meta-study Across Six European Countries", *British Journal of Political Science*, Vol. 49, No. 1, January 2019.

Bienfait, H.F. and W.E.A. van Beek, "Right and Left as Political Categories: An Exercise in 'Not-so-Primitive' Classification", *Anthropos*, Vol. 96, No. 1, 2001.

Bowler, Shaun, David Brockington and Todd Donovan, "Election System and Voter Turnout: Experiments in the United States", *The Journal of Politics*, Vol. 63, No. 3, August 2001.

Bowser, Benjamin B., "Racism: Origin and Theory", *Journal of Black Studies*, Vol. 48, No. 6, September 2017.

Bozoki, Andras and Daniel Hemedus, "An Externally Constrained Hybrid Regime: Hungary in the European Union", *Democratization*, April 2018.

Bruns, Axel and Brenda Moon, "Social Media in Australian Federal Elections: Comparing the 2013 and 2016 Campaigns", *Journalism & Mass Communication Quarterly*, Vol. 95, No. 2, 2018.

Buttigieg, Joseph A., "The Contemporary Discourse on Civil Society", *boundary 2*, Vol. 32, No. 1, Spring 2005.

Calleja, Lucie, "The Rise of Populism: The Threat to Civil Society?" *E-International Relations*, 9 February 2020, https://www.e-ir.info/pdf/81470.

Caprara, Gian Vittorio and Michele Vecchione, "On the Left and Right Ideological Divide: Historical Accounts and Contemporary Perspectives", *Advances in Political Psychology*, Vol. 39, Suppl. 1, 2018.

Carter, April, "People Power Since 1980: Examining Reasons for Its Spread, Success and Failure", *Themenschwerpunkt*, Vol. 31, No. 3, 2013.

Catellani, Patrizia and Augusta Isabella Alberici, "Does the Candidate Matter? Comparing the Voting Choice of Early and Late Deciders", *Political Psychology*, Vol. 33, No. 5, October 2012.

Chakraborty, Souvik Lal, "Gramsci's Idea of Civil Society", *International Journal of Research in Humanities and Social Studies*, Vol. 3, No. 6, June 2016.

Cho, Seok-Ju, "Voting Equilibria Under Proportional Representation", *The American Political Science Review*, Vol. 108, No. 2, May 2014.

Cho, Sundai and James W. Endersby, "Issues, the Spatial Theory of Voting, and British General Elections: A Comparison of Proximity and Directional Models", *Public Choice*, Vol. 114, No. 3/4, March 2003.

Chong, Terence, "Civil Society in Singapore: Popular Discourses and Concepts", *Sojourn: Journal of Social Issues in Southeast Asia*, Vol. 20, No. 2, October 2005.

Chong, Terence, "Embodying Society's Best: Hegel and the Singapore State", *Journal of Contemporary Asia*, Vol. 36, No. 3, 2006.

Clevers, Marijn and Zina Nimeh, *Pharaohs of the Deep State: Social Capital in an Obstinate Regime,* United Nations University Working Papers Series, #2015-056.

Colantone, Italo and Piero Stanig, "The Surge of Economic Nationalism in Western Europe", *Journal of Economic Perspectives*, Vol. 33, No. 4, Fall 2019.

Cook, E. Albert, "Conservatism in Religion", *The Harvard Theological Review*, Vol. 6, No. 2, April 1913.

Crivelli, Ericson, "The Rise of Right-Wing Populism in Brazil", *International Union Rights*, Vol. 26, No. 3, 2019.

Cronert, Axel, and Pär Nyman, "Electoral Opportunism: Disentangling Myopia and Moderation", American Political Science Association, 9 February 2021, *APSA Preprints*. doi: 10.33774/apsa-2021-s7h95.

Cunha, Patrick and Brian F. Crisp, "Ballot Spoilage as a Response to Limitations on Choice and Influence", *Party Politics*, 4 February 2021.

Cusack, Thomas R., Torben Iversen and David Sockice, "Economic Interests and the Origins of Electoral Systems", *The American Political Science Review*, Vol. 101, No. 3, August 2007.

da Cunha, Derek, "In Memoriam: Michael Leifer, 1933–2001", *Contemporary Southeast Asia*, Vol. 23, No. 1, April 2001.

Dikötter, Frank, "Racial Identities in China: Context and Meaning", *The China Quarterly*, No. 138, June 1994.

Dobel, J. Patrick, "The ethics of Resigning", *Journal of Policy Analysis and Management*, Vol. 18, No. 2, Spring 1999.

Duckitt, John, "Authoritarianism and Group Identification: A New View of an Old Construct", *Political Psychology*, Vol. 10, No. 1, March 1989.

Dumitrescu, Delia, "The Importance of Being Present: Election Posters as Signals of Electoral Strength, Evidence from France and Belgium", *Party Politics*, November 2011.

Edwards, Barry C., "Alphabetically Ordered Ballots and the Composition of American Legislatures", *State Politics and Policy Quarterly*, Vol. 15, No. 2, June 2015.

Edwards, Scott, "Political Heroes and Political Education", *The North American Review*, Vol. 264, No. 1, Spring 1979.

Elinoff, Eli, "Unmaking Civil Society: Activists Schisms and Autonomous Politics in Thailand", *Contemporary Southeast Asia*, Vol. 36, No. 3, 2014.

Enos, Ryan D., Anthony Fowler and Lynn Vavreck, "Increasing Inequality: The Effect of GOTV Mobilization on the Composition of the Electorate", *The Journal of Politics*, Vol. 76, No. 1, January 2014.

Feldman, Stanley, and Karen Stenner, "Perceived Threat and Authoritarianism", *Political Psychology*, Vol. 18, No. 4, December 1997.

Feldman, Stanley, "Enforcing Social Conformity: A Theory of Authoritarianism", *Political Psychology*, Vol. 24, No. 1, 2003.

Fine, Ben and Alfredo Saad-Filho, "Thirteen Things You Need to Know About Neoliberalism", *Critical Sociology*, Vol. 43, No. 4–5, 2017.

Fioramonti, Lorenzo, "Civil Societies and Democratization: Assumptions, Dilemmas and the South African Experience", *Theoria: A Journal of Social and Political Theory*, No. 107, August 2005.

Flinders, Matthew, and Alexandra Kelso, "Mind the Gap: Political Analysis, Public Expectations and the Parliamentary Decline Thesis", *British Journal of Politics and International Relations*, Vol. 13, No. 2, 2011.

Freire, Andre and Kats Kivitstik, "Mapping and Explaining the Use of the Left-Right Divide", *Brazilian Political Science Review*, December 2013.

Gaebler, Stefanie, Niklas Protrafka and Felix Rosel, *Compulsory Voting and Political Participation: Empirical Evidence from Austria*, ifo Working Paper No. 315, December 2019.

Glasius, Marlies, "What Authoritarianism is… and is not: A Practice Perspective", *International Affairs*, Vol. 94, No. 3, 2018.

Glucksman, Andre, "The Velvet Philosophical Revolution", *City Journal*, Winter 2010.

Goh, Daniel P. S., "Politics of the Environment in Singapore: Lessons from a 'Strange' Case", *Asian Journal of Social Science*, Vol. 29, No. 1, 2001.

Greenstein, Fred I., "Can Personality and Politics be Studied Systematically?" *Political Psychology*, Vol. 13, No. 1, March 1992.

Grice, Kevin and David Drakakis-Smith, "The Role of the State in Shaping Development: Two Decades of Growth in Singapore", *Transactions of the British Institute of Geographers*, Vol. 10, No. 3, 1985.

Guevarra, Anna Romina and Maya Arcilla, "The Source of Actual Terror: The Philippine Macho-Fascist Duterte", *Feminist Studies*, Vol. 46, No. 2, 2020.

Haselmayer, Martin, "Negative Campaigning and Its Consequences: A Review and a Look Ahead", *French Politics*, Vol. 17, 2019.

Hazama, Yasushi, "Constituency Service in Turkey: A Survey on MPs", *European Journal of Turkish Studies*, 3, 2005.

Heo, Uk and Alexander C. Tan, "Democracy and Economic Growth: A Causal Analysis", *Comparative Politics*, Vol. 33, No. 4, July 2001.

Hewison, Kevin and Garry Rodan, "The Decline of the Left in Southeast Asia", *The Socialist Register*, Vol. 30, 1994.

Hofstetter, Emily, and Elizabeth Stokoe, "Offers of Assistance in Politician-Constituent Interaction", *Discourse Studies*, Vol. 17, No. 6, December 2015.

Holbrook, Thomas M and Scott D. McClurg, "The Mobilization of Core Supporters: Campaigns, Turnout, and Electoral Composition in United States Presidential Elections", *American Journal of Political Science*, Vol. 49, No. 4, October 2005.

Horton, Peter and Garrett W. Brown, "Integrating Evidence, Politics and Society: A Methodology for the Science-Policy Interface", *Humanities and Social Sciences Communications*, 17 April 2018, https://www.nature.com/articles/s41599-018-0099-3.pdf.

Houlou-Garcia, Antoine, "Collective Wisdom, Diversity, and Misuse of Mathematics", *Revue Francaise*, Vol. 67, No. 95, 2017.

Ibrahim, Nur Amali, "Everyday Authoritarianism: A Political Anthropology of Singapore", *Critical Asian Studies*, Vol. 50, No. 2, 2018.

Indridason, Indridi H., "Proportional Representation, Majoritarian Legislatures, and Coalition Voting", *American Journal of Political Science*, Vol. 55, No. 4, October 2011.

Iversen, Torben and Max Goplerud, "Redistribution Without a Median Voter: Models of Multidimensional Politics", *Annual Review of Political Science*, Vol. 21, 2018.

Jakee, Keith and Sun Guang-Zheng, "Is Compulsory Voting More Democratic?" *Public Choice*, Vol. 129, No.1/2, October 2006.

Jayasuriya, Kanishka, "The Rise of the Right: Populism and Authoritarianism in Southeast Asian Politics", *Southeast Asian Affairs 2020*.

Johnson, Sally, M. "Personality Disorders at the Interface of Psychiatry and the Law: Legal Use and Clinical Classification", *Dialogues in Clinical Neuroscience*, Vol. 15, No. 2, June 2013.

Jones, David Martin, "Democratization, Civil Society, and Illiberal Middle-Class Structure in Pacific Asia", *Comparative Politics*, Vol. 30, No. 2, January 1998.

Jou, Willy, "The Heuristic Value of the Left-Right Schema in East Asia", *International Political Science Review*, Vol. 31, No. 3, 2010.

Kahan, Alan, "Defining Opportunism: The Writings of Eugene Spuller", *History of Political Thought*, Vol. 15, No. 3, Autumn 1994.

Karlsson, David, "Putting Party First: Swedish MPs and Their Constituencies", *Journal of Representative Democracy*, Vol. 54, No. 1, 2018.

Karp, Jeffrey A, Susan A. Banducci and Shaun Bowler, "Getting Out the Vote: Party Mobilization in a Comparative Perspective", *British Journal of Political Science*, Vol. 38, No. 1, January 2008.

Kedar, Orit, "When Moderate Voters Prefer Extreme Parties: Policy Balancing in Parliamentary Elections", *The American Policy Science Review*, Vol. 99, No. 2, May 2005.

King, Amy and Andrew Leigh, "Are Ballot Order Effects Heterogeneous", *Social Science Quarterly*, Vol. 90, No. 1, March 2009.

King, Maryon F. and Gordon C. Bruner, "Social Desirability Bias: A Neglected Aspect of Validity Testing", *Psychology and Marketing*, Vol. 17, No. 2, February 2000.

Knutsen, Oddbjorn, "The Partisan and the Value-Based Component of Left-Right Self-Placement: A Comparative Study", *International Political Science Review*, Vol. 18, No. 2, April 1997.

Koppell, Jonathan GS and Jennifer A. Steen, "The Effects of Ballot Position on Election Outcomes", *The Journal of Politics*, Vol. 66, No. 1, February 2004.

Kouba, Karren and Jakub Lysek, "What Affects Invalid Voting? A Review of Meta-Analysis", *Government and Opposition*, Vol. 54, No. 4, October 2019.

Kumarr, Suraendher, "The Politics of Controlling Labour in Singapore: Continuities and Fissures in Migrant and Citizen Labour Governance", *Journal of International & Public Affairs*, Vol. 1, No. 2, 2020.

Kużelewska, Elżbieta, "Compulsory Voting in Belgium. A Few Remarks on Mandatory Voting", *Białostockie Studia Prawnicze*, Vol. 20/A, January 2016.

Lacy, Dean and Philip Paolino, "Testing Proximity versus Directional Voting Using Experiments", *Electoral Studies*, Vol. 29, No. 3, September 2010.

Laine, Jussi, "Debating Civil Society: Contested Conceptualizations and Development Trajectories", *International Journal of Not-for-Profit Law*, Vol. 16, No. 1, September 2014.

Lau, Richard R., and Ivy Brown Rovner, "Negative Campaigning", *Annual Review of Political Science*, Vol. 12, 2009.

Lee, Terence, "Gestural Politics: Civil Society in 'New' Singapore", *Sojourn: Journal of Social Issues in Southeast Asia*, Vol. 20, No. 2, October 2005.

Lee, Yvonne C.L., "Under Lock and Key: The Evolving Role of the Elected President as a Fiscal Guardian", *Singapore Journal of Legal Studies*, December 2007.

Lewis-Beck, Michael S., "Economic Determinants of Electoral Outcomes", *Annual Review of Political Science*, Vol. 3, June 2000, https://www.annualreviews.org/doi/full/10.1146/annurev.polisci.3.1.183.

Lijphart, Arend "Unequal Participation: Democracy's Unresolved Dilemma", *The American Political Science Review*, Vol. 91, No. 1, March 1997.

Linz, Juan J., "Democracy's Time Constraints", *International Political Science Review*, Vol. 19, No. 1, January 1998.

Loh Kah Seng, "Within the Singapore Story: Use and Narrative of History in Singapore", *Crossroads: An Interdisciplinary Journal of Southeast Asian Studies*, Vol. 12, No. 2, 1998.

Mahmood, Khalid, "Hartlepool is a Wake Up Call for My Party", *Policy Exchange*, 7 May 2021, https://policyexchange.org.uk/hartlepool-is-a-wake-up-call-for-my-party/.

Marland, Alex and Tom Flanagan, "Brand New Party: Political Branding and the Conservative Party of Canada", *Canadian Journal of Political Science*, Vol. 46, No. 4, December 2013.

Marsh, David, David Richards and Martin Smith, "Unequal Plurality: Towards an Asymmetric Power Model of British Politics", *Government and Opposition*, Vol. 38, No. 3, Summer 2003.

Martin, John Levi Martin "The Authoritarian Personality, 50 Years Later: What Lessons are There for Political Psychology", *Political Psychology*, Vol. 22, No. 1, 2001.

Matthews, Mathew, Leonard Lim and Shantini Selvarajan, *Religion Morality and Conservatism in Singapore*, IPS Working Papers No. 34, May 2019 https://lkyspp.nus.edu.sg/docs/default-source/ips/ips-working-paper-34---religion-morality-and-conservatism-in-singapore.pdf.

Mathews, Mathew, Teo Kay Key, Melvin Tay and Alicia Wang, *Attitudes Towards Institutions, Politics: Key Findings from the World Values Survey*, No. 17, March 2021, https://lkyspp.nus.edu.sg/docs/default-source/ips/ips-exchange-series-17.pdf.

Matthews, Mathew, Teo Kay Key, Melvin Tay and Alicia Wang, *Lived Experiences in Singapore: Key Findings from the World Values Survey*, No. 18, July 2021, https://lkyspp.nus.edu.sg/docs/default-source/ips/ips-exchange-series-18.pdf.

McDonald, Michael D., Silvia M. Mendes and Ian Budge, "What are Elections for? Conferring the Median Mandate", *British Journal of Political Science*, Vol. 34, No. 1, January 2004.

McKay, Lawrence, "Does Constituency Focus Improve Attitudes Towards MPs? A Test for the UK", *The Journal of Legislative Studies*, Vol. 26, No. 1, March 2020.

Merieau, Eugenie, "Thailand's Deep State, Royal Power and the Constitutional Court (1997–2015)", *Journal of Contemporary Asia*, Vol. 26, No. 3, 2016.

Meredith, Marc and Yuval Salant, *Causes and Consequences of Ballot Order-Effects*, Stanford Institute for Economic and Policy Research Discussion Paper No. 03-29, February 2007, p. 24, https://siepr.stanford.edu/sites/default/files/publications/06-29_0.pdf.

Milner, Henry and Andreas Ladner, "Can PR Voting Serve as a Shelter Against Declining Turnout? Evidence from Swiss Municipal Elections", *International Political Science Review*, Vol. 27, No. 1, January 2006.

Monroe, Burt L. and Amanda G. Rose, "Electoral Systems and Unimagined Consequences: Partisan Effects of Districted Proportional Representation", *American Journal of Political Science*, Vol. 46, No. 1, January 2002.

Moral, Mert, "The Passive-Aggressive Voter: The Calculus of Casting an Invalid Vote in European Democracies", *Political Research Quarterly*, Vol. 69, No. 4, December 2016.

Murdoch, Alexandra and Kareena McAloney-Kocaman, "Exposure to Evidence of White Privilege and Perceptions of Hardships Among White UK Residents", *Race and Social Problems*, 11, 2019.

Myat, Mon Mon, "Is Politics Aung San Suu Kyi's Vocation?", *Humanities and Social Sciences Communications*, 14 May 2019, https://www.nature.com/articles/s41599-019-0258-1.

Noury, Abdul and Gerard Roland, "Identity Politics and Populism in Europe", *Annual Review of Political Science*, Vol. 23, 2020.

Oliver, J. Eric and Thomas J. Wood, "Conspiracy Theories and the Paranoid Style(s) of Mass Opinion", *American Journal of Political Science*, Vol. 58, No. 4, October 2014.

Olson, David M., "The Structure of Electoral Politics," *The Journal of Politics*, Vol. 29, No. 2, May 1967.

O'Neil, Patrick H., "The Deep State: An Emerging Concept in Comparative Politics", *Political Institutions: Non-Democratic Regimes eJournal*, November 2017, http://ssrn.com/abstract=2313375.

Park, Bill, "Turkey's Deep State", *The RUSI Journal*, Vol. 153, No. 5, 26 November 2008, https://www.tandfonline.com/doi/pdf/10.1080/03071840802521937.

Passini, Stefano, "Different Ways of Being Authoritarian: The Distinct Effects of Authoritarian Dimensions on Values and Prejudice", *Political Psychology*, Vol. 38, No. 1, February 2017.

Pattie, Charles, Todd K. Hartman and Ron Johnston, "Not all Campaigns are Created Equal: Temporal and Spatial Variability in Constituency Campaign Spending Effects in Great Britain, 1997–2015", *Political Geography*, Vol. 71, May 2019.

Phang Siew Nooi, "Decentralisation or Recentralisation? Trends in Local Government in Malaysia", *Commonwealth Journal of Local Governance*, Issue 1, May 2008.

Pieterse, Jan Nederveen, "What Do People Want? Unscrambling Populism", *Soundings: An Interdisciplinary Journal*, Vol. 102, No. 2–3, 2019.

Pracilio, Amy, *Compulsory Voting — Does It Keep the Community at Large More Connected? Have First World Countries Forgotten the Value of the Vote?* https://www.parliament.wa.gov.au/publications/tabledpapers.nsf/displaypaper/3815429c61cd31f136c4c5ae48257ac5000a65c7/$file/5429.pdf.

Protzko, John, Claire M. Zedelius and Jonathan W. Schooler, "Rushing to Appear Virtuous: Time Pressure Increases Socially Desirable Responding", *Psychological Science*, Vol. 30, No. 11, 2019.

Rahim, Lily, "Fear, Smear and the Paradox of Authoritarian Politics in Singapore", *The Conversation*, 28 September 2021, https://theconversation.com/fear-smear-and-the-paradox-of-authoritarian-politics-in-singapore-47763.

Raunio, Taipio and Taru Ruotsalainen, "Exploring the Most Likely Case for Constituency Service: Finnish MPs and the Change Towards Personalised Representation", *Journal of Representative Democracy*, Vol. 54, No. 1, 2018.

Rekkas, Marie, "The Impact of Campaign Spending on Votes in Multiparty Elections", *The Review of Economics and Statistics*, Vol. 89, No. 3, August 2007.

Riley, Jonathan, "Utilitarian Ethics and Democratic Government," *Ethics*, Vol. 100, No. 2, January 1990.

Rodan, Garry, "Civil Society Activism and Political Parties in Malaysia: Differences Over Local Representation", *Democratization*, Vol. 1, No. 5, 2014.

Rolef, Susan, "Describing, Delimiting and Defining the Job of an MP", Conference: The Twelfth Workshop of Parliamentary Scholars and Parliamentarians, Wroxton, UK, July 2015.

Rowlands, Julie and Shawn Rawolle, "Neoliberalism is Not a Theory of Everything: A Bourdeain Analysis of *Illusio* in Educational Research", *Critical Studies in Education*, Vol. 54, No. 13, 2013.

Rowley, Charles K., "The Relevance of the Median Voter Theorem", *Journal of Institutional and Theoretical Economics*, March 1984.

Sartori, Giovanni, "Politics, Ideology, and Belief Systems", *American Political Science Association*, Vol. 63, No. 2, June 1969.

Saxonberg, Steven, "The 'Velvet Revolution' and the Limits of Rational Choice Models", *Czech Sociological Review*, Vol. 7, No. 1, Spring 1999.

Schedler, Andreas and Javier Santiso, "Democracy and Time: An Invitation", *International Political Science Review*, Vol. 19, No. 1, January 1998.

Shaw, Eric, "The Labour Party and the Militant Tendency", *Parliamentary Affairs*, Vol. 42, No. 2, April 1989.

Sigelman, Lee and Mark Kugler, "Why is Research on the Effects of Negative Campaigning So Inconclusive? Understanding Citizens' Perceptions of Negativity", *The Journal of Politics*, Vol. 65, No. 1, 2003.

Sinclair, Sinclair, Margaret McConnell and Melissa R. Michelson, "Local Canvassing: The Efficacy of Grassroots Voter Mobilization", *Political Communication*, Vol. 30, No. 1, January 2013.

Singh, Shane P., "Compulsory Voting and the Voter Decision Calculus", *Political Studies*, Vol. 63, 2015.

Singh, Shane P., "Compulsory Voting and Parties' Vote-Seeking Strategies", *American Journal of Political Science*, Vol. 63, No. 1, January 2019.

Skaperdas, Stergios and Bernard Grofman, "Modelling Negative Campaigning", *American Political Science Review*, Vol. 89, No. 1, March 1995.

Solt, Frederick, "The Social Origins of Authoritarianism", *Political Research Quarterly*, Vol. 65, No. 4, December 2012.

Surridge, Paula "Britain's Choice: Polarisation or Cohesion", *The Political Quarterly*, Vol. 92, No. 1, January–March 2021, https://onlinelibrary.wiley.com/doi/epdf/10.1111/1467-923X.12943.

Takala, Tuomo Antero, "Charismatic Leadership and Power", *Problems and Perspectives in Management*, August 2004.

Tan, Kenneth Paul, "Meritocracy and Elitism in a Global City: Ideological Shifts in Singapore", *International Political Science Review*, Vol. 29, No. 1, 2008.

Tan, Netina, "Minimal Factionalism in Singapore's People's Action Party", *Journal of Current Southeast Asian Affairs*, Vol. 39, No. 1, 2020.

Temple, Michael, "New Labour's Third Way: Pragmatism and Governance", *The British Journal of Politics and International Relations*, Vol. 2, No. 3, 2000.

Thio Li-Ann, "Between Apology and Apogee, Autochthony: The 'Rule of Law' Beyond the Rules of Law in Singapore", *Singapore Journal of Legal Studies*, 2012.

Truschke, Audrey, "Hindutva's Dangerous Rewriting of History", *South Asia Multidisciplinary Academic Journal*, 24/25, 2020.

Tufuku, Darryl S., "Jesse Jackson and the Rainbow Coalition: Working Class Movement or Reform Politics?", *Humanity & Society*, Vol. 14, No. 2, 1990.

Tushnet, Mark, "Authoritarian Constitutionalism", *Cornell Law Review*, Vol. 100, No. 2, January 2015.

Urbanowski, Anne, "Al Sharpton's 2004 Presidential Campaign: Has the Reverend Lost the Faith?", *Revue LISA/LISA e-journal* [Online], Vol. IX, No. 1, 2011, 2021. URL: http://journals.openedition.org/lisa/4153; DOI: https://doi.org/10.4000/lisa.4153.

Usher, Dan, *Utilitarianism, Voting and the Redistribution of Income*, Queen's Economics Department Working Paper No. 1385, 15 June 2017.

Venugopal, Rajesh, "Neoliberalism as Concept", *Economy and Society*, Vol. 44, No. 2, 2015.

Webb, Adele, "Why are the Middle-Class Misbehaving? Exploring Democratic Ambivalence and Authoritarian Nostalgia", *Sociological Review*, Vol. 65, 2017.

Whittle, Andrea, "Making Sense of the Rise and Fall of Jeremy Corbyn: Towards an Ambiguity-Centred Perspective on Leadership", *Leadership*, Vol. 17, No. 4, August 2021.

White, Jonathan, "Left and Right as Political Resources", *Journal of Political Ideologies*, Vol. 16, No. 2, 2011.

Wickham-Jones, Mark, "Signalling Credibility: Electoral Strategy and New Labour in Britain", *Political Science Quarterly*, Vol. 120, No. 4, Winter 2005.

Williams, Laron K., "It's All Relative: Spatial Positioning of Parties and Ideological Shifts", http://web.missouri.edu/~williamslaro/It's%20All%20Relative.pdf.

Winters, Jeffrey A., "Wealth Defense and the Complicity of Liberal Democracy", *Nomos*, Vol. 58, 2017.

Yoder, Jesse, Cassandra-Handan Nader, Andrew Myers, Tobias Nowacki, Daniel M. Thompson, Jennifer A. Wu, Chenoa Yorgason and Andrew B. Hall, *How Did Absentee Voting Affect the US 2020 Election?* Stanford Institute for Economic Policy Research, Working Paper No. 21-011, March 2021.

Zeitzoff, Thomas, "How Social Media is Changing Conflict", *The Journal of Conflict Resolution*, Vol. 61, No. 9, October 2017.

Zhuo Tee, "The Special Assistance Plan: Singapore's Own Bumiputera Policy", *Equality & Democracy: Singapore Political Theory in Action*, 7 December 2017, https://equalitydemocracy.commons.yale-nus.edu.sg/2017/12/07/the-special-assistance-plan-singapores-own-bumiputera-policy/.

Mainstream, alternative and social media
AsiaOne
Atlantic
Bloomberg News
Business Times
Chicago Sun Times
CNA (Channel NewsAsia)
Economist
Facebook
Guardian
IndependentSG
Malay Mail
Mirror
Mothership SG
New Paper
New York Times
Online Citizen

Reddit
Reuters
South China Morning Post
Straits Times
Temasek Review
Today
Washington Post
Yahoo! News

INDEX

www.ingramcontent.com/pod-product-compliance
Lightning Source LLC
Chambersburg PA
CBHW050330270326
41926CB00016B/3391